Advance Praise

"Adobe Systems understands the importance of providing our Japanese-speaking customers with Japanese-capable software. The issues are complex, but Ken Lunde is able to sort them out for the reader in *Understanding Japanese Information Processing*. I expect this book to have a great impact in the field of software internationalization and localization. I feel quite fortunate having Ken Lunde on our staff at Adobe Systems."

> — Dr. John Warnock
> *CEO, Adobe Systems Incorporated*

"Creating multilingual software is a challenge in the growing global marketplace, and the task is especially daunting with Japanese—one of the world's most difficult languages. *Understanding Japanese Information Processing* is *the* resource for developers building the bridge between Japanese and Western languages."

> — Henry McGilton
> *Trilithon Software*

"*Understanding Japanese Information Processing* is a Rosetta Stone for those concerned about how Japanese is handled on computer systems. It removes the mystique and creates understanding."

> — Jun Murai, PhD
> *Keio University and WIDE Project*

"Ken Lunde's book is an essential reference for everyone developing or adapting software for handling Japanese text. It is a goldmine of useful and relevant information on fonts, encoding systems, and standards."

> — Professor Jim Breen
> *Faculty of Computing & IT, Monash University, Australia*

Understanding
Japanese Information Processing

日本語情報処理

Understanding
Japanese Information Processing

日本語情報処理

Ken Lunde

O'Reilly & Associates, Inc.
103 Morris Street, Suite A
Sebastopol, CA 95472
USA

Understanding Japanese Information Processing
by Ken Lunde

Editors: Peter Mui
Tim O'Reilly

Printing History:

September 1993:   First Edition.

This book is printed on acid-free paper with 50% recycled content, 10–15% post-consumer waste. O'Reilly & Associates is committed to using paper with the highest recycled content available consistent with high quality.

ISBN: 1-56592-043-0

Table of Contents

7: *Japanese Information Processing Techniques* *159*

8: *Japanese Text Processing Tools* *197*

Figures

Tables

3: Japanese Character Set Standards   *33*

6: Japanese Output   *129*

I: Japanese Corporate Encoding Methods   *307*

J: Character Lists and Mapping Tables   *325*

Preface

Internationalization (国際化) and localization (地方化) are hot topics these days among high-tech firms and researchers. This book is specifically about *Japanization* (日本語化), which is the localization of software for the Japanese market. It is my intention that readers will find relevant information within these pages. I include a brief description of the Japanese writing system, a thorough background of the history and current state of Japanese character sets, detailed information on code space specifications, encoding methods, code conversion techniques, Japanese input techniques, Japanese keyboard arrays, Japanese output techniques, algorithms with sample source code, tools that perform useful Japanese information processing tasks, and how to handle Japanese text using e-mail.

First let me tell you what this book is about. Expect to find plenty of platform-independent information and discussions on Japanese character sets, how Japanese is encoded and handled on computer systems, and basic guidelines and tips for developing software targeted for the Japanese market.

Now, let me tell you what this book is *not* about. Don't expect to find out how to design your own Japanese word processor, how to design your own Japanese fonts for use on your computer (I give sources for tools, though), or how to properly handle formats for Japanese numerals, currency, dates, or times. This book is not a reference manual for internationalization or localization, but should serve well as a companion to such reference works.*

It is my intention that this book become the definitive source for information relating to Japanese information processing issues. As such, this book focuses heavily on how Japanese text is handled on computer systems.

---

*A good reference manual for internationalization and localization is *Software Internationalization and Localization: An Introduction* by Emmanual Uren, Robert Howard, and Tiziana Perinotti, published by Van Nostrand Reinhold.

This book was written to fill a gap in information relating to Japanese information processing. I have attempted to do this over the past several years by maintaining a document which I call JAPAN.INF (*Electronic Handling of Japanese Text*). This document has been made publicly available through a number of anonymous FTP sites worldwide, and has gained international recognition as *the* source for information relating to Japanese text handling on computer systems. However, it is not my intention to replace JAPAN.INF with this book. This book excerpts and further develops key information from JAPAN.INF, and adds totally new material. A book format also permits presenting more material than can be displayed within the limitations of an online text file. Displaying Japanese text on many computer display devices and printers is difficult if not impossible. Even with the proper hardware and software, small configuration errors or data errors can make everything unreadable.

Time-sensitive information from JAPAN.INF is not included in this book. Such information will continue to be a part of JAPAN.INF as it is revised over the years. I also intend to make JAPAN.INF a source for corrections to this book until those corrections can be incorporated into the next printing or edition of the book. I want to be able to provide readers with timely updates to the information presented here.

Materials related to this book have been published in a number of journals: the March 1990 issue of the *CALICO Journal*; the September/October 1990 issue of *ATArashii*; the Summer 1992 issue of the *SESAME Bulletin*; and the June 1993 issue of *Computer Processing of Chinese & Oriental Languages* (CPCOL). I have also given several presentations on such material: at the University of Wisconsin-Madison on November 14, 1988, April 10, 1989, and November 27, 1989; for the International Macintosh Users Group (IMUG) on May 21, 1992 and on June 17, 1993; and at Communications Japan '93 on May 15, 1993.

Audience

Anyone interested in how Japanese text is processed on a computer will find this book useful, including those who wish to enter the field of Japanese and computers, and those who are already in the field, but need reference material. It will be useful for people using any kind of computer and any type of computer operating system: mainframe to PC, UNIX, Macintosh, and MS-DOS.

Although this book is specifically about Japanese information processing, anyone with an interest in creating multilingual software or a general interest in I18N (*internationalization*), L10N (*localization*), or J10N (*Japanization*) will learn a great deal about the issues involved in handling foreign languages on computers. This is particularly true for people interested in working with Asian languages. Information on I18N, L10N, and J10N is relatively scarce.

I assume that readers have a limited knowledge of the Japanese language and its writing system. In Chapter 1, I include material that should provide a good introduction to the language and its writing system.

Organization

Let's now preview the contents of each chapter in this book. Don't feel compelled to read this book linearly, but feel free to jump around from section to section and into the appendixes.

Chapter 1, *Overview of Japanese Information Processing*, contains an overview of the issues that are addressed by this book, and will give you an idea of what you can expect to learn. This establishes the context in which this book will become useful in your work or research.

Chapter 2, *The Japanese Writing System*, contains information directly relating to the Japanese writing system. Here you will learn about the various types of characters that compose Japanese sentences. This chapter is intended for readers who are not familiar with the Japanese language.

Chapter 3, *Japanese Character Set Standards*, describes the two classes of Japanese character set standards: electronic and non-electronic. Electronic standards are further divided into three classes: national, Asian, and international. Comparisons are drawn between these character set standards.

Chapter 4, *Japanese Encoding Methods*, contains information on how the character set standards described in Chapter 3 are encoded on computer systems. Encoding is a complex but important step in representing and manipulating human-language text in a computer. Other topics include software for converting from one Japanese code to another, and instructions on how to repair damaged Japanese text files.

Chapter 5, *Japanese Input*, contains information on how Japanese text is *input*. First I discuss Japanese input software, and describe several methods for inputting Japanese characters on computer systems. Next, we move on to the hardware necessary for Japanese input, namely the keyboard arrays used in Japan. These range from simple keyboard arrays, such as the QWERTY array, to kanji tablets containing thousands of individual keys. The end of this chapter describes dictionaries that are useful for inputting kanji when software fails.

Chapter 6, *Japanese Output*, contains information on how Japanese text is *output* to a variety of devices, namely printers and computer monitors, and includes discussions about bitmapped and outline font formats. Here you can find information relating to the latest printing technology.

Chapter 7, *Japanese Information Processing Techniques*, contains information and algorithms relating to Japanese code conversion and text handling techniques. The actual mechanics are described in detail, and, where appropriate, include algorithms written in C. The chapter ends with a brief description of three Japanese code processing tools that I have written and maintained over a period of several years. In effect, these tools show how the algorithms can be applied.

Chapter 8, *Japanese Text Processing Tools*, provides examples and brief descriptions of such tools as operating systems, input software, text editors, word processors, page layout software, online dictionaries, machine translation software, and terminal software for various platforms.

Chapter 9, *Using Japanese E-mail and News*, contains information on how Japanese text is best handled electronically over networks such as e-mail systems and news readers. Included are tips on how to ensure that what you send is received intact.

Appendix A, *Japanese Code Conversion Table*, contains a code conversion table between KUTEN, hexadecimal JIS, hexadecimal EUC, and hexadecimal Shift-JIS codes.

Appendix B, *JIS X 0208-1990 Table*, is a code table for the 6,879 characters specified in JIS X 0208-1990 indexed by KUTEN codes.

Appendix C, *JIS X 0212-1990 Table*, is a code table for the 6,067 characters specified in JIS X 0212-1990 indexed by KUTEN codes. Also included are four extra kana characters that may be added to this standard in the future.

Appendix D, *JIS Code Table Supplements*, contains a pronunciation index for JIS X 0208-1990 (JIS Level 1 only), and a radical index for JIS X 0208-1990 (JIS Level 2 kanji only) and JIS X 0212-1990. These indexes are useful in conjunction with Appendixes C and D.

Appendix E, *Jôyô Kanji List*, is a listing of the 1,945 kanji that constitute Jôyô Kanji. Appendix J includes a list of the 95 kanji that represent the difference between Tôyô Kanji and Jôyô Kanji.*

Appendix F, *Gakushû Kanji List*, is a listing of the 1,006 kanji that constitute Gakushû Kanji.

Appendix G, *Jinmei-yô Kanji List*, is a listing of the 284 kanji that constitute Jinmei-yô Kanji.

Appendix H, *Japanese Corporate Character Set Standards*, is reference material for those interested in some of the Japanese character sets developed by individual companies.

Appendix I, *Japanese Corporate Encoding Methods*, is reference material for those interested in how the character sets in Appendix H are encoded.

---

*No need to worry now as these terms and others are described later.

Appendix J, *Character Lists and Mapping Tables*, contains lists of characters and mapping tables referred to throughout the book.

Appendix K, *Software and Document Sources*, provides addresses and contact information for software and documents mentioned throughout the book. This includes machine-readable versions of most of the code fragments, mapping tables, and character lists found throughout this book.

Appendix L, *Mailing Lists*, provides information on various mailing lists that may be of interest to readers.

Appendix M, *Professional Organizations*, includes information on organizations that deal with Japanese information processing issues to varying degrees.

Appendix N, *Glossary*, defines many of the concepts and terms used throughout this book (and other books).

Appendix O, *Code Table*, contains an ASCII/JIS-Roman/EBCDIC/EBCDIK code table in binary, octal, decimal, and hexadecimal notations.

The *Bibliography* lists many useful references, most of which I used to write this book.

Conventions

In writing this book I have assumed that the reader has little or no working knowledge of written Japanese. The terms *kanji*, *kana*, *hiragana*, and *katakana* come up time and time again throughout this book. You will also encounter acronyms, such as JIS, Shift-JIS, and EUC. These terms and acronyms, along with many others, are explained in the text and again in the glossary (Appendix N). Be sure to make generous use of this glossary.

Hexadecimal values, when used in text, are prefixed with 0x, such as 0x8080. Every two hexadecimal digits beyond 0x represent a single byte. For example, 0x20 represents a one-byte value, but 0x2020 represents a two-byte value. Decimal values appear as themselves. You can also use Appendix O to convert between notations.

Throughout this book (but especially in Chapter 8) I generically use the suffix "-J" to denote a localized Japanese version of software products. In actuality, you may instead encounter the suffix 日本語版 (meaning "Japanese version"), the prefix "Kanji", or the prefix 日本語 (meaning "Japanese") in product names. I use the suffix "-J" for the sake of consistency, and because software manufacturers often change the way in which they denote the Japanese versions of their products. I also refrain from using version numbers for software described in this book (as you know, this sort of information becomes outdated very quickly). I use version numbers only when it marks a significant advancement or development stage in a product.

Throughout the book I have included in parentheses the Japanese versions of many terms, that is, how these terms are written using the standard Japanese writing system. It is my hope that those familiar with the Japanese written language may find them useful and informative as they read.

Japanese name ordering in this book, when romanized, follows the convention that is used in the West—the given name appears first, followed by the surname. When the name is written in Japanese characters—in parentheses following the romanized version—the surname appears first, followed by the given name.

Acknowledgments

I would like to take this opportunity to acknowledge numerous individuals who have made significant contributions to my work that led to the writing of this book.

First, I would like to express my deepest gratitude to Kazumasa Utashiro (歌代和正) of Software Research Associates (SRA), introduced to me by Earl Kinmonth. Through e-mail communication during the Spring of 1989 he taught me the basics of Japanese text handling, including how to send and receive Japanese text using the seven-bit JIS codes. His help inspired me to research further into this field so that I could eventually inform others about what he has taught me, plus more. He also inspired me to take my first computer programming class (Pascal) in the Summer of 1989. I was finally able to meet him in person in 1991! That experience further encouraged me to learn, on my own, C (ANSI C, that is), PostScript, Perl, and Bourne shell programming. To him goes my deepest gratitude.

I also wish to thank many at the University of Wisconsin-Madison who offered both moral and financial support in my various endeavors there which have led to my present position at Adobe Systems Incorporated. Individuals include Stephen Anderson, Donald Becker, R. Byron Bird, Arthur Chen, Edward Daub (my son's namesake), James Davis, Ezra (Sam) Diman, Naomi McGloin (マクグロイン直美), Akira Miura (三浦昭), Charles Read, Andrew Sihler, Elizabeth Steinberg, Paul Stevens, and John Street. I also wish to thank The University of Wisconsin Press, The Department of Chemical Engineering, The Department of East Asian Languages and Literature, The Department of Engineering Professional Development, and The Department of Linguistics.

I have had great pleasure working with numerous individuals at Adobe Systems who, over the time I have spent working there, have encouraged me to become even more involved in issues dealing with Japanese and computers. I especially wish to thank Masumi Abe (阿部加史), Stephen Amerige, Paul Anderson, Michiharu Ariza (有座道春), Kei Befu (別府けい), Fred Brady, Bruce Brenner, Ned Bunnell, Leo Cazares, Mary Cochran, Burwell Davis, Jim DeLaHunt, Terrence Dowling, Matt Foley, Kathleen Foster, Franky Fu (符致恩), Charles Geschke, Jerry Hall, Pei Han, Ben Hollin, Digby Horner,

Naoki Hotta (堀田直起), Ping Huey (沈依平), Marcia Israelson, Luis Jenkins, David Kelly (雷大衛), Masahiko Kozuka (小塚昌彦), David Lemon, Tom Malloy, Dan Mills, Kathe Morris, Pat Ng-Thayer, John Nogrady, Sairus Patel, David Parsons, Yumiko Ready, John Renner, Ann Robinson, Alan Sanders, Taro Tsuzuki (続木太郎), Jon von Zelowitz, Don Walker, Kevin Wandryk, John Warnock, Jim Wasco, Sharon Wienbar, Akihiko Yamamoto (山本明彦), Taro Yamamoto (山本太郎), and Andrew Yonemoto. I also wish to thank Adobe Systems for developing the PostScript tools and technologies that made producing this book possible. This book is a tribute to their technology.

Next, I would like to thank those who read through previous versions of my work, both electronic and printed, and offered suggestions for improvement. To each of them goes thanks. They include Anil Bhatia, Francis Bond, Eric Bowles, Jim Breen, Shmuel Browns, Bruce Casner, David Cowhig, Rainer Daeschler, Troy Dillard, Mark Edwards, John Findlayson, Jeffrey Friedl, Lawrence Garfield, Masashi Gomyo (五明正史), Ron Granich, Per Hammarlund, Alton Harkcom, Michael Henning, Masato Hirose (広瀬正人), Ron Hofmann, Masamichi Honda (本多正道), Jamie Hubbard, Brad Hutchings, Lars Huttar, Minoru Huttunen, Antti Karttunen, Kazuhiko Kato (加藤和彦), Robert Kerns, Akio Kido (木戸彰夫), Earl Kinmonth, Frank Klemm, Kazuya Kobayashi (小林一也), Peter Lind, David Lohrentz, Jim Loomis, Steve Madsen, Roger Martin, Mike Martinez, Dave McClane, Nathaniel McCully, Cliff Miller, James Miller, Charlie Mingo, Nobuhiro Miyatake (宮武伸裕), Takeshi Miyazaki, Jason Molenda, Katsuhiko Momoi (桃井勝彦), Koichi Mori (森浩一), Theodore Morris, Eric Nelson, Haruhiko Nishida (西田晴彦), Mikiko Nishikimi (錦見美貴子), Hisao Nojima (野島久雄), Seiichi Nomura (野村靖一), Masato Ogawa (小川雅人), Izumi Ohzawa (大沢五住), Yukihiko Okada (岡田幸彦), Hideyuki Ozaki (尾崎英之), Jamie Packer, Glen Perkins, Tad Perry, Kenji Rikitake (力武健次), Albert Saisho, Atsushi Sakurai (桜井厚), Rick Schlichting, Hiroaki Sengoku (仙石浩明), Frank Sheeran, Roger Sherman, Tomonori Shirakawa (白川友紀), Shigeo Suwa (諏訪茂男), Akio Tanaka (田中章夫), Hiroshi Tanaka (田中宏), Kyugo Tanaka (田中久吾), Brian Thomson, Hideo Tomita (富田英夫), Scott Trent, Yasuhiro (Bobby) Uraki (浦城康弘), Craig Van Degrift, Erik van der Poel, Richard Walters, Seke Wei, Jon Wiederspan, and Naoto Yagi (八木直人).

Other individuals provided me with valuable information which made writing this book possible. They include Naoko Adachi (安達直子), Joe Becker, Joe Bosurgi, Jeff Bowyer, Tim Burress, Joel Cannon, Amelia Carlson, Stephen Chung, Dan Crevier, William Davis, Tom DiCorcia, Tom Donaldson, Barbara Forsberg, Hirofumi Fujiwara (藤原博文), Kenichi Handa (半田剣一), Ruairi Hickey, Manabu Higashida (東田学), Hiroyuki Hikita (引田啓之), Ni Hongbo, Greg Hullender, Yuichi Itoda (糸田雄一), Jun-ichiro Itoh (伊藤純一郎), Alan Kastner, Yutaka Kataoka (片岡裕), Makoto Kayashima (萱島信), Akira Kon (今昭), David Lakritz, Takashi Matsuzawa, Bryan McNett, Martin Nilsson, Hiroaki Obata (小幡広昭), Junn Ohta (太田純), Stephen Palm, Tom Paquin, Martin Pauley, Rob Pike, James Roseborough, Rafael Santos, Masahiko Sato (佐藤雅彦), Ken Shibata (柴田健),

Shigeya Suzuki (鈴木茂哉), Tetsurou Tanaka (田中哲朗), Toshiyuki Takeda (武田俊之), Hiroo Yamada (山田浩大), and Shigeki Yoshida (吉田茂樹).

Special thanks go to Tim O'Reilly and Peter Mui of O'Reilly & Associates for believing in this book. Thanks go to Edie Freedman for using my idea of a blowfish on the cover (and for designing the t-shirt!). Jennifer Niederst helped me through the layout of the book. Donna Woonteiler made my writing style more consistent. Chris Reilley also deserves a lot of credit for turning my poorly designed figures into works of art. Without the editorial assistance, comments, and support from the fine folks at O'Reilly & Associates, evolving JAPAN.INF into a book would not have been fun or possible. I consider their series of computer books the best in their class, and I hope that this book can live up to that great tradition. I also thank Marilyn Rowland for creating the index.

There were several reviewers of this book. Henry McGilton deserves to be singled out for doing the very first reviews of the manuscript. His feedback and insights were invaluable to me while finishing this book. Other reviewers included Stephen Amerige, Jim Breen, Jun Murai (村井純), Steffen Schilke, Scott Trent, Kazumasa Utashiro (歌代和正), and Erik van der Poel. To all of them go my thanks.

Last but not least, I wish to thank my beloved wife, Ninik Kunti-Utami Lunde, for her incredible patience with me while I pursued my interests and a career in Japanese information processing. I apologize to her for all the mornings and nights I spent working on this book—instead of spending more time with her. To her goes all my love. I hereby dedicate this book to her, to my son, Edward Dharmaputra Lunde, and to my parents, Vernon Delano Lunde and Jeanne Mae Lunde.

Errors, Omissions, and Updates

A book containing this much highly technical information is bound to contain some errors. No doubt, these errors will be corrected in future printings or editions of this book. In the meantime, any errors will become part of JAPAN.INF. If you happen to find any errors or omissions, please send them to me through the following address:

O'Reilly & Associates, Incorporated
103 Morris Street, Suite A
Sebastopol, CA 95472
USA
800-998-9938 (phone)
707-829-0515 (phone)
707-829-0104 (facsimile)
ujip@ora.com

1

Overview of Japanese Information Processing

Much mystique surrounds how Japanese is handled on computer systems—too much, in my opinion. Much of the mystery is due to a lack of information, or simply a lack of information written in a language other than Japanese. Nevertheless, many people, like yourself, would like to know how this all works. To confirm some of your fears and speculations, Japanese text *does* require special handling on computer systems. However, it should not be mysterious after reading this book. You need only to break the *one-byte-equals-one-character* barrier—most Japanese characters are represented by more than a single byte.*

English information processing was a reality soon after the introduction of early computer systems, which were first developed in England and the United States. Adapting software to handle more complex writing systems such as those used to represent Japanese is a more recent phenomenon. This adaptation developed in various stages and continues today.

Below I list several issues that make Japanese difficult to process on computer systems:

- The Japanese writing system is a mixture of four different, but sometimes related, writing systems.

- The Japanese character set contains over 10,000 characters, many more than used in the West.

- There is no universally recognized Japanese character set standard such as ASCII for writing English.

---

*For a greater awareness (and appreciation) of some of the complexities of dealing with multiple-byte text, you might consider glancing now at the section entitled *Byte Versus Character Handling Issues* in Chapter 7.

1

- There is no universally recognized Japanese encoding method such as ASCII encoding.

- There is no universally recognized input device such as the QWERTY keyboard.

- Japanese text can be set horizontally or vertically.

You will learn later that the ASCII character set standard is not as universal as most people think. Different flavors of ASCII exist as do different ASCII encoding methods.

Multiple Writing Systems

Japanese text is typically composed of four different writing systems. It is one of the few, if not the only, languages that exhibit this characteristic. This makes Japanese quite complex, orthographically speaking, and poses several problems.* The four writing systems are *Roman characters*, *hiragana*, *katakana*, and *kanji*. You are already familiar with *Roman characters* because the English language is comprised of these—this writing system consists of the lowercase and uppercase Roman alphabet, which are the characters often found on typewriter key caps. *Hiragana* and *katakana* are native Japanese syllabaries (see Appendix N for a definition). Both represent the same set of approximately 80 sounds, and are known collectively as *kana*. *Kanji* are characters that the Japanese borrowed from the Chinese over 1,500 years ago—kanji characters number in the thousands, and usually represent pictures or meanings.

Now let's look at an example sentence composed of these four writing systems. This should serve to illustrate the different components of the Japanese writing system.

JIS等のエンコーディング方法は日本語と英語が混在しているテキストをサポートします。

In case you are curious, this sentence means "Encoding methods such as JIS can support texts that mix Japanese and English." Let's look at this sentence again, but with the Roman characters highlighted.

JIS等のエンコーディング方法は日本語と英語が混在しているテキストをサポートします。

In this case there is a single acronym, namely JIS (short for *Japanese Industrial Standard*, which refers to a specific Japanese encoding method, a topic to be covered later in this book). It is quite common to find Roman characters used for acronyms in Japanese text.

Now let's highlight the katakana characters.

JIS等のエンコーディング方法は日本語と英語が混在しているテキストをサポートします。

Katakana characters represent syllables, typically a consonant-plus-vowel combination. Katakana characters are used for writing words borrowed from other languages, usually

---

*Orthography is a linguistic term that refers to a writing system of a language.

English. Table 1-1 lists these three highlighted words along with their meaning and pronunciation.

Table 1-1: Sample Katakana

Katakana	Meaning	Pronunciation
エンコーディング	*encoding*	enkôdingu[1]
テキスト	*text*	tekisuto
サポート	*support*	sapôto

[1]The circumflex is used to denote long vowel sounds.

Note how their pronunciation closely matches that of their English counterparts, from which they were derived. This is no coincidence. It is common for the Japanese pronunciations to be spelled out with katakana characters to closely match the borrowed words.

Next we highlight the hiragana characters.

JIS等のエンコーディング方法は日本語と英語が混在しているテキストをサポートします。

Hiragana characters, like katakana described above, represent syllables. Hiragana characters are used for writing grammatical words and some verbs. Table 1-2 shows the usage or meaning of the hiragana in the above sentence.

Table 1-2: Sample Hiragana

Hiragana	Meaning/Usage	Pronunciation
の	possessive marker	no
は	topic marker	wa[1]
と	*and* (conjunction)	to
が	subject marker	ga
している	*doing* ... (verb)	shite-iru
を	object marker	o
します	*do* ... (verb)	shimasu

[1]This hiragana character is normally pronounced *ha*, but when used as a topic marker, it becomes *wa*.

That's a lot of grammatical stuff! Japanese is a postpositional language, meaning that grammatical markers such as prepositions as used in English come *after* the nouns which they modify. These grammatical markers are called *particles* (助詞).

Finally, we highlight the kanji:

JIS等のエンコーディング方法は日本語と英語が混在しているテキストをサポートします。

At first glance kanji appear to be more complex than the other characters in the sentence. This happens to be true most of the time. Kanji usually represent pictures, and always have meaning. Kanji are often called *pictographs* or *ideographs*. Kanji are also assigned one or more pronunciations, each of which is determined by context. While their pronunciation differs depending on the language (Japanese, Korean, or Chinese), kanji still have the same meaning. This makes it possible for Japanese to understand (but not necessarily to pronounce) some Chinese and Korean texts. Table 1-3 provides a listing of the highlighted kanji and kanji compounds along with their meaning.

Table 1-3: Sample Kanji and Kanji Compounds

Kanji	Meaning	Pronunciation
等	*such as ...*	nado
方法	*method*	hôhô
日本語	*Japanese*	nihongo
英語	*English*	eigo
混在	*(to) mix*	konzai

Table 1-4 lists some sample characters from each of the four writing systems used in Japan. We discuss them again in Chapters 2 and 3.

Table 1-4: Sample Japanese Characters

Roman Characters	A B C D E F G H I J ... q r s t u v w x y z
Hiragana	ぁあぃいぅうぇえぉお ... りるれろゎわゐゑをん
Katakana	ァアィイゥウェエォオ ... ロヮワヰヱヲンヴヵヶ
Kanji	亜唖娃阿哀愛挨始逢葵 ... 齶龜龜龠堯槇遙瑤凜熙

Given an average sampling of Japanese writing, one normally finds 30 percent kanji, 60 percent hiragana, and 10 percent katakana. Actual percentages depend on the nature of the text. For example, you may find a higher percentage of kanji in technical literature, and a higher percentage of katakana in the literature of fields such as computer science, which make extensive use of loan words written in katakana. Roman characters are used less frequently.

So, how many characters do you need to learn in order to read and write Japanese effectively? Well, first you will need to learn hiragana and katakana. This constitutes approximately 200 characters. You need to have general knowledge of about 1,000 kanji to read over 90 percent of the kanji in typical Japanese texts. Approximately 2,000 kanji are formally taught in the Japanese educational system.

Japanese Character Set Standards

A character set provides a common bucket of characters, if you will. You may have never thought of it this way, but the English alphabet is an example of a character set standard. It specifies 26 uppercase letters and 26 lowercase letters. Character set standards are used to ensure that we learn a minimum number of characters in order to communicate with others in society. In effect, they limit the number of characters we need to learn. There are only a handful of characters in the English alphabet, so nothing is really being limited, and as such, there really is no character set standard *per se*. In the case of Japanese, however, character set standards play an especially vital role. They specify which kanji, out of the tens of thousands in existence, are the most important to learn. The current Japanese set, called Jôyô Kanji (常用漢字), limits this number to 1,945 kanji. These character set standards were designed with education in mind, and are referred to as *non-electronic* character sets.

Character set standards designed for use on computer systems are usually larger than those used for the purposes of education, and are referred to as *electronic* character sets. Establishing electronic character set standards for use with computer systems is a way to ensure that everyone is able to view electronic documents created by someone else. ASCII is a Western character set standard, and ensures that computer systems can communicate with each other.

Electronic character set standards typically contain characters above and beyond those found in non-electronic ones. For example, the ASCII character set standard contains 94 printable characters—42 more than the lowercase and uppercase alphabet. With Japanese, there are thousands of characters in the electronic character sets in addition to the 1,945 in the standard non-electronic character set. The basic electronic Japanese character set standard, in its most current form, contains 6,879 characters, and is called JIS X 0208-1990. There are three versions of this character set, each designated by the year in which they were established: 1978, 1983, and 1990. There are three typical compatibility problems that you will encounter:

- There are 1978, 1983, and 1990 versions of the Japanese character set standard.
- These versions contain different numbers of characters.
- These versions are not 100 percent compatible with each other.

In addition, there is an extended character set standard defining 6,067 more characters (JIS X 0212-1990).

Additional incompatibility occurs because individual computer companies take these electronic character set standards one step further by defining their own set of Japanese characters. These corporate character set standards are largely, but not completely, compatible, and usually use one of the national standards as its base set. When you factor in corporate character set standards, things appear to be a big mess. This book documents these character sets, making it easier to grapple with such confusion.

Japanese Encoding Methods

Encoding is the process of mapping a character to a numeric value. By doing this, you create the ability to uniquely identify a character through its associated numeric value.

Ultimately, the computer needs to manipulate the character as a numeric value. Independent of the Japanese language or computerized implementations of any language, indexing encoded values allows a numerically-enforced ordering to be mapped on to what might otherwise be a randomly ordered natural language. While there is no universally recognized Japanese encoding method, three are commonly used: JIS, Shift-JIS, and EUC.

First, before describing these encoding methods, here's a short explanation of how memory is allocated on computer systems. Computer systems process data called *bits*. These are the most basic units of information, and can hold one of two possible values: on or off. These are usually mapped to the values 1 or 0, respectively. Bits are strung together into meaningful units called *bytes*. Bytes are usually composed of seven or eight bits. Seven bits in an array allow for up to 128 unique values; eight bits allow for up to 256. While these numbers are sufficient for representing most characters in Western writing systems, it does not even come close to accommodating large character sets whose characters number in the thousands, such as those used by the Japanese.

The first attempt to encode Japanese characters on computer systems involved the use of half-width katakana characters. This is a limited set of 63 characters that constitutes a minimal set for representing Japanese text. But there was no support for kanji. The solution to this problem, at least for Japanese, was formalized in 1978, and employed the notion of using two bytes to represent a single character. This did not eliminate the need for one-byte characters, though. The Japanese solution was to extend the notion of one-byte character encoding to include two-byte characters. This allows for text with mixed

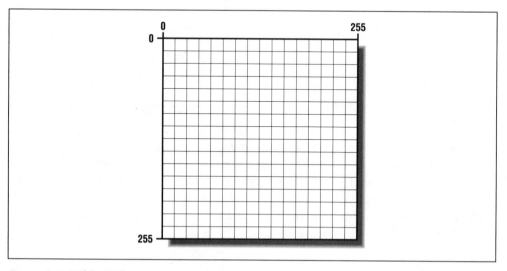

Figure 1-1: 256-by-256 matrix

one- and two-byte characters. How one- and two-byte characters are distinguished depends on the encoding method.

Two bytes equal 16 bits, and thus can provide up to 65,536 unique values. This is best visualized as a 256-row-by-256-cell matrix. See Figure 1-1 for an illustration of such a matrix.

However, not all of these 65,536 cells can be used for representing displayable characters. To enable the mixture of one- and two-byte characters within a single text stream, some characters needed to be reserved as control characters, some of which then serve as the characters that signify when a text stream shifts between one- and two-byte-per-character modes. In the case of JIS encoding, the upper limit of displayable characters was set at 8,836, which is the size of the code space made from a 94-row-by-94-cell matrix.* But why do you need to mix one- and two-byte characters anyway? To support existing one-byte encoding standards, such as ASCII, within a two-byte encoding system. One-byte encoding methods are here to stay, and it is still a rather efficient means to encode the characters necessary to write English and other languages. However, languages with large character sets, such as Japanese, require two bytes to encode characters. A mixed one- and two-byte character stream efficiently represents a mixture of English and Japanese text.

Along with discussions about character sets and encodings, you will encounter the terms *row* and *cell* again and again in this book. These refer to the axes of a matrix used to hold and encode characters. A matrix is composed of rows, and a row is made up of cells. The first byte of the character specifies the row, and the second byte specifies the cell within the row. Figure 1-2 illustrates a matrix and how characters' positions correspond to row and cell values.

In an attempt to allow for a mixture of one- and two-byte characters, several Japanese encoding methods have been developed. As you will learn in Chapter 4, these encoding methods are largely, but not completely, compatible. Some are more extensible than others, while some are more compatible than others. You will also see that there are encoding methods that use three or even four bytes to represent a single character!

The most common encoding methods are JIS, Shift-JIS, and EUC. JIS, the most basic, uses seven-bit bytes to represent characters, and requires special sequences of characters (called *escape sequences*) to shift between one- and two-byte-per-character modes. Shift-JIS and EUC (Extended UNIX Code) make generous use of eight-bit characters, and use the value of the first byte as the way to distinguish one- and multiple-byte characters.

---

*Code space refers to the area within the (usual) 256-by-256 matrix that can be used for encoding characters. Most of the figures in Chapter 4 and Appendix I illustrate code spaces that fall within the 256-by-256 matrix.

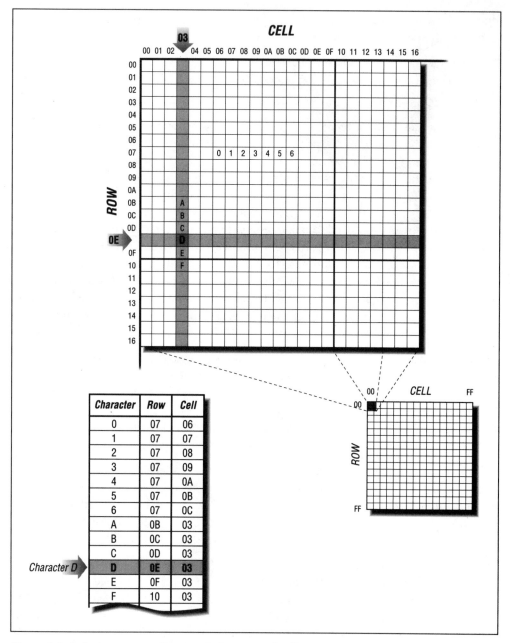

Figure 1-2: Indexing an encoding matrix by row and cell

Japanese Input

Those who type English text have the luxury of using keyboards that can hold all the keys to represent a sufficient number of characters. Japanese characters number in the thousands, though, so how does one type Japanese text? Large keyboards that hold thousands of individual keys exist, but they require special training and are difficult to use. This has led to software solutions: *front-end processors* (FEP) and *conversion dictionaries*.

Japanese text is typically input in two stages:

1) The user types raw keyboard input, which the computer interprets using the FEP and the conversion dictionary to display a list of *candidate* characters (*candidate* here refers to the character or characters that are mapped to the input string in the conversion dictionary).

2) The user selects one choice from the list of candidate characters, or requests more choices.

How well each stage is handled on your computer depends greatly on the quality (and vintage) of the input software you are using.

A front-end processor (Japanese input software) handles both of these input stages: it is so named because it grabs the user's keyboard input before any other software can use it (namely, it is the first software to process keyboard input).

The first stage of input requires keyboard input, and can take one of two usual forms:

• Transcribed Japanese using Roman characters (type "k" and "a" to get か, and so on)

• Hiragana input

The form used depends on user preference and the type of keyboard in use. The FEP usually converts transcribed Japanese into hiragana on-the-fly, so it doesn't really matter which keyboard you are using. In fact, studies show that over 70 percent of Japanese computer users use transcribed Japanese input using Roman characters.

Once the input string is complete it is then parsed in one of two ways: either by the user during input, or by a parser built into the FEP. Finally, each segment is run through a conversion process that consists of a lookup into a conversion dictionary. This is very much like a *key-value* lookup. Typical conversion dictionaries have tens of thousands of entries. It seems that the more entries, the better the conversion quality. However, if the conversion dictionary is too large, users are shown a far too lengthy list of candidates. This reduces input efficiency.

Can kanji characters be input one at a time? While single kanji input is possible, there are three basic units that can be used. These units allow you to limit the number of candidates from which you must choose. Typically, the larger the input unit, the fewer candidates. The units are as follows:

- Single kanji
- Kanji compound
- Kanji phrase

Early input programs required that each kanji be input individually (single kanji). Nowadays it is much more efficient to input kanji as they appear in compounds or even phrases. This means that you may input two or more kanji at once by virtue of inputting their combined pronunciation. For example, the kanji compound 漢字 (the two kanji for writing the word *kanji*) can be input as two separate kanji, 漢 (*kan*) and 字 (*ji*). Table 1-5 shows the two target kanji along with other kanji with the same pronunciation.

Table 1-5: Single Kanji Input

Kanji	Pronunciation	Kanji with Identical Pronunciation
漢	k a n	乾 侃 冠 寒 刊 勘 勧 巻 喚 堪 姦 完 官 寛 干 幹 患 感 慣 憾 換 敢 柑 桓 棺 款 歓 汗 漢 澗 潅 環 甘 監 看 竿 管 簡 緩 缶 翰 肝 艦 莞 観 諫 貫 還 鑑 間 閑 関 陥 韓 館 舘
字	j i	事 似 侍 児 字 寺 慈 持 時 次 滋 治 爾 璽 痔 磁 示 而 耳 自 蒔 辞

You can see that there are many other kanji with those pronunciations, so you may have to wade through a long list of candidate kanji before you find the correct one. A more efficient way is to input them as one unit, namely with the input string *kanji*, which is called a *kanji compound*. This produces a much shorter list of candidates from which to choose. Table 1-6 illustrates the two kanji input as a kanji compound along with candidate kanji compounds with the same pronunciation.

Table 1-6: Kanji Compound Input

Kanji Compound	Pronunciation	Kanji Compounds with Identical Pronunciation
漢字	k a n j i	漢字 感じ 幹事 監事 完司

Note how the list of kanji compounds is much shorter in this case. There is an even higher-level input unit called a *kanji phrase*. This is similar to inputting two or more kanji as a single compound, but adds another element, similar to a preposition in English, that makes the whole string into a phrase. An example of a kanji phrase is 漢字は, which means "the kanji."

Some of you may know of Japanese input software that claims to let you convert whole sentences at once. This is not really true. Such software allows you to *input* whole Japanese sentences, but the sentence is then parsed into smaller units, usually kanji phrases, then converted. Inputting whole sentences is just a convenience for the user.

Setting Japanese Text

Japanese text can be written in two orientations: left to right, top to bottom (*horizontal setting*, as in this book); and top to bottom, right to left (*vertical setting*). Vertical writing orientation more often than not causes problems with Western-language software. Luckily, it is generally acceptable to set Japanese text in the same horizontal orientation as most Western languages. Traditional Japanese novels and short stories are typically set vertically, but technical materials, such as science textbooks and the like, are set horizontally.

Vertically set Japanese text is not a simple matter of changing writing direction. Some characters require special handling, such as 90 degree rotation or a different position within the *em-square.** Chapter 6 provides some sample text set both horizontally and vertically, and illustrates the characters that need special attention.

In addition to the two writing directions for Japanese, there are other special text formatting considerations, such as special rules for wrapping characters at the ends of lines, special justification, and a way to annotate characters.

Basic Concepts and Terminology

Now I'll define some very basic concepts which will help carry you through this entire book. These concepts are posed as questions. After all, these are questions you might raise as you read this book. If at any time you encounter a new term, please glance at the glossary toward the back of the book: new terms are included and explained there.

What Are JISC, JIS, and JSA, and How Are They Related?

In much of the literature in the field of Japanese information processing you will quite often see references to JISC, JIS, and JSA. The most common of these is JIS, the least JISC. What these refer to can sometimes be confusing, and are often contradicted in reference works.

JISC stands for *Japanese Industrial Standards Committee* (日本工業標準調査会). This is the name of the governing body that establishes JIS standards and publishes manuals

---

*The term em-square refers to a square space whose height and width roughly corresponds to the width of the letter "M."

through JSA. The committee that develops and writes each JIS manual is composed of people from Japanese industry who have a deep technical background in the topic to be covered by the JIS manual. Committee members are listed at the end of each JIS manual.

JIS stands for *Japanese Industrial Standard* (日本工業規格), the name given to the standards used in Japanese industry. The character ㊜ is the symbol for JIS. JIS can refer to several things: to the character set standards established by JISC, to the encoding method specified in these character set standards, and even to the keyboard arrays described in JIS manuals. Context should usually make its meaning clear. The term JIS appears frequently in this book.

JSA stands for *Japanese Standards Association* (日本規格協会). This organization publishes the manuals for the JIS standards established by JISC, and generally oversees the whole process.

JIS is often used as a blanket term covering JISC, JIS, and JSA, but now you know what they *really* mean.

What Are Internationalization and Localization?

Internationalization (often abbreviated as I18N) is a blanket term referring to the process of preparing software so that it can be used by more than one culture or region. *Localization* (often abbreviated as L10N) is the process of adapting software to one specific culture or region. *Japanization* (often abbreviated J10N) is a specific instance of L10N. While this book does not necessarily address all of these issues, you will find information pertinent to internationalization and localization.

Either way, I18N or L10N are often desired by users because they provide menus and documentation written in the language of the target culture or region. They often require special character set handling because so many non-Roman based character sets require more than one byte to represent all their characters.

What Are the Multilingual and Locale Models?

There are two basic models for internationalization: the *locale model* and the *multilingual model*. The locale model implements a set of attributes for specific countries or cultures. The user must explicitely switch from one locale to another. The character sets implemented by the locale model are specific to a given culture or region.

The multilingual goes one step further by not requiring you to flip between locales—multilingual systems use a character set that contains all the characters necessary for several cultures or regions.

What Is KUTEN?

KUTEN is the transliterated form of the Japanese word 区点, which literally means "ward [and] point" (or, more intuitively, "row [and] cell"). This idea serves as an encoding-independent method for indexing characters in Japanese character set standards. A KUTEN code consists of four decimal digits—the KU (row) portion consists of two digits, and ranges from 1 to 94; likewise, the TEN (cell) portion consists of two digits, and ranges from 1 to 94. For example, the first character in the Japanese character set is 0101 in KUTEN.

When I provide lists of characters throughout this book, I usually include KUTEN and hexadecimal JIS codes. These are useful for future reference of this data (so that you don't have to hunt for the codes yourself!). KUTEN, like JIS, is used extensively throughout this book.

Appendixes C and D contain character tables for JIS X 0208-1990 and JIS X 0212-1990 (these represent the standard and supplemental Japanese character sets) indexed by KUTEN values.

What Is the Difference Between a Character and a Glyph?

Now here's a topic that is usually beaten to death! The term *character* is an abstract notion denoting a class of shapes declared to have the same meaning or form. A *glyph* is a specific instance of a character. Sometimes, more than one character can constitute a single glyph, such as the two characters *f* and *i* which can be fused together as the single entity *fi*. This glyph fi is called a *ligature*. The dollar sign is a good example of a character with several glyphs. There are four glyphs for the dollar sign, listed as follows:

- An S shape with a single vertical bar ($)
- An S shape with a single broken vertical bar ($)
- An S shape with two vertical bars ($)
- An S shape with two broken vertical bars ($)

The difference between these four glyphs is minor, but you cannot deny that they still represent the same character, namely the "dollar sign." Quite often you see a difference in glyph as a difference in typeface, as discussed below.

Japanese character set standards, JIS X 0208-1990 and JIS X 0212-1990 (I cover these later, so don't feel overwhelmed), do not define the glyph shape for the characters contained within their pages. Unfortunately, many think that the glyph shapes that appear in these manuals are the official ones. Note, however, that the official *Jôyô Kanji Table* does define the glyph shape, at least for the 1,945 kanji contained within. JSA published two manuals that do, in fact, define the glyph shape, JIS X 9051-1984 (previously called JIS C 6232-1984) and JIS X 9052-1983 (previously called JIS C 6234-1983). However, these glyph shapes have not been widely accepted in industry. It seems as though JSA has no intention of ever revising these documents—this may be their way of not enforcing glyph shape.

The one Japanese organization that has a chance in establishing a definitive Japanese glyph standard in Japan is called FDPC, which is short for *Font Development and Promotion Center* (文字フォント開発・普及センター). FDPC is a MITI (*Ministry of International Trade and Industry* (通商産業省)) funded organization, and is part of JSA. This government organization, with the help of developing members, is producing a series of Japanese outline typefaces called Heisei (平成) fonts. The first two Heisei typefaces released were Heisei Mincho W3 (平成明朝W3) and Heisei Kaku (squared) Gothic W5 (平成角ゴシックW5). In fact, the standard Japanese typeface used in the production of this book is Heisei Mincho W3. Several weights are planned. A Heisei Maru (rounded) Gothic (平成丸ゴシック) typeface and others will follow. The Heisei typefaces may soon be commonplace in the Japanese publishing industry. That is why I feel that FDPC has an opportunity to establish a glyph shape standard in Japan, at least for the characters contained in the Japanese character set standards.

What Is a Typeface?

The term *typeface* refers to the printed *style* of a glyph or character set. *Gothic* (ゴシック), which is roughly equivalent to *sans serif* in Western typography, and *mincho* (明朝) or *ming*, which is roughly equivalent to *serif* in Western typography, are the two most popular Japanese typeface styles. Table 1-7 lists some Japanese typefaces available from a leading manufacturer of font software and printer products (and my current employer!), Adobe Systems. I have included sample text.

Table 1-7: Sample Japanese Typefaces

Typeface Name	PostScript Name	Sample Text
平成明朝W3	HeiseiMin-W3	日本語文字のサンプル
平成明朝W9	HeiseiMin-W9	日本語文字のサンプル
見出明朝体MA31	MidashiMin-MA31	日本語文字のサンプル
平成角ゴシックW5	HeiseiKakuGo-W5	日本語文字のサンプル
見出ゴシック体MB31	MidashiGo-MB31	日本語文字のサンプル
じゅん101	Jun101-Light	日本語文字のサンプル

This is by no means a complete list of Japanese typeface styles. An example of another very popular Japanese typeface style is *kyokasho-tai* (教科書体), which literally means "textbook style."

What Are Half- and Full-width Characters?

The terms *half-* and *full-width* refer to the relative glyph size of characters. These terms are sometimes referred to as *hankaku* (半角) and *zenkaku* (全角), respectively. Half-width is relative to full-width. Full-width refers to the glyph size of standard Japanese characters. English characters, which appear to take up approximately half the display width of Japanese characters, are considered to be half-width by this standard. The very first Japanese characters to be processed on computer systems were half-width katakana. They have the same approximate display width as English characters. There are now full-width Roman and katakana characters. Table 1-8 shows the difference in display width between half- and full-width characters (the katakana character used as the example is pronounced *ka*).

Table 1-8: Half- Versus Full-width Characters

Katakana		Roman	
Full-width	カカカカカ	Full-width	１２３４５
Half-width	ｶｶｶｶｶ	Half-width	12345

As you can see, full-width characters occupy twice the display space as their half-width versions.

At one point in time there was a clear-cut relationship between display width of a glyph and number of bytes used to encode it—the number of bytes determined the display width. Half-width katakana characters were originally encoded with one byte. Full-width were encoded with two bytes. Now that there is a much richer choice of encoding methods available, this relationship no longer holds true. Table 1-9 lists several popular encoding methods along with the number of bytes required to represent half- and full-width characters.

Table 1-9: Half- and Full-width Character Representations

	ASCII	JIS	Shift-JIS	EUC	Unicode	ISO 10646
Full-width						
Katakana	...	2 bytes	2 bytes	2 bytes	2 bytes	2 or 4 bytes
Roman	...	2 bytes	2 bytes	2 bytes	2 bytes	2 or 4 bytes
Half-width						
Katakana	...	1 byte	1 byte	2 bytes	2 bytes	2 or 4 bytes
Roman	1 byte	1 byte	1 byte	1 byte	2 bytes	2 or 4 bytes

What Is Notation?

The term *notation* refers to a method of representing units. A distance expressed as one mile or 1.6 kilometers is, after all, the same distance. In computer science, common notations for representing the value of bytes are listed in Table 1-10, and all correspond to a different number base.

Table 1-10: Decimal 100 in Various Notations

	Base	Range	Example
Binary	2	0–1	01100100
Octal	8	0–7	144
Decimal	10	0–9	100
Hexadecimal	16	0–9 and A–F	64

While the numbers in the *Example* column all have the same underlying value, they have been expressed using different notations, and thus take on a different form. Most people use decimal notation; however, computers process information using binary notation (as discussed above, computers process *bits*, which have two possible values). Below you will find that hexadecimal notation does, however, have distinct advantages when dealing with computers.

What Is an Octet?

We already discussed the terms *bits* and *bytes*. But what about the term *octet*? At a glance, you can tell it has something to do with the number eight. An octet represents eight bits, and is an eight-bit byte. This becomes confusing when dealing with 16-bit encodings. 16 bits can be broken down into two eight-bit bytes, or two octets. 32 bits, likewise, can be broken down into four eight-bit bytes, or four octets.

Given 16 bits in a row:

```
0110010001011111
```

This string of bits can be broken down into two eight-bit units, namely octets (bytes):

```
01100100
01011111
```

The first eight bits represent 100 (0x64), and the second 95 (0x5F). All 16 bits together as one unit are usually equal to 25695 in decimal or 0x645F in hexadecimal—it may be different depending on a computer's specific architecture. Divide 25695 by 256 to get the first byte's value as a decimal octet, namely 100—the remainder from this division is the value of the second byte, which, in this case, is 95. Table 1-11 lists representations of two octets (bytes) and their 16-bit unit equivalent. This is done for you in different notations.

Table 1-11: Octets and 16-bit Units in Various Notations

Notation	First Octet	Second Octet	16-bit Unit
Binary	01100100	01011111	0110010001011111
Octal	144	137	62137
Decimal	100	95	25695
Hexadecimal	64	5F	645F

Note how going from two octets to a 16-bit unit is a simple matter of concatenation in the case of binary and hexadecimal notation. Not so with decimal notation, which requires multiplication of the first octet by 256, then addition of the second octet. The ease of going between different representations (octets versus 16-bit units) depends on the notation that you are using. Of course, concatenation is easier than two mathematical processes. This is why hexadecimal is used so frequently in computers.

2

The Japanese Writing System

Now that you have had a taste of what to expect to learn about Japanese information processing, let's begin with a thorough description of the Japanese writing system. We already touched briefly upon this subject in the introductory material, but you need to learn a bit more. After reading this chapter you should have an understanding of the types of characters used to write Japanese, namely the following four: Roman characters, hiragana, katakana, and kanji.

Each of these types of characters exhibits its own special characteristics, and usually has specific usages. This information is absolutely crucial for understanding discussions elsewhere in this book.

Roman Characters

Roman characters (ローマ字) used in Japanese texts are the same as those used in Western texts, namely the 52 lowercase and uppercase characters of the alphabet. Also included are the ten numerals zero through nine. Table 2-1 lists the Roman characters, for the sake of completeness.

Table 2-1: Roman Characters

Lowercase	abcdefghijklmnopqrstuvwxyz
Uppercase	ABCDEFGHIJKLMNOPQRSTUVWXYZ
Numerals	0123456789

There is really nothing special about these characters. The Japanese do not use them differently from Western languages. They are most often used in tables (numerals) or in acronyms (alphabet). The Japanese, too, find acronyms a convenient way of abbreviating names of organizations and such.

Hiragana

Hiragana (平仮名) are characters that represent sounds, specifically syllables. A syllable is generally composed of a consonant plus a vowel—sometimes just a vowel will do. In Japanese, there are five vowels: *a, i, u, e,* and *o*; and 14 basic consonants: *k, s, t, n, h, m, y, r, w, g, z, d, b,* and *p.* It is important to understand that hiragana are a *syllabary*, not an alphabet—you cannot decompose a hiragana character into a part that represents the vowel and a part that represents the consonant. Hiragana (and katakana, covered in the next section) is one of the only true syllabaries still in common use today. Table 2-2 illustrates a matrix containing the basic and extended hiragana syllabary.

Table 2-2: The Hiragana Syllabary

	k	s	t	n	h	m	y	r	w	g	z	d	b	p
a	あ[1]	か	さ	た	な	は	ま	や[1]	ら	わ[1]	が	ざ	だ	ば	ぱ
i	い[1]	き	し	ち	に	ひ	み		り	ゐ[2]	ぎ	じ	ぢ	び	ぴ
u	う[1]	く	す	つ[1]	ぬ	ふ	む	ゆ[1]	る		ぐ	ず	づ	ぶ	ぷ
e	え[1]	け	せ	て	ね	へ	め		れ	ゑ[2]	げ	ぜ	で	べ	ぺ
o	お[1]	こ	そ	と	の	ほ	も	よ[1]	ろ	を[3]	ご	ぞ	ど	ぼ	ぽ
n	ん[4]														

[1]Several hiragana have smaller versions, and are as follows (in parentheses you will find the normal version): ぁ (あ), ぃ (い), ぅ (う), ぇ (え), ぉ (お), っ (つ), ゃ (や), ゅ (ゆ), ょ (よ), and ゎ (わ).

[2]Two hiragana, ゐ and ゑ, are no longer commonly used.

[3]The hiragana を is pronounced as *o*, not *wo*.

[4]The hiragana ん is used to close syllables, and is pronounced like *n*.

Notice that some cells do not contain any characters. These sounds are no longer used in Japanese, and thus no longer need a character to represent them. Also, the first block of characters is set in a five-by-ten matrix. This is sometimes referred to as the *50 Sounds Table* (50音表), so named because it has a capacity of 50 cells. The other blocks of characters are the same as those in the first block, but with *diacritic marks.*

Diacritic marks serve to annotate characters with additional information—usually a variant pronunciation. In the West you commonly see accented characters such as á, à, â, ä, ã, and å. The accents are diacritic marks.

In Japanese there are two diacritic marks: *nigori* and *maru.* The nigori (濁り) appears as two short strokes (ﾞ) in the upper-right corner of some kana characters. Nigori serves to *voice* the consonant portion of the kana character to which it is attached. Voicing is a linguistic term referring to the vibration of the vocal bands while pronouncing a consonant. Examples of voiceless consonants include *k*, *s*, and *t*. Their voiced counterparts are *g*, *z*, and *d*, respectively. Hiragana *ka* (か) becomes *ga* (が) with the addition of the nigori mark. The *b* sound is a special case of a voiced *h* in Japanese. The maru (丸) appears as a small open circle (゚) in the upper-right corner of kana characters that begin with the *h* consonant. It transforms this *h* consonant into a *p* sound.

Hiragana were derived by cursively writing kanji, but no longer carry the meaning of the kanji from which they were derived. Table 2-4 lists the kanji from which the basic hiragana characters were derived.

Hiragana are used to write grammatical words, inflectional endings for verbs and adjectives, and some nouns. They can also be used as a fallback in case you forget how to write a kanji—the hiragana that represent the pronunciation of a kanji are used in this case. In summary, hiragana are used to write native Japanese words. The following characters represent the standard hiragana character set as listed in the basic Japanese character set standard:

ぁあぃいぅうぇえぉおかがきぎくぐけげこごさざしじ
すずせぜそぞただちぢっつづてでとどなにぬねのはば
ぱひびぴふぶぷへべぺほぼぽまみむめもゃやゅゆょよ
らりるれろゎわゐゑをん

Note how these characters have a *cursive* or *calligraphic* look to them (cursive and calligraphic refer to a smoother, handwritten style of characters). Keep these shapes in mind while we move on to katakana.

Katakana

Katakana (片仮名), like hiragana, are a syllabary, and represent the same set of sounds as hiragana. Their usage, however, differs from hiragana. Where hiragana are used to write native Japanese words, katakana are used primarily in two ways: to write words of foreign origin, called *gairaigo* (外来語), and for emphasis—similar to the use of italics to represent foreign words and to express emphasis in English. For example, the Japanese word for *bread* is written パン and pronounced *pan*. It was borrowed from the Portugese word *pāo*, which is pronounced sort of like *pown*. Katakana are also used to write foreign names. Table 2-3 illustrates the basic and extended katakana syllabary.

Table 2-3: The Katakana Syllabary

	k	s	t	n	h	m	y	r	w	g	z	d	b	p
a	ア[1]	カ[1]	サ	タ	ナ	ハ	マ	ヤ[1]	ラ	ワ[1]	ガ	ザ	ダ	バ	パ
i	イ[1]	キ	シ	チ	ニ	ヒ	ミ		リ	ヰ[2]	ギ	ジ	ヂ	ビ	ピ
u	ウ[1]	ク	ス	ツ[1]	ヌ	フ	ム	ユ[1]	ル		グ	ズ	ヅ	ブ	プ
e	エ[1]	ケ[1]	セ	テ	ネ	ヘ	メ		レ	ヱ[2]	ゲ	ゼ	デ	ベ	ペ
o	オ[1]	コ	ソ	ト	ノ	ホ	モ	ヨ[1]	ロ	ヲ[3]	ゴ	ゾ	ド	ボ	ポ
n	ン[4]														

[1] Several katakana have smaller versions, and are as follows (in parentheses you will find the normal version): ァ (ア), ィ (イ), ゥ (ウ), ェ (エ), ォ (オ), ヵ (カ), ヶ (ケ), ッ (ツ), ャ (ヤ), ュ (ユ), ョ (ヨ), and ヮ (ワ).

[2] Two katakana, ヰ and ヱ, are no longer commonly used.

[3] The katakana ヲ is pronounced as *o*, not *wo*.

[4] The katakana ン is used to close syllables, and is pronounced like *n*.

Katakana were derived by extracting a single portion of a whole kanji, and, like hiragana, no longer carry the meaning of the kanji from which they were derived. If you compare several of these characters to some kanji, you may recognize common shapes. Table 2-4 lists the basic katakana characters along with the kanji from which they were derived.

Table 2-4: The Kanji Used to Derive Katakana and Hiragana

Katakana	Kanji		Hiragana	Katakana	Kanji		Hiragana
ア	阿	安	あ	ノ	乃		の
イ	伊	以	い	ハ	八	波	は
ウ	宇		う	ヒ	比		ひ
エ	江	衣	え	フ	不		ふ
オ	於		お	ヘ	部		へ
カ	加		か	ホ	保		ほ
キ	幾		き	マ	万	末	ま
ク	久		く	ミ	三	美	み
ケ	介	計	け	ム	牟	武	む
コ	己		こ	メ	女		め
サ	散	左	さ	モ	毛		も
シ	之		し	ヤ	也		や
ス	須	寸	す	ユ	由		ゆ
セ	世		せ	ヨ	与		よ
ソ	曽		そ	ラ	良		ら
タ	多	太	た	リ	利		り
チ	千	知	ち	ル	流	留	る
ツ	川		つ	レ	礼	禮	れ

Katakana	Kanji	Hiragana	Katakana	Kanji		Hiragana
テ	天	て	ロ	呂		ろ
ト	止	と	ワ	和		わ
ナ	奈	な	ヰ	井	為	ゐ
ニ	二　仁	に	ヱ	恵		ゑ
ヌ	奴	ぬ	ヲ	乎	遠	を
ネ	祢　禰	ね	ン	尓	无	ん

Note how many of the kanji from which katakana and hiragana characters were derived are the same, and how the shapes of several hiragana/katakana pairs are similar. In fact, many katakana are nearly identical to kanji, and can usually be distinguished by their smaller size. Katakana can usually be distinguished from kanji in that they are usually found in strings containing other katakana. Table 2-5 shows some examples of this phenomenon.

Table 2-5: Katakana and Kanji With Similar Shapes

Katakana	Kanji	Katakana	Kanji	Katakana	Kanji
エ	工	ト	ト	ム	ム
カ	力	ニ	二	メ	メ
タ	夕	ヒ	ヒ	ロ	口

The following characters represent the standard katakana character set as contained in the basic Japanese character set standard:

ァアィイゥウェエォオカガキギクグケゲコゴサザシジ
スズセゼソゾタダチヂッツヅテデトドナニヌネノハバ
パヒビピフブプヘベペホボポマミムメモャヤュユョヨ
ラリルレロヮワヰヱヲンヴヵヶ

Katakana, unlike hiragana, have a squared, more rigid feel to them. Structurally speaking, they are quite similar in appearance to kanji, which we discuss next.

Kanji

The single most complex writing system used by the Japanese is called *kanji* (漢字). The word kanji literally means "Chinese character." These characters were borrowed from the Chinese over 1,500 years ago. To grasp the concept of kanji, one must first understand the magnitude of such a writing system. The 26 characters of the English alphabet (52 characters, if one counts both lowercase and uppercase) seem quite limiting compared to the tens of thousands of kanji in current use by the Japanese and other Asian countries. It is well documented that the Japanese borrowed the Chinese script over the course of a millennium. What is *not* well known is that while the Japanese were borrowing from the Chinese, the Chinese were, themselves, adding to the total number of characters in their language by creating new characters. This means that the Japanese were able, in essence, to capture and freeze a segment of Chinese history every time they borrowed from the Chinese. Kanji were not usually borrowed as individual characters, but as compounds containing two or more kanji.

Before we begin discussions about the history of kanji, and how kanji are composed, let's take some time to illustrate some examples of kanji. The following characters represent the first row of 94 kanji in the standard Japanese character set standard:

亜唖娃阿哀愛挨姶逢葵茜穐悪握渥旭葦芦鯵梓圧斡扱宛
姐虻飴絢綾鮎或粟袷安庵按暗案闇鞍杏以伊位依偉囲夷
委威尉惟意慰易椅為畏異移維緯胃萎衣謂違遺医井亥域
育郁磯一壱溢逸稲茨芋鰯允印咽員因姻引飲淫胤蔭

A noteworthy characteristic of kanji is that they can be quite complex (believe it or not, they can get even more complex than the 94 shown above!). Kanji are composed of *radicals*, which can be thought of as building-blocks. Radicals are discussed later in this chapter, in the section *The Structure of Kanji*.

The Pronunciation of Kanji

Kanji are usually assigned one or more pronunciations—also known as *readings*. The terms *pronunciation* and *reading* are used interchangeably.

The typical kanji has at least two pronunciations—some have more. For example, the kanji 生, whose meaning relates to "life," has 27 pronunciations—most of which are found in Japanese given names, which typically have unusual pronunciations. No matter what their pronunciation, they still have approximately the same meaning.

Kanji pronunciations come from two sources:

* Native Japanese pronunciation
* Borrowed (and approximated) Chinese pronunciation

The native Japanese pronunciation was how the Japanese pronounced a word before the Chinese influenced their language and writing system. The native Japanese pronunciation is called the *KUN reading* (訓読み).

The borrowed Chinese pronunciation is the Japanese language approximation of the native Chinese pronunciation of a kanji.* These borrowed approximate pronunciations are called *ON readings* (音読み), ON being the word for "sound." If a particular kanji was

---

* Some people believe that the Chinese pronunciations are closer to Cantonese than to Mandarin Chinese.

borrowed more than once, multiple pronunciations can result. Table 2-6 lists several kanji along with their respective pronunciations.

Table 2-6: Kanji and Their Pronunciations

Kanji	Meaning	ON Readings	KUN Readings
剣	*sword*	ken	akira, haya, tsurugi, tsutomu
窓	*window*	sô	mado
車	*car*	sha	kuruma
万	*10,000*	ban, man	katsu, kazu, susumu, taka, tsumoru, tsumu, yorozu
生	*life, birth*	sei, shô	ari, bu, fu, fuyu, haeru, hayasu, i, ikasu, ikeru, ikiru, iku, ki, mi, nama, nari, nori, o, oki, ou, susumu, taka, ubu, umareru, umu, yo
店	*store, shop*	ten	mise

So how does one go about deciding which pronunciation to use? Good question! As you learned earlier, the Japanese borrowed kanji as compounds of two or more kanji, and use the ON reading for such compounds. Conversely, when these same kanji appear in isolation, the KUN reading is used. Table 2-7 provides some examples of individual kanji and kanji compounds.

Table 2-7: Kanji and Kanji Compounds

Kanji Compound	Meaning	Pronunciation
自動車	*automobile*	jidôsha (ON readings)
車	*car*	kuruma (KUN reading)
剣道	*Kendo*	kendô (ON readings)
剣	*sword*	tsurugi (KUN reading)

As with all languages, there are always exceptions to rules! Sometimes you find kanji compounds that use KUN readings for one or all kanji. You may also find kanji in isolation that use ON readings. Table 2-8 lists some examples.

Table 2-8: Irregular Uses of Kanji Pronunciations

Kanji Compound	Meaning	Pronunciation
重箱	*nest of boxes*	jûbako (ON plus KUN reading)
湯桶	*bath ladle*	yutô (KUN plus ON reading)
窓口	*ticket window*	madoguchi (KUN plus KUN reading)
単	*simple, single*	tan (ON reading)

Japanese personal names tend to use the KUN readings even though they are in compounds. For instance, 藤本 is pronounced *fujimoto* rather than *tôhon*.

The Structure of Kanji

Kanji are composed of smaller, primitive units called *radicals*, which are used as building blocks. Radicals are the most basic meaningful units of kanji. 214 radicals are used for writing kanji. Several radicals stand alone as single, meaningful kanji. Table 2-9 provides some examples of radicals along with several kanji that can be written with them.

Table 2-9: Radicals and Kanji Made From Them

Radical	Variant	Stand-alone	Meaning	Examples
木		yes	*tree*	本札朴朶李材条杲林枦栞棚森橋
火	灬	yes	*fire*	灯灰灸災炎点無然熊熟熱燃燭爛
水	氵	yes	*water*	氷永汁江汲沢泉温測港源溢澡濯
辵	辶	no	*running*	辷込辻辺迪迄迅迎近返迚連週還

Note how each radical is placed within kanji—they are stretched or squeezed so that all of the radicals that constitute a kanji fit into the general shape of a square. Also note how radicals are positioned within kanji, namely on the left, right, top, or bottom.

Radicals, in turn, are composed of smaller units called *strokes*. A radical can consist of one or more strokes. Sometimes a single stroke is considered a radical. There is even one stroke that is considered a single kanji: 一, the kanji that represents the number one. Figure 2-1 shows how a typical kanji is composed of radicals and strokes.

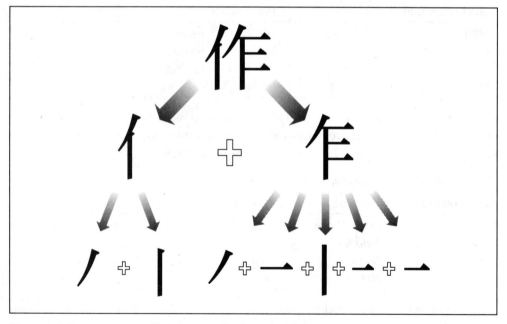

Figure 2-1: Decomposition of kanji into radicals and strokes

There are many classifications of kanji, but four are most common: pictographic, ideographic, logical compounds, and phonetic compounds. *Pictographic* (象形文字), the most basic, are little pictures, and usually look much like the object they represent. Table 2-10 lists examples of pictographic kanji.

Table 2-10: Pictographic Kanji

Kanji	Meaning
日	*sun*
月	*moon*
山	*mountain*
火	*fire*
木	*tree*
車	*car, cart*
口	*mouth*

Whereas pictographic kanji represent concrete objects, *ideographic characters* (指事文字) represent abstract concepts or ideas (as the name suggests), such as numbers and directions. Table 2-11 lists examples of ideographic kanji.

Table 2-11: Ideographic Kanji

Kanji	Meaning
上	*up*
下	*down*
中	*center, middle*
一	*one*
二	*two*
三	*three*

Pictographic and ideographic kanji can be combined to represent more complex pictures, and usually reflect the combined meaning of its individual elements. These are called *logical compounds* (会意文字). Table 2-12 lists examples of logical compounds.

Table 2-12: Logical Compounds

Kanji	Components	Meaning
林	木 + 木	*woods*
森	木 + 木 + 木	*forest*
明	日 + 月	*clear, bright*

Phonetic compounds (形声文字) account for more than 90 percent of all kanji. They usually have at least two components, one to indicate pronunciation, and the other to denote basic meaning. Table 2-13 provides examples that all use the same base *pronunciation* component.

Table 2-13: Phonetic Compounds With a Common Pronunciation Component

Kanji	Meaning	Pronunciation	Meaning Part	Pronunciation Part
銅	*copper*	dô	金 (*metal*)	同 (dô)
洞	*cave*	dô	氵 (*water*)	同 (dô)
胴	*torso*	dô	月 (*organ*)	同 (dô)
恫	*threat*	dô	忄 (*heart*)	同 (dô)

Note that each uses the 同 radical (dô) for its pronunciation component. Table 2-14 lists several kanji that use the same base *meaning* component.

Table 2-14: Phonetic Compounds With a Common Meaning Component

Kanji	Meaning	Pronunciation	Meaning Part	Pronunciation Part
雰	*fog*	fun	雨 (*rain*)	分 (fun)
雲	*cloud*	un	雨 (*rain*)	云 (un)
震	*shake*	shin	雨 (*rain*)	辰 (shin)
霜	*frost*	sô	雨 (*rain*)	相 (sô)

Note that each uses the 雨 ("rain") radical for its meaning component. The 雨 radical is another example of a radical that can stand alone as a single kanji.

Kanji are subsequently combined with other kanji as words to form more complex ideas or concepts. These are called *compounds* or *kanji compounds* (熟語). Table 2-15 lists a few examples. Note that you can decompose words into pieces, each piece being a single kanji with its own meaning.

Table 2-15: Kanji Compounds

Compound	Meaning	Component Kanji and Their Meaning
日本	*Japan* (the country)	日 means *sun*, and 本 means *origin*
短刀	*short sword*	短 means *short*, and 刀 means *sword*
酸素	*oxygen*	酸 means *oxygen*, and 素 means *element* (*the element oxygen*)
曲線	*curve*	曲 means *curved*, and 線 means *line* (*curved line*)
剣道	*Kendo*	剣 means *sword*, and 道 means *path* (*the way of the sword*)
自動車	*automobile*	自 means *self*, 動 means *moving*, and 車 means *car*
火山	*volcano*	火 means *fire*, and 山 means *mountain* (*fire mountain*)

There, that should have given you a sense of how kanji are constructed and how they are combined with other kanji to form compounds. But how did they come to be used in Japan? These and other questions are answered next.

The History of Kanji

This section provides some historical context to explain the history of kanji, and how they came to be used in Japan.

There is no evidence to suggest that there was any writing system in place in Japan prior to the introduction of the Chinese script. In fact, it is quite common for writing systems to develop relatively late in the history of languages. A writing system as complex as Chinese is not really an ideal choice for borrowing, but perhaps this was the only writing system from which the Japanese could choose at the time.

The Japanese borrowed kanji from the Chinese between 222 AD and 1279 AD. During this millennium of borrowing, the Chinese increased their inventory of kanji nearly three-fold. Table 2-16 illustrates the number of kanji that existed in Chinese at different periods.

Table 2-16: The Number of Chinese Characters During Different Periods

Year (AD)	Number of Kanji
100	9,353
227–239	11,520
480	18,150
543	22,726
751	26,194
1066	31,319
1615	33,179
1716	47,021
1919	44,908
1969	49,888

This table clearly indicates that the Chinese, over a period of about 2,000 years, increased their inventory of kanji by roughly a factor of five (from 9,353 to 49,888). As you can see, the Japanese were borrowing from the Chinese even while the Chinese were still creating new kanji.

The Japanese began borrowing the Chinese script over 1,500 years ago. This massive borrowing took place in three different waves. Several kanji were borrowed repeatedly at different periods, and the pronunciation of each kanji was also borrowed again. This led to different pronunciations for a given kanji depending on which word or words it appeared in, due to dialectal and diachronic differences in China.*

The first wave of borrowing took place sometime between 222 and 589 AD via Korea, during the Six Dynasties Period in China. Kanji borrowed during this period were those used primarily in Buddhist terminology. During this period, the Chinese had between 11,520 and 22,726 kanji.

The second wave took place between 618 and 907 AD, during the T'ang Dynasty in China. Kanji borrowed during this period were those used primarily for government and in Confucianism terminology. During this period, the Chinese had between 22,726 and 26,194 kanji.

The third wave occurred somewhere between 960 and 1279 AD, during the Song Dynasty in China. Kanji borrowed during this period were those used in Zen terminology. The Chinese had between 31,319 and 33,179 kanji by this period.

During all three waves of borrowing, most kanji were borrowed as *compounds* of two or more kanji, rather than as isolated characters. It is in this context that you find differences in pronunciation of a particular kanji depending on what word it appears in. For example, the kanji 万, meaning "ten thousand," can be found in kanji compounds with either the pronunciation *man* or *ban*, that is, 万一 (*man + ichi*) and 万歳 (*ban + zai*—yes, the actual kanji compound for *banzai*!). This *(m)an/(b)an* alternation would indicate to a linguist that these two words were probably borrowed at different periods.

The first two waves of borrowing had the most significant impact on the Japanese lexicon, which accounts for the dual Chinese pronunciation of many kanji (lexicon simply refers to the individual words that constitute a language). The third wave of borrowing had very little effect on the Japanese lexicon.

Over time, Chinese characters have been simplified. Such simplifications have been different depending on the culture using them. For example, kanji (or *banzi*, as they are called in Chinese) in their traditional form are still being used in Taiwan—their most widely used character set standard is called *Big Five*. The same holds true for Korea, whose character set standard is called KS C 5601-1992 (kanji are called *hanja* in Korean). Also, kanji in an even more simplified form than found in Japanese are being used in Mainland China—their character set standard is called GB 2312-80. A great number of kanji are used in an identical form in Japan, Taiwan, Korea, and Mainland China, so you will find a lot of commonality. Table 2-17 illustrates several kanji in both simplified and

---

Dialectal and *diachronic* are linguistic terms. Dialectal refers to different flavors of a language that are usually spoken in different regions. Diachronic refers to linguistic changes that occur between different periods. *Synchronic*, a related term, refers to changes that exist during the same period.

traditional form (KUTEN values are given followed by hexadecimal JIS values in parentheses).

Table 2-17: Simplified and Traditional Kanji Forms

Traditional	Simplified (Japan)	Simplified (Mainland China)
廣 5502 (5722)	広 2513 (392D)	广 5678 (5488)
兒 4927 (513B)	児 2789 (3B79)	儿 4925 (5139)
兩 4932 (5140)	両 4630 (4E3E)	两 1608 (3028)[1]
氣 6170 (5D66)	気 2104 (3524)	气 6167 (5D63)
豐 7620 (6C34)	豊 4313 (4B2D)	丰 1613 (302D)[1]
國 5202 (5422)	国 2581 (3971)	国 2581 (3971)
學 5360 (555C)	学 1956 (3358)	学 1956 (3358)
點 8358 (735A)	点 3732 (4540)	点 3732 (4540)

[1] The KUTEN and hexadecimal JIS codes given here correspond to the JIS X 0212-1990 code table.

In case you are wondering, those codes, KUTEN and hexadecimal JIS, are indexes to the characters in Table 2-17. I used those codes to illustrate that each of the kanji has a unique encoding within the same character set standard. These and other codes are described in Chapter 4.

Both the simplified and traditional forms of kanji can coexist within the same character set standard, and the above pairs are such examples—most of them are part of the basic Japanese character set standard, namely JIS X 0208-1990. The two exceptions can be found in JIS X 0212-1990. You can see that some simplifications are more extreme than others.

Such simplifications in Japan have led to variants of many characters, and in some character sets both the simplified and traditional forms are included (the examples given above are such cases). As an extreme example, let's examine the JIS X 0208-1990 kanji 剣 (KUTEN 2385, and JIS 0x3775), whose five variant kanji are also encoded within the same character set standard. These variants are listed in Table 2-18 (KUTEN values are given followed by hexadecimal JIS values in parentheses).

Table 2-18: Kanji Variants in the Same Character Set

Kanji

劍 4988 (5178)
劒 4989 (5179)
劔 4990 (517A)
剱 4991 (517B)
釼 7863 (6E5F)

Finally, the Japanese have created their own kanji. These are known as *kokuji* (国字), literally meaning "national characters," or more intuitively, "Japanese-made kanji." Kokuji behave like true kanji, following the same rules of structure—namely that they are composed of radicals and strokes, and can be combined with one or more other kanji to form compounds or words. These kanji were created out of a need for characters not borrowed from China. In fact, many kokuji were borrowed by the Chinese! Most kokuji are used to represent indigenous Japanese plants and fish. They are also used quite frequently in Japanese place and personal names.

Approximately 200 kokuji have been identified in the basic Japanese character set standard, namely JIS X 0208-1990. There are even more in the supplemental set, namely JIS X 0212-1990. Table 2-19 provides a few examples of kokuji (KUTEN values are given followed by hexadecimal JIS values in parentheses):

Table 2-19: Examples of Kokuji

Kokuji	Pronunciations	Meaning
峠 3829 (463D)	tôge	*mountain pass*
働 3815 (462F)	hataraku, dô	*to work*
畑 4010 (482A)	hata, hatake	*dry field*
鰯 1683 (3073)	iwashi	*sardine*
粂 2309 (3729)	kume	Used in personal names
枠 4740 (4F48)	waku	*frame*
榊 2671 (3A67)	sakaki	A species of tree called *sakaki*
凩 4962 (515E)	kogarashi	*cold, wintry wind*

More kokuji were created when the Japanese isolated themselves from the rest of the world for approximately 250 years: from the mid-1600s to the late 1800s. Without direct influence from China, the Japanese resorted to creating their own kanji as necessary.

3

Japanese Character Set Standards

Japanese character sets can be classified into two basic types: *non-electronic* and *electronic*. Non-electronic refers to a character set established without regard to how it would be processed on computer systems, if at all. Electronic refers to being electronically encoded, that is, that such character sets were specifically designed for processing on computer systems. You will find that the characters contained in non-electronic sets constitute a subset of the characters contained in electronic character sets.

After reading this chapter, you should be able to distinguish which characters constitute a particular character set, and how each of these character sets relates to the others.

Non-electronic Character Set Standards

Long before there were any electronic character set standards in Japan (or even before the concept of an electronic character set standard existed!), several non-electronic ones existed. These were the first attempts to limit the number of kanji used in Japan.

All of these non-electronic character sets include only kanji. Since everyone is expected to learn hiragana and katakana, there is a need to limit only the number of kanji, which can number in the tens of thousands. These character sets include *Jôyô Kanji* (preceded by *Tôyô Kanji*)—the 1,945 kanji designated by the Japanese government as the ones to be used in public documents such as newspapers; *Gakushû Kanji* (preceded by *Kyôiku Kanji*)—the 1,006 kanji formally taught during the first six grades in Japanese schools; and *Jinmei-yô Kanji*—the 284 kanji sanctioned by the Japanese government for use in writing personal names. The growth and development of these character sets are listed in Table 3-1 (note that some were renamed).

Table 3-1: Evolving Kanji Counts for Various Non-electronic Character Set Standards

Year	Tôyô Kanji	Kyôiku Kanji	Jinmei-yô Kanji
1946	1850[1]		
1948		881	
1951			92
1976			120
1977		996 (Gakushû Kanji)	
1981	1945 (Jôyô Kanji)		166
1990			284
1992		1006[2]	

[1]The corresponding glyph chart (当用漢字字体表) was published in 1949, and likewise, the corresponding pronunciation table (当用漢字音訓表) was published in 1948.
[2]This was established in 1989, but was not fully implemented until 1992.

There is some overlap between these character sets. Gakushû Kanji is a subset of Jôyô Kanji (likewise, Kyôiku Kanji was a subset of Tôyô Kanji).

Table 3-2 shows how you write the names of these character sets in native Japanese orthography, and tells you what they really mean.

Table 3-2: The Names and Meanings of Japanese Non-electronic Character Set Standards

Character Set	In Japanese	Meaning
Tôyô Kanji	当用漢字	Common use kanji
Jôyô Kanji	常用漢字	Everyday use kanji
Kyôiku Kanji	教育漢字	Instructional kanji
Gakushû Kanji	学習漢字	Educational kanji
Jinmei-yô Kanji	人名用漢字	Personal name use kanji

While this table appears to show that the Gakushû Kanji list gained only 10 kanji between 1977 and 1992, the list also experienced some internal shifts. Gakushû Kanji and Kyôiku Kanji are broken down into six sets of kanji, each one corresponding to the grade of school during which they are formerly taught. Table 3-3 shows the six grade levels on the left, along with the number of kanji taught during each one—this is done for Kyôiku Kanji and both versions of Gakushû Kanji.

Table 3-3: The Development of Gakushû Kanji

Grade	1958 (881)[1]	1977 (996)	1992 (1,006)
1	46	76	80
2	105	145	160
3	187	195	200

[1]Kyôiku Kanji was not divided into the six grade levels until 1958.

Grade	1958 (881)	1977 (996)	1992 (1,006)
4	205	195	200
5	194	195	185
6	144	190	181

The general trend shown by Table 3-3 is that more kanji are now taught in the earlier grades.

Appendixes E through G contain complete listings of Jôyô Kanji, Gakushû Kanji, and Jinmei-yô Kanji character sets.

Electronic Character Set Standards

Proliferation of computers necessitated the creation of electronic character set standards. The first multiple-byte national electronic character set standard in Asia was a Japanese electronic character set established on January 1, 1978 by the Japanese Standards Association (JSA), and was named JIS C 6226-1978. Other Asian countries, such as Korea and China, followed suit by copying the Japanese solution, and in some cases copied more than just the encoding method or arrangement of characters. For example, in the case of the Chinese Big Five character set, it was claimed that the Chinese (in Taiwan) borrowed several bitmapped glyphs from JIS C 6226-1978. Anyway, JIS C 6226-1978 went through two revisions to eventually become JIS X 0208-1990 on September 1, 1990. On October 1, 1990, a supplemental Japanese character set standard called JIS X 0212-1990 was also established.

Five electronic character sets are widely used in Japan, and are considered the "national" character sets. They are ASCII, JIS-Roman, half-width katakana, JIS X 0208-1990 (and its predecessors), and JIS X 0212-1990. Next, Asian character set standards are covered, which, while not used in Japan, show how similar concepts of large character sets are used in other Asian countries, such as Korea, Mainland China, and Taiwan. Finally, this chapter ends with a discussion of international character set standards, namely Unicode, ISO 10646, and XCCS, and describes how they relate to the national character sets, and when applicable, how they relate to each other.

National Character Set Standards

Character set standards described in this section constitute those maintained by the government or a government-sanctioned organization within a given country, and are considered the standard character sets for such countries. In addition, such character set standards usually form the foundation from which others are derived (as you will see later in this chapter).

Table 3-4 summarizes the national character sets described in this section along with the number and types of characters implemented by each.

Table 3-4: Japanese National Character Set Standards

	JIS Level 1 Kanji[1]	JIS Level 2 Kanji[1]	Non-kanji	Control Codes
ASCII/JIS-Roman			94	34
Half-width katakana			63[2]	
JIS C 6226-1978	2,965	3,384	453	
JIS X 0208-1983	2,965	3,388	524	
JIS X 0208-1990	2,965	3,390	524	
JIS X 0212-1990	5,801[3]		266	

[1]The terms JIS Level 1 kanji and JIS Level 2 kanji have not been described yet. They refer simply to the two groups of kanji characters that make up JIS X 0208-1990 and its past versions. JIS Level 1 kanji contains frequently used kanji, whereas JIS Level 2 kanji contains less frequently used kanji. JIS X 0212-1990 only has one group of kanji, though.

[2]Some implementations have 64—the extra character is a half-width space.

[3]This set of 5,801 kanji is more properly referred to as *supplemental kanji*.

ASCII

Most readers of this book are probably familiar with the ASCII character set standard, so it is a good place to begin the discussion of character set standards, and will serve as a point of reference. This character set is covered in this book because it is quite often mixed with Japanese characters within a text stream. Note, however, that the ASCII character set standard is not specific to Japanese. ASCII is an acronym for *American Standard Code for Information Interchange*. The definition of the ASCII character set standard is described in the documents ISO 646-1991* and ANSI X3.4-1986.† ANSI X3.4-1986 describes the United States version of the ASCII character set.

The ASCII character set is composed of 128 characters. The printable ASCII character set standard consists of 94 characters. There are also 34 other characters, which include a space character and many control characters (such as tab, escape, shift-in, and so on). Table 3-5 lists the 94 printable ASCII characters.

Table 3-5: The ASCII Character Set

Lowercase Roman	`abcdefghijklmnopqrstuvwxyz`
Uppercase Roman	`ABCDEFGHIJKLMNOPQRSTUVWXYZ`
Numerals	`0123456789`
Symbols	`!"#$%&'()*+,-./:;<=>?@[\]^_`{|}~`

---

*ISO is short for *International Standards Organization*.

†ANSI is short for *American National Standards Institute*.

These same printable characters are also used in EBCDIC, an encoding method covered in the next chapter. The binary nature of computers allows these 128 characters to be represented with seven bits, but because computers evolved along processing information in eight-bit segments, these 128 ASCII characters are usually represented by either seven or eight bits. Other character sets incorporate these characters, often encoded as two bytes.

There are also nine extended ASCII character sets. These character sets contain the ASCII character set as their common base plus additional characters. Extended ASCII character sets are used to represent other writing systems, such as Arabic, Hebrew, and Cyrillic. There is also an extensive collection of additional Roman characters. These characters are usually additional symbols and accented versions of Roman characters.

Eight-bit ASCII representations can handle 128 more characters than seven-bit representations. The documents ISO 8859 Parts 1 through 9 (*Information Processing—8-bit Single-byte Coded Graphic Character Sets*) describe the character sets that can be encoded in the additional 128 positions when an eight-bit ASCII representation is used. Table 3-6 lists the contents of each of the nine parts of ISO 8859.

Table 3-6: The Nine Parts of ISO 8859

	Date	Contents
Part 1	1987	Latin alphabet No. 1
Part 2	1987	Latin alphabet No. 2
Part 3	1988	Latin alphabet No. 3
Part 4	1988	Latin alphabet No. 4
Part 5	1988	Latin/Cyrillic alphabet
Part 6	1987	Latin/Arabic alphabet
Part 7	1987	Latin/Greek alphabet
Part 8	1988	Latin/Hebrew alphabet
Part 9	1989	Latin alphabet No. 5

Table 3-7 lists some examples of characters from Latin alphabet No. 1.

Table 3-7: The Extended ASCII Character Set—ISO 8859 Part 1—Examples

Lowercase Roman	àáâãäåæçèéêëìíîïñòóôõöùúûüøÿ
Uppercase Roman	ÀÁÂÃÄÅÆÇÈÉÊËÌÍÎÏÑÒÓÔÕÖÙÚÛÜ
Symbols	¡¢£¤¥§©®ª º«»¬ ¯¨°µ¶ß•Ø÷±

These, as you probably expect, are not that useful for working with Japanese text. This just shows you what is available. Note again that these extended ASCII character sets require eight bits for encoding.

JIS-Roman

The Japanese have developed their own version of the ASCII character set called JIS-Roman (JISローマ字). JIS-Roman, like ASCII, consists of 94 printable characters, but three of them replace the standard ASCII characters. The three characters that differ are:

ASCII		JIS-Roman	
\	(backslash)	¥	(yen sign)
~	(tilde)[1]	‾	(overbar)
¦	(broken bar)[2]	|	(bar)

[1]The position of the tilde may vary depending on the implementation.
[2]Some implementations of ASCII may use a bar instead of a broken bar—this is a glyph issue.

Table 3-8 shows the 94 printable JIS-Roman characters.

Table 3-8: The JIS-Roman Character Set

Lowercase Roman	`abcdefghijklmnopqrstuvwxyz`
Uppercase Roman	`ABCDEFGHIJKLMNOPQRSTUVWXYZ`
Numerals	`0123456789`
Symbols	`!"#$%&'()*+,-./:;<=>?@[¥]^_`{|}‾`

Since the difference between ASCII and JIS-Roman is only so minor, they are treated as the same throughout this book. You will also find that most terminal software supports one or the other. This means that terminals which support only JIS-Roman display the ASCII backslash as the JIS-Roman yen sign. For systems that require the backslash, such as MS-DOS for directories, the yen sign is used instead. You will also find that most Japanese software supports JIS-Roman instead of ASCII. It is possible that the computer supports both ASCII and JIS-Roman. Changing the display from JIS-Roman to ASCII (and vice versa), though, may be as simple as changing the display font. You will see in the next chapter that this is because ASCII and JIS-Roman occupy the same encoding space.

A document called JIS X 0201-1976, *Code for Information Interchange* (情報交換用符号), contains the definition of the JIS-Roman character set standard. This JIS manual is identical to ISO 646-1991 except that it contains the extensions for JIS-Roman and half-width katakana.

Half-width Katakana

The first attempt by the Japanese to adapt their writing system to computer systems was in the creation of half-width katakana. These characters formed a limited set of characters that could be easily encoded on early computer systems. They also took up the same amount of display space as ASCII characters. This collection of 63 half-width katakana characters is defined in the document JIS X 0201-1976, and consists of the basic katakana characters along with enough punctuation marks and symbols to write the most basic Japanese text.* Table 3-9 contains all the characters of this character set.

Table 3-9: The Half-width Katakana Character Set

Katakana	ｦｧｨｩｪｫｬｭｮｯｱｲｳｴｵｶｷｸｹｺｻｼｽｾｿﾀﾁﾂﾃﾄﾅﾆﾇﾈﾉﾊﾋﾌﾍﾎﾏﾐﾑﾒﾓﾔﾕﾖﾗﾘﾙﾚﾛﾜﾝ
Symbols	｡｢｣､･ﾞﾟｰ

Sometimes a half-width space character is part of this character set, which brings the total to 64 characters.

These characters occupy half the display space of the equivalent full-width katakana found in JIS X 0208-1990 (described below). The katakana characters of JIS X 0208-1990 are known as full-width characters. Full-width, in this case, translates to roughly a square space, meaning that the character space is roughly the same in both width and height. Half-width characters are the same height as full-width characters, but occupy half the width. In addition, the voiced and semi-voiced counterparts of katakana are not included in the half-width katakana character set. The voiced mark (゛) called *nigori* and the semi-voiced mark (゜) called *maru* are used to create additional katakana characters. Nigori and maru are treated as separate characters in half-width katakana. Table 3-10 clearly shows the relationship between half- and full-width katakana characters, and how nigori and maru marks are treated as separate characters.

Table 3-10: Nigori Versus Maru and Full- Versus Half-width

	ka	ga (voiced ka)	ha	pa (semi-voiced ha)
Full-width	カ カ カ カ カ	ガ ガ ガ ガ ガ	ハ ハ ハ ハ ハ	パ パ パ パ パ
Half-width	ｶ ｶ ｶ ｶ ｶ	ｶﾞ ｶﾞ ｶﾞ ｶﾞ ｶﾞ	ﾊ ﾊ ﾊ ﾊ ﾊ	ﾊﾟ ﾊﾟ ﾊﾟ ﾊﾟ ﾊﾟ

When the ASCII/JIS-Roman and half-width katakana character set standards are combined into one larger collection of characters, this newly-formed character set standard is often called ANK, for *Alphabet, Numerals, and Katakana.*

JIS X 0208-1990

The first attempt by the Japanese to create an electronic character set standard that better represented their written language was developed in 1978. This is the first electronic character set standard to include kanji, and included thousands of them. This character set standard is also significant in that it broke the one-byte-equals-one-character barrier.

The title of this standard is *Code of the Japanese Graphic Character Set for Information Interchange* (情報交換用漢字符号), and was established on September 1, 1990. The current version of this standard, JIS X 0208-1990, is considered the most basic and defini-

---

*JIS X 0201-1976 was reaffirmed in 1989.

tive description of the Japanese character set. This character set standard enumerates 6,879 characters as standard characters. The character space is arranged in a 94-row-by-94-cell matrix. Rows 1 through 8 are reserved for non-kanji, rows 9 through 15 are unassigned and free, rows 16 through 84 are reserved for kanji, and rows 85 through 94 are unassigned and free. Table 3-11 provides a much more detailed description of how characters are allocated to each of its 94 rows.

Table 3-11: The JIS X 0208-1990 Character Set

Row	Number of Characters	Content
1	94	Miscellaneous symbols
2	53	Miscellaneous symbols
3	62	Numerals 0–9, lowercase and uppercase Roman characters
4	83	Hiragana
5	86	Katakana
6	48	Lowercase and uppercase Greek characters
7	66	Lowercase and uppercase Cyrillic characters
8	32	Line-drawing elements
9–15	0	Unassigned (free)
16–47	2,965	JIS Level 1 kanji
48–83	3,384	JIS Level 2 kanji
84	6	Additional kanji[1]
85–94	0	Unassigned (free)

[1]The six kanji in row 84 are usually considered to be part of JIS Level 2 kanji, so the typical number that one would see is 3,390 kanji in JIS Level 2 kanji, and thus includes row 84.

There are 6,355 kanji in this character set. The kanji are broken into two distinct sections. The first section is called *JIS Level 1 kanji* (JIS第一水準漢字), and the kanji within it are arranged by ON (Chinese) reading.* The second section of kanji, called *JIS Level 2 kanji* (JIS第二水準漢字), are arranged by radical, then number of strokes. The six additional kanji in row 84 are arranged by radical, then number of strokes, like JIS Level 2 kanji. JIS Levels 1 and 2 kanji are mutually exclusive—each contains no characters found in the other—together they constitute a set of unique kanji.

A complete code table for the characters that make up JIS X 0208-1990 can be found in Appendix B. Also, Appendix D provides a pronunciation index for JIS Level 1 kanji, and a radical index for JIS Level 2 kanji.

---

*Some kanji do not have an ON reading. In these cases they are arranged by their KUN (Japanese) reading.

If you still haven't quite grasped the Japanese writing system, you must be wondering what all this means (I don't blame you!). The following listing should help out. It provides a graphic description for the first and last characters from each of the above groups of characters (note that the complete list for numerals and additional kanji is given).

Miscellaneous symbols	、。，・：；？！ ... ∬Å‰♯♭♪†‡¶○
Numerals	0 1 2 3 4 5 6 7 8 9
Roman characters	A B C D E F G H I J ... q r s t u v w x y z
Hiragana	ぁあぃいぅうぇえぉお ... りるれろゎわゐゑをん
Katakana	ァアィイゥウェエォオ ... ロヮワヰヱヲンヴヵヶ
Greek characters	Α Β Γ Δ Ε Ζ Η Θ Ι Κ ... ο π ρ σ τ υ φ χ ψ ω
Cyrillic characters	А Б В Г Д Е Ё Ж З И ... ц ч ш щ ъ ы ь э ю я
Line-drawing elements	─│┌┘└├┼┴ ... ┣┥╋┝┱┛┷
JIS Level 1 kanji	亜唖娃阿哀愛挨姶逢葵 ... 瓦亙鰐詫藁蕨椀湾碗腕
JIS Level 2 kanji	弌丐丕个丱丶丼丿乂乖 ... 齦齧齬齪齷齲齶龕龜龠
Additional kanji	堯槇遙瑤凜熙

Now for more explanations. Symbols include punctuation marks, mathematical signs, and various brackets and parentheses. Numerals and Roman characters are what one would normally find in the ASCII character set (less symbols)—these are full-width, not half-width. The hiragana and katakana characters are full-width, not half-width. Cyrillic and Greek characters are included, since many Japanese technical works include occasional Russian or Greek words. The line-drawing elements are used for building charts on a per-character basis.

This character set standard was first established on January 1, 1978 as JIS C 6226-1978, modified for the first time on September 1, 1983 as JIS X 0208-1983, and modified again on September 1, 1990 as JIS X 0208-1990. This character set is widely implemented on a variety of platforms. Encoding methods for JIS X 0208-1990 include Shift-JIS, EUC, and JIS. These three encoding methods are covered in Chapter 4.

Now for some history. You may sometimes encounter systems and documentation that are based on earlier versions of JIS X 0208-1990, the most likely of which is JIS X 0208-1983. That standard, originally known as JIS C 6226-1983, did, in fact, exist. On March 1, 1987, JSA decided to rename many JIS standards from a "C" to an "X" designation (don't ask me why). JIS C 6226-1983, with no substantive changes, was renamed to JIS X 0208-1983.

Since its conception in 1978, this character set standard has experienced a slight increase in the total number of characters. Table 3-12 lists how characters are allocated to each row in JIS C 6226-1978. Note that rows 2, 8, and 84 differ from JIS X 0208-1990.

Table 3-12: The JIS C 6226-1978 Character Set

Row	Number of Characters	Content
1	94	Miscellaneous symbols
2	14	Miscellaneous symbols
3	62	Numerals 0–9, lowercase and uppercase Roman characters
4	83	Hiragana
5	86	Katakana
6	48	Lowercase and uppercase Greek characters
7	66	Lowercase and uppercase Cyrillic characters
8–15	0	Unassigned (free)
16–47	2,965	JIS Level 1 kanji
48–83	3,384	JIS Level 2 kanji
84–94	0	Unassigned (free)

Table 3-13 does the same for JIS X 0208-1983. Note that only row 84 differs from JIS X 0208-1990.

Table 3-13: JIS X 0208-1983 Character Set

Row	Number of Characters	Content
1	94	Miscellaneous symbols
2	53	Miscellaneous symbols
3	62	Numerals 0–9, lowercase and uppercase Roman characters
4	83	Hiragana
5	86	Katakana
6	48	Lowercase and uppercase Greek characters
7	66	Lowercase and uppercase Cyrillic characters
8	32	Line-drawing elements
9–15	0	Unassigned (free)
16–47	2,965	JIS Level 1 kanji
48–83	3,384	JIS Level 2 kanji
84	4	Additional kanji
85–94	0	Unassigned (free)

More detailed information about the differences between JIS C 6226-1978, JIS X 0208-1983, and JIS X 0208-1990 can be found in Appendix J.

JIS X 0212-1990—A Supplemental Character Set

A supplemental Japanese character set standard was established by JISC on October 1, 1990, and specified 6,067 characters, 5,801 of which are kanji. These characters are in addition to those found in JIS X 0208-1990, but like that character set standard, is composed of a 94-row-by-94-cell character space. Also like JIS X 0208-1990, rows 1 through 15 are reserved for non-kanji, rows 16 through 84 are reserved for kanji, and rows 85 through 94 are unassigned and free.

The official title of JIS X 0212-1990 is *Code of the Supplementary Japanese Graphic Character Set for Information Interchange* (情報交換用漢字符号—補助漢字). Table 3-14 lists how characters are allocated to each of its 94 rows.

Table 3-14: JIS X 0212-1990 Character Set

Row	Number of Characters	Content
1	0	Unassigned (reserved)
2	21	Diacritics and miscellaneous symbols
3–5	0	Unassigned (reserved)
6	21	Greek characters with diacritics
7	26	Eastern European characters
8	0	Unassigned (reserved)
9–11	198	Miscellaneous alphabetic characters
12–15	0	Unassigned (reserved)
16–77	5,801	Supplemental kanji
78–84	0	Unassigned (reserved)
85–94	0	Unassigned (free)

The 5,801 kanji are arranged by radical then stroke count (like JIS Level 2 kanji of JIS X 0208-1990). When this data is merged with JIS X 0208-1990, you see that there are now 12,156 unique standard kanji, and 12,946 total standard characters. However, very few software systems use these 6,067 supplemental characters. The latest version of Mule, a powerful multilingual text editor, is an example of a program that supports the encoding of the JIS X 0212-1990 character set standard. Much of the difficulty in supporting JIS X 0212-1990 is the poor availability of fonts that include its characters set.

The following list illustrates the first and last ten characters in each category of characters listed above:

Miscellaneous Symbols	˘ ˇ ¸ ‥ ″ ‾ ˛ ° ˜ ′ ... ¡ ¦ ¿ º ª ©®™ ¤ Nº
Greek Characters	Ά Έ Ή Ί Ϊ Ό Ύ Ϋ Ώ ά ... ή ί ΐ ϊ ό ς ύ ϋ ΰ ώ
Eastern European Characters	Ђ Ѓ Є Ѕ І Ї Ј Љ Њ Ћ ... ѕ і ї ј љ њ ћ ќ ў џ
Alphabetic Characters	Æ Đ Ħ IJ Ł Ŀ Ŋ Ø Œ Ŧ ... ŭ ů ű ŵ ý ÿ ŷ ź ž ż
Supplemental Kanji	ㄅ ㄟ ㄊ ㄦ ㄡ 丟 乖 两 丨 丫 ... 龑 龒 龔 龘 龝 龞 歃 龢 龣 龥

A complete code table for the characters that make up JIS X 0212-1990 can be found in Appendix C. Also, a radical index for the 5,801 kanji of JIS X 0212-1990 can be found in Appendix D.

A committee may eventually add four unique katakana characters to JIS X 0212-1990. They are as follows:

Katakana	Pronunciation
ヷ	va
ヸ	vi
ヹ	ve
ヺ	vo

These four characters, although rarely employed, are used for writing foreign words and can already be found in at least one corporate character set standard (Apple90, described in Appendix H). Space for these four characters has already been allocated in JIS X 0212-1990—if accepted for inclusion into this character set standard, they will be placed in row 5 beginning at cell 87. Table 3-15 illustrates these proposed changes.

Table 3-15: Proposed Change to the JIS X 0212-1990 Character Set

Row	Number of Characters	Content
1	0	Unassigned (reserved)
2	21	Diacritics and miscellaneous symbols
3–4	0	Unassigned (reserved)
5	4	Katakana
6	21	Greek characters with diacritics
7	26	Eastern European characters
8	0	Unassigned (reserved)
9–11	198	Miscellaneous alphabetic characters
12–15	0	Unassigned (reserved)
16–77	5,801	Supplemental kanji
78–84	0	Unassigned (reserved)
85–94	0	Unassigned (free)

There have been recent discussions about how one may go about extending the current encodings to handle the new supplemental characters introduced with JIS X 0212-1990. Incorporating these characters into JIS encoding was trivial: a new two-byte character escape sequence (explained in Chapter 4) for this new set of characters was determined. It is not possible to encode these additional characters in Shift-JIS code because there is no space left. EUC does not suffer from this problem of limited encoding space, and in Chapter 4 you will learn how JIS X 0212-1990 is supported by EUC.

Relationships Between National Character Set Standards

You already read about the slight difference between ASCII and JIS-Roman. With only one exception, the character set standards JIS X 0208-1990 and JIS X 0212-1990 contain no characters found in the other—together they are designed to form a larger collection of characters. These two characters are as follows:

JIS X 0208-1990	JIS X 0212-1990
⺨ 0126 (213A)	⺨ 1617 (3031)

The characters are the same, with identical meanings, and are used in the same way—it is really only a glyph difference. In JIS X 0208-1990 it is treated as a non-kanji character (in a row of miscellaneous symbols), but in JIS X 0212-1990 it is treated as a kanji. This character, in both instances, is pronounced *shime*, and means "deadline."

The internal structures of JIS X 0208-1990 and JIS X 0212-1990 share several qualities, the most notable being that they both consist of a 94-row-by-94-cell character space for a maximum number of 8,836 encoded characters. Thus, they both occupy the same character *space*. Furthermore, the non-kanji characters of both standards are allocated to rows 1 through 15, and the kanji characters are allocated to rows 16 through 84 (that is not to say that all those rows are currently filled, but that they have been allocated for such classes of characters). Chapter 4 discusses how computer systems can distinguish between these two character sets.

Another interesting aspect of these standards is how the non-kanji are arranged so that one could easily superimpose one set onto the other with no overlap of used character positions. This would make it fully possible to merge rows 1 through 15 of both standards with no filled character positions overlapping. In fact, the four katakana characters that may eventually be added to JIS X 0212-1990 are positioned such that they would appear immediately after the katakana in JIS X 0208-1990.

One last thing to mention about the relationship between these two character set standards is that there are 28 kanji in JIS X 0212-1990 that were in JIS C 6226-1978, but were replaced with different glyphs in JIS X 0208-1983. Table J-2 in Appendix J lists these 28 character pairs.

Asian Character Set Standards

As you learned earlier, Japan was the first Asian country to develop and implement a multiple-byte national character set and encoding. The other major Asian countries—Mainland China, Taiwan, and Korea—soon followed with their own. To give you a feeling for how similar other Asian character set standards are to JIS X 0208-1990, this section briefly describes the current versions of the most widely used Asian character set standards, and draws comparisons between them and JIS X 0208-1990.

Table 3-16 summarizes the Asian character set standards covered in this section. Similarities to Japanese character set standards are discussed later.

Table 3-16: Asian Character Set Standards

	Country	Level 1 Kanji	Level 2 Kanji	Non-kanji
KS C 5601-1992	Korea	2,350[1]	4,888	986
GB 2312-80	Mainland China	3,755	3,008	682
Big Five	Taiwan	5,401	7,652	470

[1]In this case, these 2,350 characters are *hangul*, the native Korean alphabet.

KS C 5601-1992 (Korea)

The latest Korean character set standard, specified in the document KS C 5601-1992, enumerates 8,224 characters. There are 4,888 kanji (or *hanja*, as the Koreans call them) arranged by pronunciation, 2,350 *hangul* arranged by pronunciation, and other symbols. Table 3-17 lists the characters that constitute KS C 5601-1992.

Table 3-17: KS C 5601-1992

Row	Number of Characters	Content
1	94	Miscellaneous symbols
2	69	6 abbreviations, 63 miscellaneous symbols
3	94	KS C 5636, the Korean version of ASCII character set (similar to JIS-Roman)
4	94	Basic hangul elements
5	68	Lowercase and uppercase Roman numerals 1–10, 48 lowercase and uppercase Greek characters
6	68	Line-drawing elements
7	79	Abbreviations
8	91	13 phonetic symbols, 28 circled hangul elements, circled lowercase Roman characters, circled numerals 1–15, 9 fractions
9	94	16 phonetic symbols, 28 parenthesized hangul elements, parenthesized lowercase Roman characters, parenthesized numerals 1–15, 5 superscripts, 4 subscripts
10	83	Hiragana
11	86	Katakana
12	66	Lowercase and uppercase Cyrillic characters
13–15	0	Unassigned
16–40	2,350	Hangul
41	0	Unassigned
42–93	4,888	Kanji (*hanja*)[1]
94	0	Unassigned

[1]Sometimes written *hancha*.

The kanji and hangul are arranged by pronunciation.

Hangul refers to the native Korean writing system. Each hangul character is usually composed of vowel and consonant sounds, and thus can be considered a syllabary, similar to hiragana and katakana. However, the individual vowel and consonant sounds can be extracted from each hangul character, so it is really an alphabetic writing system. Note that the individual vowel and consonant sounds cannot be extracted from hiragana or katakana, so they are not considered an alphabetic writing system, but true syllabaries.

The kanji specified in this character set standard are considered to be in the traditional form. Some examples of simplified versus traditional kanji are listed in Chapter 2.

This Korean character set standard is similar to JIS X 0208-1990; it contains the same set of hiragana and katakana characters (but in different rows). Although hangul are not considered to be kanji, they do begin at row 16, like the kanji in JIS X 0208-1990.

GB 2312-80 (The People's Republic of China)

This national character set standard, established in 1981 by The People's Republic of China, enumerates 7,445 characters. Its official name is *Code of Chinese Graphic Character Set for Information Interchange—Primary Set*. Table 3-18 lists how characters are allocated to each row.

Table 3-18: GB 2312-80

Row	Number of Characters	Content
1	94	Miscellaneous symbols
2	72	Numerals 1–20 with period, parenthesized numerals 1–20, circled numerals 1–10, parenthesized kanji numerals 1–20, uppercase Roman numerals 1–12
3	94	ASCII character set (full-width)
4	83	Hiragana
5	86	Katakana
6	48	Lowercase and uppercase Greek characters
7	66	Lowercase and uppercase Cyrillic characters
8	63	26 accented vowels, 37 *bopomofo* characters
9	76	Line-drawing elements
10–15	0	Unassigned
16–55	3,755	Level 1 kanji
56–87	3,008	Level 2 kanji
88–94	0	Unassigned

Level 1 kanji are arranged by pronunciation. Level 2 kanji are arranged by radical then stroke count. *Bopomofo* are symbols used to represent standard pronunciations in

Chinese. Its name is derived from the first four sounds in that set of symbols, namely *b*, *p*, *m*, and *f*.

Mainland China also has a single-byte character set similar to ASCII and JIS-Roman. It is called GB-Roman, and is defined in the document called GB 1988-80. GB 1988-80 is often used in conjunction with GB 2312-80.

Some of the similarities between this character set standard and JIS X 0208-1990 are astonishing. First, note how the allocation of rows 4 through 7 (hiragana, katakana, Greek, and Cyrillic characters) is identical to the allocation of those rows in JIS X 0208-1990. Also, like JIS X 0208-1990, rows 1 through 15 are reserved for non-kanji. And finally, kanji are divided into two levels, with the first level arranged by pronunciation, and the second level by radical then stroke count.

Big Five (Taiwan)

Big Five is the most widely implemented character set standard used in Taiwan, and was established in May 1984 by the Institute of Information Industry of Taiwan. Unlike the other Asian character set standards its character space is set in a 94-row-by-157-cell matrix, for a maximum capacity of 14,758 cells. The Big Five character set standard specifies 13,523 standard characters, but other implementations may have a different number. I must warn you that Big Five is not a national standard, but it is used much more widely than the national standards of Taiwan, such as CNS 11643-1986. Table 3-19 lists the character allocation of the Big Five character set.

Table 3-19: The Big Five Character Set

Row	Number of Characters	Content
1	157	2 abbreviations, 155 miscellaneous symbols
2	157	9 kanji for measurements, 9 abbreviations, 21 line-drawing elements, numerals 0–9, upper-case Roman numerals 1–10, Chinese numerals 1–12, lowercase and uppercase Roman characters (except for w-z), 38 miscellaneous symbols
3	156	lowercase Roman characters w-z, 48 lowercase and uppercase Greek characters, 37 bopomofo characters, 4 accents, 33 abbreviations for control characters, circled numerals 1–10, parenthesized numerals 1–10, lowercase Roman numerals 1–10
4–38	5,401	Level 1 kanji
39–40	0	Unassigned
41–89	7,652	Level 2 kanji[1]
90–94	0	Unassigned

[1] CNS 11643-1986 has only 7,650 characters in Level 2 kanji.

The kanji in each level are arranged by increasing stroke count, and then by radical (the opposite of the ordering found in JIS Level 2 kanji of JIS X 0208-1990 and JIS X 0212-1990—their kanji are ordered by radical *then* by increasing number of strokes).

The authors of *An Introduction to Chinese, Japanese, and Korean Computing* claim that the designers of the Big Five code actually copied many kanji from the JIS standard. Many kanji exist in both Chinese and Japanese, but there are some subtle glyph differences between them. The Big Five contains many non-Chinese versions of kanji (and not the actual Chinese equivalent), and no attempt was made to remedy this problem.

International Character Set Standards

Organizations and corporations have been developing international character set standards in an attempt to include most of the world's written languages into a single superset of characters. These should be of interest to you since they all include thousands of Japanese characters.

Table 3-20 lists the international character set standards covered in this section. Note that the first two use as their base JIS X 0208-1990 and JIS X 0212-1990. JIS83 below refers to JIS X 0208-1983.

Table 3-20: International Character Set Standards

	Subset	Additional Kanji	Other Characters	User-defined
ISO 10646	12,156[1]	8,746	13,266	16,384
Unicode	12,156[1]	8,746	13,266	16,384
XCCS	JIS83	382	3,687	

[1]This is a combination of JIS X 0208-1990 (6,355 kanji) and JIS X 0212-1990 (5,801 kanji).

ISO 10646 and Unicode

The International Standards Organization (ISO) and the Unicode Consortium have jointly developed a multilingual character set designed to combine the majority of the world's character set standards into one larger set of characters. ISO named this standard ISO 10646. The characters have two- and four-byte representations according to this standard.

The Unicode Consortium calls their standard *Unicode*, and has a 16-bit representation (for all practical purposes, 16 bits are two bytes). Unicode is a subset of ISO 10646, and fits into what is called the *Basic Multilingual Plane* (BMP) of ISO 10646. It is called the BMP because ISO 10646 is composed of cubes of planes—a plane is a two-dimensional object. The only characters defined in either standard are those in the BMP. This character set was constructed in an attempt to unify all kanji from various national standards into a single set of approximately 20,902 kanji which support Chinese (both simplified and traditional), Japanese, and Korean. This unified set of kanji is known as CJK (Chinese, Japanese, and Korean). This effort is known as *Han Unification*. The Han comes from the Chinese pronunciation of the kanji 漢—in Japanese it is pronounced *kan*. Note this is not true unification of kanji due to the source separation rule (to be explained below).

Unicode and two-byte ISO 10646 both contain 65,536 character positions. As of this writing, 34,168 of these have been assigned characters. The character space for Unicode can be thought of as a 256-row-by-256-cell matrix. Table 3-21 details, by row, how many characters are currently assigned to Unicode.

Table 3-21: The Unicode and ISO 10646 Character Set

Row	Number of Characters	Content
1–17	2,300	Alphabets
18	240	Hangul alphabet
19–30	0	Unassigned
31–32	478	Latin and Greek precombined forms
33–40	1,376	Symbols
41–48	0	Unassigned
49–52	842	CJK auxiliaries
53–78	6,656	Hangul
79–160	20,902	CJK unified ideographs
161–224	0	User-defined characters
225–249	0	Private Use Area
250–251	302	CJK ideograph compatibility
252–254	650	Presentation forms
255–256	422	Compatibility and specials

The actual number of characters in Unicode is constantly changing as of this writing, so expect changes in the future. The characters on this list applicable to this book are the 20,902 kanji. The remaining characters, for the most part, are beyond the scope and interest of this book.

These 20,902 kanji are a result of merging or *unifying* many character set standards into one larger repertoire of characters. According to Volume 2 of *The Unicode Standard: Worldwide Character Encoding*, the kanji contained in the character set standards listed in Table 3-22 have been unified.

Table 3-22: Character Sets Included in Unicode Kanji Set

Character Set Standard	Country of Origin	Number of Kanji
ANSI Z39.64-1989 (EACC)	USA	13,481
Big Five	Taiwan	13,053
CCCII, Level 1	Taiwan	4,808
CNS 11643-1986	Taiwan	13,051
CNS 11643-1986 User Characters	Taiwan	3,418
GB 2312-80	Mainland China	6,763
GB 12345-90	Mainland China	2,176
GB 7589-87	Mainland China	7,327
GB 7590-87	Mainland China	7,039
General Use Characters for Modern Chinese	Mainland China	41
GB 8565-89	Mainland China	287
GB 12052-89	Mainland China	94
JEF (Fujitsu)[1]	Japan	3,149
JIS X 0208-1990	Japan	6,355
JIS X 0212-1990	Japan	5,801
KS C 5601-1992	Korea	4,888
KS C 5657-1991	Korea	2,856
PRC Telegraph Code	Mainland China	±8,000
Taiwan Telegraph Code	Taiwan	9,040
Xerox Chinese	USA	9,776

[1] I don't know how the Unicode Consortium came up with 3,149 kanji in JEF. Appendix H shows that there are 4,039 kanji in JEF that are above and beyond those in JIS X 0208-1990.

This list contains approximately 121,403 kanji, but when the Han Unification rules are applied, they become 20,902 unique characters. These kanji are subsequently arranged by radical then total stroke count (similar to the ordering of JIS Level 2 kanji of JIS X 0208-1990). So what is Han Unification anyway? Han Unification is the process of eliminating redundant characters among the approximately 121,403 kanji that are represented in Table 3-22. The basic process of unification involves the merging of characters that have identical or nearly identical structure, and have the same meaning. For example, the two kanji in Table 3-23 have similar structure, similar enough, in fact, to unify them. However, they have unique meanings, so unification does not take place.

Table 3-23: Example of Ununified Kanji

Kanji	Meaning
土	*earth*
士	*scholar, knight*

However, characters such as those in Table 3-24 have been unified.

Table 3-24: Example of a Unified Kanji

Kanji	Meaning	Source Set	Encoding
父	*father*	JIS X 0208-1983	4167 (4963)
父	*father*	JIS X 0208-1990	4167 (4963)

Note how their structures are nearly identical, and that they have the same meaning. They share the same encoding, but come from different versions of the JIS X 0208 character set standard. The earlier versions of JIS X 0208 are not considered one of the Japanese sources—only JIS X 0208-1990 and JIS X 0212-1990 are used.

Han Unification is performed using a three-dimensional model. The X axis (semantic) separates characters by their meaning. The Y axis (abstract shape) separates a character on the X axis into its abstract shapes. Traditional and simplified forms of a particular kanji fall into the same Y axis. The Z axis (typeface) separates a character into glyph differences. Only Z axis differences are unified under the rules of Han Unification. Table 3-24 provides an example of a Z axis difference—such glyphs are unified under the Han Unification rules. Glyph differences are usually found when using different typefaces to produce the same character. The same character in different languages may also appear differently. Figure 3-1 illustrates the three-axis model used for Han Unification.

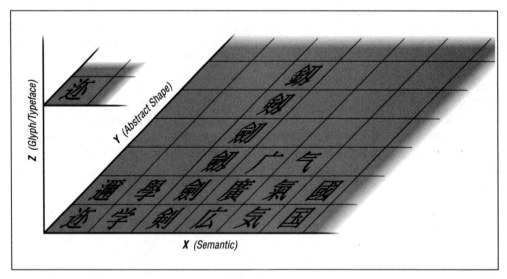

Figure 3-1: Three-axis model for Han Unification

There is also the *source separation* rule. First, there are four sources from which the Unicode kanji set is derived: Japanese, Korean, Mainland Chinese, and Taiwanese character sets. For example, there are two Japanese character sets in the Japanese source: JIS

X 0208-1990 and JIS X 0212-1990. The source separation rule states that unification of two characters cannot take place if they have unique encoded positions within a single source. Table 3-25 lists the kanji 剣 and its five variants—all of these characters have unique code positions in JIS X 0208-1990, and are thus not unified. The source separation rule is to ensure that round-trip conversion is successful. JIS X 0208-1990 and JIS X 0212-1990 contain many kanji that could potentially be unified: the kanji in Table 3-25 is a single example.

Table 3-25: Six Kanji From JIS X 0208-1990 That Are Not Unified

剣	2385	(3775)
劍	4988	(5178)
劎	4989	(5179)
剱	4990	(517A)
劔	4991	(517B)
釼	7863	(6E5F)

Much of the Han Unification work was performed in China, and I have observed that some of the kanji ordering is biased toward Chinese. There are instances of kanji being classified under the wrong radical, at least from a Japanese perspective. Most of these happen to be kanji (or variants thereof) that are unique to Japanese character set standards. For example, the kanji 歯 (meaning "tooth") is classified under the radical 止 in the Unicode kanji set. For Japanese, this kanji is just the simplified version of 齒, which is itself a radical. Japanese would expect to find the kanji 歯 listed under the 齒 radical, not under 止. This is one reason why the Japanese are not particularly pleased with the results of Han Unification.

For additional information regarding the Unicode character set or Han Unification, refer to *The Unicode Standard: Worldwide Character Encoding*, available in two volumes. The first volume contains information about the rules for Han Unification, and lists all the non-kanji characters of Unicode. The second volume contains detailed information on the kanji implemented in the Unicode standard. The ISO 10646 manual is also available, and contains similar information.

XCCS

Xerox Corporation developed what they call the *Xerox Character Code Standard* (XCCS) as their own attempt at a multilingual character set standard. This character set standard currently contains over 10,000 characters: 6,735 of these are kanji, mainly from JIS X 0208-1983. Of the remaining 382 kanji, 360 are IBM select kanji.

The character space for this standard is arranged into a 256-row-by-256-cell matrix, much like Unicode and ISO 10646. Each row of this matrix is considered a character set, and each character set can hold a maximum of 188 characters. Table 3-26 illustrates how characters are assigned to each of its character sets.

Table 3-26: The XCCS Character Set

Row	Number of Characters	Content
1	179	Roman characters and punctuation
2–33	0	Not used (control character area)
34	150	Japanese punctuation and math symbols
35	180	Japanese and math symbols
36	87	Extended Roman alphabet
37	126	Hiragana and bopomofo
38	86	Katakana
39	105	Greek characters
40	180	Cyrillic characters
41	120	Forms and mosaic characters
42	168	Runic and Gothic characters
43	48	Extended Cyrillic characters
44–46	0	Unassigned (reserved)
47	24	Decorated rules
48	94	Vertically-set Japanese symbols
49–116	6,349	JIS C 6226-1978 kanji
117	27	1 parenthesized kanji, 14 circled katakana, 12 circled kanji
118	4	JIS X 0208-1983 kanji
119	68	16 diamond enclosed numbers, 52 circled lowercase and uppercase letters
120–127	382	Extended kanji
128–161	0	Not used (control character area)
162–213	0	Unassigned (reserved for Chinese)
214–224	0	Unassigned (reserved)
225	72	Arabic characters
226	48	Hebrew characters
227	149	International Phonetic Alphabet (IPA)
228	54	Korean hangul elements
229	115	Georgian and Armenian alphabets
230	89	Devanagari alphabet
231–235	0	Unassigned (reserved)
236	39	General and technical symbols 3
237	151	Extended ITC Dingbats 2 and general symbols
238	179	ITC Dingbats 1
239	188	General and technical symbols 2
240	188	General and technical symbols 2
241	77	Ligatures and field format symbols
242	187	Accented Latin characters 1

Row	Number of Characters	Content
243	42	Accented Latin characters 2
244	188	Accented Greek characters 1
245	42	Accented Greek characters 2
246	94	Initial, medial, and final Arabic characters
247–253	0	Unassigned (reserved)
254	143	Variant representations for graphic characters
255	0	Not used (private use area)
256	0	Not used (character set select code)

Xerox plans to add more character sets to XCCS, including Arabic, Farsi, Hebrew, Hindi, Chinese, and Korean.

Non-electronic Versus Electronic Character Set Standards

Non-electronic character sets relate to JIS X 0208-1990 (and earlier versions) in a variety of ways. This just shows how electronic character set standards attempt to follow and keep pace with non-electronic character set standards.

All of the Tôyô Kanji characters were included in JIS Level 1 kanji of JIS C 6226-1978. When Jôyô Kanji was introduced in 1981, the additional 95 kanji and subsequent glyph changes forced the creation of JIS X 0208-1983 (first called JIS C 6226-1983, then changed to the new designation in 1987)—those extra 95 characters had to be made part of JIS Level 1 kanji (22 simplified and traditional kanji pairs exchanged code positions between JIS Level 1 kanji and JIS Level 2 kanji). Table J-3 in Appendix J contains the 95 kanji that were added to Tôyô Kanji in 1981 in order to become Jôyô Kanji.

The kanji specified in Jinmei-yô Kanji, on the other hand, could appear in either JIS Levels 1 or 2 kanji, so that is why four kanji were appended in 1983, and two in 1990. Here are the four kanji appended to JIS Level 2 kanji in 1983 to create JIS X 0208-1983:

堯 8401 (7421)
槇 8402 (7422)
遙 8403 (7423)
瑤 8404 (7424)

And here are the two kanji that were appended to JIS Level 2 kanji in 1990 to create JIS X 0208-1990:

凜 8405 (7425)
熙 8406 (7426)

There is no relationship between Gakushû Kanji and electronic character sets except for the fact that Gakushû Kanji is a subset of Jôyô Kanji.*

Figure 3-2 illustrates how the current versions of the non-electronic character sets relate to each other, and to JIS Levels 1 and 2 kanji of JIS X 0208-1990.

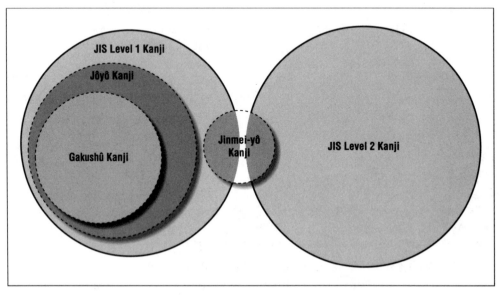

Figure 3-2: Relationships between electronic and non-electronic character set standards

Advice to Developers

Software developers should, at a minimum, support ASCII/JIS-Roman, half-width katakana, and the characters defined in the document JIS X 0208-1990. Whether or not to support JIS X 0212-1990 is a difficult question. These characters are not used often, if at all, by the casual user, yet they are standardized characters. I once conducted a study in which I calculated the percentage of JIS Level 2 kanji in a variety of electronically en-coded Japanese text. After analyzing approximately 500,000 characters, I found that less than 1/10th of one percent of the characters were JIS Level 2 kanji! You can be assured that the frequency of usage is even lower for the kanji in JIS X 0212-1990. However, when a JIS X 0212-1990 character is required by a user, support for that character set standard becomes indispensable. So, you may ask, what does this mean for me? Well, if you wish to write software that is extendable, I highly suggest supporting both JIS X 0208-1990 and JIS X 0212-1990. Support for JIS X 0212-1990 implies the support for JIS or EUC encoding—Shift-JIS encoding does not support these extra characters.

---

*This means that Gakushû Kanji is a subset of JIS Level 1 kanji.

What about ISO 10646 and Unicode? As I mentioned earlier, the character set defined by those standards is still in flux. I am not saying that supporting ISO 10646 or Unicode is a poor choice for software developers, but that developers should be cautious about jumping into something new. These character set standards, however, should be taken quite seriously once their character set has stabilized. PenPoint by GO Corporation and Plan 9 by AT&T Bell Laboratories are operating systems that currently support the Unicode character set. Other manufacturers have similar plans.

4

Japanese Encoding Methods

In this chapter you will learn how character set standards presented in the previous chapter are encoded for use on computer systems. To recap what you learned earlier, *encoding* is the mapping of a character to a numeric value. While there is no universally recognized Japanese encoding method, you will learn that JIS, Shift-JIS, and EUC are the most commonly used. Note that this discussion applies only to the electronic character set standards (for example, it applies to JIS X 0208-1990 and JIS X 0212-1990, but *not* to Jôyô Kanji, Gakushû Kanji, Jinmei-yô Kanji, or their predecessors).

There are three basic Japanese encoding methods:

- JIS
- Shift-JIS
- EUC (Extended UNIX Code)

If, after reading this chapter, you understand these encoding methods and how they relate to each other, one goal of this book has been achieved. If you absorb the other information in this chapter, great! Otherwise, treat the rest as reference material, and use it as needed.

Encoding methods covered in this chapter fall into one of three possible types:

- Modal
- Non-modal
- Fixed-width

Modal encoding methods require *escape sequences* or special characters for switching between one- and two-byte-per-character modes, different character sets, or different versions of the same character set. Modal encoding methods use a two-stage encoding process. The first stage is the mode switching initiated by the escape sequence. The second stage is the handling of the actual bytes that represent the characters. Modal encoding methods typically use seven-bit bytes. One example of modal encoding is JIS encoding.

Non-modal encoding methods, on the other hand, make use of the numeric value of a text stream's bytes for deciding when to switch between one- and two-byte-per-character modes. These encoding methods usually make liberal use of eight-bit bytes (that is, the eighth bit of a byte is turned on). Examples include Shift-JIS and EUC packed format. Non-modal encodings typically use less space than modal and fixed-width encoding methods to represent the same characters. This is one reason why they are often used for internal processing purposes.

Fixed-width encoding methods use the same number of bytes to represent all the characters available in a character set. There is no switching between one- and two-byte-per-character modes. This encoding method simplifies searching, indexing, and sorting of text, but can use up a lot of space. Examples of fixed-width encoding include ASCII, EUC complete two-byte format, Unicode, 10646.UCS-2, and 10646.UCS-4.

Note that not all of the encodings for the character set standards described in this chapter have been fully implemented—they have been defined by appropriate agencies, corporations, or committees so that their implementation, once it begins, is simplified.

National Encoding Methods

This is probably one of the most important sections of this book, and lays the foundations for your complete understanding of the various Japanese encoding methods, so be sure to take some extra time to read and study this material well. Some of the encoding methods described here, namely JIS, Shift-JIS, and EUC, will serve as a basis for drawing comparisons between other encodings, and for discussions that appear later in this book.

Table 4-1 lists the Japanese national character sets along with the encoding methods that support them.

Table 4-1: Japanese National Character Set Standards and Their Encoding Methods

	JIS	Shift-JIS	EUC	Other
ASCII/JIS-Roman	*yes*	*yes*	*yes*	ASCII, EBCDIC, and EBCDIK
Half-width katakana	*yes*	*yes*	*yes*	EBCDIK
JIS C 6226-1978	*yes*	*yes*	*yes*	
JIS X 0208-1983	*yes*	*yes*	*yes*	
JIS X 0208-1990	*yes*	*yes*	*yes*	
JIS X 0212-1990	*yes*	*no*	*yes*	

It may be argued that encodings such as JIS and Shift-JIS, in a strict sense, describe only the encoding for characters in JIS X 0208-1990 (and its earlier versions) or JIS X 0212-1990 (but not for Shift-JIS)—I include ASCII/JIS-Roman and half-width katakana when appropriate because such text streams typically contain those characters as well. The definition of EUC actually includes all of these character sets.

ASCII/JIS-Roman Encoding

ASCII and JIS-Roman are considered different character set standards, but they share the same encoding. The definition of the encoding method for the ASCII character set is found in the document called ISO 646-1991. Likewise, the encoding method for JIS-Roman encoding is found in the document called JIS X 0201-1976.* The ASCII/JIS-Roman encoding method specifies that seven bits be used, which in turn allows for 128 uniquely encoded characters. Of these 128 encoded characters, 94 consist of the ASCII/JIS-Roman character set, and are printable, meaning that they are displayed on the screen with something other than just white space. The remaining 34 characters are non-printing, meaning that they are either control characters or white space. *White space* refers to characters such as tabs and spaces. Table 4-2 lists the encoding ranges for the characters, printable and non-printable, in ASCII/JIS-Roman encoding.

Table 4-2: ASCII and JIS-Roman Encoding Specifications

	Decimal	Hexadecimal	Octal
Control characters	0–31	00–1F	000–037
Space character	32	20	040
Graphic characters	33–126	21–7E	041–176
Delete character	127	7F	177

Note that these values can be represented with only seven bits (the importance of this is explained later in this chapter). Briefly, this allows the mixture of the ASCII and half-width katakana character sets with eight-bit bytes. A more graphic representation of the ASCII/JIS-Roman encoding method can be found in Figure 4-1.

The extended ASCII character set encoding defined by ISO 8859 makes use of all eight bits, so more of the 256 possible characters available with eigth bits can be encoded with graphic characters. The first 128 character positions are reserved for the ASCII character set and control characters, but the additional 128 character positions made possible with the eighth bit can vary. Exactly which characters are encoded in this extended ASCII character set depends on the implementation. The extended ASCII characters specified in each of these nine parts fall into the range 0xA1–0xFF. However, not all encoded positions in this range are used by every part of ISO 8859.

---

*Until March, 1987 this was called JIS C 6220-1976.

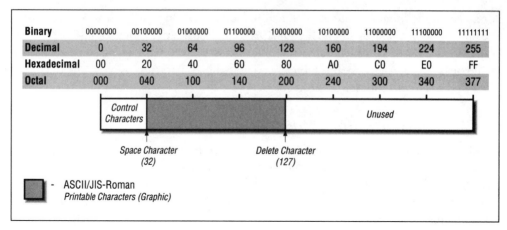

Figure 4-1: ASCII/JIS-Roman encoding table

Figure 4-2 illustrates the encoding range for ASCII and extended ASCII as defined in the nine parts of ISO 8859.

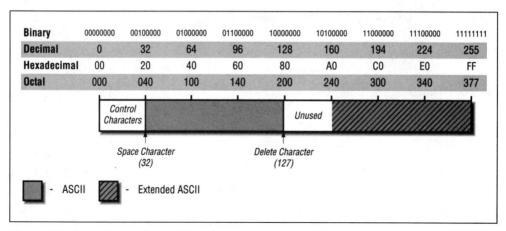

Figure 4-2: ISO 8859 encoding table

Most of the Japanese encoding methods, especially those used as internal codes for computer systems, make generous use of eight-bit characters. This makes it very difficult to mix characters from ISO 8859's nine parts with Japanese since they all fall into the same encoded range. Some computer platforms deal with this much better than others. The Apple Macintosh handles this problem quite well simply by changing the font.

EBCDIC/EBCDIK Encoding

IBM developed their own single-byte character set standard called EBCDIC (*Extended Binary-Coded-Decimal Interchange Code*). The number and type of printable characters are the same as ASCII, but the encoding for EBCDIC differs greatly. The main difference is that EBCDIC requires eight bits for full representation, whereas ASCII and JIS-Roman require only seven bits. Table 4-3 lists the specifications for EBCDIC.

Table 4-3: EBCDIC Encoding Specifications

	Decimal	Hexadecimal	Octal
Control characters	0–63	00–3F	000–077
Space character	64	40	100
Graphic characters	65–239	41–EF	101–357
Numerals	240–249	F0–F9	360–371
Undefined	250–254	FA–FE	372–376
Control character	255	FF	377

The EBCDIC encoding method is not used as often as the encoding for ASCII/JIS-Roman, and appears to be slowly becoming obsolete. EBCDIC is included in these pages for the sake of completeness, and because three of the encoding methods to follow include EBCDIC as a subset (they are IBM DBCS-Host, JEF, and KEIS encoding methods—all of these are corporate encoding methods). Figure 4-3 illustrates the encoding space for EBCDIC encoding.

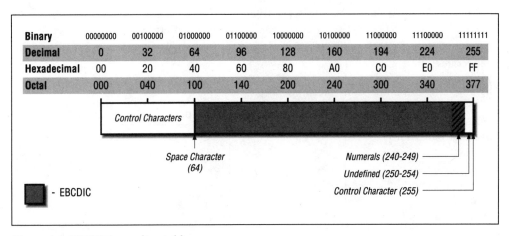

Figure 4-3: EBCDIC encoding table

There is also an encoding called EBCDIK, which stands for *Extended Binary-Coded-Decimal Interchange Kana* code. It is an EBCDIC encoding that contains uppercase Roman characters, numerals, symbols, half-width katakana, and control characters (note that there are no lowercase Roman characters). Table 4-4 shows the encoding ranges for the characters in EBCDIK.

Table 4-4: EBCDIK Encoding Specifications

	Decimal	Hexadecimal	Octal
Control characters	0–63	00–3F	000–077
Space character	64	40	100
Graphic characters	65–239	41–EF	101–357
Numerals	240–249	F0–F9	360–371
Undefined	250–254	FA–FE	372–376
Control character	255	FF	377

Note how the encoding space is identical to that of EBCDIC (see Figure 4-3). Characters are scattered in a rather random way throughout the graphic character space, and not all positions have characters assigned to them.

For a complete listing of EBCDIC and EBCDIK characters and their code positions, see Appendix O.

Half-width Katakana Encoding

Half-width katakana characters have been encoded in a variety of ways. As single-byte characters, they are encoded in two ways. These two methods are described in the document JIS X 0201-1976. Table 4-5 illustrates the one-byte encoding methods for this small collection of characters.

Table 4-5: Half-width Katakana Encoding Specifications

	Decimal	Hexadecimal	Octal
Seven-bit half-width katakana			
Byte range	33–95	21–5F	041–137
Eight-bit half-width katakana			
Byte range	161–223	A1–DF	241–337

JIS encoding uses both of these encoding methods. Shift-JIS encoding also makes use of only the eight-bit half-width katakana encoding method. EUC encoding takes a different approach, and encodes these characters with two bytes. Each of these encoding methods is discussed later in this chapter. Table 4-6 gives the EUC encoding specifications for half-width katakana.

Table 4-6: EUC Half-width Katakana Encoding Specifications

	Decimal	Hexadecimal	Octal
EUC half-width katakana (packed format)			
First byte	142	8E	216
Second byte range	161–223	A1–DF	241–337
EUC half-width katakana (complete two-byte format)			
First byte	0	00	000
Second byte range	161–223	A1–DF	241–337

Note how the second byte range is identical to the eight-bit half-width katakana range in the previous table—EUC simply prepends a byte.

Figure 4-4 illustrates the encoding space for the half-width katakana character set in the various encodings.

Now note how eight-bit half-width katakana and seven-bit ASCII/JIS-Roman can coexist within the same eight-bit one-byte encoding space. When these two character sets are mixed, the newly formed character set is called ANK (*Alphabet, Numerals, and Katakana*), as illustrated in Figure 4-5.

KUTEN Encoding

Before I discuss JIS encoding, I would like to discuss KUTEN encoding. This section title is a sort of misnomer in that KUTEN is not really an encoding *per se*, but rather an *indexing* method (the Japanese version of TEX is the only software I know of that can process KUTEN codes internally). The word KUTEN (区点) itself refers to the row and cell of a matrix. KU (区) means "row" or "ward," and TEN (点) means "cell" or "point." The documents JIS X 0208-1990 and JIS X 0212-1990 use KUTEN to index each character. KUTEN is used primarily as an encoding-independent way to represent characters within a specified matrix size, usually 94-by-94.

The encoding methods described so far more or less fall into the area of single-byte encodings (with the exception of EUC encoded half-width katakana). Now we enter into the area of multiple-byte encodings. KUTEN is important since it provides a good introduction to the encoding of multiple-byte characters.

In the case of the JIS character set standards, KUTEN values can range from 1 to 94 (decimal notation). This constitutes a 94-row-by-94-cell matrix, with a total capacity of

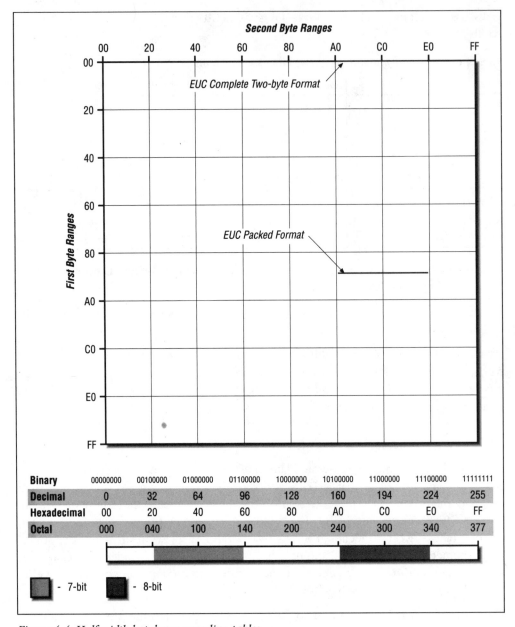

Figure 4-4: Half-width katakana encoding tables

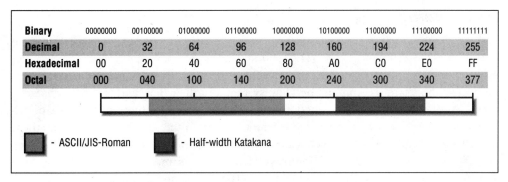

Binary	00000000	00100000	01000000	01100000	10000000	10100000	11000000	11100000	11111111
Decimal	0	32	64	96	128	160	194	224	255
Hexadecimal	00	20	40	60	80	A0	C0	E0	FF
Octal	000	040	100	140	200	240	300	340	377

- ASCII/JIS-Roman   - Half-width Katakana

Figure 4-5: Half-width katakana plus ASCII/JIS-Roman encoding table

8,836 cells. Table 4-7 shows a formal representation of the KUTEN ranges. Note how it can be expressed in notations other than decimal.

Table 4-7: KUTEN Encoding Specifications

	Decimal	Hexadecimal	Octal
First byte range	1–94	01–5E	001–136
Second byte range	1–94	01–5E	001–136

Figure 4-6 illustrates the 94-row-by-94-cell matrix as used by KUTEN indexing. You will quite often see this 94-by-94 matrix as the dimensions of other encoding spaces.

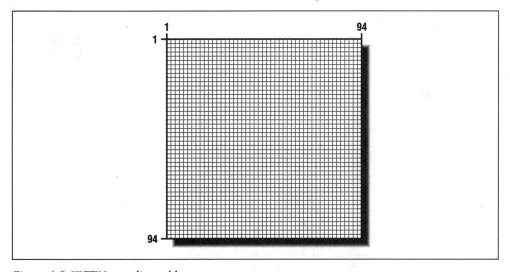

Figure 4-6: KUTEN encoding table

JIS Encoding

The Japanese Standards Association (JSA) promulgated character set standards known as JIS (JIS X 0208-1990 and JIS X 0212-1990 are the major ones.). JIS encoding handles several versions and types of the Japanese character set, most of which consist of seven-bit codes, and share a common encoding system, but their one- and two-byte character escape sequences differ. This encoding method is *modal*, namely in that escape sequences are used to switch between different modes. In the case of JIS encoding, these modes are typically one- and two-byte representations, but there are other modes, such as different character sets, or different versions of the same character set. An escape sequence consists of the escape character (0x1B) plus other characters. ISO 2022-1993 and JIS X 0202-1991 contain tables that list the escape sequences for a variety of character sets.

JIS encoding is not very efficient for internal storage or processing on computer systems. It is used more as an information interchange code for moving information between computer systems. This is called an *external* code. There are, however, some software and environments that process JIS encoding internally, such as Mule, Nemacs, and some versions of Japanese TEX. Many other programs can create JIS encoded data, but do not necessarily process JIS encoding internally.

JIS and KUTEN are related more closely than you would think. JIS is the encoded value, and KUTEN is an encoding-independent way of indexing characters.

Escape sequences should be fully contained within a line—they should not span newlines or carriage returns. If there are any two-byte characters on a line, there should be at least one two-byte character escape sequence and one one-byte character escape sequence. If the last character on a line is represented by two bytes, a one-byte character escape sequence should follow before the line terminates. If the first character on a line is represented by two bytes, a two-byte character escape sequence should precede it. Not all these procedures are necessary, but they are useful because they ensure that small communication errors do not render an entire Japanese document unreadable—each line becomes self-contained. These escape sequences are also known as *kanji-in* and *kanji-out*. Kanji-in corresponds to a two-byte character escape sequence, and kanji-out corresponds to a one-byte character escape sequence.

JIS is the primary encoding method used for electronic transmission (for instance, e-mail) because it typically contains seven-bit characters.* This is why JIS encoding is often referred to as a seven-bit encoding method. The eight bit is still there, but unused. Table 4-8 lists the code specifications for the JIS encoding method along with the escape sequences for different versions and types of the Japanese character set.

---

*Some network paths strip the eighth bit from characters—these can usually be repaired, though, as you will see later in this chapter.

Table 4-8: JIS Encoding Specifications

	Decimal	Hexadecimal	Octal
Two-byte character escape sequences			
JIS C 6226-1978[1]	27 36 64	1B 24 40	033 044 100
JIS X 0208-1983[2]	27 36 66	1B 24 42	033 044 102
JIS X 0208-1990[3]	27 38 64 27 36 66	1B 26 40 1B 24 42	033 046 100 033 044 102
JIS X 0212-1990[4]	27 36 40 68	1B 24 28 44	033 044 050 104
Two-byte characters			
First byte range	33–126	21–7E	041–176
Second byte range	33–126	21–7E	041–176
One-byte character escape sequences			
JIS-Roman[5]	27 40 74	1B 28 4A	033 050 112
JIS-Roman[6]	27 40 72	1B 28 48	033 050 110
ASCII[7]	27 40 66	1B 28 42	033 050 102
Half-width katakana[8]	27 40 73	1B 28 49	033 050 111
JIS7 half-width katakana			
Byte range	33–095	21–5F	041–137
JIS8 half-width katakana			
Shift-out	14	0E	016
Byte range	161–223	A1–DF	241–337
Shift-in	15	0F	017
ASCII/JIS-Roman			
Byte range	33–126	21–7E	041–176

[1] Represented graphically as <ESC> $ @.

[2] Represented graphically as <ESC> $ B.

[3] Represented graphically as <ESC> & @ <ESC> $ B.

[4] Represented graphically as <ESC> $ (D.

[5] Represented graphically as <ESC> (J.

[6] Represented graphically as <ESC> (H. This is improperly used on some implementations as the one-byte character escape sequence for JIS-Roman. The correct sequence to use is <ESC> (J. According to the document JIS X 0202-1991, it is actually the one-byte character escape sequence for the Swedish character set. It is a good idea for software to recognize, but not to generate, this one-byte character escape sequence.

[7] Represented graphically as <ESC> (B.

[8] Represented graphically as <ESC> (I.

The two-byte character escape sequence for JIS C 6226-1978 is commonly referred to as Old-JIS, and the one for JIS X 0208-1983 as New-JIS. I have monitored e-mail discussions in which several people recommended that the JIS X 0208-1983 two-byte escape sequence also be used for JIS X 0208-1990. This is not its official two-byte escape sequence, but since the difference between these two characters sets lies in only two kanji, there seems to be no compelling reason to use a separate escape sequence for both. This is more an issue of practicality, but this behavior may change in the future.

Let's take a look at some JIS encoded material to see exactly how this encoding method works. The example string is かな漢字, which means "kana [and] kanji." The encoded values are in hexadecimal notation.

Character String				か	な	漢	字			
Escape Sequences	<ESC>	$	B					<ESC>	(	J
Encoded Values	1B	24	42	242B	244A	3441	3B7A	1B	28	4A

In the above example, the first escape sequence signals a switch in mode to the JIS X 0208-1983 character set (two-byte-per-character mode); then the four characters are displayed. To terminate the line, a one-byte character escape sequence is used (in this case it is the one for switching to the JIS-Roman character set).

You have already learned that JIS encoding makes use of seven bits for representing two-byte characters. The actual encoded range corresponds to that used for representing the ASCII character set. Thus, the encoded values for the kanji in the above example can be represented with ASCII characters. Let's look at that example again, but with some additional data: the ASCII characters.

Character String				か	な	漢	字			
Escape Sequences	<ESC>	$	B					<ESC>	(	J
Encoded Values	1B	24	42	242B	244A	3441	3B7A	1B	28	4A
ASCII Characters				$+	$J	4A	;z			

JIS encoding also supports half-width katakana, and has two different methods called JIS7 and JIS8. JIS7 encoding has all eighth bits masked; JIS8 does not share this restriction. JIS7 and JIS8 half-width katakana encodings are not widely used in products, so it is questionable whether all software should necessarily generate such codes. It is, however, important that software recognize and deal with them appropriately.

JIS7 encoding is identical to JIS encoding, but with the addition of another escape sequence for shifting into half-width katakana mode. This method is defined in the document JIS X 0202-1991. This means that a document containing two-byte Japanese, one-byte ASCII, and half-width katakana characters may make use of at least three escape sequences, one for shifting into each of the three modes or character sets.

The encoding range for JIS8 includes eight-bit bytes (its range is 161–223, and is identical to the half-width katakana range in Shift-JIS encoding), and uses the ASCII SI (shift-in) and SO (shift-out) control characters. To begin a half-width katakana sequence, you must use the SO character, and to end it, the SI character. The text stream must also be in one-byte-per-character mode.

Figure 4-7 illustrates the encoding space for JIS.

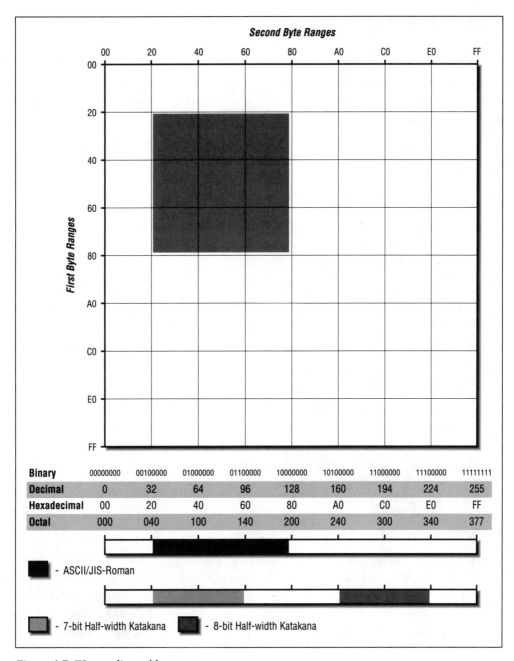

Figure 4-7: JIS encoding tables

Shift-JIS Encoding

Shift-JIS encoding, developed by Microsoft Corporation, is widely implemented as the internal code for a variety of platforms including Japanese PCs and KanjiTalk (漢字 Talk)—the Japanese operating system for Apple Macintosh. Shift-JIS is sometimes referred to as MS (for Microsoft) Kanji or SJIS (short form of Shift-JIS). Historically, Shift-JIS was so named because of the way the code positions for two-byte characters *shifted* around the code positions for half-width katakana—Japanese PC users originally used only half-width katakana, so Shift-JIS was developed in order to maintain backward compatibility.

The following list provides more examples of computer platforms and environments that process Shift-JIS code internally:

Epson PCs
Fujitsu FM-R series PCs
HP MPE/iX
HP-UX
IBM 5550
IBM DOS J/V
IBM PS/55
Japanese TEX (ASCII version)
KanjiTalk (Macintosh)
Mule
NEC PC-9800/9801 series PCs
Nemacs
Panasonic Panacom M series PCs
PS/2 running AIX 1.2/1.3 (requires a system extension)
RISC System/6000 running AIX 3.1.5 (requires a system extension)
RISC System/6000 running AIX 3.2.0 & later
Sony NEWS
Toshiba J-3100 series PCs

Here is how Shift-JIS encoding works. A two-byte-per-character mode in Shift-JIS is initiated with a byte having a decimal value ranging between 129–159 or 224–239 (0x81– 0x9F or 0xE0–0xEF). This byte is subsequently treated as the first byte of an expected two-byte sequence. The following (second) byte must have a decimal value ranging between 64–126 or 128–252 (0x40–0x7E or 0x80–0xFC). Note that the first byte's range falls entirely in the extended ASCII character set—in the eight-bit character set with the high-order bit on. Note that Shift-JIS also encodes half-width katakana and ASCII/JIS-Roman. Table 4-9 lists the code specifications for Shift-JIS.

Table 4-9: Shift-JIS Encoding Specifications

	Decimal	Hexadecimal	Octal
Two-byte characters			
First byte ranges	129–159, 224–239	81–9F, E0–EF	201–237, 340–357
Second byte ranges	64–126, 128–252	40–7E, 80–FC	100–176, 200–374
Half-width katakana			
Byte range	161–223	A1–DF	241–337
ASCII/JIS-Roman			
Byte range	33–126	21–7E	041–176

Now let's take a look at some Shift-JIS encoded material to illustrate just how this encoding method works. The example string is かな漢字, which was used in the previous section on JIS encoding. The encoded values are in hexadecimal notation.

Character String	か	な	漢	字
Encoded Values	82A9	82C8	8ABF	8E9A

Note that no escape sequences are used in this example—this is typical of non-modal encodings, and produces a much tighter encoding. There is, however, no ASCII representation for the two bytes that constitute these characters.

Shift-JIS encoding does not support the characters defined in JIS X 0212-1990. There is simply not enough encoding space left to include these characters, and there is currently no plan to extend Shift-JIS in a manner such that JIS X 0212-1990 can be included. See Figure 4-8 for an illustration of the Shift-JIS encoding space.

Some definitions (in particular, corporate definitions) of Shift-JIS also contain encoding blocks for user-defined characters or even an encoded position for a half-width katakana space character. Such encoding blocks and encoded positions are not useful if true information interchange is desired, because they are encoded in such a way that they do not convert to encoded positions in other Japanese encoding methods (that is, JIS and EUC). Table 4-10 lists these non-standard Shift-JIS encoding blocks and encoded positions.

Table 4-10: Shift-JIS User-defined Character Encoding Specifications

	Decimal	Hexadecimal	Octal
Two-byte user-defined characters			
First byte range[1]	240–252	F0–FC	360–374
Second byte ranges	64–126, 128–252	40–7E, 80–FC	100–176, 200–374
Half-width katakana			
Space character	160	A0	240

[1]Some implementations have a smaller user-defined character range.

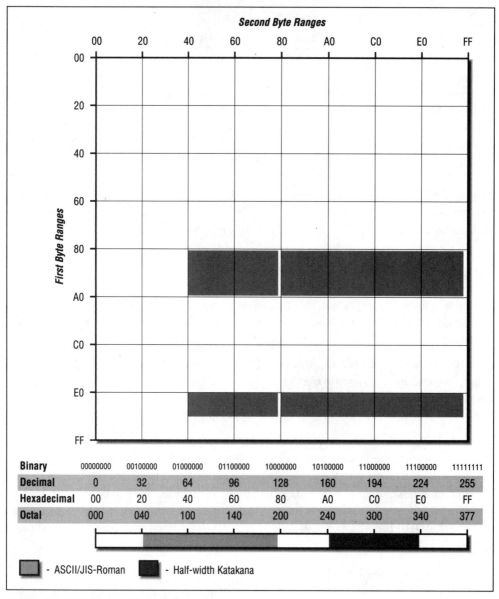

Figure 4-8: Shift-JIS encoding tables

Note how the second byte range is unchanged from the standard definition of Shift-JIS—only the first byte range is different.

Figure 4-9 illustrates the standard Shift-JIS encoding space along with the user-defined character area.

Shift-JIS Versus JIS Encoding

The relationship between Shift-JIS and JIS is not very apparent, and requires the use of a somewhat complex conversion algorithm, examined in detail in Chapter 7. Figure 4-10 illustrates the Shift-JIS encoding space and how it relates to JIS (note that the half-width

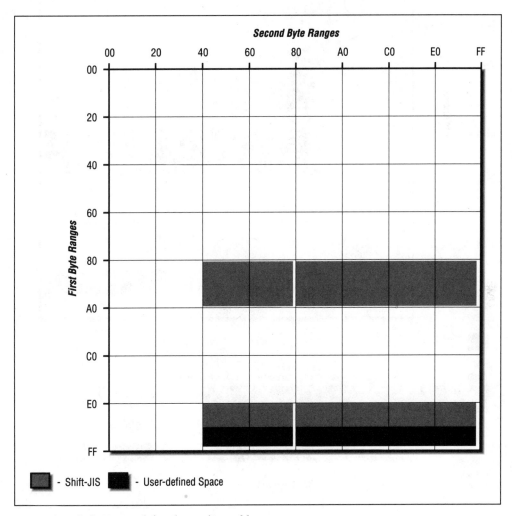

Figure 4-9: Shift-JIS user-defined encoding table

katakana encoding as used with Shift-JIS encoding is identical to that used in JIS8, and that the ASCII/JIS-Roman encoding as used with Shift-JIS encoding is identical to that used with JIS).

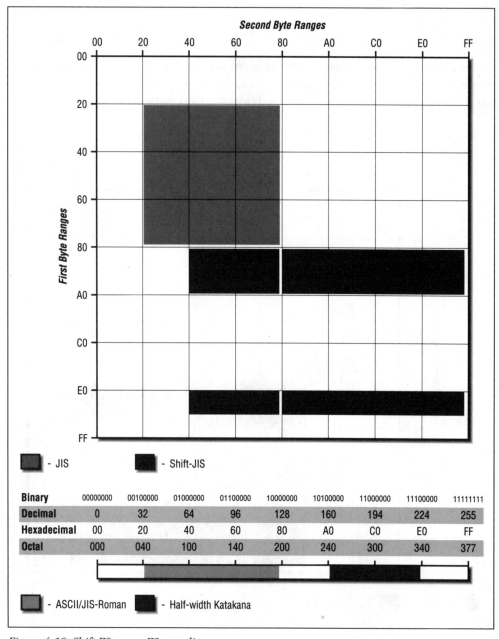

Figure 4-10: Shift-JIS versus JIS encoding

EUC Encoding

EUC (Extended UNIX Code) encoding is implemented as the internal code for most UNIX workstations configured to support Japanese. EUC is also known as UJIS (short for *UNIXized JIS*) and AT&T JIS. The definition of EUC comes from the document called ISO 2022-1993.

EUC is not special to Japanese encoding—it was developed as a method for handling multiple character sets, Japanese or otherwise, within a single text stream. The full definition of EUC is quite rich and supports multiple-byte encoding, but the specific implementations used for Japanese systems usually fall into two specific types: *EUC packed format* and *EUC complete two-byte format*. These Japanese definitions of EUC were standardized in 1991 by three organizations: The Open Software Foundation (OSF), UNIX International (UI), and UNIX System Laboratories Pacific (USLP). This standardization has subsequently made it easier for other developers to implement Japanese systems, and at the same time reinforced the use of EUC encoding.

The current trend in software development is to produce systems that process EUC—it is much more extensible than Shift-JIS. The following computer operating systems and software process EUC internally:

ANS (Amiga Nihongo System)
HP-UX
Japanese TEX
JDIC
JLE (Sun Microsystems' Japanese Language Environment)
JREADER
KG (Kanji Guess)
MOKE (Mark's Own Kanji Editor)
Mule
NEC EWS
Nemacs
Omron LUNA
RISC System/6000 running AIX 3.2.0 & later
Sony NEWS
X11R5
YKH (Yaki Kemono Hosuto)

Japanese EUC implementations use one specific instance of multiple-width and one specific instance of fixed-width encoding.

The full definition of EUC consists of four code sets. Code set 0 is always set to the ASCII character set or a country's own version thereof (that is, JIS-Roman for Japan). The remaining code sets are defined as a set of variants from which each country can select. You will learn about how the Japanese implemented EUC later in this chapter.

There are several reserved code positions in EUC that cannot be used to encode graphic characters. These code positions and ranges consist of the space character, the delete character, and two independent ranges of control characters. Table 4-11 shows these code ranges in more detail.

Table 4-11: EUC Reserved Code Ranges and Positions

	Decimal	Hexadecimal	Octal
Control set 0	0–31	00–1F	000–037
Space character	32	20	040
Delete character	127	7F	177
Control set 1	128–159	80–9F	200–237

The above limitation then permits two ranges for encoding graphic characters, namely 0x21–0x7E (94 characters) and 0xA0–0xFF (96 characters). The second range, at least for the Japanese implementation, is usually limited to the range 0xA1–0xFE as a way to stay compatible with encodings that support ranges of only 94 characters, such as JIS. Table 4-12 lists these two encoding ranges in other notations.

Table 4-12: EUC Graphic Character Encoding Ranges

	Decimal	Hexadecimal	Octal
First code range	33–126	21–7E	041–176
Second code range	160–255	A0–FF	240–377

There are also two special characters: SS2 and SS3. SS2 stands for *Single Shift 2*, and is used as a prefix to every character in code set 2. Likewise, SS3 stands for *Single Shift 3*, and is used as a prefix to every character in code set 3. Table 4-13 lists them in three notations. These will become important later when we discuss code sets 2 and 3.

Table 4-13: EUC SS2 and SS3 Characters

	Decimal	Hexadecimal	Octal
SS2	142	8E	216
SS3	143	8F	217

Table 4-14 illustrates the multiple-width representation of the four EUC code sets along with their possible permutations (hexadecimal notation is used here for the sake of space).

Table 4-14: EUC Multiple-width Representations

	Variant 1	Variant 2	Variant 3
Code set 0	21–7E		
Code set 1	A0–FF	A0–FF + A0–FF	A0–FF + A0–FF + A0–FF
Code set 2	8E + A0–FF	8E + A0–FF + A0–FF	8E + A0–FF + A0–FF + A0–FF
Code set 3	8F + A0–FF	8F + A0–FF + A0–FF	8F + A0–FF + A0–FF + A0–FF

The highlighted permutations are those implemented for Japanese. This representation is often referred to as EUC packed format. Also, there can be as many variants of this representation as needed to represent a given country's character set. For example, Chinese may use parts of Variant 3 because some character sets require more than two bytes for representation.

There are two fixed-width EUC representations: 16- and 32-bit. Table 4-15 describes the 16-bit code space.

Table 4-15: EUC 16-bit Fixed-width Representations

	Variant 1	Variant 2
Code set 0	00 + 21-7E	
Code set 1	80 + A0–FF	A0-FF + A0-FF
Code set 2	00 + A0-FF	21–7E + A0–FF
Code set 3	80 + 21–7E	A0-FF + 21-7E

Again, the highlighted permutations indicate those implemented for Japanese. This representation is often referred to as EUC complete two-byte format. Note that the SS2 and SS3 characters are not used in this representation. The 32-bit representation gets very long, and since it is not implemented for Japanese, there is no need to illustrate its code ranges.

Note that EUC encodes half-width katakana using two bytes rather than one, and that it includes a very large user-defined character space. Large enough, in fact, that EUC implements the JIS X 0212-1990 character set by placing it into this user-defined character space.

The official definition of Japanese EUC specifies the character sets to be assigned to each of the four EUC code sets. These assignments are illustrated in Table 4-16.

Table 4-16: Japanese EUC

	Character Set	Display Width	Number of Bytes
Code set 0	ASCII or JIS-Roman	1	1
Code set 1	JIS X 0208-1990	2	2
Code set 2	Half-width katakana	1	1[1]
Code set 3	JIS X 0212-1990	2	2[1]

[1]The number of bytes does not include the SS2 and SS3 characters—only those within proper encoding ranges are used in the byte count.

The display widths in the above table correspond to the number of columns occupied by each character in a code set. A display width value of 1 corresponds to what the Japanese call half-width, and a display width value of 2 corresponds to what the Japanese call full-width.

EUC Packed Format

The most commonly encountered Japanese EUC implementation is the multiple-width version. This is also known as the *packed format*.

As you already learned, EUC consists of four code sets: the primary code set (code set 0) which is the ASCII/JIS-Roman character set, and three supplemental code sets (code sets 1, 2, and 3) which can be specified by the user and are usually used for non-Roman characters. Table 4-17 lists the code specifications for all the code sets of EUC in packed format.

Table 4-17: EUC Packed Format Encoding Specifications

	Decimal	Hexadecimal	Octal
Code set 0 (ASCII/JIS-Roman)			
Byte range	33–126	21–7E	041–176
Code set 1 (JIS X 0208-1990)			
First byte range	161–254	A1–FE	241–376
Second byte range	161–254	A1–FE	241–376
Code set 2 (Half-width katakana)			
First byte	142	8E	216
Second byte range	161–223	A1–DF	241–337

	Decimal	Hexadecimal	Octal
Code set 3 (JIS X 0212-1990)			
First byte	143	8F	217
Second byte range	161–254	A1–FE	241–376
Third byte range	161–254	A1–FE	241–376

See Figure 4-11 for an illustration of the EUC packed format encoding space. Note how it requires a three-dimensional encoding space.

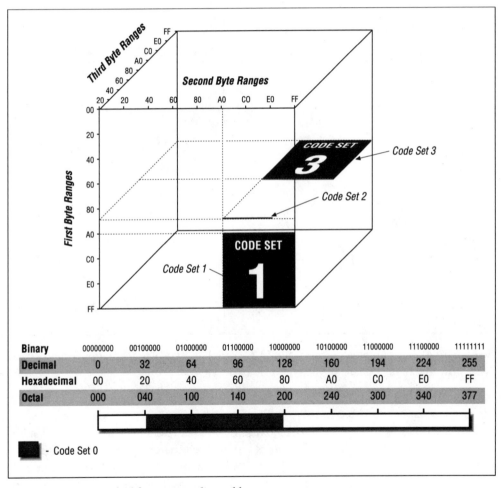

Figure 4-11: EUC packed format encoding tables

EUC Complete Two-byte Format

The 16-bit fixed-length Japanese implementation of EUC is called the *complete two-byte format*. This version of EUC encoding is not commonly encountered. In this implementation of EUC, all code sets, including code set 0, are represented by two bytes. This approach can make it easier for software to handle the characters since they can expect all characters to consist of two bytes (that is, 16 bits)—no switching between multiple byte representations is required. Fixed-width codes are also called *process codes*. Using process codes facilitates sorting, searching, and indexing, since all characters are encoded similarly.

Table 4-18 lists the code specifications for EUC in complete two-byte format.

Table 4-18: EUC Complete Two-byte Format Encoding Specifications

	Decimal	Hexadecimal	Octal
Code set 0 (ASCII/JIS-Roman)			
First byte	0	00	000
Second byte range	33–126	21–7E	041–176
Code set 1 (JIS X 0208-1990)			
First byte range	161–254	A1–FE	241–376
Second byte range	161–254	A1–FE	241–376
Code set 2 (Half-width katakana)			
First byte	0	00	000
Second byte range	161–223	A1–DF	241–337
Code set 3 (JIS X 0212-1990)			
First byte range	161–254	A1–FE	241–376
Second byte range	33–126	21–7E	041–176

See Figure 4-12 for an illustration of the EUC complete two-byte format encoding space. Note how all characters are represented by two bytes.

You may have noticed that, for each byte of some of the code sets, EUC permits up to 96 characters (that is, the range of 0xA0–0xFF). So why are the above code listings set in a smaller encoding space (namely 0xA1–0xFE, or 94 characters instead of 96)? As stated earlier, this is done for the sake of compatibility with character sets and encodings (most notably, JIS) that are based on a 94-row-by-94-cell matrix. This is not to say that code positions 0xA0 or 0xFF are invalid, but that there are most likely no characters encoded in those positions.

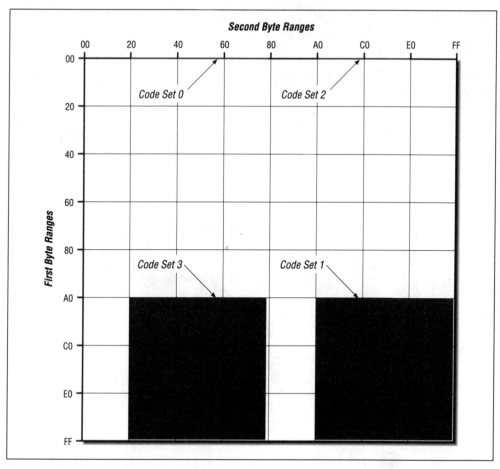

Figure 4-12: EUC complete two-byte format encoding table

Let's now take a peek at some EUC encoded material to see how this encoding method works. The example string is かな漢字, which was used in previous sections. Like before, the encoded values are in hexadecimal notation.

Character String	か	な	漢	字
Encoded Values	A4AB	A4CA	B4C1	BBFA

Like Shift-JIS, there are no escape sequences used here. The above example is representative of both EUC packed and EUC complete two-byte formats.

EUC Versus JIS Encoding

EUC encoding is closely related to JIS encoding. In fact, every character that can be encoded by JIS can be converted to a EUC encoded equivalent. This leads to better information interchange. The following figures draw comparisons between JIS encoding and the two forms of EUC encoding: EUC packed format (Figure 4-13) and EUC complete two-byte format (Figure 4-14).

In most cases, EUC is simply JIS with the high bit set. This is discussed in more detail in Chapter 7.

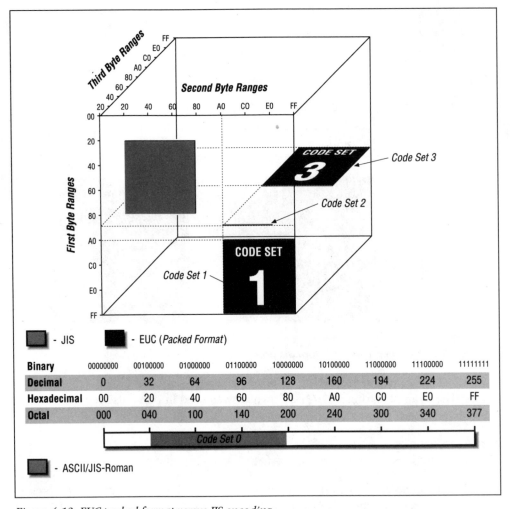

Figure 4-13: EUC packed format versus JIS encoding

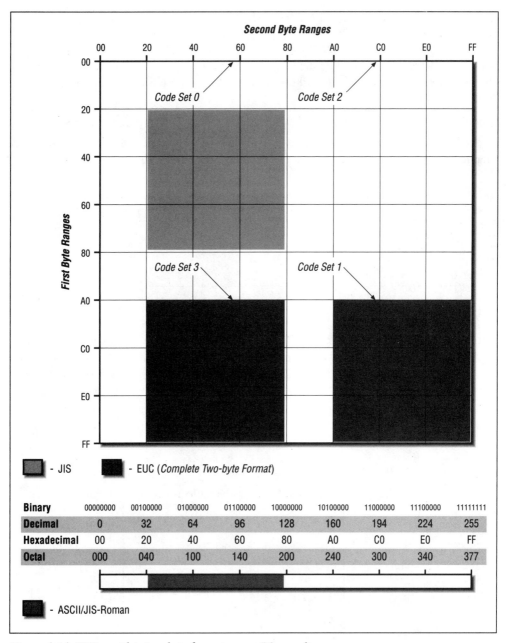

Figure 4-14: EUC complete two-byte format versus JIS encoding

Asian Encoding Methods

Included here are listings of the encoding methods used for the other Asian character set standards, namely KS C 5601-1992, GB 2312-80, and Big Five. You will note that many of the encoding methods to be described in this section are identical to Japanese ones we have already covered..

Table 4-19 lists the Asian character set standards along with the encoding methods that support them. The basic encoding methods include JIS, Shift-JIS, and EUC. For one of the character sets, Big Five, its encoding is similar, but not identical, to EUC encoding.

Table 4-19: Asian Character Set Standards and Their Encoding Methods

	JIS	Shift-JIS	EUC
KS C 5601-1992	yes	no	yes
GB 2312-80	yes	no	yes
Big Five	no	no	yes

KS C 5601-1992 Encoding

The Korean character standard, KS C 5601-1992, is encoded very similar to JIS X 0208-1990. It departs only in that there is no encoding method comparable to Shift-JIS. This means that you should expect to find an encoding like JIS (uses escape sequences to shift between one- and two-byte characters—modal), and one like EUC (extensive use of eight-bit characters, and the values of each byte are used to determine whether characters consist of one or two bytes—non-modal). Table 4-20 lists the JIS-like encoding for KS C 5601-1992. This is called the seven-bit encoding.

Table 4-20: KS C 5601-1992 Seven-bit Encoding Specifications

	Decimal	Hexadecimal	Octal
Two-byte character escape sequence KS C 5601-1992[1]	27 36 40 67	1B 24 28 43	033 044 050 103
Two-byte characters (KS C 5601-1992)			
First byte range	33–126	21–7E	041–176
Second byte range	33–126	21–7E	041–176
One-byte character escape sequence ASCII[2]	27 40 66	1B 28 42	033 050 102

---

[1]Represented graphically as <ESC> $ (C.
[2]Represented graphically as <ESC> (B.

	Decimal	Hexadecimal	Octal
One-byte characters (ASCII)			
Byte range	33–126	21–7E	041–176

Likewise, Table 4-21 lists the EUC-like encoding for KS C 5601-1992. The document called KS C 5861-1992 actually describes the EUC encoding for Korean text. This is called the eight-bit encoding.

Table 4-21: KS C 5601-1992 Eight-bit Encoding Specifications

	Decimal	Hexadecimal	Octal
Two-byte characters (KS C 5601-1992)			
First byte range	161–254	A1–FE	241–376
Second byte range	161–254	A1–FE	241–376
One-byte characters (ASCII)			
Byte range	33–126	21–7E	041–176

GB 2312-80 Encoding

The encoding for the GB 2312-80 is nearly identical to KS C 5601-1992 except that there is an additional one-byte character set supported, namely GB 1988-80, which is the Chinese equivalent to JIS-Roman. It will be called GB-Roman here. Like KS C 5601-1992, there is also no encoding method comparable to Shift-JIS used.

Table 4-22 lists the seven-bit encoding for GB 2312-80.

Table 4-22: GB 2312-80 Seven-bit Encoding Specifications

	Decimal	Hexadecimal	Octal
Two-byte character escape sequence GB 2312-80[1]	27 36 40 65	1B 24 28 41	033 044 050 101
Two-byte characters (GB 2312-80)			
First byte range	33–126	21–7E	041–176
Second byte range	33–126	21–7E	041–176

---

[1]Represented graphically as <ESC> $ A.

	Decimal	Hexadecimal	Octal
One-byte character escape sequences			
ASCII[2]	27 40 66	1B 28 42	033 050 102
GB-Roman[3]	27 40 84	1B 28 54	033 050 124
One-byte characters (ASCII/GB-Roman)			
Byte range	33–126	21–7E	041–176

[2]Represented graphically as <ESC> (B.
[3]Represented graphically as <ESC> (T.

Table 4-23 lists the eight-bit encoding for GB 2312-80. Note the similarity to EUC encoding (EUC code sets 0 and 1, that is), and that this encoding is identical to KS C 5601-1992, described above.

Table 4-23: GB 2312-80 Eight-bit Encoding Specifications

	Decimal	Hexadecimal	Octal
Two-byte characters (GB 2312-80)			
First byte range	161–254	A1–FE	241–376
Second byte range	161–254	A1–FE	241–376
One-byte characters (ASCII/GB-Roman)			
Byte range	33–126	21–7E	041–176

Big Five Encoding

The Big Five encoding has much in common with EUC code sets 0 and 1, the main difference being that there is an additional encoding block. This is required since the Big Five character set contains over 13,000 characters—EUC code set 1 simply cannot encode that many characters. Table 4-24 illustrates its encoding specifications.

Table 4-24: Big Five Encoding Specifications

	Decimal	Hexadecimal	Octal
Two-byte characters (Big Five)			
First byte range	161–254	A1–FE	241–376
Second byte ranges	64–126, 161–254	40–7E, A1–FE	100–176, 241–376
One-byte characters (ASCII)			
Byte range	33–126	21–7E	041–176

Figure 4-15 illustrates the Big Five encoding table.

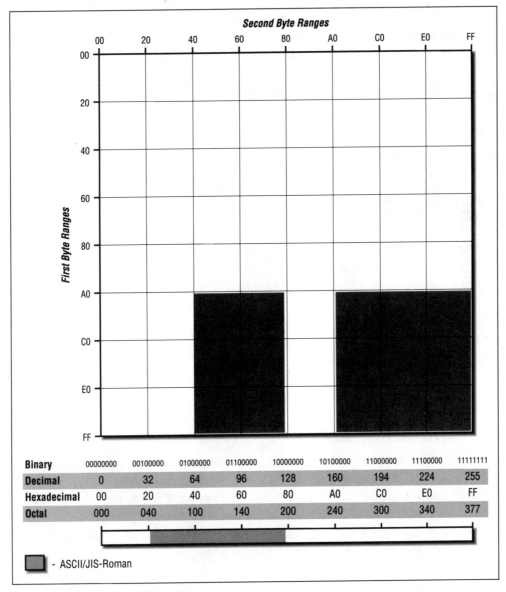

Figure 4-15: Big Five encoding table

Comparing Japanese and Other Asian Encoding Methods

The repertoire of characters, especially kanji, in the Asian character set standards overlap considerably, although the ordering of the characters is markably different. This means that any attempt at conversion between them must be done with mapping tables, and there may be cases when characters in one character set standard do not exist in another.

Table 4-25 lists the encoded values for the two kanji 漢 and 字. I am listing them under two encoding methods which are the closest to what they actually use. Note how there is no correspondence between the encodings of these two characters in the different character sets.

Table 4-25: Kanji Encoded in Different Asian Character Sets

	Seven-bit Encoding	Eight-bit Encoding
Japanese (JIS X 0208-1990)		
漢	3441	B4C1
字	3B7A	BBFA
Korean (KS C 5601-1992)		
漢	7953	F9D3
字	6D2E	EDAE
Chinese (GB 2312-80)		
汉[1]	3A3A	BABA
字	5756	D7D6
Chinese (Big Five)		
漢	...	BA7E
字	...	A672

[1]The character 汉 is the simplified version of the character 漢.

International Encoding Methods

So far you have learned about three basic encoding methods: JIS, Shift-JIS, and EUC. These encoding methods are shared by most of the Japanese national and corporate encoding methods since the character sets they support are nearly identical. In this section you will see radically different encoding methods, ones for encoding a much larger repertoire of characters. Table 4-26 lists the international character set standards along with the encoding methods that support them.

Table 4-26: International Character Set Standards and Their Encoding Methods

	JIS	Shift-JIS	EUC	Other
Unicode	*no*	*no*	*no*	*Unicode*[1]
ISO 10646	*no*	*no*	*no*	*10646.UCS-2 or 10646.UCS-4*[1]
XCCS	*no*	*no*	*no*	*XCCS*[2]

[1]These encoding methods are fixed-width: all characters are represented by the same number of bytes.
[2]This encoding method is modal: special character sequences (or a single character in some cases) are used to switch between one- and two-byte-per-character modes.

ISO 10646/Unicode Encoding

ISO 10646 defines two encoding methods. The first method is the 32-bit form, referred to as 10646.UCS-4 (Universal Character Set containing four bytes). The second is the 16-bit form, referred to as 10646.UCS-2 (Universal Character Set containing two bytes). Note that the second method is identical to the encoding used for Unicode. A 16-bit representation can encode up to 65,536 unique code points. A 32-bit representation, on the other hand, can encode up to 4,294,967,296 unique characters.

These encodings are not modal and do not alter the byte count for each character. All 16 or 32 bits are used for representing characters. Control code ranges, which are usually forbidden in other encodings, are valid for encoding characters. Table 4-27 shows the encoding space for both 10646.UCS-2 and 10646.UCS-4.

Table 4-27: Unicode and ISO 10646 Encoding Specifications

	Decimal	Hexadecimal	Octal
10646.UCS-2 and Unicode			
First byte range	0–255	00–FF	000–377
Second byte range	0–255	00–FF	000–377
10646.UCS-4			
First byte	0	00	000
Second byte	0	00	000
Third byte range	0–255	00–FF	000–377
Fourth byte range	0–255	00–FF	000–377

Since Unicode and ISO 10646 allocate the entire encoding space for characters, it makes no sense to include a diagram showing either the encoding space or how it compares to JIS encoding. You will see in the following section that this encoding space is divided into four zones, each one containing one of four different classes of characters.

The following is an example of some Japanese text encoded in 10646.UCS-2. The same representation holds true for Unicode encoding—10646.UCS-2 and Unicode encodings are identical.

Character String	か	な	漢	字
Encoded Values	304B	306A	6F22	5B57

Next, you see the same characters, but encoded in 10646.UCS-4. Note how every character has bytes with the value 0x0000 prepended.

Character String	か	な	漢	字
Encoded Values	0000304B	0000306A	00006F22	00005B57

UTF is another encoding method developed for Unicode and ISO 10646 text. UTF stands for UCS (Universal Character Set) Transformation Format, and is a method for encoding 16- or 32-bit representations so that the data can be passed more reliably as text streams or in e-mail messages. Plan 9, which is described in Chapter 8, is a distributed operating system that uses UTF to encode Unicode text.

ISO 10646/Unicode Encoding Versus JIS Encoding

There is no clean conversion algorithm between the Unicode kanji set and JIS X 0208-1990 (and JIS X 0212-1990, for that matter). What is required is a set of hard-coded mapping tables—luckily, there is a source of such tasks.

The Unicode Consortium developed a tab-delimited database file in text file format that contains cross listings between the Unicode kanji set and the major Asian character set standards such as JIS X 0208-1990 and JIS X 0212-1990. This file is approximately 1MB in size, and is available through anonymous FTP. It is called `cjkxref.fix`. If you do not have FTP access, this file can also be obtained directly from the Unicode Consortium. See Appendix K for FTP sites and contact information for the Unicode Consortium.

Unicode Zones

The Unicode Standard defines zones. These zones allocate particular classes of characters to particular regions of the encoding table. The zones within Unicode (that is, the Basic Multilingual Plane of ISO 10646) in two-byte format are listed in Table 4-28.

Table 4-28: Unicode Zones

	Decimal	Hexadecimal	Octal
A-zone (19,903 positions)			
First byte range	0–77	00–4D	000–115
Second byte range	0–255	00–FF	000–377
I-zone (20,992 positions)			
First byte range	78–159	4E–9F	116–237
Second byte range	0–255	00–FF	000–377

	Decimal	Hexadecimal	Octal
O-zone (16,384 positions)			
First byte range	160–223	A0–DF	240–337
Second byte range	0–255	00–FF	000–377
R-zone (8,190 positions)			
First byte range	224–255	E0–FF	340–377
Second byte range	0–255	00–FF	000–377

There is nothing magical about these zones: they simply show what type of characters can be allocated to different encoding blocks within the Unicode encoding space. "A" stands for *Alphabets* (alphabets are encoded in the A-zone), "I" stands for *Ideographs* (kanji are sometimes called ideographs), "O" stands for *Open*, and "R" stands for *Restricted*. Figure 4-16 illustrates these four Unicode zones.

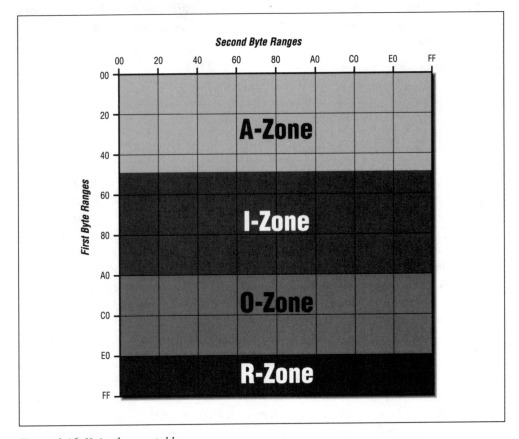

Figure 4-16: Unicode zone table

XCCS Encoding

The XCCS (Xerox Character Code Standard) encoding space is similar to Unicode and ISO 10646 as discussed above. Under this encoding method, every character can be represented by two bytes. The definition of the code space does include the entire 256-row-by-256-cell matrix: however, not all 65,536 code positions are valid for characters. Table 4-29 lists the specifications.

Table 4-29: XCCS Encoding Specifications

	Decimal	Hexadecimal	Octal
XCCS			
First byte range	0–255	00–FF	000–377
Second byte range	0–255	00–FF	000–377

Certain code ranges, such as those used for control characters, are invalidated by making them reserved or unused. We can modify the specifications to take this into account, as illustrated in Table 4-30.

Table 4-30: Modified XCCS Encoding Specifications

	Decimal	Hexadecimal	Octal
XCCS			
First byte ranges	0, 33–126, 161–254	00, 21–7E, A1–FE	000, 041–176, 241–376
Second byte ranges	33–126, 161–254	21–7E, A1–FE	041–176, 241–376

Now you have learned about the valid encoding ranges for characters in the XCCS character set, but how are text strings handled? The encoding used by XCCS makes use of what Xerox calls the *CSselect, CharSet8, CharSet16, Char8Code,* and *Char16Code* identifiers. This encoding method is *modal,* meaning that these special sequences of characters are used to shift between character sets and the number of bytes expected for each character. In the case of JIS encoding, which is also modal, the escape character was a vital part of an escape sequence. In the case of XCCS, the last character representable with eight bits, namely 0xFF (255), is used as the key for switching modes. This character is called CSselect.

XCCS supports variable length encoding, ranging from 8 to 16 bits per character. CSselect is similar to an escape character in that it signals that a change in mode is about to take place—either a different number of expected bytes or a different character set altogether. As discussed above, CSselect has the value 0xFF. Each CSselect character signifies an expected eight-bit length encoding. This means that two CSselect characters indicate an expected 16-bit encoding to follow.

The CharSet character comes in two flavors: *CharSet8* and *CharSet16*. These are similar to the final portion of an escape sequence as used in JIS encoding—it identifies the character set to be used. CharSet8 is used when eight-bit encoded characters follow, and CharSet16 is used when 16-bit encoded characters follow. The default CharSet is 0x00—in the case of CharSet8, this default is eight-bit ASCII, but for CharSet16, the default is 16-bit Japanese. The default encoding length is eight-bit—any string not beginning with CSselect is treated as CharSet8 equals 0x00, and for all practical purposes, is ASCII encoding. Selecting a CharSet8 value other than 0x00 usually indicates a row in the JIS X 0208-1983 character set.

The CharCode is used to represent characters, and again comes in two flavors: *Char8Code* and *Char16Code*. Char8Code is a single byte, and Char16Code is two bytes (two Char8Codes).

There are many ways to encode a text string in XCCS encoding. Let's now turn our attention to some XCCS encoded material. The example string is かな漢字, the same as that used in previous examples. The encoded values are in hexadecimal notation.

The first example is a simple ASCII string. Here you see how it is encoded according to the XCCS specifications.

Character String			a	b	c	d	e
CS8Declaration	FF	00					
Char8Code Values			61	62	63	64	65

Recall that the default CharSet8 value is 0x00, so the same string could be encoded as follows without a CS8Declaration:

Character String	a	b	c	d	e
Char8Code Values	61	62	63	64	65

Let's now move to some examples using the Japanese text string. Here is an example using eight-bit XCCS encoding. Note that only one 0xFF character is used in the CS8Declaration, which signifies eight-bit encoding.

Character String			か	な			漢			字
CS8Declaration	FF	24			FF	34		FF	3B	
Char8Code Values			2B	4A			41			7A

Note how the second byte in the CS8Declaration (the CharSet8 byte) is the same as the first byte when it is JIS encoded. The bytes which are used to represent these characters correspond to the second byte when it is JIS encoded.

Finally, here is an example of 16-bit XCCS encoding:

Character String				か	な	漢	字
CS16Declaration	FF	FF	00				
Char16Code Values				242B	244A	3441	3B7A

Since 0x00 is the default value for CharSet16, and indicates the Japanese character set, the above example could have been represented as follows without the CharSet16 character:

Character String			か	な	漢	字
CS16Declaration	FF	FF				
Char16Code Values			242B	244A	3441	3B7A

Note how two CSselect characters are used here to signal the 16-bit encoding.

XCCS encoding can be rather confusing, so let's summarize here what you have learned in this section:

- The number of CSselect characters (0xFF) indicates the encoding length (one indicates eight-bit and two indicates 16-bit).
- The default encoding length is eight-bit.
- The default CharSet8 value is 0x00 (ASCII).
- The default CharSet16 value is 0x00 (Japanese).
- The CharSet8 value for Japanese text indicates the row if it were JIS encoded. The Char8Code indicates the cell.

Conversion of Japanese Text

Conversion of Japanese text requires that you alter the numeric values of the bytes used to represent each character. There are a wide variety of Japanese code conversion programs available. Some are portable across platforms, and some are not. Software developers who intend to introduce products into the Japanese market must make their software as flexible as possible—meaning that software should be able to handle more than one Japanese encoding method. This is not to say that such software should be able to process all possible encodings internally, but that it should have the ability to read and write as many encodings as possible, which will result in better information interchange among various platforms.

Earlier in this chapter you may have noticed how JIS encoding can support the encoding of the 1978, 1983, and 1990 versions of JIS X 0208 by using different escape sequences. In Appendix J you will find material illustrating the differences between these versions of JIS X 0208. Should Japanese code conversion programs account for these differences? I don't recommend it. Shift-JIS and EUC encodings support JIS X 0208 without any method for designating its version. Any conversion from JIS to Shift-JIS or EUC encoding will remove the information that indicates which version of JIS X 0208 is used in the text. Likewise, converting from Shift-JIS or EUC to JIS encoding requires that an arbitrary version of JIS X 0208 be selected because a two-byte character escape sequence must be used for properly encoding the text.

I have written a FreeWare tool in ANSI C called `jconv.c`, which changes the Japanese code within a text file. This tool handles Shift-JIS, EUC, and JIS codes. I distribute this tool in the form of source code so that other programmers may benefit from the algorithms used to convert between the various Japanese codes, and so that it can be compiled on a variety of platforms. This tool has many useful features: error checking, the ability to automatically detect an input file's Japanese code, the ability to manually specify the input file's code, selective conversion of half-width katakana to their full-width equivalents, a help page, automatic JIS encoding repair, and command-line argument support. The source code for this tool is available through anonymous FTP. A more complete description of this tool, including its help page, can be found in Chapter 7.

I have also written a Macintosh port of this tool, called JConv, described above (made from the same source code!). It supports a very minimal Macintosh interface, but works well. This tool is also FreeWare, and comes with the source code. It, too, is available through anonymous FTP.

Other Japanese code conversion tools are available. They all perform roughly the same tasks, but in different ways. Some are more portable than others. Other such tools include nkf (Network Kanji Filter), KC, MacKC (based on KC), ASLKConvert, and pkf (Perl version of nkf). These Japanese code conversion tools are available on a number of anonymous FTP sites.

Repairing Damaged Japanese Text

Japanese text files can be damaged in different ways depending on which Japanese encoding was used in the file in question. JIS encoded text is usually damaged by unfriendly mailers (and news readers) that remove control characters including the all too important escape character. EUC and Shift-JIS encoded files make generous use of eight-bit characters, and many mailers (and news readers) are not what I would call *eight-bit clean*, meaning that they turn off the eighth bit of every byte. This has the effect of scrambling such encoded files, and renders the text unreadable. You will see that this type of damage is relatively easy to repair since the remaining characters that constitute a valid escape sequence can serve as the context for properly reinserting the escape characters.

Let's first discuss the repair procedure for JIS encoded files. One might receive Japanese e-mail messages or read articles in Japanese on Usenet News which have had their escape characters stripped out by unfriendly e-mail or news reading software. This is a very annoying problem since one usually must throw out such e-mail message or articles, or else suffer through the grueling task of manually inserting the escape characters. For example, look at the following strings. First is a Japanese text string as it should appear when displayed properly, and below it is how it may appear if it is corrupted.

| Original | これは和文の文章の例で、それはEnglishの文章の例です。 |
| Corrupted JIS | B3$1$OOBJ8$NJ8>O$NNc$G!"$=1O(JEnglish$B$NJ8>ONNcG$9!#(J |

I have written a tool to repair these damaged JIS encoded files by simply scanning for the printable character portions of the escape sequences left intact, keeping track of the state of the stream (that is, whether it is in one- or two-byte-per-character mode), and then using this as the context for inserting escape characters in the proper places. The tool that makes use of the routines for repairing damaged JIS encoded files is called `jconv.c`, which was described briefly in the previous section; its full description is in Chapter 7.

Unfortunately, there is no elegant way of repairing Shift-JIS and EUC files which have had their eighth bits stripped. Manual repair of EUC is not terribly difficult; you simply need to insert whole one- and two-byte escape sequences (not just the escape character) around chunks of Japanese text.* The only problem is detecting which bytes are used to compose two-byte characters—this is where human intervention is required. The following is the same Japanese string used in the above JIS sample, but this time you see how it would appear if the eighth bits were stripped from an EUC encoded version. Compare it with the corrupt JIS string above—the crucial context-forming strings, namely $B and (J, are missing.

| Original | これは和文の文章の例で、それはEnglishの文章の例です。 |
| Corrupted EUC | $3$1$OOBJ8$NJ8>ONNcG!"$=$1$OEnglish$NJ8>ONNcG$9!# |

Doing the same for Shift-JIS is possible. See the example strings below.

| Original | これは和文の文章の例で、それはEnglishの文章の例です。 |
| Corrupted Shift-JIS | 1 j M a 6 L 6 M L a E A ; j MEnglish L 6 M L a E 7 B |

Depending on the capabilities of your Japanese terminal emulation software, this corrupt Shift-JIS string could also appear as the following:

| Corrupted Shift-JIS | 1jMa6L6MLaEA;jMEnglishL6MLaE7B |

The above example is different from the first example of corrupted Shift-JIS encoding in that it does not contain spaces as place holders for the control characters.

---

*This transforms the file into JIS encoded text—remember that EUC is simply escape sequence-less JIS with the eighth bit of both bytes turned on.

The EUC and Shift-JIS repair solution should be interactive with the user. There is too much judgement involved, and a human is needed to guide the repair process. I hope to develop such a tool in the future.

Advice to Developers

The information presented in this chapter may have given you the impression that Japanese encoding is a real mess. However, you should have found that there are three basic Japanese encoding methods: JIS, Shift-JIS, and EUC. Each of these is more or less compatible with the others. In Chapter 7, I discuss Japanese code conversion algorithms that allow you to convert between them.

Now, which Japanese encoding method should you choose for your products? My recommendation to software developers is that they should favor EUC encoding internally in their systems, and JIS encoding for information interchange (for example, e-mail transmission). The decision to use EUC should come from a desire to anticipate future trends in Japanese software needs. You may recall that Shift-JIS encoding cannot support the JIS X 0212-1990 character set standard, but EUC and JIS encodings can. If this character set standard becomes more widely accepted (and desired!) in the marketplace, the software developers who have chosen EUC as the internally processed Japanese code for their products will have the easiest time adding support for the JIS X 0212-1990 character set. It is for this very same reason that I strongly believe that Shift-JIS will eventually be superseded by EUC for most systems in the future.

Newly designed operating systems and software seem to be steering toward EUC encoding anyway, so it would appear that there are some people out there who are, in fact, looking ahead, and anticipating the future needs of users.

Companies that are interested in a more global market for their products are seriously considering Unicode. In fact, there are several Unicode-based systems currently available or under development, such as Plan 9 and PenPoint. Any Japanese implementation must have the capability to convert between Unicode and the three Japanese encoding methods you learned about in this chapter. This conversion process requires the use of mapping tables. Such conversion tables are provided by the Unicode Consortium (see Appendix K for information on obtaining these mapping tables). I have discovered errors in these mapping tables, so they should always be checked and verified prior to implementation.

I mentioned earlier that Shift-JIS cannot be extended to handle the characters in JIS X 0212-1990. Systems that process Shift-JIS, such as Macintosh and Microsoft Windows-J, seem to be moving toward Unicode as a way to support these additional 6,000 or so characters.

5

Japanese Input

In earlier chapters you learned most of what you need to know about the Japanese writing system, character set standards, and encoding methods. Now it is time for you to learn something about how to input the several thousand characters in the Japanese character set standards.

Because of the vast number of characters defined in Japanese character set standards, there is no simple solution like direct keyboard input such as you would find in the West. Instead, you will find that Japanese input methods fall into two categories:

- A direct method that uses the actual encoded value of the target character

- An indirect (and usually more convenient) means of obtaining the encoded value of the target character or characters, usually by typing out the pronunciation on a keyboard

You will see that the indirect input methods are more commonly used, and rightly so, since they usually involve the pronunciation of a character, which is more intuitive. After all, speakers of Japanese learn characters by their pronunciation. There are characters, however, that are not commonly known by speakers of Japanese, and these are input by other means. All of the different input methods are covered in this chapter.

To facilitate the explanations to come, at least two examples will be provided per input method. In most cases, the two examples are the kanji 漢 and 字 (the two kanji for writing the word *kanji*). Other characters will be substituted when appropriate.

There is an easy explanation for why so many different input methods are required for handling Japanese text. First, it is nearly impossible to fit thousands of characters on a keyboard. Mind you, such keyboards do exist, but they are not designed for the casual operator, and do not contain all the character set standards covered in Chapter 3 (an example of this type of keyboard is described below). This forced the Japanese to develop more efficient means of Japanese input. Second, Japanese text, as you learned in Chapter 4, is encoded in a variety of ways. This makes using the encoded value of a character in each encoding method a viable method for input.

Japanese Input Software

This chapter is intended to describe Japanese input in a platform- and software-independent way. What you learn here can then be applied to a wider variety of Japanese input programs, possibly even ones that have yet to be developed.

Unlike English, which permits direct keyboard entry for the majority of characters, there are two ways to input Japanese characters: direct and indirect. Input by encoded value is a direct means of input, and unambiguously allows you to access Japanese characters. However, this is quite unintuitive. How would you like to memorize the value 0x3775 for the kanji 剣? Now imagine doing this for thousands of kanji. While input by pronunciation may yield more than one candidate character from which you must choose, it is (in a seeming paradox) the most productive and most widely used method. Figure 5-1 illustrates the four possible stages of Japanese input: it shows how the flow of input information travels, and how different input methods and keyboards interface at each stage.

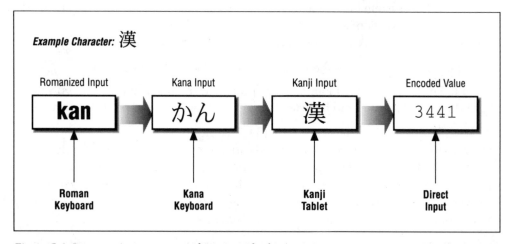

Figure 5-1: Japanese input stages and input method interaction

Japanese input software is usually referred to as an *FEP*, which stands for *front-end processor*. The FEP is so named because it grabs the keyboard input, processes the input, then sends it to the application or other software. Typically, the FEP runs as a separate process in its own input window, largely independent of the underlying application.

MS-DOS-based systems, at least the Japanese versions thereof, have several such Japanese input systems from which you can choose. These include VJE-γ, ATOK, Katana (刀),

and EGBridge. Some industrious people have even adapted UNIX-based Japanese input software so that they can run under non-Japanese MS-DOS systems. One such example is the adaption of a program called SKK for use with MOKE, a Japanese text editor described in Chapter 8. Macintosh-based systems (that is, those running KanjiTalk, the Japanese operating system) offer several Japanese input software systems such as MacVJE, MacVJE-γ, EGBridge, Katana, TurboJIP, Wnn, and ことえり (*kotoeri*). SweetJam is an example of a Macintosh FEP that does not require the KanjiTalk operating system. UNIX offers FEP software such as SKK, Wnn, Canna, and kinput2. UNIX versions are available from a variety of anonymous FTP sites. Most of these Japanese input programs are described in more detail in Chapter 8.

Most Japanese input software systems run as separate processes from programs such as text editors or word processors. This allows you to use a single Japanese input program with many text editors and word processors. It can also allow the use of more than one Japanese input program (not simultaneously, though, but by switching between them with a special key stroke, menu item, or control panel).

Many of these Japanese input systems allow you to emulate others. For example, MacVJE for Macintosh allows you to emulate EGBridge, ATOK, Wnn, and TurboJIP keyboard commands. Some others offer the same flexibility. This may prove to be useful, especially when using multiple platforms where the Japanese input software you prefer to use is not available on the current platform. However, the emulation may not be complete. For example, EGBridge for Macintosh can emulate MacVJE, but its emulation does not have the same set of functions. Expect to find slight differences—after all, EGBridge is only *emulating* the other input software.

All Japanese input software shares many similar qualities. Although there are other tasks, of course, the input software must provide a method to perform the following basic operations:

- Switch between Japanese and English writing modes
- Convert the input string into a mixture of kana, kanji, and Roman characters
- Select from a list of candidate characters
- Accept the selected or converted string

The ability to switch between writing modes is necessary because Japanese text can be composed of both Japanese and English text. Most input programs do not input kanji characters directly, so a key stroke is used to tell the input software to convert the input text and, because many kanji and kanji compounds share the same pronunciation, it is necessary to list all the kanji or kanji compounds with the same pronunciation. The user then selects the kanji or kanji compound that they intended to input. Finally, the converted input string is sent to the application (this is called *accepting* the input string).

Table 5-1 lists several popular Japanese input programs and the keystrokes used to perform the above input tasks. The "Xfer" and "Nfer" keystrokes in Table 5-1 refer to special keys sometimes found on keyboards.

Table 5-1: Keystrokes for Common Japanese Input Tasks

Operations	VJE-γ	Wnn	Canna	SKK
Japanese ⇒ English	Cmd-space	F3	Xfer or C-o	l
English ⇒ Japanese	Cmd-space	F3	Xfer or C-o	C-j
Conversion	space or C-c	C-w or C-z	Xfer or space	uppercase
Candidate Selection	arrows	up/down arrows	arrows	space
Accepting	return or F10	C-l	Nfer or return	C-j

As you can see, the basic input tasks are common among these various Japanese input programs, but the keystrokes used to invoke them are different. These and other Japanese input programs are described in Chapter 8.

Our discussion will proceed from the most widely used input method to the least widely used. Since most symbols and kana can be input directly, these discussions focus primarily on the input of kanji, and the problems inherent in that process. Kanji are problematic because they number in the thousands, and thus require an indirect method of input.

Kana Versus Romanized Input

Before we actually dive into Japanese input, it is important to mention that there are two ways to provide input to Japanese input software: romanized and kana. Ultimately, most Japanese input software requires kana input, which means that there must be a mechanism in place for converting, on-the-fly, romanized Japanese strings into kana. Almost all (if not all) such software has such a mechanism which permits Western keyboard arrays, such as QWERTY, to be used to input Japanese text.

Table 5-2 lists the basic set of kana characters (hiragana, in this case) along with the keystroke or keystrokes necessary to produce them. Some Japanese input software supports optional keystrokes, and they are listed in parentheses.

Table 5-2: Keystrokes to Produce Kana Characters

あ	a	い	i	う	u	え	e	お	o
か	k a	き	k i	く	k u	け	k e	こ	k o
が	g a	ぎ	g i	ぐ	g u	げ	g e	ご	g o
さ	s a	し	s i (s h i)	す	s u	せ	s e	そ	s o
ざ	z a	じ	z i (j i)	ず	z u	ぜ	z e	ぞ	z o
た	t a	ち	t i (c h i)	つ	t u (t s u)	て	t e	と	t o
だ	d a	ぢ	d i	づ	d u	で	d e	ど	d o
な	n a	に	n i	ぬ	n u	ね	n e	の	n o

は	h a	ひ	h i	ふ	h u (f u)	へ	h e	ほ	h o
ば	b a	び	b i	ぶ	b u	べ	b e	ぼ	b o
ぱ	p a	ぴ	p i	ぷ	p u	ぺ	p e	ぽ	p o
ま	m a	み	m i	む	m u	め	m e	も	m o
や	y a			ゆ	y u			よ	y o
ら	r a	り	r i	る	r u	れ	r e	ろ	r o
わ	w a	ゐ	w i			ゑ	w e	を	w o
ん	n (n n)								

There are also combinations of two kana characters that require special romanization. These consist of one of the above kana plus the small versions of や (*ya*), ゆ (*yu*), and よ (*yo*). These are listed in Table 5-3. Like Table 5-2, optional keystrokes are listed in parentheses.

Table 5-3: Keystrokes to Produce Special Kana Characters

きゃ	k y a	きゅ	k y u	きょ	k y o
ぎゃ	g y a	ぎゅ	g y u	ぎょ	g y o
しゃ	s y a (s h a)	しゅ	s y u (s h u)	しょ	s y o (s h o)
じゃ	z y a (j a)	じゅ	z y u (j u)	じょ	z y o (j o)
ちゃ	t y a (c h a)	ちゅ	t y u (c h u)	ちょ	t y o (c h o)
ぢゃ	d y a	ぢゅ	d y u	ぢょ	d y o
にゃ	n y a	にゅ	n y u	にょ	n y o
ひゃ	h y a	ひゅ	h y u	ひょ	h y o
びゃ	b y a	びゅ	b y u	びょ	b y o
ぴゃ	p y a	ぴゅ	p y u	ぴょ	p y o
みゃ	m y a	みゅ	m y u	みょ	m y o
りゃ	r y a	りゅ	r y u	りょ	r y o

These three small kana characters, や, ゆ, and よ, can sometimes also be generated by either typing an "x" before their pronunciation (for example, や can be input with the three-character string "xya") or by pressing the shift key while typing their pronunciation. Check the documentation of your Japanese input software to find out which method is supported. Also check the documentation for romanization tables similar to those above, that specify other special combinations that can be used.

Writing a roman-to-kana conversion routine is not that difficult. Sometimes the authors of such programs encourage others to use their routines, and most Japanese input software that is freely available comes with source code. A perl version of a roman-to-kana conversion library called `romkan.pl` is available through anonymous FTP (`romkan.pl` requires the perl library file called `jcode.pl` to function). See Appendix K for more information.

Input by Pronunciation

The most frequently used Japanese input method is by pronunciation. There are three basic units by which Japanese input can be converted into kanji:

- Single kanji

- Kanji compound (a string of two or more kanji)

- Kanji phrase (a string of one or more kanji followed by a postposition)

You may have heard of Japanese input programs that claim to be able to convert whole sentences at once. In fact, what they are actually describing is the ability to *input* whole Japanese sentences, but these sentences are parsed into smaller units, usually kanji phrases, and then converted. This often introduces parsing errors, and it is up to the user to adjust each phrase. More about this at the end of this section.

For example, if you want to input the phrase 漢字は (meaning "the kanji"), you have three choices: you can input each character, you can input a phrase as a compound, or you can input a phrase as a string of characters. Table 5-4 shows how you can input each character one at a time, and how this results in candidates, from which you may choose, for each character.

Table 5-4: Input by Pronunciation (Single Kanji)

Target Character	Roman Input String	Kana Input String	Candidates
漢	k a n (n)[1]	か ん	乾 侃 冠 寒 刊 勘 勧 巻 喚 堪 姦 完 官 寛 干 幹 患 感 慣 憾 換 敢 柑 桓 棺 款 歓 汗 漢 潤 潅 環 甘 監 看 竿 管 簡 緩 缶 翰 肝 艦 莞 観 諫 貫 還 鑑 間 閑 関 陥 韓 館 舘
字	j i	し ゛	事 似 侍 児 字 寺 慈 持 時 次 滋 治 爾 璽 痔 磁 示 而 耳 自 蒔 辞
は	h a	は	…[2]

[1] Whether you need to type one or two ns depends on your Japanese input software.
[2] The character は resolves itself—no conversion is necessary.

Table 5-5 illustrates how you can input this phrase as a kanji compound plus the following hiragana, and how a shorter list of candidates results.

Table 5-5: Input by Pronunciation (Kanji Compound)

Target Character(s)	Roman Input String	Kana Input String	Candidates
漢字	k a n j i	か ん し ゛	漢字 感じ 幹事 監事 完司
は	h a	は	...[1]

[1]The character は resolves itself—no conversion is necessary.

Note how the candidate list became shorter, thus making selection among them much easier. Table 5-6 shows the effect of inputting the entire phrase as one long string of characters. The ability to perform this type of conversion depends on the quality of your Japanese input software.

Table 5-6: Input by Pronunciation (Phrase)

Target String	Roman Input String	Kana Input String	Candidates
漢字は	k a n j i h a	か ん し ゛ は	漢字は 感じは 幹事は 監事は 完司は

A kana-to-kanji conversion dictionary (仮名漢字変換辞書) makes all this possible. Most Japanese input systems are based on a conversion dictionary that takes kana strings as input, and then converts them into strings containing a mixture of kanji and kana. The conversion dictionary uses a key (the pronunciation) to look up possible replacement strings (candidates). Quite often a single search key has multiple replacement strings assigned to it. Conversion dictionaries typically contain tens of thousands of entries.

Several kanji even have multiple pronunciations assigned to them. How many really depends on the conversion dictionary used by your Japanese input software. For example, the kanji 日 can have up to nine unique pronunciations, depending on the context (and the conversion dictionary!). They are び (*bi*), ひ (*hi*), に (*ni*), ぴ (*pi*), か (*ka*), じつ (*jitsu*), にち (*nichi*), につ (*nitsu*), and たち (*tachi*). While this is an extreme example, this phenomenon is not unique.

As you saw above, the most widely used and most efficient method for inputting kanji by pronunciation is to handle them as kanji compounds or kanji phrases, not as single characters. If you desire a single kanji, it is often more efficient to input it as a compound or phrase, then delete the unwanted character or characters.

Up to this point we have dealt primarily with kanji. What about the other characters? Well, as you have seen, kana can be input more or less directly. Symbols and other miscellaneous characters may also be input using a pronunciation. Table 5-7 provides examples of symbols along with their candidates.

Table 5-7: Input by Pronunciation for Non-kanji Characters

Target Character	Roman Input String	Kana Input String	Candidates
〒[1] 】	yuubin(n) kakko	ゆ う ひ ゛ ん か っ こ	郵便 〒 括弧 （ 〔 〔 ｛ 〈 《 「 『 【 ） 〕 〕 ｝ 〉 》 」 』 】

[1]The character 〒 is not a kanji, but a postal code symbol.

Note how kanji compounds are also listed as candidates.

Almost all Japanese input programs use their own unique conversion dictionary or dictionaries. This means that no two input programs behave the same. Luckily, such software allows the user to create a user dictionary in which new search keys can be created, and candidate replacement strings assigned. Whether or not there is a logical ordering in a conversion dictionary depends on the dictionary itself. Entries are typically ordered by pronunciation (remember that the *key* for lookup is usually kana, which implies ordering by pronunciation). The *values* associated with the keys are typically ordered by their relative frequency of use—more obscure kanji or kanji compounds appear further down the list of candidates. It is quite common to find Japanese input programs that include a *learning function* (学習機能). This learning function allows the subtle rearrangement of values associated with keys. The default value for a particular key can change depending on how often the user selects a given candidate. For example, if the default key for the input string けん (pronounced *ken*) is 犬 (meaning "dog"), and if I constantly select the candidate 剣 (the kanji I use for my given name), 剣 eventually becomes the default value associated with the key けん. Exactly when the default changes depends on the software—sometimes only one occurrence is necessary.

More advanced Japanese input systems implement parsers that use grammatical information for making decisions. This allows users to input whole Japanese sentences by pronunciation, then let the software slice the input into units that are manageable for conversion. Like I mentioned earlier, errors in parsing can be quite common.

Input by Radical

Most software that you will encounter allows only JIS Level 2 kanji to be input by radical. This is because JIS Level 2 kanji are arranged by radical, and it is trivial to cut up this collection of characters into sets of kanji indexed by the same radical. Some input methods allow users to input *all* encoded kanji by radical, even those in JIS Level 1 kanji.*

Table 5-8 shows examples of input by radical, using two kanji from JIS Level 2 kanji.

Table 5-8: Input by Radical

Target Kanji	Radical	Candidates
漢	氵	水 氷 永 氾 汀 汁 求 汎 汐 汕 汗 汚 汝 汞 江 池 汢 汨 汪 汰 汲 汳 決 汽 汾 沁 沂 沃 沈 沌 沐 漢 滝 滞 滬 滲 滷 滸 etc.
字	子	子 孔 孕 字 存 孚 孛 孜 孝 孟 季 孥 学 孩 孤 孫 孰 孱 孳 孵 孺

More sophisticated software displays a graphic listing of the 214 radicals. These 214 radicals actually came from a Chinese dictionary called 康熙字典, which is dated 1716. However, other methods exist. Each of the 214 radicals has a name or number assigned to it. Some of these radicals even have variants, most of which have unique names. The number represents the relative order within the set of radicals. For example, the last radical is assigned the number 214. You may encounter Japanese input software that requires that radicals be input by either their name or number. Table 5-9 gives some examples of radicals along with their names and numbers.

Table 5-9: Radicals With Their Names and Numbers

Radical	Radical Name	Meaning	Radical Number
一	いち (ichi)	*one*	1
丨	ぼう (bô)	*bar*	2
女	おんな (onna)	*woman*	38
子	こ (ko)	*child*	39
疒	やまいだれ (yamaidare)	*illness enclosure*	104
石	いし (ishi)	*stone*	112
貝	かい (kai)	*shell*	154
鳥	とり (tori)	*bird*	196
鼻	はな (hana)	*nose*	209

Appendix D provides a complete listing of the 214 radicals, with their names.

---

*Two examples of software that allows this are ことえり (*kotoeri*), which is included with Apple's KanjiTalk 7.1, and MOKE 2.1.

Input by Stroke Count

In most cases, a given kanji has a unique number of strokes. This allows for an input method where the number of strokes is entered by the user, and all the candidate kanji for that stroke count are displayed for selection. However, there are a select few whose actual number of strokes is arguable (this difference is typically a single stroke). Good software accounts for these differences, and allows the user to input the kanji under multiple stroke counts. Also note that stroke count occasionally depends on the glyph shape. For example, an input system based on the JIS C 6226-1978 character set behaves strangely if the JIS X 0208-1990 character set is swapped.

Table 5-10 shows a candidate list for two different stroke counts.

Table 5-10: Input by Stroke Count

Target Kanji	Stroke Count	Candidates
漢	13	愛 葦 飴 暗 意 違 溢 碓 園 煙 猿 遠 鉛 塩 嫁 暇 禍 嘩 蛾 雅 解 塊 慨 碍 蓋 該 較 隔 楽 滑 褐 蒲 勧 寛 幹 感 漢 頑 棄 義 詰 *etc.*
字	6	旭 扱 安 伊 夷 衣 亥 芋 印 因 吋 宇 羽 迂 臼 曳 汚 仮 会 回 灰 各 汗 缶 企 伎 危 机 気 吉 吃 休 吸 朽 汲 兇 共 匡 叫 仰 曲 刑 圭 血 件 伍 交 光 向 后 好 江 考 行 合 此 艮 再 在 旨 死 糸 至 字 寺 次 而 耳 自 *etc.*

Input by Multiple Criteria

Some tools were specifically designed to input kanji or other characters with more than one of the above input methods. This is very useful because a user can significantly narrow a search by giving more than one indirect input criterion.

Just like a typical bibliographic search, the more search parameters you provide to the software, the shorter the candidate list becomes. However, don't expect to find very many programs, other than dedicated Japanese character dictionary software, that accept multiple search criteria.

As you will learn in the next section, inputting Japanese (or non-Japanese) characters by their encoded value or dictionary number is a direct method, and always results in a single character match.

Input by Encoded Value

This Japanese input method is based on fixed values for each character, namely their encoded value. This is a direct means for input, and is usually used as a last resort for input. This means that one can unambiguously (that is, with no candidates) input a single character. Note that it is most common to use hexadecimal values when inputting characters, with the exception of KUTEN, which uses four decimal digits.

This input method makes use of the encoded values of the target characters. As most systems process only a single code internally, yet accept different encoded values, some sort of conversion between codes is still being performed. For example, many systems can accept both hexadecimal JIS and Shift-JIS codes since they can be easily distinguished from one another—they occupy separate encoding blocks.

Most Japanese input software includes character tables indexed by one or more of these encoding methods. Some programs even have these character indexing tables built in so that you need not consult the printed documentation.

Many front-end processors allow the user to select which encoding to use for inputting kanji, and those which are really good automatically detect which code the user has selected. This is simple for JIS and Shift-JIS as they occupy different code spaces, but KUTEN and EUC pose special problems. Some implementations require that a period or other delimiter separate the KU from the TEN of a KUTEN code. Input by EUC code is very rare.

Table 5-11 lists two kanji with their values in a variety of encodings, listed from left to right in decreasing frequency of usage.

Table 5-11: Input by Encoded Value

	KUTEN	Hex JIS	Hex Shift-JIS	Hex EUC	Hex Unicode	Dictionary Number[1]
漢	2033	3441	8ABF	B4C1	6F22	05193
字	2790	3B7A	8E9A	BBFA	5B57	02108

[1]These numbers refer to those found in the dictionary called 最新JIS漢字辞典, which is discussed later in this chapter.

Most Japanese input systems provide at least two of these input methods, usually KUTEN and hexadecimal JIS. Sometimes the encoding method supported by the software you are running is another option. For example, systems that process Shift-JIS internally, such as KanjiTalk, provide code input by KUTEN, hexadecimal JIS, and hexadecimal Shift-JIS codes.

Input by Postal Code

Japanese postal codes (郵便番号) consist of three digits. Some conversion dictionaries include keys that correspond to these postal codes, and the values associated with those keys are strings that represent the place or places for which the postal codes are used. Table 5-12 includes some examples of postal code input.

Table 5-12: Input by Postal Code

Postal Code	Candidate Locations
001	北海道札幌市北区
500	岐阜県岐阜市
999	山形県酒田市, 山形県最上郡, 山形県上山市, 山形県飽海郡, 山形県北村山郡, 山形県尾花沢市, 山形県長井市, 山形県西置賜郡, *etc.*

Japanese place names, especially for the non-native speaker of Japanese, are difficult to learn. Japanese addresses usually contain postal codes, and for those who use Japanese input software that supports this type of input, much digging in dictionaries to find out how to pronounce and thus enter each kanji can be avoided.

Input by Association

Input by association (連想入力) is an older Japanese input method, and is often referred to as the two stroke input method (2ストローク入力方式). It is unlike input by pronunciation in that there is only one kanji associated with each pair of key strokes—no candidate selection is required.

Input by association works by associating two characters, usually kana, to a single kanji. These two kana are usually associated with the kanji by pronunciation or meaning. For example, the two katakana ハハ (pronounced *haha*) are associated with the kanji 母, whose pronunciation happens to be *haha*.

Needless to say, this input method has a long learning curve, but skilled word processor operators can use this input method quite effectively.

There are many in Japan who feel that input by *unassociation* (無連想入力) is better. This means that the relationship between the kanji and its two key strokes is arbitrary. In fact, such an input method has been developed, and has quite a following. It is called Tcode, and is available for a variety of systems, such as UNIX, MS-DOS, and Macintosh. There is even a Tcode mailing list. See Appendixes K and L for more information on obtaining Tcode or joining the Tcode Mailing List. See Chapter 8 for more information on Tcode itself.

In-line Conversion

Japanese input programs typically provide their own input window since they run as a separate process from the application in which the Japanese text will be inserted. Japanese input takes place in the dedicated window, is then sent to the current application, and finally is pasted into the current cursor position. As you can expect, this is far from ideal since you must look at both the current cursor position *and* the FEP input window. The solution to this problem is called *in-line conversion* (インライン変換). There are standard protocols developed by FEP manufacturers which can be used in applications such that Japanese input and conversion can take place at the cursor position, not in a dedicated window in an inconvenient location on the screen.

Many Japanese word processors come bundled with an FEP, and this usually means in-line conversion support, at least for the bundled FEP. Read the product literature to find out whether there is in-line conversion support for a particular FEP. Nisus and Solo Writer, for example, provide in-line conversion support for three FEPs: ことえり (*kotoeri*), MacVJE, and EGBridge.

Japanese Input Hardware

Our discussion continues with a description of several keyboard arrays in use in Japan, with figures so that comparisons can be drawn between them. Keyboard arrays covered here are divided into four categories:

- Two non-Japanese keyboard arrays (QWERTY and Dvorak)
- One kanji keyboard array (kanji tablet)
- Four kana keyboard arrays (JIS, New-JIS, Thumb-shift, and 50 Sounds)
- Two romanized keyboard arrays (M-style and High-speed Roman)

The market for dedicated Japanese word processors experiences enormous flux in keyboard designs and usage. It seems that for every new computer model a hardware manufacturer introduces to the market, the same manufacturer may introduce two or three dedicated Japanese word processor models. These word processors are much like computers, but the basic software for word processing is usually fixed (that is, not upgradable).

Actual computer systems are designed for more general usage, so there is less variety in keyboard arrays. In fact, some dedicated Japanese word processor keyboards may have more than one keyboard array imprinted on its keys. This is done by imprinting more than one character on a key. I once owned and used two dedicated Japanese word processors: the NEC 文豪ミニ5G and the NEC 文豪ミニ7H.* On the tops of their keys

---

*The kanji compound 文豪 is pronounced *bungô*, and means "literary master."

were imprints for the QWERTY array and the JIS array; on the sides of the keys were imprints for the 50 Sounds array.

The intent of this chapter is not to teach you how to use these keyboard arrays effectively, but rather to tell you a little bit about them and their characteristics.

Western Keyboard Arrays

Western keyboard arrays are used quite commonly for Japanese input because the typical Japanese input methods allow for the user to input text phonemically with the use of Roman characters (the Japanese input software subsequently converts this romanized input into kana characters, typically hiragana characters). In fact, one study claimed that over 70 percent of Japanese computer users input Japanese with Roman characters. This is not to say that keyboard arrays designed specifically for Japanese do not exist, but as you will see in the following sections, there are many to choose from.

QWERTY Array

The most widely used keyboard in the world is known as the *QWERTY* keyboard array, so named because its first six alphabetic keys are for the characters *q, w, e, r, t,* and *y*. It was originally developed so that frequently used keys were spaced far from each other. In the days of mechanical typewriters, having such keys in close proximity to each other would often result in a jam. However, most keyboards today are not mechanical, but electrical, so the original need for spacing out highly used keys is no longer valid.

The QWERTY keyboard array is so well entrenched that it is doubtful that it will ever be replaced. Figure 5-2 illustrates the basic QWERTY keyboard array.

Figure 5-2: The QWERTY keyboard array

Dvorak Array

There have been attempts at replacing the QWERTY keyboard array by providing an improved layout of keys, but none of them has succeeded to date. One such attempt was called the *Dvorak* keyboard array, developed in the 1930s by August Dvorak and William Dealey. Keys on the Dvorak keyboard array are positioned such that approximately 70 percent of all English words can be typed with the fingers in the home position. Compare this with only 32 percent in the case of the QWERTY keyboard array. See Figure 5-3 for an illustration of the Dvorak keyboard array.

To date, the Dvorak keyboard array has not succeeded in replacing the QWERTY array. This just goes to show that efficiency does not always make an item more appealing.

Figure 5-3: The Dvorak keyboard array

Kanji Keyboard Arrays

The first Japanese keyboards that were able to accommodate the Japanese writing system were called *kanji tablets*. These were huge keyboards that contained thousands of individual keys.

The document called JIS X 6003-1989, *Keyboard Layout for Japanese Text Processing*, defines a keyboard array that contains a total of 2,160 individual keys. The kanji tablet shown in Figure 5-4 is 60 keys wide by 36 keys deep (it is also available in another orientation with fewer keys). The 780 most frequently used kanji are in Level 1, 1,080 additional kanji are in Level 2, and 300 non-kanji are in the remaining keys.

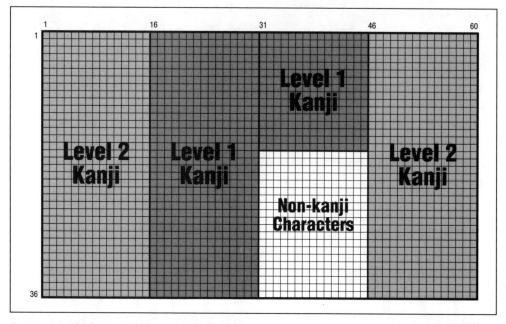

Figure 5-4: The kanji tablet array

Some Japanese corporations have even defined their own kanji tablet layouts, but this type of Japanese input device is quickly becoming obsolete. Japanese input software has developed to the point that much smaller keyboard arrays, such as those already discussed, are more efficient and easier to learn.

Kana Keyboard Arrays

The keyboard arrays discussed in this section have kana imprinted on their keys. One word of caution, though: just because such keyboard arrays are considered standard doesn't mean that they have been widely accepted in the Japanese marketplace. Like the QWERTY array in the West, the Japanese have a similar keyboard array called the JIS array—one that is not very efficient, yet is the most commonly used and learned.

JIS Array

The document called JIS X 6002-1985 (formerly JIS C 6233-1980), *Keyboard Layout for Information Processing Using the JIS 7 Bit Coded Character Set*, specifies what is known as the JIS keyboard array (JIS配列). This keyboard array is the most widely used in Japan (besides the QWERTY array, that is), and can be found with almost every computer system sold there. This standard also defines that the QWERTY array be superimposed on the keys of the keyboard (incidentally, this is how one accesses numerals).

The JIS array is not terribly efficient for Japanese input. Keys are arranged such that all four banks are required for Japanese input. This means that users must move their fingers a lot during typing, and to shift mode in order to access numerals, which are imprinted on the fourth bank of keys along with kana. In addition, the keys are not logically arranged, so it is difficult to memorize the positions. Figure 5-5 provides an illustration of the JIS array.

Note that the nigori (ﾞ) and maru (ﾟ) marks have their own keys. This means that characters such as が (hiragana *ga*) must be input as the two keystrokes か (hiragana *ka*) and ﾞ (nigori mark). The same character が can be input as the two keystrokes *g* and *a* in the case of the QWERTY and other Roman keyboard arrays.

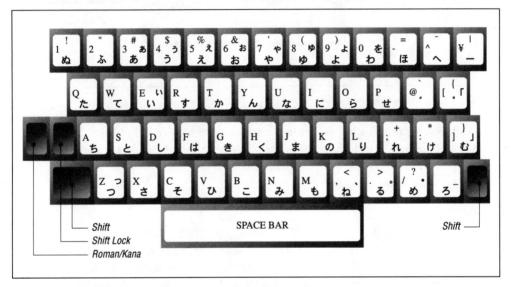

Figure 5-5: The JIS keyboard array

New-JIS Array

The document called JIS X 6004-1986, *Basic Keyboard Layout for Japanese Text Processing Using Kana-Kanji Translation Method*, specifies what is known as the New-JIS keyboard array (新JIS配列). This keyboard array, too, specifies that the QWERTY array be superimposed on the keyboard keys.

The kana on the keyboard are arranged on the first three banks of keys, and each key holds up to two kana (a shift key is required to access all the kana). This allows the input of numerals without the use of a mode change. Figure 5-6 illustrates the New-JIS keyboard array.

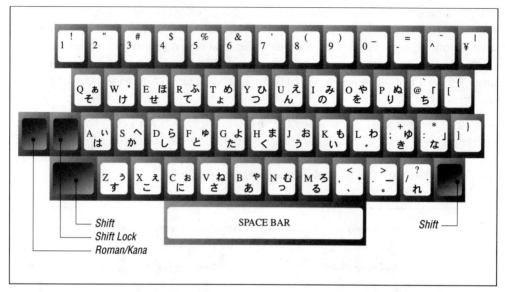

Figure 5-6: The New-JIS keyboard array

Although this keyboard array seems to be an improvement over the JIS array, it has not been widely accepted in industry. To put it mildly, it failed to replace the standard JIS array (covered above). You will see that its design is similar in some ways to Fujitsu's Thumb-shift array, described next.

Thumb-shift Array

In an attempt to improve the input of Japanese text on computers, Fujitsu developed a keyboard known as the Thumb-shift array (親指シフト配列). It is very similar in design and concept to the New-JIS array, but has a slightly different keyboard arrangement, and places two special modifier keys in the vicinity of the user's thumbs (these act to *shift* the keyboard to access more characters).

Like the New-JIS array, the Thumb-shift array assigns two kana characters per key for the first three banks of keys (the fourth bank of keys is reserved for numerals and symbols), but diverges in how the nigori (゛) and maru (゜) marks are applied to kana characters. This is where the thumb-shift keys play a vital role.

The two thumb-shift keys each serve different functions. The left thumb-shift key converts the default character into the version that includes the nigori mark. The right thumb-shift key simply shifts the keyboard so that the second character on the key is input. Table 5-13 illustrates some keys, and shows how to derive all possible characters from them (secondary characters for each are in parentheses).

Table 5-13: The Effect of the Thumb-shift Keys

Key	No Thumb-shift	Left Thumb-shift	Right Thumb-shift
は （み）	は	ば	み
と （お）	と	ど	お
せ （も）	せ	ぜ	も
け （ゆ）	け	げ	ゆ

The trickery used by this keyboard array is that all the characters that can be modified by the nigori mark are placed in the *no thumb-shift* location of each key (that is, the default character). There is a special key used for modifying a character with a maru mark. Figure 5-7 illustrates the Thumb-shift keyboard array in all its glory.

The Thumb-shift keyboard array is probably one of the most widely used in Japan (behind the QWERTY and JIS arrays, that is). In fact, other manufacturers have licensed it for use with their own computer systems.

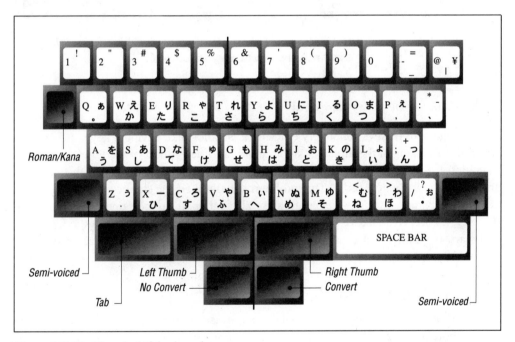

Figure 5-7: The Thumb-shift keyboard array

50 Sounds Array

As you may recall from discussions in Chapter 2, the term *50 Sounds* (50音) refers to the size of the matrix that holds the basic kana character set. The 50 Sounds array (50音配列) is based on this matrix. On one side of the matrix are five vowels: *a*, *i*, *u*, *e*, and *o*. On the other side of the matrix are nine consonants: *k, s, t, n, h, m, y, r,* and *w.* On the same side as the consonants is also a place that represents no consonant, where the vowels can stand alone. This arrangement of kana characters was then used as the basis for a Japanese keyboard array. This array is illustrated in Figure 5-8.

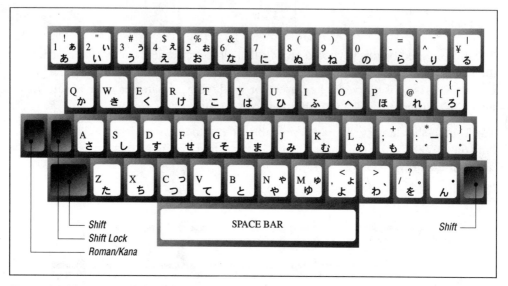

Figure 5-8: The 50 Sounds keyboard array

This arrangement of keys is not very efficient: it is almost like having a keyboard array in which the 26 letters of the alphabet are arranged in order—most of the time is spent just searching for keys. In fact, there *are* Western keyboard arrays on which the keys are arranged in alphabetical order! This problem is multiplied for Japanese, which requires nearly 50 separate keys! This keyboard array also suffers from the same problems of the JIS array, namely that all four banks of keys are required for kana, and that the nigori (˙) and maru (˚) marks require separate keys. Needless to say, this keyboard array is not very widely used in Japan.

Roman Character Keyboard Arrays

Keyboard arrays appearing in this section make use of Roman characters rather than kana—there are a smaller number of Roman characters than kana, and these keyboard designs take advantage of that fact. These are unlike the QWERTY and Dvorak keyboard arrays described above in that they are optimized for Japanese input. Both keyboard arrays presented in this section are of very recent design, and share similar qualities (they were both developed by NEC, and are used on NEC machines).

M-style Array

Developed by NEC in the early 1980s, the M-style array (M式配列) defines not only a keyboard, but also a new Japanese input method. The "M" in the name of this keyboard array comes from the last name of its designer, Masasuke Morita (森田正典), a senior engineer at NEC. He has even written two books about this keyboard array and input method. I had a chance to try out the M-style keyboard array connected to two different machines in 1988 while in Japan. I was impressed with the feel of the keyboard, and the efficiency of input. This keyboard array is also used for the TRON (The Real-time Operating system Nucleus) Project.

This keyboard array makes use of only 19 keys for inputting Japanese text. Five are vowels, namely *a*, *i*, *u*, *e*, and *o*. The remaining 14 are consonants, namely *k*, *s*, *t*, *n*, *h*, *g*, *z*, *d*, *b*, *m*, *y*, *r*, *w*, and *p*. There are, of course, additional keys for the remaining seven characters necessary for inputting English text (*q*, *l*, *j*, *f*, *c*, *x*, and *v*). Memorizing the locations for 19 keys is easier than 26 for English, and considerably easier than the nearly 50 required for kana keyboard arrays.

See Figure 5-9 for an example of the M-style keyboard array.

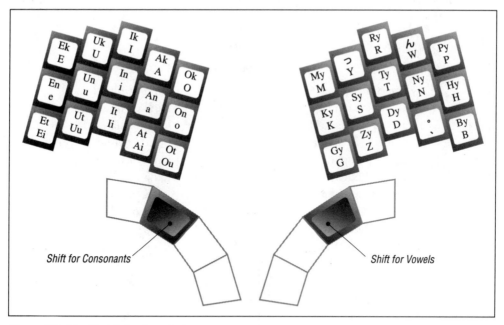

Figure 5-9: The M-style keyboard array

At first glance you should notice that the keyboard has a unique design—this is to make it more comfortable to use (less strain on the hands). Next, you should have noticed that the vowels are on the left set of keys, and the consonants are on the right set of keys.

Japanese is a syllable-based language,* so this vowel and consonant key arrangement provides a right-to-left typing rhythm.

The most important feature of this keyboard array and input system is that the user decides which parts of the input string are to be converted to kanji, which to hiragana, and which to katakana. There are three banks of vowel keys, and each bank can also shift to provide even more variations. These different banks specify the target character type for the input segments. With conventional input software the user simply inputs a string of characters, then lets the software decide which parts convert to kanji, and which parts remain as hiragana—this can lead to misconversions.

There are three banks of vowel keys. Each bank contains five keys, one for each of the five Japanese vowels. In addition, a vowel-shift key is located near the user's right thumb. This, in effect, gives you six banks of vowel keys with each bank having a unique purpose. The consonant keys permit only two states, shifted by the consonant-shift key located near the user's left thumb.

The shifted state for the consonant keys in general adds a *y* element. This is used to make combinations such as ぎょ (*gyo*) or しゅ (*shu*). Table 5-14 illustrates how the consonant keys shift, and their purpose. Note that some of the shifted versions are not used for kanji input, such as っ and ん.

Table 5-14: The M-style Keyboard Array's Consonant Keys

Unshifted	Use	Shifted	Use
G	kanji or hiragana	Gy	kanji or hiragana
Z	kanji or hiragana	Zy	kanji or hiragana
D	kanji or hiragana	Dy	kanji or hiragana
、	comma (punctuation)	。	period (punctuation)
B	kanji or hiragana	By	kanji or hiragana
K	kanji or hiragana	Ky	kanji or hiragana
S	kanji or hiragana	Sy	kanji or hiragana
T	kanji or hiragana	Ty	kanji or hiragana
N	kanji or hiragana	Ny	kanji or hiragana
H	kanji or hiragana	Hy	kanji or hiragana
M	kanji or hiragana	My	kanji or hiragana
Y	kanji or hiragana	っ	hiragana
R	kanji or hiragana	Ry	kanji or hiragana
W	kanji or hiragana	ん	hiragana
P	kanji or hiragana	Py	kanji or hiragana

---

*Well, to be more precise, it is a *mora*-based language, but that is beyond the scope of this book.

The shifted state for the vowel keys is a bit more complex, and requires more detailed tables. Some banks of vowel keys are designed to generate hiragana, not kanji. See Table 5-15 to find out how this works.

Table 5-15: The M-style Keyboard Array's Vowel Keys

Unshifted

1st Bank	Use	2nd Bank	Use	3rd Bank	Use
Ei	kanji (long vowel)	e	hiragana	E	kanji (single vowel)
Uu	kanji (long vowel)	u	hiragana	U	kanji (single vowel)
Ii	kanji (long vowel)	i	hiragana	I	kanji (single vowel)
Ai	kanji (long vowel)	a	hiragana	A	kanji (single vowel)
Ou	kanji (long vowel)	o	hiragana	O	kanji (single vowel)

Shifted

1st Bank	Use	2nd Bank	Use	3rd Bank	Use
Et	kanji (+ ち/つ/っ)	En	kanji (+ ん)	Ek	kanji (+ き/く/っ)
Ut	kanji (+ ち/つ/っ)	Un	kanji (+ ん)	Uk	kanji (+ き/く/っ)
It	kanji (+ ち/つ/っ)	In	kanji (+ ん)	Ik	kanji (+ き/く/っ)
At	kanji (+ ち/つ/っ)	An	kanji (+ ん)	Ak	kanji (+ き/く/っ)
Ot	kanji (+ ち/つ/っ)	On	kanji (+ ん)	Ok	kanji (+ き/く/っ)

Okay, but what happened to katakana? The M-style keyboard must be shifted into a special state for katakana input to be in effect. Katakana input is quite similar to kanji input in that you can use different vowel keys as short cuts. Some of the vowel keys change in ways that speed katakana input.

Table 5-16 shows how the M-style keyboard array can be used to specify which characters convert to kanji, and how many kanji to select during conversion. The examples all share the same pronunciation, namely *daku*.

Table 5-16: Comparisons Between M-style, Roman, and Kana Input

Word	M-style Input	Conventional Roman Input	Conventional Kana Input
駄句	D A K U	d a k u	た ゛ く
諾	D Ak	d a k u	た ゛ く
抱く	D A K u	d a k u	た ゛ く
だく	D a K u	d a k u	た ゛ く

A lot (but not all) of the ambiguity that you will see in conventional Japanese input methods is remedied by the M-style input method.

The M-style keyboard is standard equipment on many of NEC's dedicated Japanese word processing systems.

High-speed Roman Array

NEC also developed a keyboard array, partly based on the M-style array, called the High-speed Roman array (快速ローマ字配列). It is set into a conventional keyboard shape, though. The keys are basically set into the same arrangement as with the M-style array, but without extra vowel keys and the special vowel and consonant modifier keys for distinguishing kanji from kana during input. Figure 5-10 provides an illustration of the High-speed Roman array.

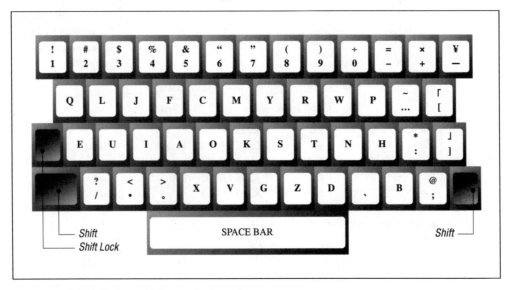

Figure 5-10: The High-speed Roman keyboard array

For those who use a Macintosh computer, I have experimented with rearranging the keyboard resources within the System file (using ResEdit, the standard resource editor for the Macintosh computer) such that this keyboard array can be used for Japanese input (it gave me a chance to experiment with this keyboard array without purchasing special hardware). Modifying keyboard arrays in software is something that almost every platform allows, and this keyboard array can be easily implemented. In fact, you can purchase software kits that allow you to accomplish this more easily. One such kit is called MacQWERTY, distributed by Nisus Software. These kits usually come with stickers to apply to your keys that represent the new keyboard layout. The standard resource editor for the Macintosh, ResEdit, can also be used to modify the keyboard layout in software.

Other Input Hardware

What has been described so far falls into the category of keyboard arrays. That is, keys are used to input kana and Roman characters. Other more recent hardware methods such as pen input do not require use of conventional keys. Optical character recognition

(OCR) is another input system which deals with the problem of transcribing already printed information. Finally, there are voice input systems.

This area is rapidly changing. Any mentioning of specifics may make this section obsolete. I do, however, list some systems that use these input systems just to give you a taste for what has been developed. I plan to include more specific information about products in JAPAN.INF, the online companion to this book.

Pen Input

GO Corporation developed a pen-based operating system and programming environment called PenPoint. PenPoint does not require the use of conventional keys, but instead uses a tablet on which the user physically *writes* what is intended. Pen input depends on another technology, namely optical character recognition (to be covered next).

GO Corporation has enhanced their pen-based operating system to handle Japanese through the use of Unicode. PenPoint is described in more detail in Chapter 8.

Other pen input products include MacHandwriter II by CIC, the Sony PalmTop computer, and Microsoft Windows-Pen.

Optical Character Recognition

Several OCR systems currently accept Japanese character input although there are, of course, limitations. The clearer and larger the typefaces, the more reliable such a system is. Some systems do not recognize all the characters in JIS X 0208-1990 (for instance, some recognize only JIS Level 1 kanji), and some are restricted to certain Japanese typeface styles.

You encounter OCR systems more frequently in the West where recognition of a much smaller collection of characters is done. The recognition of thousands of individual characters becomes much more difficult, particularly when each one is fairly complex in structure. There are currently efforts to recognize handwritten Japanese characters.

MacReader plus by Media Drive Laboratory is an example of OCR software that handles Japanese and English text. It runs under KanjiTalk on Macintosh computers.

Voice Input

Voice input systems require users to register their voice patterns so that the voice recognition software can more predictably match the user's voice input with correct character strings. Of course, a voice input system is customized for a specific user, so no others can effectively use voice input unless the system is trained to recognize the new voice.

Voice-driven software is now becoming more widespread, so expect more sophisticated systems to enter the market. If you think your office environment is distracting now, you can look forward to the joys of entire buildings full of people yelling at their computers!

Japanese Character Dictionaries

Dictionaries are another useful resource for inputting Japanese characters. Yes, usually good old-fashioned books! In fact, Appendixes B through D of this book, to some extent, can fill this purpose. What you will find in those appendixes are listings of the characters in JIS X 0208-1990 and JIS X 0212-1990 followed by pronunciation and radical indexes. The dictionaries discussed in this section go one step further in helping you to find characters from those Japanese character set standards.

Japanese character dictionaries fall into two categories: 1) conventional dictionaries that give you information such as pronunciation, some kanji compounds in which the character occurs, and perhaps even a short definition—these were not designed with computers in mind; and 2) specialized dictionaries that give you information, such as pronunciations, one or more encoded values with which to input the character, and perhaps other information, such as some compounds in which it occurs. Needless to say, conventional dictionaries are most useful to the casual student or scholar of the language, but specialized dictionaries are a valuable resource for the computer user, and typically contain all the characters in one or more Japanese character set standards, such as JIS X 0208-1990 or JIS X 0212-1990. The largest conventional Japanese character dictionary is called 大漢和辞典, and contains 50,294 kanji. This dictionary is published as a 13-volume set, and is quite expensive.*

Dictionaries that include the encoded value of characters prove their usefulness when you are trying to input a particular character, usually a kanji, and the input software you are using just doesn't seem to know it exists. Mind you, there are kanji that are not included in any of the JIS character set standards, but those are few and far between. There are many characters, such as JIS Level 2 kanji, that usually cannot be input by pronunciation, and the user must resort to input by encoded value. Most input software provides a mechanism for code input, and most systems come with manuals that contain a JIS table indexed by encoded value. The usefulness of JIS tables is limited. Remember that JIS Level 1 kanji are arranged by pronunciation, so forget trying to find a character there by its radical. JIS Level 2 kanji, on the other hand, are arranged by radical, so this makes finding characters a bit easier. However, there are times that you may wish to use other means, such as pronunciation for a JIS Level 2 kanji, total stroke number, or radical for a JIS Level 1 kanji. This is when a specialized Japanese character dictionary becomes invaluable. They go beyond the JIS tables in that they offer two or more methods to index all the characters in the JIS character set standards. I highly recommend purchasing at least one of these reference works. Below I describe the two that I have grown to prefer.

---

*You can also order a large poster called これが5万字 (meaning "this is 50,000 characters") that illustrates these 50,294 kanji. Appendix K has ordering information.

The two specialized dictionaries I use contain different sets of characters, offer different methods of locating characters, and provide a different set of information once you find the target character. The first dictionary, called パソコンワープロ漢字辞典 (*Personal Computer and Word Processor Kanji Dictionary*), allows you to index all the characters found in JIS X 0208-1983 (*not* the 1990 version) by pronunciation, radical, and total number of strokes, and provides hexadecimal JIS, hexadecimal Shift-JIS, KUTEN, and the two printable ASCII characters that correspond to the two hexadecimal JIS bytes. The second dictionary, called 最新JIS漢字辞典 (*The Latest JIS Kanji Dictionary*), allows you to index all the characters in JIS X 0208-1990 and JIS X 0212-1990 by radical and pronunciation, and provides hexadecimal JIS and KUTEN values for JIS X 0208-1990 characters, and only the KUTEN value for JIS X 0212-1990 characters. I find both of these references indispensable for my work and study. See the Bibliography for complete information on these dictionaries.

Another useful specialized dictionary is called 大漢語林. It includes all the characters of JIS X 0208-1990 and JIS X 0212-1990, and provides information similar to that provided in 最新JIS漢字辞典, except much more detailed. This dictionary is rather expensive, so unless you expect to make use of these dictionaries quite often, the less expensive ones described above may be better for the short-term.

Electronic dictionaries are a more recent phenomenon. Some are conventional, some are specialized, and some are even a combination of both. These electronic dictionaries may take the form of online dictionary software for your computer or as a hand-held device. The programs for your computer are described in Chapter 8. One of the most popular hand-held models is the Canon WordTank. Seiko Instruments and other companies also manufacture these devices. See Appendix K for more information.

So, what about the corporate character set standards that are described in Appendix H? Most companies that develop their own Japanese character set standards also publish a kanji dictionary that allows you to index all of its special characters. I have such dictionaries for JEF, FMR Kanji, HP Kanji, NEC Kanji, and KEIS. Some are more useful than others. For example, the one for HP Kanji is the same as the JIS standard, except that it lists the Shift-JIS, JIS, and KUTEN values—this doesn't help you much in finding obscure kanji. The set published by NEC is superb, and allows you to search by radical, pronunciation, total number of strokes, and encoded value. The moral of the story is that you should look before you buy (or else get a recommendation from someone). I am sure there are dictionaries available for the other corporate character set standards described in this book.

There are other such dictionaries available, too. Some of these are listed in the Bibliography at the end of this book. I urge you to select one that suits your needs, and contains enough indexing information to find characters quickly. I found a set that works well for me; now it's your turn.

6

Japanese Output

We now come to the point where we discuss how Japanese text is output to devices such as printers and computer monitors. You just learned the various ways in which Japanese text can be input, but now comes the time when you must display or print that text. Printers can range from low-resolution, dot-matrix printers to high-resolution photo imagesetters. Computer monitors are usually low-resolution devices.

No matter what output device is being used, whether it is a computer monitor, a dot-matrix printer, or even a high-resolution photo imagesetter, the most basic unit of output is either a *pixel* (in the case of computer monitors) or a *dot* (in the case of printers). The resolution of both types of devices is usually expressed in units called *dpi*, short for dots-per-inch. The most commonly used printers are 300-dpi laser printers, although inexpensive 600-dpi printers are just beginning to emerge. The most commonly used computer monitors have a 72-dpi resolution.

Just what is considered high- or low-resolution depends on your background. To people who use a 1270-dpi photo imagesetter, 600-dpi and below are considered low-resolution, but those who just moved from a dot-matrix printer to a 300-dpi laser printer may think that they now have a high-resolution printer. As you can see, it's all relative.

This book deals with many typographic issues specific to Japanese text. If you are remotely interested in typography in general, I suggest that you get the books entitled *The Elements of Typographic Style* by Robert Bringhurst, published by Hartley & Marks, and *Stop Stealing Sheep & find out how type works* by Erik Spiekermann and E.M. Ginger, published by Adobe Press. There are also catalogs that are more like magazines such as *Font & Function* by Adobe Systems and *U&lc* (Upper & lowercase) by International

Typeface Corporation (ITC). Good typography crosses all cultural and language barriers, and these publications serve as excellent references.

Before we begin this discussion, I would like to mention that I work for Adobe Systems in Japanese Font Production, and feel compelled to provide some sort of disclaimer here. Much of the material in this chapter relates to software developed by Adobe Systems, thus many of the discussions may seem biased toward their technology. I feel that the software solutions for Japanese output that Adobe Systems provides are among the best—that is why I decided to work for them. That is also why I make such software recommendations to you.

Japanese Fonts

One of the most important aspects of Japanese output is the availability of fonts. Fonts form the basis of document writing—no matter which writing system is involved—and are available in a variety of formats. Although the internal representation of characters in these formats differs considerably, the final result, whether printed or output to a computer monitor, is simply a bitmapped font.

A typical Japanese font today consists of the characters from JIS X 0208-1990 (or previous versions). Just a few years ago Japanese fonts that supported JIS Level 2 kanji were uncommon—now you can expect to find Japanese fonts that support the additional 5,801 kanji and 266 non-kanji specified in JIS X 0212-1990.

Selecting the point size of a particular font is probably one of the most common tasks you perform on a computer. The size of a font is usually described in units called points. A *point* is a term used in typography that represents a measurement that is approximately 1/72 of an inch.* This means that a 72-point kanji is roughly one inch wide and one inch tall. 10- and 12-point fonts are the most common point sizes used in text. This text is set in 10-point ITC Garamond Light.

Three major Japanese type foundries have the design expertise and human resources necessary to design Japanese typefaces that contain thousands of characters. They are Morisawa (モリサワ), Shaken (写研), and Ryobi (リョービ). Japanese type was originally cast in metal, but the trend is moving toward digital type.

Bitmapped Fonts

The first Japanese fonts were bitmapped. This means that each character is constructed from a matrix, each cell of which could be turned on or off. The limitation of this font

---

*The actual measurement represented by a point is exactly 1/72.27 of an inch.

format is that they are usually restricted to a single point size. Any scaling applied to a bitmapped font may produce irregular-looking results (the *jaggies*, as many call them). See Figure 6-4 on page 143 for an example of a scaled 12-point bitmapped character.

One of the most commonly used bitmapped font formats is called BDF, short for *Bitmap Distribution Format*. This font format was developed by Adobe Systems, and is the standard bitmapped font format used on most UNIX-based systems. It is quite easy to use BDF fonts. In fact, many people have used freely available Japanese BDF fonts for use in developing their own software. Figure 6-1 is the BDF description for the character 剣— these data are for a 24-by-24 dot-matrix pattern, which is graphically illustrated in Figure 6-2.

```
STARTCHAR 3775          3ffec6
ENCODING 14197          318cc6
SWIDTH 1002 0           318cc6
DWIDTH 24 0             318cc6
BBX 24 24 0 -2          318cc6
BITMAP                  3ffcc6
018007                  318cc6
018006                  0340c6
0360e6                  033006
0318c6                  061806
060cc6                  0c1c06
0c06c6                  180c06
1866c6                  300c3e
37f0c6                  c0000c
c180c6                  ENDCHAR
218cc6
```

Figure 6-1: Sample BDF character description

You must be wondering how to interpret this BDF data. Table 6-1 lists the keywords along with a brief description.

Table 6-1: BDF Keyword Descriptions

Keyword	Example	Description
STARTCHAR *name*	STARTCHAR 3775	Character name (3775 is hexadecimal JIS)
ENCODING *n*	ENCODING 14197	Encoding of character (14197 is decimal JIS)
SWIDTH *x y*	SWIDTH 1002 0	Scaled width expressed as a vector
DWIDTH *x y*	DWIDTH 24 0	Device width expressed as a vector
BBX *w h x y*	BBX 24 24 0 -2	The bounding box for the character
BITMAP	BITMAP	Beginning of bitmapped pattern description
ENDCHAR	ENDCHAR	End of character description

The actual bitmapped data for each character entry of a BDF file that describes 24-by-24 dot-matrix patterns consists of 24 lines of six characters each. Each line represents 24 pixels, and each character represents four pixels. Each of these six characters can have a value in the ranges 0x0–0x9 or 0xA–0xF. This allows for up to 16 unique values, which is the total number of unique patterns that can be produced with four pixels. Table 6-2 illustrates these 16 values as binary patterns.

Table 6-2: The 16 Unique Binary Patterns From BDF Data

Value	Binary Pattern	Value	Binary Pattern
0	0000	8	1000
1	0001	9	1001
2	0010	A	1010
3	0011	B	1011
4	0100	C	1100
5	0101	D	1101
6	0110	E	1110
7	0111	F	1111

Let's take a look at the first line of the BDF character description shown in Figure 6-1:

```
018007
```

The binary pattern that represents these data corresponds to the pixel pattern—zeros correspond to white pixels, and ones correspond to black pixels. Table 6-3 illustrates how these binary patterns correspond to pixel patterns.

Table 6-3: Binary and Pixel Patterns for BDF Data

BDF Data	0	1	8	0	0	7
Binary Pattern	0000	0001	1000	0000	0000	0111
Pixel Pattern	□□□□	□□□■	■□□□	□□□□	□□□□	□■■■

Note how there are 24 pixels across (and 24 such lines). Compare this pixel pattern to what you see in the first row of pixels in Figure 6-2. In fact, it is more efficient to read these binary patterns two characters at a time into a byte. A byte can hold a binary pattern eight digits long. For example, the first two characters, 01, are read into a single byte, and its binary pattern is 00000001.

If you are interested in how to make use of Japanese BDF fonts in your own programs, I suggest that you obtain the source code for KD (Kanji Driver), a Japanese terminal emulation program written by Izumi Ohzawa (大沢五住). Many people have used the KD source code as a reference for writing programs that make use of Japanese BDF fonts. The KD distribution comes with the complete source code. For a more complete description on BDF files, contact Adobe Systems' Adobe Developer Support to obtain the document entitled *Glyph Bitmap Distribution Format (BDF) Specification*. This document is also available through anonymous FTP as a PostScript file—you simply download this file to a PostScript printer to get the document. See Appendix K for more information.

Figure 6-2 is an example of 24-by-24 and 16-by-16 dot-matrix patterns for the character 剣. These dot-matrix patterns were taken directly from the JIS manuals called JIS X 9052-1983 and JIS X 9051-1984, respectively. These manuals may become useful if your system does not support all the characters in JIS X 0208-1990.* I once put them to use when I used EGWord Version 2.2 by Ergosoft on the Macintosh several years ago—that word processing software supported only JIS Level 1 kanji (versions of EGWord after 2.2 included support for JIS Level 2 kanji).

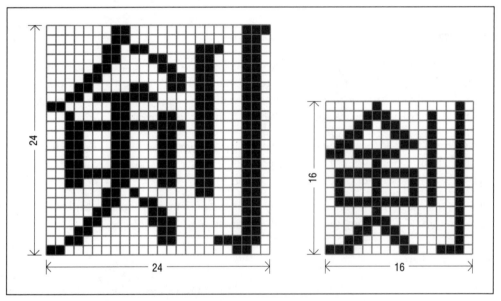

Figure 6-2: Japanese bitmapped characters

There are even higher resolution bitmapped fonts available, such as 32-by-32, 48-by-48, 56-by-56, and so on. Canon (キヤノン) and Dainippon Printing (大日本印刷) in Japan are sources for higher resolution bitmapped Japanese fonts. You can even find similar sized fonts at anonymous FTP sites, usually in the form of BDF files. For those who need to handle more kanji than found in JIS X 0208-1990, the Wnn Consortium has made a

---

*Note that these manuals are based on JIS X 0208-1983.

freely available JIS X 0212-1990 bitmapped font (in BDF format). A Japan-based company called Yinu System also sells JIS X 0212-1990 bitmapped fonts (in BDF format) in a variety of sizes. This now makes it possible to develop programs that graphically support the JIS X 0212-1990 character set. See Appendix K for more information.

Obviously, the larger the dot-matrix pattern, the more memory such a font requires, especially when producing a bitmapped Japanese font that contains several thousand characters. There is also the problem of having to design a complete set of characters for every dot-matrix size needed.

It must be stated, however, that bitmapped fonts do have their merits. More advanced font technologies, which you will learn about next, may produce poor quality results at small point sizes and on low resolution output devices such as computer monitors. With bitmapped fonts, the user can have hand-tuned fonts for commonly used point sizes. For example, Adobe Systems typically provides bitmapped fonts, at 10-, 12-, 14-, 18-, and 24-point, with their outline font packages.

Parametric Fonts

The first step of improving the internal representation of fonts was to use vectors to define their shapes mathematically. As a result, parametric fonts are also known as vector fonts. Each character is broken down into primitive elements, and these elements then form a library of instructions for describing the shape of a character.

Parametric fonts do not provide very pleasing typographic results, especially when printed at large point sizes. However, parametric fonts are scalable, so they were one step ahead of fixed-size, unscalable bitmapped fonts.

AIN Technologies in Japan manufacturers Japanese parametric fonts in a variety of styles. See Appendix K for information on how to contact AIN Technologies.

Outline Fonts

During the early 1980s there was a revolution in the publishing industry. This revolution was made possible by the advent of PostScript, the page-description programming language developed by Adobe Systems. PostScript allows for the seamless mixture of text and graphics, and, with the development of laser printers, brought high-quality publishing capability to many more people than before. Now, for under $10,000 (U.S.), anyone can purchase the necessary hardware and software to produce high-quality Japanese text by themselves.* As far as Japanese is concerned, the PostScript language supports a font format that can represent characters as scalable outlines.

---

*A list of hardware and software is listed at the end of this chapter, so hang on!

There is another page-description language called TrueImage, developed by Microsoft, which supports a scalable font format known as TrueType. These outline font formats are discussed in greater detail below.

Japanese fonts of more recent vintage are constructed from *outlines*. This means that each character is described mathematically as a collection of line segments, arcs, and curves. This outline is then filled, and when it is output to computer monitors or printers, it is scaled to the selected point-size, then rendered to the output device.* A single outline font can be used at any conceivable size and resolution. The design process is also simplified in that the designer need not worry about the point size of the font, and thus does not need to design more than a single point size.

Figure 6-3 is an example of a character from an outline font. The outline is constructed from line segments and curves. The anchor points that describe the outline are marked with small black squares along the actual outline of the character. The offline control points that define the Bézier curves are represented by small black circles with lines drawn to their respective anchor points. In this example, the character 剣 from Heisei Kaku Gothic W5 (平成角ゴシックW5) is used.

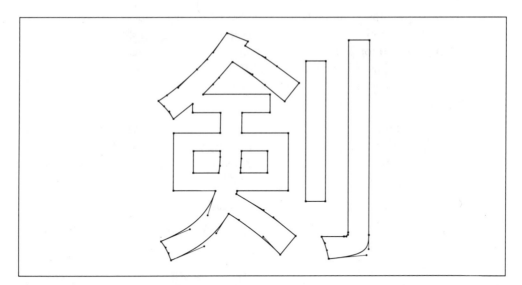

Figure 6-3: Japanese outline character

Currently, the two most commonly used outline font technologies are PostScript and TrueType. Their primary difference lies in that PostScript uses Bézier curves, and TrueType uses quadratic splines. Exactly what this means is well beyond the scope of

---

*In case you are wondering, *rendering*, or scan converting or rasterizing, is the process of converting a scaled outline to a bitmapped image—the outline format is only for more efficient internal representation.

this book, but Bézier curves require fewer control points for representation—this leads to fonts that require less disk storage space.

PostScript Fonts

PostScript is a powerful page description language backed by a programming language. As a programming language, PostScript is syntactically similar to FORTH. As a page description language, PostScript supports both graphics and text, and, to render text effectively, requires support for fonts.

PostScript supports several font formats. The most widely used format is called Type 1. The Type 1 font format is, strictly speaking, a small and stylized language outside of the standard PostScript language. Other font formats include Type 0, Type 3, Type 4, Type 5, and Type 42 (there is no Type 2 font format).

Type 0 fonts are composite fonts, which are made up of two or more descendant fonts. A *composite* font constitutes a hierarchical structure in which huge character sets can be handled. A *descendant* font can be Type 1, Type 3, or even Type 0 fonts.* PostScript Japanese fonts are Type 0 fonts.

Type 1 fonts are the most commonly found. Type 1 fonts use a special, restricted subset of PostScript, which allows for a more compact (and faster printing) font. The Type 1 font format is typically used for all roman fonts issued by Adobe Systems. It is also the format specified by an ISO standard called ISO 9541-1993 (*Font Information Interchange*), parts 1, 2, and 3. A Japanese version of this standard is in the process of being created, and will be published as a series of four JIS manuals.

Type 3 is a user-defined font format. Type 3 fonts are much like Type 1 fonts, but allow for more complex outlines, such as logos and designs, and permit the use of the full range of PostScript operators. Type 3 fonts are not that common, and do not work with Adobe Type Manager (ATM) software, discussed later in this chapter.

Type 4 fonts are Type 1 fonts, but are disk-based rather than printer-resident.

Type 5 fonts are actually Type 1 fonts compressed in a special way for storage within printer ROMs.

Type 42 fonts are actually TrueType fonts with a PostScript *wrapper* so that they can reside within PostScript printers, and act much like PostScript fonts. Why Type 42? What happened to Type 6 through 41?†

---

*A Type 0 font made up of Type 0 descendant fonts is said to be a *nested* composite font.

†It is rumored that 42 was chosen by an unidentified (Apple) employee who was being humorous. In the *Hitchhiker* series of books (by Douglas Adams, published by Pocket Books), a god-like computer named Deep Thought is asked to find the answer to the Ultimate Question of Life, the Universe and Everything. After computing for thousands of years, this computer returns the answer 42.

Table 6-4 summarizes these six font formats with a brief description of their purpose.

Table 6-4: The Six PostScript Font Formats

Font Type	Description
Type 0	Composite font format
Type 1	The basic and most widely-used font format
Type 3	User-defined font format
Type 4	Disk-based font format (actually a Type 1 font stored in a way that saves RAM)
Type 5	ROM-based font format (actually a Type 1 font stored in a special compressed format for ROM storage)
Type 42	A TrueType font with a PostScript *wrapper*.

PostScript Japanese fonts are actually collections of composite fonts that support various character sets and encoding methods. They also have special naming conventions not found in other fonts offered by Adobe Systems. A Japanese font name consists of several parts: font name, weight, character set, encoding, and writing direction. Table 6-5 shows possible values for each of these parts.

Table 6-5: PostScript Japanese Font Name Conventions

Font Name	Weight	Character Set[1]	Encoding[6]	Writing Direction
Ryumin	Light	83pv[2]	RKSJ[7]	H
GothicBBB	Medium	Add[3]	EUC[8]	V
FutoMinA101	Bold	Ext[4]		
MidashiGo	MB31	NWP[5]		
HeiseiMin	W3			
etc.	*etc.*			

[1] When the character set is not specified, the default is the standard JIS character set.

[2] 83pv stands for *JIS X 0208-1983 plus verticals*, and represents the Apple character set (Apple83), which also contains the vertically set characters. The writing direction is always specified as -H because most of the character are horizontal.

[3] The Add character set represents a version of the FMR Kanji character set.

[4] The Ext character set represents the NEC Kanji character set.

[5] The NWP character set, short for *NEC Word Processor*, represents the NEC Kanji character set as used on NEC Japanese word processors.

[6] When the encoding is not specified, the default is JIS encoding.

[7] RKSJ stands for *Roman, Kana, and Shift-JIS*.

[8] EUC, as you might have expected, stands for Extended UNIX Code. The only recognized EUC code set is code set 1, namely JIS X 0208-1990.

Note that not all possibilities in this matrix are supported. The following are examples of some full PostScript Japanese font names for the typeface called HeiseiMin-W3:

```
HeiseiMin-W3-H
HeiseiMin-W3-V
HeiseiMin-W3-Add-H
HeiseiMin-W3-Add-V
HeiseiMin-W3-Ext-H
HeiseiMin-W3-Ext-V
HeiseiMin-W3-NWP-H
HeiseiMin-W3-NWP-V
HeiseiMin-W3-EUC-H
HeiseiMin-W3-EUC-V
HeiseiMin-W3-RKSJ-H
HeiseiMin-W3-RKSJ-V
HeiseiMin-W3-Add-RKSJ-H
HeiseiMin-W3-Add-RKSJ-V
HeiseiMin-W3-Ext-RKSJ-H
HeiseiMin-W3-Ext-RKSJ-V
HeiseiMin-W3-83pv-RKSJ-H
```

Compare them with Table 6-5 to find out what character sets and encoding methods each one supports.

A sampling of Adobe PostScript Japanese typefaces is shown in Table 6-6. These typefaces are licensed from the original designer, then produced by Adobe Systems or their font tools licensees to conform to the PostScript Japanese font specifications.

Table 6-6: Sample PostScript Japanese Typefaces

Typeface Name	PostScript Name	Font Vendor	Sample Text
リュウミンL-KL	Ryumin-Light	Morisawa	日本語文字のサンプル
平成明朝W3	HeiseiMin-W3	FDPC[1]	日本語文字のサンプル
平成明朝W9	HeiseiMin-W9	FDPC[1]	**日本語文字のサンプル**
太明朝体A101	FutoMinA101-Bold	Morisawa	日本語文字のサンプル
見出明朝体MA31	MidashiMin-MA31	Morisawa	**日本語文字のサンプル**
中ゴシック体BBB1	GothicBBB-Medium	Morisawa	日本語文字のサンプル
平成角ゴシックW5	HeiseiKakuGo-W5	FDPC[1]	**日本語文字のサンプル**
太ゴシック体B101	FutoGoB101-Bold	Morisawa	**日本語文字のサンプル**
見出ゴシック体MB31	MidashiGo-MB31	Morisawa	**日本語文字のサンプル**
じゅん101	Jun101-Light	Morisawa	日本語文字のサンプル

[1]FDPC, if you recall from earlier material, stands for Font Development & Promotion Center (文字フォント開発・普及センター).

I know, some of those typefaces look the same, especially the first two. Let me assure you that they are not: when set at a larger point size, they look quite different. The main difference is in the shapes of the serifs (the terminals of the strokes). You may also notice a difference in weight. Let's take a closer look at a character set at 150-point in the first two typefaces, Ryumin-Light and HeiseiMin-W3.

Ryumin-Light   **HeiseiMin-W3**

Do they still look the same? I don't think so. Ryumin-Light has flared strokes, whereas HeiseiMin-W3 has squared ones.

For more information on PostScript fonts, I can suggest some further reading material. The Type 1 font format is described in the book entitled *Adobe Type 1 Font Format*, written by Adobe Systems and published by Addison-Wesley. For more information on handling Japanese fonts under PostScript, I suggest reading the Japanese edition of the *PostScript Language Tutorial & Cookbook*, written by Adobe Systems and published by ASCII Corporation in Japan. An additional 30 pages or so that are not found in the English version provide a tutorial on handling Japanese fonts. The *PostScript Language Reference Manual*, second edition, also written by Adobe Systems and published by Addison-Wesley, provides a complete description of the PostScript language, including information on Type 0 and Type 3 fonts. Finally, for an excellent tutorial on the PostScript language, I suggest *Thinking in PostScript*, written by Glenn Reid and published by Addison-Wesley. *PostScript by Example*, written by Henry McGilton and Mary Campione and published by Addison-Wesley, is also an excellent tutorial, and has a chapter on fonts, including a superb tutorial on composite fonts. Complete information on these books can be found in the Bibliography.

For those interested in the PostScript page-description language, I suggest contacting Adobe Systems' PostScript Developer Association for more information. Their contact information can be found in Appendix K. They offer several levels of membership. I also suggest obtaining some or all of the books about PostScript listed above.

Companies that manufacture PostScript Japanese fonts include Adobe Systems, Information Control Laboratory (ICL), Morisawa, FontWorks, and TypeBank.

There are projects underway to provide freely available PostScript Japanese fonts. One such project is at Tokyo University (東京大学), and the results of their project are available through anonymous FTP. See Appendix K for more information.

TrueType Fonts

TrueType fonts, like PostScript fonts, are described as outlines, and as such are scalable. Curves are represented as quadratic splines. TrueType fonts are just now able to reside on printer hard disks (or in RAM or ROM) because Adobe Systems' Type 42 font format provides a PostScript wrapper for TrueType fonts.

TrueType fonts are available for the MS-DOS and Macintosh platforms. The UNIX platform currently does not provide support for TrueType fonts.

Many TrueType fonts are also available in Type 1 format—many type vendors market their fonts in both formats to appeal to those dedicated to a particular format.

TrueType Japanese fonts are a more recent addition to TrueType font technology, and are currently usable on the Macintosh platform. In fact, KanjiTalk 7.1 (the Japanese operating system for Macintosh) comes with seven TrueType-J fonts. These fonts require approximately 20–40 percent more disk space than the equivalent PostScript Japanese fonts. If disk space is at a premium in your environment, PostScript Japanese fonts are probably a better choice.

Creating Your Own Fonts

If you are interested in creating your own typefaces (that is, rolling your own), by all means endeavor to do so. Be aware, however, that designing typefaces requires special skills, and lots of time, especially for a Japanese typeface that contains thousands of characters. Designing a Japanese typeface in outline format is almost never an individual task, but the result of a group effort. It would literally take several years for an individual to design a Japanese typeface. This should not stop you from trying, though. Sometimes you may need just to add a few characters to an existing Japanese typeface. It is also not enough to be able to design characters, but that all the characters you design for a typeface match each other in both style and weight.

Several font editors are commercially available. One of the most prominent is Fontographer, developed by Altsys Corporation. Fontographer is available for Macintosh and MS-DOS (running Microsoft Windows) platforms, and lets you create fonts for virtually any platform (Macintosh, MS-DOS, UNIX, and so on)—even if the version of Fontographer you are running is not designed for that platform. Fontographer also handles TrueType fonts, and is available as a Japanese version (Japanese-language interface only). Fontographer also lets you create either Type 1 or TrueType fonts from the same data. Others font editors include FontStudio by Letraset, and Ikarus M by URW.

All of the font editors described above can create only single-byte encoded fonts. Altsys is currently developing software called Altsys Rollup that will let you create PostScript Japanese fonts. That is, two-byte encoded fonts that contain thousands of characters. When released, Altsys Rollup will be the first commercially available software that can make PostScript Japanese fonts.

There are also tools, such as Metamorphosis Professional by Altsys, that convert fonts from one format to another (for example, from TrueType to Type 1 format). There are two things to keep in mind when doing this sort of font format conversion:

- The license agreement included with some font software states that the data must not be converted to other formats—this is a *legal* issue.

- The conversion process often strips out the hints which allow the font data to rasterize better at small point sizes and at low resolutions—this is a *quality* issue.

These issues may be reasons for *not* modifying font data. Fonts *are* software (that is, programs—the PostScript language, or a subset thereof, constitutes a complete programming language), and as such are copyrightable. So why do such tools exist? Well, not all fonts fall under restrictions for conversion to other formats, and many fonts are in the public domain.

Printer Output

Several years ago you could print Japanese using only bitmapped fonts. In fact, some printers required that the bitmapped characters be resident in the printer hardware itself. As discussed above, bitmapped fonts are not ideal these days for printing high-quality Japanese text. Fortunately, there are now many ways you can improve the quality of printed and displayed Japanese text.

Printers can range from low-resolution, dot-matrix printers to high-resolution photo imagesetters. Printers can also have PostScript support, which means that they contain a PostScript interpreter—we discuss why this is important later in this section.

At the beginning of this chapter, I stated that everything comes down to resolving a font into dots or pixels when printing or displaying is performed. Ultimately, every font is resolved into a bitmap. For outline fonts, printing speed and performance is heavily dependent on where the outlines are scaled and subsequently rendered into bitmapped fonts. The characters can be rendered on the computer, then sent to the printer; or, the instructions for rendering can be sent to the printer, which can subsequently render the characters. The latter is usually faster, but both should provide the same results as long as the software performing the rendering is the same. Hardware and software for both methods is described below.

PostScript Japanese Printers

One of the very first solutions for obtaining high-quality Japanese output was to obtain a PostScript Japanese printer. One of the most common ones was (and still is) the Apple LaserWriter IINTX-J, a PostScript Level One printer with composite font support. The Apple LaserWriter IINTX-J comes with a hard disk containing two PostScript Japanese fonts, Ryumin-Light and GothicBBB-Medium. There are also many PostScript Japanese printers that now have five PostScript Japanese fonts. These fonts include the two listed above (sometimes in ROM rather than on a hard disk) plus FutoMinA101-Bold, FutoGoB101-Bold, and Jun101-Light. Companies such as Apple Computer, Canon, Dainippon Screen, DEC, Electronics for Imaging, Linotype-Hell, Oki Electric, and Varityper manufacture PostScript Japanese printers. These range from laser printers to high-resolution photo imagesetters. Other companies, such as LaserMaster Corporation, manufacture PostScript-compatible Japanese printers.

Adobe Systems released PostScript Level Two to the marketplace in the latter part of 1991. PostScript Level Two has built in support for composite fonts (Type 0 fonts). However, this support does not automatically give you the ability to use Japanese fonts since there need to be special system files resident in ROM or on the hard disk—it does, though, make it easier for printer manufacturers to produce PostScript Japanese printers (they license those special system files from Adobe Systems).

Pre-Level Two versions of PostScript, now called PostScript Level One, did not have composite font support (exceptions being PostScript Japanese Level One printers such as the Apple LaserWriter IINTX-J mentioned above).

No matter which version of PostScript you may be using, if the font you are attempting to use is resident on the printer (resident here refers to being in ROM or on the printer's hard disk), the font is rendered on the printer. Just to give you an example of the size of a PostScript file compared to sending bitmapped data to the printer from the computer, see the following text, which is a very minimal PostScript file for printing my Japanese pen-name (小林剣) set vertically at 200-point:

```
%!                              % This indicates a PostScript file.
/Ryumin-Light-V findfont        % Find the font, Ryumin-Light-V, in the font directory
                                % Note that the -V at the end indicates a vertical font.
200 scalefont                   % Scale the font to 200-point.
setfont                         % Make this scaled font the current font.
306 720 moveto                  % Move 4.25 inches right and 10 inches up.
<3E2E 4E53 3775> show           % Show the characters whose codes are in <>.
showpage                        % Print the page.
```

The above PostScript example provides the instructions to the PostScript interpreter resident on the printer. The printer renders the characters per the instructions. Compare that with a file that contains bitmapped data for 200-point characters, which may be up to 100 times as large. It should be obvious which is faster to send from the computer to the printer.

However, not everyone, especially individual users, has enough money to purchase a PostScript Japanese printer, so there are software solutions, such as ATM-J (Adobe Type Manager, Japanese version), which render Japanese fonts on the computer, then send them to the printer. While this obviously takes much longer to print, the results are the same.

Adobe Type Manager (ATM)

Adobe Systems developed a font rendering program called Adobe Type Manager (ATM), which is basically the font rendering software used in a PostScript interpreter. ATM resides on the computer, which allows users to place printer fonts on the computer and to use them with ATM for high-quality computer monitor output. ATM is also used for printing to printers on which the fonts are not resident. ATM works with non-PostScript printers, too. The first versions of ATM could handle only Roman fonts, but late in 1991 Adobe Systems released ATM-J, the Japanese version of ATM. This software package comes with two PostScript Japanese fonts, which the user installs on their computer hard disk.

If the typeface is resident on both the computer and printer, ATM-J (and ATM) does not render the characters, but lets the printer do it instead. For display, ATM-J (and ATM) is used to render point sizes for which a bitmapped font is not installed.

Figure 6-4 illustrates the kanji 剣 printed at 216-point (scaled) in three ways: using a 12-point bitmapped font, on a screen display with ATM-J turned on (72-dpi), and printer output with ATM-J turned on (300-dpi). Notice the difference ATM-J makes in the output quality of the character. The same figure applies to TrueType, which is covered next.

Figure 6-4: The effect of ATM-J on a 216-point kanji

As of this writing, you can purchase 14 Adobe PostScript Japanese fonts that work with ATM-J—this number is expected to grow. ATM-J is a superset of ATM, meaning that it can also be used for Roman fonts. However, SuperATM, described later in this chapter, has functionality that is not yet part of ATM-J. ATM-J currently runs on any Macintosh running KanjiTalk (the Japanese operating system) and on PCs running Microsoft Windows-J.

TrueType

TrueType font rendering technology is basically the same as ATM in that it renders character outlines on the computer, then uses the resulting bitmapped fonts for both display and printing. The TrueType software is embedded into the Macintosh OS starting with System 7, so you always have TrueType capability.

Like ATM, TrueType began as a Roman-fonts-only technology. In mid-1992, Apple released Kanji TrueType, which included two TrueType Japanese typefaces: 本明朝-M and 平成角ゴシック. Late in 1992, Apple released KanjiTalk 7.1, which includes seven TrueType Japanese typefaces—the two listed above plus Osaka, 平成明朝, 丸ゴシック-M, 中ゴシックBBB, and リュウミンライト-KL.

TrueType-J fonts use an excellent font caching mechanism that makes subsequent displays of characters very fast.

Other Printing Methods

Many of you may not have access to the above printing methods, probably because you do not use a platform that is supported by the printing software (ATM-J and TrueType), or do not have access to a PostScript Japanese printer. Fortunately, you will usually find that the Japanese text processing software you are using comes with at least a limited way to output Japanese text to a printer.

There are freely available Japanese printing kits, such as kanjips and jenscript (Japanese version of enscript). These programs take Japanese text files as input, and format them for printing. These printing kits often come bundled with a minimal set of bitmapped fonts, but you are not limited to those.

Besides PostScript, there are other typesetting and page-description languages in use today. Examples include ditroff, triroff, troff, and TEX. Some of these, such as TEX, have Japanese versions available. In fact, there are many slightly different versions of TEX available, such as NTT and ASCII versions. Japanese TEX makes use of fonts from Dainippon Printing.

The material in this chapter concentrates on PostScript because it produces a quality printed page on almost any output device, and because the most commonly available outline fonts are in PostScript format. These others can be made to generate PostScript.

Computer Monitor Output

Being able to output Japanese text on a computer monitor is a very basic requirement. Without this ability, how would you go about processing Japanese text?

A computer monitor screen image consists of pixels, with each pixel representing a basic unit of display. In the case of monochrome displays, each pixel can be either white or black.

As we discussed above, ATM-J and Kanji TrueType can be used to provide high-quality output for display devices. There is also Display PostScript (DPS), which is like ATM but has the whole range of PostScript available.* DPS provides what is known as WYSIWYG (*What You See Is What You Get*), namely that what is displayed on the screen is what you will get when printed. Currently, some IBM, DEC, NeXT, and SGI workstations support DPS.

The X Window System for UNIX is a graphical user interface, and as such, handles the display of a variety of fonts. It is usually necessary to use a special window for Japanese output, such as a kterm, exterm, or equivalent.

Vertically-set Japanese Text

Japanese, like Chinese, is traditionally set vertically. Columns start at the right of the page, and work their way left. Also, books are read from what in the West is considered the back of the book. Fortunately, it is also acceptable to set Japanese text horizontally, and to read books in "Western" orientation. There are, however, a few punctuation marks and kana characters that require special handling, such as their positioning within the em-square.

PostScript's flexible text handling capabilities allow you to set Japanese text vertically. Whether or not you can actually do this depends upon the application you are using. The underlying PostScript Japanese fonts have such support.

Let's look at some examples of Japanese text set horizontally and vertically, including some of those characters that require special vertical handling.

---

*ATM has only the font handling routines of PostScript at its disposal.

Horizontally Set

普通の「DTPシステム」は縦書きレイアウトをサポートしていますが、簡単なワープロやテキストエディターはサポートしません。縦書きのサポートの為にはフォントも必要です。全てのポストスクリプト日本語フォントには縦書きフォントも含まれています。

Vertically Set

普通の「DTPシステム」は縦書きレイアウトをサポートしていますが、簡単なワープロやテキストエディターはサポートしません。縦書きのサポートの為にはフォントも必要です。全てのポストスクリプト日本語フォントには縦書きフォントも含まれています。

Table 6-7 illustrates how some characters change their orientation or positioning within the em-square depending on whether they are being set horizontally or vertically (the em-squares have been highlighted for easier comparison).

Table 6-7: Sample Japanese Characters That Require Special Vertical Handling

Description	Horizontal	Vertical
Japanese period	。	。
Japanese comma	、	、
Extended vowel mark	ー	｜
Opening parenthesis	「	﹁
Closing parenthesis	」	﹂
Small katakana *i*	ィ	ィ
Small katakana *o*	ォ	ォ

Software that allows for vertically set Japanese often lets you edit text vertically—this is a new experience for those not accustomed to it. The cursor is often a horizontal bar, and moves top to bottom then right to left. Some software lets you enter and edit text horizontally, but will print vertically.

External Character Handling

In Appendixes H and I we cover corporate-defined characters within corporate character sets. I state there that these characters, called *gaiji* (外字) in Japanese, do not convert very well between different character set standards. These are referred to here as *external characters* (外 means "external," and 字 means "character"), meaning that they fall outside the range of *standard* characters. External characters can be separated into two distinct categories:

- User-defined characters

- Corporate-defined characters

You will learn about corporate-defined characters in Appendixes H and I—they are usually specific to a particular corporation's Japanese character set standard, and do not include only kanji. User-defined characters are those that a single user creates for personal use. Again, they are not limited to kanji.

Both types of external characters pose problems when information interchange is necessary. The target encoding or character set may not support certain characters that are used in a file. This is especially true for user-defined characters, which are usually specific to a single person's environment. Even JIS X 0212-1990 characters can be considered external characters if the target system does not support their use.* Some claim that Unicode is a solution to this problem. While this appears to be true at first glance (after all, there are nearly 21,000 kanji to pick and choose from!), I have found that there are approximately 1,000 JEF kanji that are not part of the Unicode kanji set.

The success of printing or displaying external characters depends on the fonts you are using. If the font that you have chosen has the proper external character, you should get proper output. If you need to use a corporate-defined character set, you most likely have access to fonts that correspond to it.

A problem arises when printing user-defined characters. In the case of bitmapped fonts, it is usually possible to create a new bitmapped character, then add it to the repertoire of characters in the font. However, creating a new outline character is a bit more tedious as it requires much more design skill (you may even have to create a corresponding bitmapped character!). Character design software such as Fontographer (described earlier in this chapter) can be used to create your own bitmapped and outline fonts.

So, what can you do about this problem? Unfortunately, there is no elegant solution. A solution would need to somehow allow for the successful transmission of user- and corporate-defined characters to systems that do not support such characters. Even large character sets do not have all corporate-defined characters, and that doesn't even touch upon the problem of user-defined characters. A necessary step in finding a solution might be to embed character data, both bitmapped and outline, into files when they are transmitted. This includes a mechanism for detecting which characters are user-defined. The first person or company to offer a platform-independent gaiji solution will be rewarded well by the Japanese computer industry.

---

*For example, in Shift-JIS encoding, which does not support JIS X 0212-1990, they are considered external characters.

Special Japanese Text Formatting Functions

In addition to the different writing modes for Japanese text (horizontal and vertical), there are some special formatting considerations such as hyphenation and justification. For example, Japanese text does not follow Roman-language style hyphenation rules.

Japanese Hyphenation

Japanese requires special handling for the ends of lines, which is called *Japanese hyphenation*. In Japanese this is 禁則処理 (*kinsoku shori*), which literally means "prohibited [character] processing." There are certain characters that should not begin a new line and, likewise, there are characters that should not end a line. There are similar rules in English, but they are much more important in Japanese because there are no spaces between words (this is sometimes referred to as *Japanese word wrap*)—punctuation marks are treated like any other character.

Table 6-8 lists the characters that should not begin a new line. These include characters such as punctuation marks, closing quotes, and closing parentheses. The characters in the first rank have priority in processing. Some software handles only some ranks.

Table 6-8: Characters Prohibited From Beginning Lines

Rank	Characters
1	、 。 , . : ; ? ! ' ") 〕] 〉 } 〉 》 」 』 】
2	々 ー ー あ い う え お つ や ゆ よ わ ア イ ウ エ オ ツ ャ ユ ヨ ワ カ ケ
3	゛ ゜ ヽ ヾ ゝ ゞ ― - ゜ ´ ″ ℃ %

Table 6-9 lists the characters that should not end a line. These are basically opening quotes and opening parentheses, and are ranked into two groups.

Table 6-9: Characters Prohibited From Terminating Lines

Rank	Characters
1	' " (〔 [{ 〈 《 「 『 【
2	¥ $ ¢ £ @ § 〒 #

There are three types of Japanese hyphenation. The first type is known as *wrap-up hyphenation* (追込み禁則処理). Wrap-up hyphenation works by moving characters that are prohibited from beginning a new line back up to the end of the previous line. It can also move a character from the following line up such that characters that are prohibited from ending a line do not actually end a line. The following are examples:

Original Texts

日本語の一文字を七ビットの二バイトのコードで表現する方法には新ＪＩＳ
、旧ＪＩＳ、日電漢字等があります。

これらのコードを用いた文章では日本語テキストの前後に「漢字イン」、「
漢字アウト」という二つのエスケープ・シーケンスを使用することにより、
その中が日本語であることを示します。

Wrap-up Hyphenated

日本語の一文字を七ビットの二バイトのコードで表現する方法には新ＪＩＳ、
旧ＪＩＳ、日電漢字等があります。

これらのコードを用いた文章では日本語テキストの前後に「漢字イン」、「漢
字アウト」という二つのエスケープ・シーケンスを使用することにより、そ
の中が日本語であることを示します。

The second type of Japanese hyphenation is called *wrap-down hyphenation* (追出し禁則処理). It works by forcing characters that are prohibited from ending a line down to the next line. Another possibility is for a character to wrap down to the following line so that it appears before a character that is prohibited from beginning a line. The following texts are examples of this type:

Original Texts

日本語の一文字を七ビットの二バイトのコードで表現する方法には新ＪＩＳ
、旧ＪＩＳ、日電漢字等があります。

これらのコードを用いた文章では日本語テキストの前後に「漢字イン」、「
漢字アウト」という二つのエスケープ・シーケンスを使用することにより、
その中が日本語であることを示します。

Wrap-down Hyphenated

日本語の一文字を七ビットの二バイトのコードで表現する方法には新ＪＩ
Ｓ、旧ＪＩＳ、日電漢字等があります。

これらのコードを用いた文章では日本語テキストの前後に「漢字イン」、
「漢字アウト」という二つのエスケープ・シーケンスを使用することによ
り、その中が日本語であることを示します。

The third type of Japanese hyphenation is called *dangling hyphenation* (ぶら下がり禁則処理). It is similar to wrap-up hyphenation, but instead of adjusting the intercharacter spaces of punctuation to accommodate an extra character on the line, the character is left hanging out on the right margin. These characters appear to dangle off the end of the line, hence its name. Some implementations can dangle more than one character. Dangling hyphenation is often provided as an option for wrap-up hyphenation. The following is an example:

Original Text

日本語の一文字を七ビットの二バイトのコードで表現する方法には新ＪＩＳ、旧ＪＩＳ、日電漢字等があります。これらのコードを用いた文章では日本語の前後に漢字イン、漢字アウトという二つのエスケープ・シーケンスを使用することにより、その中が日本語であることを示します。

Dangle Hyphenated

日本語の一文字を七ビットの二バイトのコードで表現する方法には新ＪＩＳ、旧ＪＩＳ、日電漢字等があります。これらのコードを用いた文章では日本語の前後に漢字イン、漢字アウトという二つのエスケープ・シーケンスを使用することにより、その中が日本語であることを示します。

Proper application of Japanese hyphenation is crucial if a program is to succeed in the Japanese market. Some vendors have implemented all the types described above, and let the user select which one or ones to use. It is up to the software how this feature is implemented—there are no standards *per se*.

Japanese Justification

In the West we usually think of justification in terms of making the ends of lines for a paragraph adjusted such that they line up on their right sides. This is usually done by either adjusting the spacing between words in a sentence, or by adjusting the spacing between every letter in the sentence. The same principle holds true for Japanese text, but since Japanese words are strung together with no spaces interspersed, adjusting the spacing between individual characters is required. Under most implementations, Japanese characters, kana and kanji, are monospaced—every character occupies the same amount of space. Kana should properly be proportionally spaced, and systems seem to be moving in that direction. Sophisticated typesetting systems already have this capability. Roman characters are typically proportionally spaced, meaning that the widths of characters differ depending on their shape. The English textface used in this book is proportionally spaced, but you will occasionally find a monospaced font used for code samples or other purposes.

However, there are special ways to justify Japanese text, on a much more smaller scale than the text of paragraphs. This is known as *Japanese justification* (均等割付). This technique is most often used when listing Japanese names. Table 6-10 provides an example of a list of Japanese names justified in various ways.

Table 6-10: Examples of Japanese Justification

Unjustified	Justified Narrow	Justified Wide
久保田久美子	久保田久美子	久 保 田 久 美 子
小林剣	小　林　　剣	小　　　林　　　剣
山本太郎	山　本　太　郎	山　　本　　太　　郎
藤本みどり	藤　本　み　どり	藤　本　み　ど　り

Note how the justification takes place within units such as small text blocks, and that the characters are all adjusted such that they line up equally on both sides.

Ruby Characters

Ruby (ルビ) characters are simply very small kana characters that appear above (or sometimes below) one or more kanji, and act to annotate characters by indicating their pronunciation—this often helps readers to understand the word better. Ruby characters are sometimes referred to as *furigana* (振り仮名) or as *glosses*. Ruby characters are often seen in Japanese texts. Rarely used kanji or kanji compounds usually have ruby characters above them—no one in Japan can pronounce all kanji.* Children's books use them much more extensively. Kana are learned first, then kanji. These small annotations written in kana allow Japanese children (and foreigners who are learning to read Japanese) to learn the readings of kanji.

Table 6-11 provides some examples of kanji compounds annotated with ruby characters.

Table 6-11: Japanese Characters Annotated With Ruby Characters

Ruby Characters	かんじ 漢字	かぶしきがいしゃ 株式会社	はんちゅう 範疇
Pronunciation	kanji	kabushikigaisha	hanchû
Meaning	*kanji*	*incorporated*	*category*

There are also special uses for ruby characters. These are called *pseudo ruby* (疑似ルビ) characters. For example, katakana words can be annotated with ruby characters that are actually small kanji—these are often used to indicate the Japanese equivalent of loan words. Kanji compounds can also be annotated with ruby characters that are small Roman characters. Table 6-12 lists some examples of pseudo ruby characters.

---

*It is possible to understand the meaning of kanji without necessarily knowing their pronunciation.

Table 6-12: Japanese Characters Annotated With Pseudo Ruby Characters

Pseudo Ruby Characters	拳　　銃　　　　　　　　　　　　　計　算　機　　　　　　　　　　N　E　C		
	ピストル	コンピュータ	日本電気
Pronunciation	pisutoru	konpyûta	nippondenki
Meaning	*pistol*	*computer*	*NEC*

You may find Japanese word processing software that handles ruby characters, but it is a more usual feature of page layout software.

Advice to Developers

This section presents my personal recommendation on the purchase of Japanese publishing hardware and software, and describes of some of the latest font technology being developed by Adobe Systems.

Obtaining a Japanese Publishing System

After reading the material in this chapter, you should be well convinced that using outline fonts for Japanese output is the best choice for high-quality output. Just a few years ago you would need to spend several tens of thousands of dollars to produce high-quality Japanese output. Believe it or not, you can now purchase an entire hardware and software system for producing high-quality Japanese text for just under $10,000 (U.S.). The actual price may fluctuate depending on how many Japanese typefaces you need and other factors (for example, you may already own some of the hardware or software). My recommendations for a basic Japanese publishing system are listed in Table 6-13.

Table 6-13: Japanese Publishing System Hardware and Software Recommendations

Hardware/Software	Description	Estimated Cost
Printer	600-dpi PostScript Level 2	$ 2,000
Japanese typefaces	Gothic and mincho in text and display weights	$ 2,500
Roman typefaces	Adobe Type on Call with typeface purchases	$ 1,000
CPU	Macintosh computer (4MB RAM/80MB HD)	$ 1,000
Font rendering software	ATM-J (Adobe Systems)	$ 300
Japanese operating system	System 7.1 and Japanese Language Kit (Apple)	$ 300
Japanese layout software	Aldus PageMaker-J (Aldus)	$ 1,000
Japanese word processor	Nisus (Nisus Software)	$ 300
Japanese graphics software	Adobe Illustrator-J (Adobe Systems)	$ 1,000

See Appendix K for sources of these products. MacSTATION in Japan and Qualitas Trading Company in the U.S. distribute most of the software on this list. The hardware is not specific to Japanese processing.

If you cannot fit even the most basic outline font software into your budget, there are, fortunately, sources for bitmapped fonts, many of them freely obtainable from anonymous FTP sites. Japanese operating systems usually provide a basic set of Japanese fonts. Some, like KanjiTalk 7.1 (Macintosh), even come with Japanese outline fonts.

Software Recommendations

You may be wondering which outline font format to use: PostScript or TrueType. Most of what I covered focused on PostScript fonts. I suggest working with PostScript fonts, and there are a number of reasons for this. First, Adobe Systems' whole corporate direction lies in the further development of the PostScript language and its supported font formats, so by using PostScript you are likely to be using more advanced font technologies much sooner—companies that develop TrueType fonts often make their livelihood in other ways, so they may not be as committed to advancing the technology. Second, most printing bureaus accept only documents formatted using PostScript fonts. High-end users, who generally insist on the highest quality fonts, tend to prefer PostScript over TrueType. TrueType fonts are not without their merits, however. On Macintosh, TrueType fonts are very easy to install. Also, TrueType Japanese fonts use an excellent disk caching mechanism.

What *should* happen in the future is a merging of PostScript and TrueType technologies so that it does not matter which font format is being used—this sort of internal processing should be invisible to the casual user anyway. You have already read about such an example—the Type 42 font format that provides a PostScript wrapper for TrueType fonts. Both font technologies, hopefully, will have equal footing in all major platforms. This is rapidly turning into a reality, at least on the Macintosh platform. As an example, Apple Computer is about to add Adobe Type 1 font rendering support to its operating system.

Advanced Typeface Technologies

In closing this chapter, I would like to briefly mention four new typeface technologies recently announced or released by Adobe Systems. You will notice that some of these technologies build on others.

Multiple Master Typefaces

Multiple Master technology is an extension to the Type 1 Font Format described earlier in this chapter. This technology allows for the dynamic *interpolation* of a typeface's attributes, such as width, weight, optical size, and style. Multiple Master fonts are a big design effort, and require that many master outlines be made for each character. Just how many master outlines depends on the number of design axes. Table 6-14 illustrates the relationship between design axes and master outlines.

Table 6-14: Multiple Master Design Axes and Number of Corresponding Master Outlines

Number of Design Axes	Number of Master Outlines
1	2
2	4
3	8
4	16

These master outlines are interpolated to produce a particular font instance. Think of a single axis where one end contains a light version of a character, and the other end contains a bold version of the same character. Now traverse along the axis. The closer you get to the end containing the bold version, the bolder the character becomes. Now imagine doing this with four axes! Let's take a look at a two-axis Multiple Master character. Table 6-15 illustrates the four master designs of the letter "A." The two axes are for weight and width.

Table 6-15: Sample Character for a Two-axis Multiple Master Font

	Condensed	Extended
Light	A	A
Bold	**A**	**A**

The number of axes relates to the number of dimensions. For example, a typeface with a single design axis is represented by a straight line, and a line needs two points to be defined. Extend this all the way up to four design axes, at which time you get a hypercube (four dimensions). Needless to say, designing a Multiple Master font is a great task, but is possible. For those of you who are so inclined, the latest version of Fontographer by Altsys allows you to create Multiple Master fonts.

These techniques can also be applied to a Japanese font. Table 6-16 illustrates several intermediate instances of a kanji from a single-axis Multiple Master font—the axis is for weight. The two master designs are located at each extreme.

Table 6-16: Sample Kanji for a One-axis Multiple Master Font With Interpolation

Light	⇔	Bold

京 京 京 京 京 京 京 京 京 京 京

Unfortunately, there are no Multiple Master Japanese fonts available as of this writing. Design of a Japanese font is itself a large project—making a Multiple Master Japanese font is much more work!

SuperATM

SuperATM is an extension to ATM, and makes use of the Multiple Master technology described above. Well, to be a bit more clear, SuperATM is font substitution technology. So, you may ask, what problem does SuperATM attempt to solve? Consider a case in which someone gives you a document, but you do not have the typefaces which were used to create it. What usually happens is that the computer substitutes Courier, a mono-spaced font (this is Courier) which totally destroys the layout and line breaks of the document. SuperATM solves this problem by using Multiple Master technology to gener-ate typefaces with identical metrics, but is otherwise very close to those used in the document. SuperATM uses two generic Multiple Master fonts to accomplish this feat: one is a serif font, and the other is sans serif. So how are SuperATM and Multiple Master different? When you select a different weight, width, optical size, or even style for a Multiple Master font, the interpolation ratios are applied to every character in the type-face. In the case of SuperATM, however, the matching of metrics is done at the character, not typeface, level. This means that every character in a substituted font may have a unique interpolation ratio. SuperATM uses a database of metrics information to accom-plish this.

Adobe Acrobat

The primary goal of Adobe Acrobat is to achieve document portability (you may have heard about it under its code name *Carousel* while it was under development). This is more or less the same as information interchange, but carried a step further. This further step is to preserve the *look-and-feel* of a document across platforms. This includes the typefaces (font substitution technology is key here), graphics, and even color. No longer will you need the application that created the document, and no longer will Courier be used to replaced missing fonts. You may have guessed that Adobe Acrobat uses SuperATM technology to accomplish part of its goal.

Adobe Acrobat works by interpreting a PostScript file—these can come from a variety of sources. Adobe Acrobat then outputs a new file that conforms to PDF specifications (PDF stands for Portable Document Format). PDF files contain only seven-bit ASCII characters, so they are easily transported to different platforms. Acrobat Distiller is the program that converts PostScript files to PDF files. Acrobat Reader, which will be available for plat-forms such as Macintosh, UNIX, MS-DOS, and so on, is used to view PDF files.

The PDF specifications are available in the book entitled *Portable Document Format Reference Manual*, written by Tim Bienz and Richard Cohen and published by Addison-Wesley. An excellent guide to using Adobe Acrobat is *Beyond Paper: the official guide to Adobe Acrobat*, written by Patrick Ames and published by Adobe Press. See the Bibliog-raphy for more information.

Multiple Master, SuperATM, and Adobe Acrobat technologies do not apply to Japanese fonts at this time, but the next two font technologies do.

Adobe Type Composer

Adobe Type Composer is software that allows you to rearrange the characters of Japanese typefaces, and also let's you add new characters to the same—PostScript Japanese typefaces, that is. Adobe Type Composer has three basic functions:

- Add new characters to an existing Japanese typeface in the user-defined character range

- Substitute characters from one Japanese typeface for another Japanese typeface

- Change the baseline for proportional Roman fonts

Here is what each of these functions can do for you. First, you can add new characters, up to a maximum of 2,256 (this is composed of 12 rows of 188 characters each), to existing PostScript Japanese fonts. You can either create or purchase additional characters, and add them to encoded positions of a font. Second, you can substitute the kana characters or some select symbols with another of a different style. Since kana characters constitute over 70 percent of typical Japanese text, you can dramatically change the look-and-feel simply by using different kana characters. This is an inexpensive way to add more functionality to a smaller Japanese type library. Let's look at some Japanese text. The block on the left is set in a single Japanese typeface, whereas the block on the right uses a different typeface for the kana.

HeiseiMin-W3	**HeiseiMin-W3 and Jun101-Light**
普通の和文フォントは明朝体とゴシック体ですが、スペシャルなフォントもあります。例えば、丸ゴシック体、楷書体、毛筆体、および教科書体というフォントに人気があります。	普通の和文フォントは明朝体とゴシック体ですが、スペシャルなフォントもあります。例えば、丸ゴシック体、楷書体、毛筆体、および教科書体というフォントに人気があります。

See what I mean? The abundance of kana clearly allows you to change the look-and-feel of Japanese texts. Of course, this mixing of typefaces can be performed by most word processing software simply by selecting the kana and changing them to another font. But what about software, such as text editors, that allow only a single font selection per document? That is an instance when this functionality is crucial.

Adobe Type Composer makes it more feasible for font manufacturers (and individual designers) to produce kana-only fonts for mixing with kanji from a different typeface.

Adobe Type Composer software currently rearranges only the `83pv-RKSJ-H` character set and encoding, which is used on the Macintosh platform. This means that the user-defined character area pertains only to Shift-JIS (RKSJ) encoded fonts.

CID-keyed Fonts

CID-keyed fonts are the latest font technology announced by Adobe Systems. CID stands for Character ID, and is a new character and glyph access type.

There are two components to a CID-keyed font: a file that contains the outline descriptions along with other data necessary to properly render them (such as hint information), and a set of CMap (character map) files that are used to establish code to CID mappings, and to use CIDs to index into the file containing the outline descriptions.

The file that contains the outline descriptions assigns a unique character ID (CID) for every character in the character set. This character ID is independent of any encoding. Table 6-17 provides an example of a few character IDs along with a graphic representation of the characters that are associated with them.

Table 6-17: Character IDs and Their Graphic Representations

CID	Character
1	(space)
...	(*thousands of character IDs omitted*)
7474	堯
7475	槇
7476	遙
7477	瑤
...	(*hundreds of character IDs omitted*)
8284	凜
8285	熙

The CMap files contain information that associates encoded values with character IDs. In many cases, an encoding range is associated with a character ID range. The following are example lines taken from an imaginary CMap file that uses JIS encoding:

```
100 begincidrange
... (98 CID ranges omitted)
<7421> <7424> 7474
<7425> <7426> 8284
endcidrange
```

Note how the encoding ranges are associated with a range of character IDs. Here is how it works: the encoding range is specified by two encoded values, one for each end of the encoding range. In the case above, the two ranges are 0x7421 to 0x7424 and 0x7425 to 0x7426. The character ID associated with each range indicates the starting point from which encoded positions are associated with character IDs. For example, the two ranges listed above will make the associations between encoded values and character IDs, as listed in Table 6-18.

Table 6-18: Encoded Values Versus Character IDs

Encoded Value	Character ID
<7421>	7474
<7422>	7475
<7423>	7476
<7424>	7477
<7425>	8284
<7426>	8285

Note how two lines of a CMap file can be used to associate many characters with their character IDs. In the case of a complete row of characters, such as the range 0x3021 to 0x307E (94 characters), the following single line can be used:

```
<3021> <307E> 1125
```

This is just a taste of what the CID-keyed fonts offer. This technology will allow developers to make Japanese fonts much more easily, smaller, and more efficiently than before. CID-keyed fonts are also portable across platforms. The document entitled *Adobe CMap and CIDFont Files Specification* describes CID-keyed fonts in more detail.

Adobe Type 1 Coprocessor

The Adobe Type 1 Coprocessor (T1C) is an ASIC (Application Specific Integrated Circuit) developed by Adobe Systems for use under license by their PostScript OEMs (Original Equipment Manufacturer). This chip is essentially a hardware version of Adobe Systems' ATM renderer, which significantly accelerates the rasterization of Type 1 fonts. It was developed primarily to improve the performance of PostScript output devices that support Asian fonts by reducing the time it takes to process their complex character outline descriptions.

The first commercial products to support the Adobe Type 1 Coprocessor are Oki Electric's series of PostScript Level 2 Japanese printers: the ML800PSII LT, ML801PSII and ML801PSII+F. They were introduced to the market in January 1993.

Contact Adobe Developer Support for more information on these and other technologies being developed by Adobe Systems.

7

Japanese Information Processing Techniques

As you learned in previous chapters, Japanese character set standards have many ways in which each is unique, but that some effort was made to keep their encoding methods somewhat compatible. This becomes increasingly important when you are dealing with Japanese code and text processing on multiple platforms—not all computer systems use the identical Japanese encoding method. Shift-JIS encoding is typically used on MS-DOS-based machines, EUC encoding on UNIX-based machines, and JIS encoding for electronic transmission, such as e-mail. Faced with the difficulties of converting Japanese text between various encodings, I personally developed tools for performing such conversions.

A new aspect to programming and operating systems is the ability to use what is known as the *locale model*. The locale model is a system that predefines many attributes that are language- and culture-specific, such as the maximum number of bytes per character, date formats, time formats, currency formats, and so on. The actual attributes are located in a library or locale object file and are loaded when required. The locale model as defined by X/Open's XPG4 (*X/Open Portability Guide 4*) and IEEE's POSIX (Portable Operating System Interface) contains several categories of features: code set information, time and date formats, numeric formatting, collation information, and so on.

A locale name is divided into two parts. The first part refers to languages and code sets (En for English, ja for Japanese, and so on). The second part refers to countries (US for USA, JP for Japan, and so on). The locale ja_JP refers to Japanese as used in Japan, and would include a Japanese code set, a yen sign (¥) for the currency symbol, and so on.

The locale `ja_US` refers to Japanese as used in the U.S., but would include a dollar sign ($) for the currency symbol. For more information on the locale model, I suggest that you obtain three *X/Open CAE Specifications* books (CAE stands for *Common Applications Environment*), and *X/Open Guide: Internationalisation Guide*. See the Bibliography for more information on these books.

Another future programming trend are variables and data structures that use *wide* and *multiple-byte* characters. A wide character can be like Unicode, in which each character is defined as a 16-bit entity. A multiple-byte character is one which is represented by more than one byte. (The difference between a 16-bit character and a character represented by two eight-bit bytes is almost non-existent.) Unicode claims to use 16-bit characters since every character in its encoding can be represented by 16 bits. In the case of other encodings, such as JIS or EUC, characters are represented by one, two, or more bytes, so the concept of multiple-byte works better.

The algorithms and techniques listed in this chapter do not make use of the locale model nor wide and multiple-byte character data structures since most compilers (and programming languages, for that matter) currently do not have the ability to handle them. Until the locale model becomes more widely implemented, it may be necessary to write your own input and output mechanisms to handle issues such as representing two or more bytes as a single character.

I first discuss and list the algorithms for actual byte value conversion (this is the heart of the Japanese code conversion process). However, that is not all that is required. Next, I move on to text stream handling, which serves as the wrapper for the code conversion routines. I continue with an explanation and listing of miscellaneous algorithms, such as half- to full-width katakana conversion and automatic code detection. Finally, I wrap up this chapter with information about handling multiple bytes as a single unit for operations such as text insertion, text deletion, and text searching.

In most cases, workable C source code along with an explanation of the algorithm is provided. Feel free to use these code fragments in your own programs—that is why they are included in this book. These same functions and code fragments are used in the three Japanese code processing tools described later in this chapter. I am sure that you may have a better way to implement the code samples in this chapter. The code samples that I provide here may not be the most efficient code, but are workable. Feel free to adapt what you find here to suit your own programming style or taste. The entire source code for these algorithms are available in machine-readable form at an anonymous FTP site. See Appendix K for more details.

Code Conversion Algorithms

It is very important to understand that only the encoding methods for the national character sets are mutually compatible, and work quite well for round-trip conversion.* The corporate-defined characters and character sets include characters that do not map to anything in the national character set standards. When dealing with JIS, Shift-JIS, and EUC encodings, analytic methods can be used to perform the conversion—this involves mathematical operations that are applied equally to *every* character represented under an encoding method. This is known as *algorithmic conversion*. However, character set standards such as ISO 10646 and Unicode require mapping tables (used when a one-to-one correspondence between two encodings is not available, or when no conversion algorithm exists). This is also known as *hard-coded conversion*. Hard-coded conversion deals with every character on a case-by-case basis. Table 7-1 provides some examples of algorithmic and hard-coded conversion (for brevity, all numbers are expressed in hexadecimal notation).

Table 7-1: Algorithmic Versus Hard-coded Conversion

Character	Algorithmic (JIS to EUC)	Hard-coded (Unicode to JIS)
小	Add 0x80 to each byte (JIS 3E2E ⟹ EUC BEAE)	Unicode 5F0F maps to JIS 3E2E
林	Add 0x80 to each byte (JIS 4E53 ⟹ EUC CED3)	Unicode 6797 maps to JIS 4E53
剣	Add 0x80 to each byte (JIS 3775 ⟹ EUC B7F5)	Unicode 5263 maps to JIS 3775

Figure 7-1 illustrates this difference between algorithmic and hard-coded conversion. Note how algorithmic conversion alters every character in the same way—they are in the same relative position in the new encoding. However, hard-coded conversion introduces apparent randomness. Each character code conversion is treated as a special case.

The code conversion techniques in this section cover the three basic Japanese encoding methods: JIS, Shift-JIS, and EUC. Information on conversion to and from KUTEN is also covered.

It is best to treat the corporate encoding methods as exceptional cases. It is also best to avoid using such encoding methods and character sets if your software requires the maximum amount of flexibility and information interchange.

The following sections contain more detailed information about dealing with the conversion of these Japanese encoding methods. The first two conversion algorithms require the use of functions for maximum efficiency (at least, when writing in C). The other types of conversion use these functions or simple assignment statements.

---

*The only possible exceptions lie in user-defined characters, which do not exist in all encodings; and the JIS X 0212-1990 character set standard, which is not encoded by Shift-JIS.

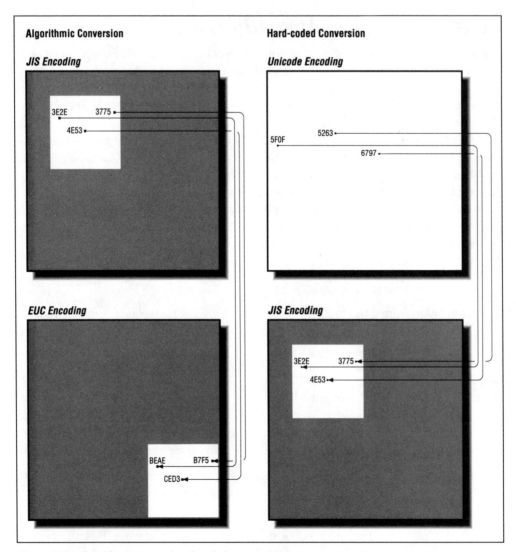

Figure 7-1: Algorithmic versus hard-coded conversion

JIS to Shift-JIS Conversion

Conversion from JIS to Shift-JIS requires the use of the following conversion algorithm (given in C code), or its equivalent. A call to this function must pass variables for both bytes to be converted, and pointers are used to return the values back to the calling statement. Here is the algorithm:

```
         void jis2sjis(int *p1, int *p2)
         {
Line 1     unsigned char c1 = *p1;
Line 2     unsigned char c2 = *p2;
Line 3     int rowOffset = c1 < 95 ? 112 : 176;
Line 4     int cellOffset = c1 % 2 ? (c2 > 95 ? 32 : 31) : 126;

Line 5     *p1 = ((c1 + 1) >> 1) + rowOffset;
Line 6     *p2 += cellOffset;
         }
```

Assuming that variables have been defined already, a typical call to this function may take the following form:

```
    jis2sjis(&p1,&p2);
```

Table 7-2 provides a step-by-step listing of the conversion process used in the above function. The target character is 漢 (from the word kanji). Its JIS code is 52-65, and the Shift-JIS code is 138-191. Changes are highlighted.

Table 7-2: JIS to Shift-JIS Conversion Example

Variable	Line 1	Line 2	Line 3	Line 4	Line 5	Line 6
c1	52	52	52	52	52	52
c2	...	65	65	65	65	65
rowOffset	...	...	112	112	112	112
cellOffset	...	...	...	126	126	126
*p1	52	52	52	52	138	138
*p2	65	65	65	65	65	191

Now for some explanation by line number:

Line 1   The variable c1 is assigned the value of the object to which *p1 points. In this case, it is the value of the first byte, namely 52.

Line 2   The variable c2 is assigned the value of the object to which *p2 points. In this case, it is the value of the second byte, namely 65.

Line 3   The variable `rowOffset` is initialized by testing a condition. This condition is whether the value of the variable `c1` is less than 95. If its value is less than 95, `rowOffset` is initialized to 112. Otherwise, it is initialized to 176. As `c1` is less than 95 in the example, `rowOffset` is initialized to 112.

Line 4   The variable `cellOffset` is initialized by testing one or more conditions. The first condition is whether the variable `c1` is odd. If this first condition is not met, `cellOffset` is initialized to 126. If this first condition is met, another condition is tested. If the variable `c2` is greater than 95, `cellOffset` will be initialized to 32; 31 otherwise. As `c1` is not odd in the example, `cellOffset` is initialized to 126.

Line 5   The object to which `*p1` points is assigned the value of adding 1 to `c1` (52 + 1 = 53), performing a right-shift, which is like dividing a number by two and throwing away the remainder (53 / 2 = 26), then finally adding `rowOffset` (26 + 112 = 138).

Line 6   The object to which `*p2` points is assigned the value of adding `cellOffset` to itself (126 + 65 = 191).

It is also very important to be able to detect the escape sequences used in JIS encoding—this is covered later. Escape sequences signal the software when to change modes. Good software should also keep track of the current n-byte-per-character mode so that redundant escape sequences can be ignored (and absorbed). Remember that Shift-JIS encoding does not use escape sequences, so you will have to make sure that they are not written to the resulting output file.

Shift-JIS to JIS Conversion

Conversion from Shift-JIS to JIS is not as simple as just reversing the above algorithm, but requires the use of the following dedicated conversion algorithm (given again in C code), or its equivalent. A call to this function must pass variables for both bytes to be converted, and pointers are used to return the values back to the calling statement.

```
        void sjis2jis(int *p1, int *p2)
        {
Line 1      unsigned char c1 = *p1;
Line 2      unsigned char c2 = *p2;
Line 3      int adjust = c2 < 159;
Line 4      int rowOffset = c1 < 160 ? 112 : 176;
Line 5      int cellOffset = adjust ? (c2 > 127 ? 32 : 31) : 126;

Line 6      *p1 = ((c1 - rowOffset) << 1) - adjust;
Line 7      *p2 -= cellOffset;
        }
```

Assuming that variables have been defined already, a typical call to this function may take the following form:

```
sjis2jis(&p1,&p2);
```

Table 7-3 provides a step-by-step table of the conversion process used in the above function. The target character is 漢 again. Its Shift-JIS code is 138-191, and its JIS code is 52-65. Changes are highlighted.

Table 7-3: Shift-JIS to JIS Conversion Example

Variable	Line 1	Line 2	Line 3	Line 4	Line 5	Line 6	Line 7
c1	138	138	138	138	138	138	138
c2	...	191	191	191	191	191	191
adjust	...	...	0	0	0	0	0
rowOffset	...	...	...	112	112	112	112
cellOffset	...	...	...	...	126	126	126
*p1	138	138	138	138	138	52	52
*p2	191	191	191	191	191	191	65

Now for some explanation by line number:

Line 1 The variable c1 is assigned the value of the object to which *p1 points. In this case, it is the value of the first byte, namely 138.

Line 2 The variable c2 is assigned the value of the object to which *p2 points. In this case, it is the value of the second byte, namely 191.

Line 3 The variable adjust is assigned the value 0 or 1, depending on the result of a test. This test checks whether the value of the variable c2 is less than 159. If the result of this test is true, then the variable adjust is assigned the value 1, otherwise it is assigned the value 0. In this example, the variable c2 is 191, which is not less than 159, so adjust is assigned the value 0.

Line 4 The variable rowOffset is initialized by testing a condition. This condition is whether the value of the variable c1 is less than 160. If its value is less than 160, rowOffset is initialized to 112. Otherwise, it is initialized to 176. As c1 is less than 160 in the example, rowOffset is initialized to 112.

Line 5 The variable cellOffset is initialized by testing one or more conditions. The first condition is whether the variable c1 is odd. If this first condition is not met, cellOffset is initialized to 126. If this first condition is met, another condition is tested. If the variable c2 is greater than 127, cellOffset will be initialized to 32; 31 otherwise. As c1 is not odd in the example, cellOffset is initialized to 126.

Line 6   The object to which `*p1` points is assigned the value of subtracting `rowOffset` from c1 (138 − 112 = 26), performing a left-shift, which is equivalent to multiplying a number by two (26 × 2 = 52), then finally subtracting `adjust` (52 − 0 = 52).

Line 7   The object to which `*p2` points is assigned the value of subtracting `cellOffset` from itself (191 − 126 = 65).

Again, it is also very important to be able to properly insert escape sequences into JIS encoded text streams. Be sure that redundant escape sequences are not written.

JIS to EUC and EUC to JIS Conversion

EUC is what I often refer to as *escape sequence-less JIS with the eighth bit set.* Some e-mail transport systems (and news readers) strip the eighth bits from e-mail messages—if one sends an EUC encoded file through such mailers, the file is considered damaged because it is transformed into escape sequence-less JIS. This should indicate to you that conversion to and from JIS and EUC is a simple matter of subtracting or adding 128 (0x80) to both bytes—this has the effect of turning the eighth bit on or off. Although the conversion of bytes is a simple process, one must properly detect and insert escape sequences for JIS encoded text.

First, we assume two variables, one for holding each of the two bytes to be converted:

```
int p1,p2;
```

I am not showing how you go about assigning the initial values to these variables—I assume here that they contain appropriate values.

Converting JIS to EUC is a simple matter of using the following two assignment statements in C:

```
p1 += 128;
p2 += 128;
```

These assignment statements have an effect of adding 128 (0x80) to the current values of the variables p1 and p2. These statements could also have been written as follows:

```
p1 = p1 + 128;
p2 = p1 + 128;
```

Both styles do the same thing. C simply has a shorthand method for doing these sort of variable assignments. There are even other shorthand methods for turning the eighth bit on or off.

Next, converting EUC to JIS requires the following two statements (or their equivalent):

```
p1 -= 128;
p2 -= 128;
```

These assignment statements have an effect of subtracting 128 (0x80) from the current value of the variables p1 and p2. That's really all there is to do.

JIS to KUTEN and KUTEN to JIS Conversion

Conversion from JIS to KUTEN is a matter of subtracting 32 (0x20) from each of the JIS bytes. Similarly, conversion from KUTEN to JIS is a matter of adding 32 (0x20) to each of the KUTEN bytes (or, more properly, adding 32 (0x20) to the KU and 32 (0x20) to the TEN). This may not be very useful for converting Japanese text since KUTEN is not typically used internally to represent characters on computer systems—there are exceptions, of course. It may often be useful to determine the KUTEN value for Japanese characters, such as for indexing into a dictionary whose entries are listed by KUTEN code.

To convert from JIS to KUTEN, use the following assignment statements:

```
p1 -= 32;
p2 -= 32;
```

The reverse conversion (KUTEN to JIS) uses the following assignment statements:

```
p1 += 32;
p2 += 32;
```

JIS and KUTEN are related more closely than you would think. They are different only in the fact that JIS is the encoded value, which does not happen to begin at value 1, and that KUTEN represents an encoding-independent way of indexing characters within the 94-by-94 character matrix. The only software system I know of that processes Japanese characters by KUTEN values is the Japanese version of TEX, a typesetting language—for other systems it is just not very efficient nor practical to process KUTEN codes internally.

Shift-JIS to EUC and EUC to Shift-JIS Conversion

There is no need to explain elaborately how one goes about converting Shift-JIS to EUC here. What you have already learned should be sufficient. You simply need to use JIS encoding as the middle ground. The only exceptional handling that is required is for half-width katakana, which require a one-byte representation in Shift-JIS, but a two-byte representation in EUC. The relationship between them is useful to know—the second byte of EUC encoded half-width katakana is the same as the Shift-JIS equivalent. Converting Shift-JIS half-width katakana to EUC is a matter of prepending a byte with the value of 142 (0x8E) before each half-width katakana byte. Likewise, converting EUC encoded half-width katakana to Shift-JIS is a simple matter of removing the first byte, namely 142 (0x8E). Note that escape sequence handling is not required in this case.

Other Code Conversion Types

What you have learned already is enough to guide you through additional code conversion types, so we haven't covered every type of code conversion. Table 7-4 details how to implement other conversions. The values used in Table 7-4 are in decimal notation.

Table 7-4: Code Conversion Matrix

From / To	JIS	Shift-JIS	EUC	KUTEN
JIS	...	`jis2sjis`	+ 128	− 32
Shift-JIS	`sjis2jis`	...	`sjis2jis` then + 128	`sjis2jis` then − 32
EUC	− 128	− 128 then `jis2sjis`	...	− 160
KUTEN	+ 32	+ 32 then `jis2sjis`	+ 160	...

`jis2sjis` refers to the JIS to Shift-JIS code conversion algorithm; likewise, `sjis2jis` refers to the Shift-JIS to JIS code conversion algorithm—both were described in detail earlier in this chapter. The numbers prefixed with either + or − mean that you must add or subtract those amounts, in decimal, from both bytes. Also note in the table how JIS is often used as the middle ground for code conversion. This does not mean such implementation is absolutely necessary, but I find it efficient to do so.

Text Stream Handling Algorithms

This section provides example code conversion algorithms for handling a Japanese text stream, and shows you how to apply them. These algorithms fall into four basic types:

- Seven- to eight-bit   (JIS to EUC or JIS to Shift-JIS)
- Eight- to seven-bit   (EUC to JIS or Shift-JIS to JIS)
- Eight- to eight-bit   (EUC to Shift-JIS or Shift-JIS to EUC)
- Seven- to seven-bit   (Between different JIS escape sequences, such as JIS C 6226-1978 to JIS X 0208-83)

Each of these text stream conversion types requires special handling, such as the proper handling of escape sequences in JIS encoding. Each algorithm is described below as workable C code.

Keeping track of the current n-byte-per-character mode is very important when dealing with JIS encoded data. Adding this support to your software serves the following purposes:

- Allows you to recognize and remove redundant escape sequences
- Ensures that lines terminate in a one-byte-per-character mode
- Ensures that the file terminates in a one-byte-per-character mode

This list may not seem very important to you now, but as you begin to encounter JIS encoded files with redundant or missing escape sequences, you will soon appreciate it.

The functions that appear in this section all use a common set of C #define statements, as follows:

```
#define NL          10
#define CR          13
#define ESC         27
#define SS2         142
#define TRUE        1
#define FALSE       0
#define SJIS1(A)    ((A >= 129 && A <= 159) || (A >= 224 && A <= 239))
#define SJIS2(A)    (A >= 64 && A <= 252)
#define HANKATA(A)  (A >= 161 && A <= 223)
#define ISEUC(A)    (A >= 161 && A <= 254)
```

In addition, they all assume that file variables have been established. The following are sufficient, and are used for the input and output streams, but you still need to write code to assign a file or text stream to these variables.

```
FILE *in;
FILE *out;
```

In addition, when the input stream is JIS encoded, it is useful to be able to absorb escape sequences, and to detect whether the n-byte-per-character mode needs to change (redundant escape sequences should be ignored, and the n-byte-per-character mode should not be changed). The following C function, called SkipESCSeq(), is used by some of the C functions described later, and performs the task of absorbing escape sequences.

```
int SkipESCSeq(FILE *in,int temp,int *intwobyte)
{
  int tempdata = *intwobyte;         /* For storing intwobyte value. */

  if (temp == '$' || temp == '(')    /* If temp is second byte of escape sequence. */
    fgetc(in);                       /* Read in, absorb third byte. */
  if (temp == 'K' || temp == '$')    /* If temp is part of a two-byte character escape
                                        sequence. */
    *intwobyte = TRUE;               /* Set intwobyte to TRUE. */
```

```
  else                           /* Else if temp is part of a one-byte character
                                    escape sequence. */
    *intwobyte = FALSE;          /* Set intwobyte to FALSE. */
  if (tempdata == *intwobyte)    /* If the n-byte-per-character mode remained the
                                    same. */
    return FALSE;                /* Return FALSE to the calling statement. */
  else                           /* Or else if the n-byte-per-character mode
                                    changed. */
    return TRUE;                 /* Return TRUE to the calling statement. */
}
```

Note that this function returns a value to the calling statement which indicates whether the n-byte-per-character mode was altered. Some calling statements may ignore this value. A call to this function takes the following form:

```
SkipESCSeq(in,temp,&intwobyte);
```

Eight- to Seven-bit Conversion

When converting from an eight-bit encoding to a seven-bit one, besides the obvious code conversion, you must take care to properly insert escape sequences into the text stream. Here you will see an example that handles Shift-JIS to JIS conversion.

A call to this function takes the following form:

```
shift2seven(in,out,incode,ki,ko);
```

The parameter ki stores a string corresponding to a two-byte character escape sequence, less the escape character. Likewise, the parameter ko stores a string corresponding to a one-byte character escape sequence, less the escape character.

Here is the C function for converting a JIS encoded text stream to Shift-JIS encoding. Notice that this function does not return any information to the calling statement—it merely reads in the data as one text stream, and outputs to another text stream.

```
void shift2seven(FILE *in,FILE *out,int incode,char ki[],char ko[])
{
  int p1;                          /* First byte. */
  int p2;                          /* Second byte. */
  int intwobyte = FALSE;           /* The n-byte-per-character mode. Initially
                                      set to one-byte-per-character mode. */

  while ((p1 = fgetc(in)) != EOF) {   /* Read one byte into p1 until end-of-file is
                                         detected. */

    if (p1 == NL || p1 == CR) {       /* If EOL is detected. */
      if (intwobyte) {                /* And if in two-byte-per-character mode. */
        intwobyte = FALSE;            /* Switch to one-byte-per-character mode. */
        fprintf(out,"%c%s",ESC,ko);   /* Print one-byte escape sequence. */
      }
```

```
        fprintf(out,"%c",p1);              /* Print EOL character. */
    }
    else if (SJIS1(p1)) {                  /* If p1 in Shift-JIS range. */
        p2 = fgetc(in);                    /* Read next byte into p2. */
        if (SJIS2(p2)) {                   /* If p2 in Shift-JIS range. */
            sjis2jis(&p1,&p2);             /* Convert to JIS. */
            if (!intwobyte) {              /* If in one-byte-per-character mode. */
                intwobyte = TRUE;          /* Change to two-byte-per-character mode. */
                fprintf(out,"%c%s",ESC,ki); /* Print two-byte escape sequence. */
            }
        }
        fprintf(out,"%c%c",p1,p2);         /* Print p1 and p2. */
    }
    else if (HANKATA(p1)) {                /* If p1 is in half-width katakana range. */
        han2zen(in,&p1,&p2,incode);        /* Convert p1 to full-width. */
        sjis2jis(&p1,&p2);                 /* Convert Shift-JIS to JIS. */
        if (!intwobyte) {                  /* If in one-byte-per-character mode. */
            intwobyte = TRUE;              /* Change to two-byte-per-character mode. */
            fprintf(out,"%c%s",ESC,ki);    /* Print two-byte escape sequence. */
        }
        fprintf(out,"%c%c",p1,p2);         /* Print p1 and p2. */
    }
    else {                                 /* Or else any other data. */
        if (intwobyte) {                   /* If in two-byte-per-character mode. */
            intwobyte = FALSE;             /* Switch to one-byte-per-character mode. */
            fprintf(out,"%c%s",ESC,ko);    /* Print one-byte escape sequence. */
        }
        fprintf(out,"%c",p1);              /* Print p1. */
    }
  }
  if (intwobyte)                           /* If the stream ends in two-byte-per-
                                              character mode. */
    fprintf(out,"%c%s",ESC,ko);            /* Print one-byte escape sequence. */
}
```

Seven- to Eight-bit Conversion

Properly handling conversion from a seven-bit code to an eight-bit encoding requires that escape sequences be recognized, handled, then absorbed. The example code provided below handles conversion of a JIS encoded text stream to Shift-JIS encoding. Another example is JIS to EUC conversion.

A call to this function takes the following form:

```
seven2shift(in,out);
```

Here is the C function for converting a JIS encoded text stream to Shift-JIS encoding. Notice that this function does not return any information to the calling statement—it merely reads in a text stream, and outputs to another text stream.

```
void seven2shift(FILE *in,FILE *out)
{
  int temp;                            /* Temporary data. */
  int p1;                              /* First byte. */
  int p2;                              /* Second byte. */
  int intwobyte = FALSE;               /* The n-byte-per-character mode.
                                          Initially set to one-byte-per-character
                                          mode. */

  while ((p1 = fgetc(in)) != EOF) {    /* Read one byte into p1 until end-of-file
                                          is detected. */
    if (p1 == ESC) {                   /* If escape character is detected. */
      temp = fgetc(in);                /* Read next byte to temp. */
      SkipESCSeq(in,temp,&intwobyte);  /* Absorb escape sequence, then change
                                          n-byte-per-character mode if necessary. */
    }
    else if (p1 == NL || p1 == CR) {   /* Or else if end-of-line is detected. */
      if (intwobyte)                   /* If in two-byte-per-character mode. */
        intwobyte = FALSE;             /* Change to one-byte-per-character
                                          mode. */

      fprintf(out,"%c",p1);            /* Print end-of-line character. */
    }
    else {                             /* If any other data. */
      if (intwobyte) {                 /* If in two-byte-per-character mode. */
        p2 = fgetc(in);                /* Read next byte into p2. */
        jis2sjis(&p1,&p2);             /* Convert from JIS to Shift-JIS. */
        fprintf(out,"%c%c",p1,p2);     /* Print p1 and p2. */
      }
      else                             /* If in one-byte-per-character mode. */
        fprintf(out,"%c",p1);          /* Print p1. */
    }
  }
}
```

Eight- to Eight-bit Conversion

Conversion between eight-bit codes, while it does not require the handling of escape sequences, does require special treatment of certain character sets, in particular, half-width katakana. As you may recall from Chapter 4, these characters are encoded with one byte in Shift-JIS encoding, but with two bytes in EUC encoding. Also included in this algorithm is the ability to convert half-width katakana to full-width versions—this is accomplished by calling the function han2zen(), which is listed later in this chapter.

This function requires two text streams (one for input and one for output), a variable for storing information on the encoding used in the input stream (this is used for converting half-width katakana to full-width, if desired), and a variable for storing a decision whether to convert half-width katakana to full-width.

A call to this function takes the following form:

```
euc2shift(in,out,incode,tofullsize);
```

The parameter `incode` stores a value that indicates the input file's encoding. This is used if the `han2zen()` function is called. The parameter `tofullsize` stores a value that indicates whether the user wants to convert half-width katakana to full-width versions.

Here is the C function for converting an EUC encoded text stream to Shift-JIS encoding. Notice that this function does not return any information to the calling statement—it merely reads in one text stream, and outputs to another text stream.

```
void euc2shift(FILE *in,FILE *out,int incode,int tofullsize)
{
  int p1;                              /* First byte. */
  int p2;                              /* Second byte. */

  while ((p1 = fgetc(in)) != EOF) {    /* Read one byte into p1 until end-of-file is
                                          detected. */
    if (ISEUC(p1)) {                   /* If p1 is in EUC range. */
      p2 = fgetc(in);                  /* Read next byte into p2. */
      if (ISEUC(p2)) {                 /* If p2 is in EUC range. */
        p1 -= 128;                     /* Convert p1 to JIS. */
        p2 -= 128;                     /* Convert p2 to JIS. */
        jis2sjis(&p1,&p2);             /* Convert JIS to Shift-JIS. */
      }
      fprintf(out,"%c%c",p1,p2);       /* Print p1 and p2. */
    }
    else if (p1 == SS2) {              /* If first byte of EUC half-width katakana is
                                          detected. */
      p2 = fgetc(in);                  /* Read next byte into p2. */
      if (HANKATA(p2)) {               /* If p2 is in half-width katakana range. */
        p1 = p2;                       /* Assign p1 the value p2. */
        if (tofullsize) {              /* If user selected half-width to full-width
                                          conversion. */
          han2zen(in,&p1,&p2,incode);  /* Convert to full-width. */
          fprintf(out,"%c%c",p1,p2);   /* Print p1 and p2. */
        }
        else {                         /* Or else if user did not select conversion. */
          fprintf(out,"%c",p1);        /* Print p1. */
        }
      }
    }
```

```
      else                               /* Else if p2 is not in half-width katakana
                                         range. */
         fprintf(out,"%c%c",p1,p2);      /* Print p1 and p2. */
    }
    else                                 /* If any other data. */
       fprintf(out,"%c",p1);             /* Print p1. */
  }
}
```

Seven- to Seven-bit Conversion

Conversion between seven-bit codes results in exchanging escape sequences for one character set to another (for instance, from JIS C 6226-1978 to JIS X 0208-1983). One must also take care to recognize and ignore redundant escape sequences, which are sometimes generated by poorly designed Japanese terminal software. It is important to eliminate these redundant escape sequences as they may cause problems if the file is damaged—redundant escape sequences severely hamper the repair process.

A call to this function takes the following form:

```
seven2seven(in,out,ki,ko);
```

The parameter ki stores a string corresponding to a two-byte character escape sequence, less the escape character. Likewise, the parameter ko stores a string corresponding to a one-byte character escape sequence, less the escape character.

Here is the C function for converting a JIS encoded text stream to another JIS encoding. Notice that this function does not return any information to the calling statement—it merely reads in one text stream, and outputs to another text stream.

```
void seven2seven(FILE *in,FILE *out,char ki[],char ko[])
{
  int temp;                         /* Temporary data. */
  int p1;                           /* First byte. */
  int p2;                           /* Second byte. */
  int change;                       /* Whether the n-byte-per-character mode
                                    has changed. */
  int intwobyte = FALSE;            /* The n-byte-per-character mode. Initially
                                    at one-byte-per-character mode. */

  while ((p1 = fgetc(in)) != EOF) { /* Read one byte to p1 until EOF detected. */
    if (p1 == ESC) {                /* If escape character is detected. */
      temp = fgetc(in);             /* Read next byte into temp. */
      change = SkipESCSeq(in,temp,&intwobyte);  /* Absorb the escape sequence,
                                    and change the n-byte-per-character mode
                                    if necessary. The variable change stores a
                                    value that indicates whether a change in
                                    the n-byte-per-character mode occurred.*/
```

```
      if ((intwobyte) && (change))        /* If in two-byte-per-character mode, and if
                                              it was a change in n-byte-per-character
                                              mode. */
          fprintf(out,"%c%s",ESC,ki);      /* Print two-byte escape sequence. */
      else if (change)                     /* Or else if in one-byte-per-character mode,
                                              and if it was a change in the n-byte-per-
                                              character mode. */
          fprintf(out,"%c%s",ESC,ko);      /* Print one-byte escape sequence. */
    }
    else if (p1 == NL || p1 == CR) {       /* Else if EOL is detected. */
      if (intwobyte) {                     /* And if in two-byte-per-character mode. */
        intwobyte = FALSE;                 /* Switch to one-byte-per-character mode. */
        fprintf(out,"%c%s",ESC,ko);        /* Print one-byte escape sequence. */
      }
      fprintf(out,"%c",p1);                /* Print EOL character. */
    }
    else {                                 /* Or else any other data. */
      if (intwobyte) {                     /* And if in two-byte-per-character mode. */
        p2 = fgetc(in);                    /* Read next byte into p2. */
        fprintf(out,"%c%c",p1,p2);         /* Print both bytes. */
      }
      else                                 /* Else if in one-byte-per-character mode. */
        fprintf(out,"%c",p1);              /* Print p1. */
    }
  }
  if (intwobyte)                           /* If stream ends in two-byte-per-character
                                              mode. */
      fprintf(out,"%c%s",ESC,ko);          /* Print one-byte escape sequence. */
}
```

Miscellaneous Algorithms

This section covers three miscellaneous algorithms that are useful, but are not directly associated with either code conversion or text stream handling, as covered in the two previous sections.

The first algorithm is for the automatic detection of the input file's encoding. Some software requires that you specify the encoding method used by the input file: many people who use Japanese code conversion utilities may not be familiar with the various Japanese encoding methods. If you do not know, all you can do is guess. The Japanese code detection algorithm examines the input file in order to determine the encoding method. This usually makes it unnecessary to specify the input file's encoding method. However, there are times when the input file's encoding may be ambiguous—the Shift-JIS and EUC encoding spaces overlap considerably, for example.

The second algorithm converts half-width katakana into their full-width counterparts. Some environments do not provide half-width katakana support, so this algorithm converts these characters into their full-width versions, which are more commonly supported. This algorithm is also quite useful as a filter for outgoing e-mail transmissions to ensure that information interchange is maintained on the receiving end.

The third and last algorithm repairs damaged JIS encoded files; that is, files which had their escape sequences stripped out by unfriendly e-mail or news reading software. I occasionally received e-mail in this damaged format, and spent a lot of time reinserting those lost escape characters. This algorithm is simply a way to automate this repair process.

The C functions described in this section use the following C #define statements in addition to those listed in the previous section:

```
#define NEW         1
#define OLD         2
#define NEC         3
#define EUC         4
#define SJIS        5
#define EUCORSJIS   6
#define ASCII       7
#define ISMARU(A)   (A >= 202 && A <= 206)
#define ISNIGORI(A) ((A >= 182 && A <= 196) || (A >= 202 && A <= 206) ||
                     (A == 179))
```

Japanese Code Detection

This algorithm is useful for automatically detecting the Japanese encoding used in a Japanese text file. This is useful when you receive Japanese text files with various encodings: it is not always obvious what encoding a given text file uses, so it is easier to let the software decide for you.

This C function requires only an input stream as a parameter, but returns a value to the calling statement indicating what Japanese code, if any, was detected. This value can either specify the Japanese encoding detected or that none was detected (or was ambiguous). If Japanese encoding was detected, possible values include JIS C 6226-1978 (also called Old-JIS), JIS X 0208-1983 (also called New-JIS), NEC Kanji (also called NEC-JIS), EUC (packed format), and Shift-JIS. It also returns special values if no Japanese encoding was detected, or if the Japanese encoding was ambiguous (Shift-JIS and EUC overlap considerably, and it is possible to encounter text streams that may be ambiguous). I use this algorithm in two of the tools described at the end of this chapter, namely jconv.c and jcode.c. A typical call to this function takes the following form:

```
DetectCodeType(in);
```

Below is a C function for detecting the Japanese encoding of an input stream. Most of the statements check encoded value ranges. The results of these checks are then used to determine whether a particular encoding has been detected in the stream. JIS encoding is easily detected by the occurrence of escape characters along with other characters that constitute a valid two-byte character escape sequence.

```
int DetectCodeType(FILE *in)
{
  int c = 0;                          /* For reading bytes. Initially set to
                                         zero for safety. */
  int whatcode = ASCII;               /* The detected code. Initially set to
                                         ASCII, which assumes no Japanese. */

  while ((whatcode == EUCORSJIS || whatcode == ASCII) && c != EOF) {
                                      /* Continue to read bytes as long as
                                         the input code is ambiguous (EUC or
                                         Shift-JIS) or no Japanese, and until
                                         end-of-file is detected. */
    if ((c = fgetc(in)) != EOF) {     /* Read one byte into c until end-of-
                                         file is detected. */
      if (c == ESC) {                 /* If c is escape character (maybe JIS
                                         code). */
        c = fgetc(in);                /* Read next byte to c. */
        if (c == '$') {               /* If c is dollar sign (possible two-byte
                                         character escape sequence). */
          c = fgetc(in);              /* Read next byte to c. */
          if (c == 'B')               /* JIS X 0208-1983. */
            whatcode = NEW;           /* New-JIS detected. */
          else if (c == '@')          /* JIS C 6226-1978. */
            whatcode = OLD;           /* Old-JIS detected. */
        }
        else if (c == 'K')            /* NEC Kanji. */
          whatcode = NEC;             /* NEC Kanji detected. */
      }
      else if ((c >= 129 && c <= 141) || (c >= 143 && c <= 159))
        whatcode = SJIS;              /* Shift-JIS detected. */
      else if (c == SS2) {            /* If c is SS2 (for EUC half-width
                                         katakana). */
        c = fgetc(in);                /* Read next byte to c. */
        if ((c >= 64 && c <= 126) || (c >= 128 && c <= 160) || (c >=
                                         224 && c <= 252))
          whatcode = SJIS;            /* Shift-JIS detected. */
        else if (c >= 161 && c <= 223)
          whatcode = EUCORSJIS;       /* Ambiguous (Shift-JIS or EUC). */
      }
      else if (c >= 161 && c <= 223) {
        c = fgetc(in);                /* Read next byte to c. */
        if (c >= 240 && c <= 254)
          whatcode = EUC;            /* EUC detected. */
```

```
       else if (c >= 161 && c <= 223)
          whatcode = EUCORSJIS;                /* Ambiguous (Shift-JIS or EUC). */
       else if (c >= 224 && c <= 239) {
          whatcode = EUCORSJIS;                /* Ambiguous (Shift-JIS or EUC). */
          while (c >= 64 && c != EOF && whatcode == EUCORSJIS) {
            if (c >= 129) {
               if (c <= 141 || (c >= 143 && c <= 159))
                  whatcode = SJIS;             /* Shift-JIS detected. */
               else if (c >= 253 && c <= 254)
                  whatcode = EUC;              /* EUC detected. */
            }
            c = fgetc(in);                     /* Read next byte to c. */
          }
       }
       else if (c <= 159)
          whatcode = SJIS;                     /* Shift-JIS detected. */
    }
    else if (c >= 240 && c <= 254)
       whatcode = EUC;                         /* EUC detected. */
    else if (c >= 224 && c <= 239) {
       c = fgetc(in);                          /* Read next byte to c. */
       if ((c >= 64 && c <= 126) || (c >= 128 && c <= 160))
          whatcode = SJIS;                     /* Shift-JIS detected. */
       else if (c >= 253 && c <= 254)
          whatcode = EUC;                      /* EUC detected. */
       else if (c >= 161 && c <= 252)
          whatcode = EUCORSJIS;                /* Ambiguous (Shift-JIS or EUC). */
    }
  }
}
 return whatcode;                              /* Return the detected code to the
                                                 calling statement. */

}
```

Half- to Full-width Katakana Conversion

It sometimes is necessary to convert half-width katakana to their full-width counterparts. This is most useful as a filter to ensure that no half-width katakana characters are included within e-mail messages. It is also useful when you need to move files from one platform to another and the new platform does not support half-width katakana characters.

There is no simple conversion algorithm that you can use to accomplish this task. In fact, such conversion requires a mapping table between half- and full-width katakana (hard-coded conversion), as well as special handling to accommodate the nigori and maru, the marks that modify kana characters. You see, these marks are encoded as a separate character in the half-width katakana character set, but in the case of full-width katakana, they are integrated with katakana characters within the same encoded character.

The following C code is a function called `han2zen()` that represents the algorithm for converting half-width katakana to their full-width counterparts, and includes proper handling for the nigori and maru marks. You saw an example call to this function earlier in this chapter.

```c
void han2zen(FILE *in,int *p1,int *p2,int incode)
{
    int tmp = *p1;                /* Value of p1. */
    int junk;                     /* For handling temporary data. */
    int maru = FALSE;             /* For handling characters with the maru mark. */
    int nigori = FALSE;           /* For handling characters with the nigori mark. */
    int mtable[][2] = {           /* Data structure for mapping half-width katakana
                                     to full-width versions in Shift-JIS encoding. */
    {129,66},{129,117},{129,118},{129,65},{129,69},{131,146},{131,64},
    {131,66},{131,68},{131,70},{131,72},{131,131},{131,133},{131,135},
    {131,98},{129,91},{131,65},{131,67},{131,69},{131,71},{131,73},
    {131,74},{131,76},{131,78},{131,80},{131,82},{131,84},{131,86},
    {131,88},{131,90},{131,92},{131,94},{131,96},{131,99},{131,101},
    {131,103},{131,105},{131,106},{131,107},{131,108},{131,109},
    {131,110},{131,113},{131,116},{131,119},{131,122},{131,125},
    {131,126},{131,128},{131,129},{131,130},{131,132},{131,134},
    {131,136},{131,137},{131,138},{131,139},{131,140},{131,141},
    {131,143},{131,147},{129,74},{129,75}
    };

    if (incode == SJIS) {         /* If input code is Shift-JIS. */
        *p2 = fgetc(in);          /* Read next byte into p2. */
        if (*p2 == 222) {         /* If p2 is 222, the nigori mark. */
            if (ISNIGORI(*p1))    /* If p1 is a character that can be modified by the
                                     nigori mark. */

                nigori = TRUE;    /* Set nigori to TRUE. */
            else                  /* If p1 is not a character that can be modified by
                                     the nigori mark. */

                ungetc(*p2,in);   /* Put p2 back into input stream. */
        }
        else if (*p2 == 223) {    /* If p2 is 223, the maru mark. */
            if (ISMARU(*p1))      /* If p1 is a character that can be modified by the
                                     nigori mark. */

                maru = TRUE;      /* Set maru to TRUE. */
            else                  /* If p1 is not a character that can be modified by
                                     the maru mark. */

                ungetc(*p2,in);   /* Put p2 back in input stream. */
        }
        else                      /* If p2 is any other value. */
            ungetc(*p2,in);       /* Put p2 back into input stream. */
```

```
}
else if (incode == EUC) {              /* If input code is EUC. */
  junk = fgetc(in);                    /* Read next byte into junk. */
  if (junk == SS2) {                   /* If the variable junk is SS2, we have another half-
                                          width katakana. */

    *p2 = fgetc(in);                   /* Read next byte into p2. */
    if (*p2 == 222) {                  /* If p2 is 222, the nigori mark. */
      if (ISNIGORI(*p1))               /* If p1 is a character that can be modified by the
                                          nigori mark. */

        nigori = TRUE;                 /* Set nigori to TRUE. */
      else {                           /* If p1 is not a character that can be modified by
                                          the nigori mark. */

        ungetc(*p2,in);               /* Put p2 back in input stream. */
        ungetc(junk,in);             /* Put junk back in input stream. */
      }
    }
    else if (*p2 == 223) {            /* If p2 is 223, the maru mark. */
      if (ISMARU(*p1))                /* If p1 is a character that can be modified by the
                                          nigori mark. */

        maru = TRUE;                  /* Set maru to TRUE. */
      else {                          /* If p1 is not a character that can be modified by
                                          the maru mark. */

        ungetc(*p2,in);             /* Put p2 back in input stream. */
        ungetc(junk,in);           /* Put junk back in input stream. */
      }
    else {                            /* If p2 is any other value. */
      ungetc(*p2,in);              /* Put p2 back in input stream. */
      ungetc(junk,in);            /* Put junk back in input stream. */
    }
  }
  else                                /* If junk is any other value. */
    ungetc(junk,in);              /* Put junk back in input stream. */
}
if (HANKATA(tmp)) {                    /* Checks to see if tmp is in half-width katakana
                                          range. */
  *p1 = mtable[tmp - 161][0];        /* Calculates first byte using mapping table. */
  *p2 = mtable[tmp - 161][1];        /* Calculates second byte using mapping table. */
}
if (nigori) {                         /* Code to transform kana into kana with nigori. */
  if ((*p2 >= 74 && *p2 <= 103) || (*p2 >= 110 && *p2 <= 122))
    (*p2)++;
  else if (*p1 == 131 && *p2 == 69)
    *p2 = 148;
}
else if (maru && *p2 >= 110 && *p2 <= 122)   /* Code to transform kana into
                                          kana with maru. */

  *p2 += 2;
}
```

JIS Encoding Repair

JIS encoded files often become damaged or corrupt from software that strips out escape characters. Some programs have a tendency to filter out control characters from files, and the escape character (0x1B), which is an essential part of JIS encoding, is a control character. Luckily, there are ways to repair corrupted JIS encoded files.

You can make a few assumptions before you proceed to repair damaged JIS encoded files. The first assumption is that the text stream begins, and also ends, in a one-byte-per-character mode. In addition, each line begins and ends in a one-byte-per-character mode. The next assumption is that the other characters that make up a complete escape sequence are still intact. These may include such strings as $@, $B, (J, and (B. Depending on the *n*-byte-per-character mode, you need to scan for different strings.

While in one-byte-per-character mode, you need only to scan for the strings $B or $@, which should signify the beginning of a two-byte-per-character mode. The chances of encountering such strings of characters while in one-byte-per-character mode are quite low (but can happen!). You need to repair such string occurrences by inserting an escape character immediately before the string that determined the context for it (in this case, either $B or $@). The current mode is then shifted to two-byte-per-character.

While in two-byte-per-character mode, you need to scan for the strings (J and (B. Also, since you are in two-byte-per-character mode, you must scan two characters, then compare them to the search strings. The two bytes that represent the strings (J and (B are within the JIS encoding space, but have no characters assigned to them. This means that you should never run into those strings other than when they are part of a damaged escape sequence. Like before, you need to insert an escape character right before the string that was found (in this case, either (J or (B). The current mode is then shifted to one-byte-per-character.

Other processing may be necessary if you reach the end of a line, but are still in a two-byte-per-character mode. You must then insert a whole escape sequence.

The following C function represents an algorithm for automatically inserting escape sequences into a damaged JIS encoded file. Note that undamaged escape sequences are also recognized by this C function. A modified version of this function is used in one of the Japanese code processing tools (jconv.c) described at the end of this chapter.

```
void repairjis(FILE *in,FILE *out)
{
  int p1;                          /* First byte. */
  int p2;                          /* Second byte. */
  int p3;                          /* Third byte. */
  int shifted_in = FALSE;          /* The n-byte-per-character mode. Initially set
                                      to one-byte-per-character mode. */
```

```
while ((p1 = getc(in)) != EOF) {      /* Read one byte into p1 until end-of-file is
                                         detected. */
  if (shifted_in) {                   /* If in two-byte-per-character mode. */
    if (p1 == ESC) {                  /* If p1 is escape character. */
      p2 = getc(in);                  /* Read next byte into p2. */
      if (p2 == '(') {                /* If p2 is (. */
        p3 = getc(in);                /* Read next byte into p3. */
        switch (p3) {                 /* Case statement for p3. */
          case 'J' :                  /* JIS-Roman. */
          case 'B' :                  /* ASCII. */
          case 'H' :                  /* False JIS-Roman. */
            shifted_in = FALSE;       /* Change to one-byte-per-character mode. */
            break;
          default :                   /* Do nothing if other value. */
            break;
        }
        fprintf(out,"%c%c%c",p1,p2,p3);   /* Print the escape sequence. */
      }
    }
    else if (p1 == '(') {             /* If p1 is (. */
      p2 = getc(in);                  /* Read next byte into p2. */
      switch (p2) {                   /* Case statement for p2. */
        case 'J' :                    /* JIS-Roman. */
        case 'B' :                    /* ASCII. */
        case 'H' :                    /* False JIS-Roman. */
          shifted_in = FALSE;         /* Change to one-byte-per-character mode. */
          fprintf(out,"%c%c%c",ESC,p1,p2);   /* Print the repaired escape
                                                sequence. */
          break;
        default :                     /* If any other value. */
          fprintf(out,"%c%c",p1,p2);  /* Print p1 and p2. */
          break;
      }
    }
    else {                            /* If any other data. */
      p2 = getc(in);                  /* Read next byte into p2. */
      fprintf(out,"%c%c",p1,p2);      /* Print p1 and p2. */
    }
  }
  else {                              /* If in one-byte-per-character mode. */
    if (p1 == ESC) {                  /* If p1 is escape character. */
      p2 = getc(in);                  /* Read next byte into p2. */
      if (p2 == '$') {                /* If p2 is a dollar sign. */
        p3 = getc(in);                /* Read next byte into p3. */
        switch (p3) {                 /* Case statement for p3. */
          case 'B' :                  /* JIS X 0208-1983. */
          case '@' :                  /* JIS C 6226-1978. */
            shifted_in = TRUE;        /* Change to two-byte-per-character mode. */
```

```
                break;
            default :                    /* Do nothing if other value. */
                break;
        }
        fprintf(out,"%c%c%c",p1,p2,p3);   /* Print the escape sequence. */
    }
}
else if (p1 == '$') {              /* If p1 is a dollar sign. */
    p2 = getc(in);                /* Read next byte into p2. */
    switch (p2) {                 /* Case statement for p2. */
        case 'B' :                /* JIS X 0208-1983. */
        case '@' :                /* JIS C 6226-1978. */
            shifted_in = TRUE;    /* Change to two-byte-per-character mode. */
            fprintf(out,"%c%c%c",ESC,p1,p2);   /* Print the repaired escape
                                                 sequence. */
            break;
        default :                 /* If any other value. */
            fprintf(out,"%c%c",p1,p2);        /* Print p1 and p2. */
            break;
    }
}
else                              /* If any other data. */
    fprintf(out,"%c",p1);        /* Print p1. */
        }
    }
}
```

Byte Versus Character Handling Issues

Most Western encoding methods have the luxury of assuming that one character can equal one byte, so inserting, deleting, and searching text becomes a simple matter of comparing one byte to another. However, this is not the case with encodings that require more than one byte to represent a single character, such as those used for representing Japanese text. Life gets much more complex! A multiple-byte character is still a *character*. Consider it as an "atomic" unit. After all, you would gawk at Western style software that split characters into four-bit units for some strange design reason. What I discuss below falls into what I would call Japanese *text* processing algorithms, because such behavior is what one would expect from programs such as text editors, word processors, and the like.

What you should learn from this section is that a multiple-byte character should *never* be broken down into its component bytes. This whole discussion points out the best reason for using fixed 16- or 32-bit representations inside your software—you deal with atomic units. The topics to follow are examples of areas in which many text processing programs fail to handle multiple-byte characters properly. There are many examples of programs that fall into this category—unless a program was specifically designed to handle multiple-byte characters, it is doubtful that multiple-byte characters are handled properly. For example, Microsoft Word (for Macintosh) is one of the most popular word processing programs ever, but fails to handle two-byte characters properly.

Character Deletion

It is quite likely that you will encounter text processing software that deletes only one byte of a two-byte character. Those that have been properly adapted to Japanese are able to detect whether the character in front of the insertion point is represented by two bytes, and subsequently deletes both bytes. This problem can be avoided if you remember to press the delete key twice when dealing with two-byte characters. If you are not careful, loss of data can result.

Let's take a closer look at this problem. Below is a sample Shift-JIS encoded Japanese text string. The first process that will be applied is the deletion of the last character. One example deletes a *character* (two bytes), and the other deletes a single *byte*. Finally, we add another character, namely 典, at the insertion point. Note how the undeleted first byte affects the interpretation of the added character (the encoded value of this added character is highlighted).

	Graphic Representation	Shift-JIS Representation			
Original String	漢字辞書	漢	字	辞	書
		8ABF	8E9A	8EAB	8F91
Correctly Deleted	漢字辞	漢	字	辞	
		8ABF	8E9A	8EAB	
Character Added	漢字辞典	漢	字	辞	典
		8ABF	8E9A	8EAB	**9354**
Incorrectly Deleted	漢字辞	漢	字	辞	
		8ABF	8E9A	8EAB	8F
Character Added	漢字辞諸T	漢	字	辞	諸　　T
		8ABF	8E9A	8EAB	8F**93**　**54**

A lack of synch occurs when the first byte of a two-byte character is left behind. Any two-byte characters that follow will be interpreted incorrectly—their first byte will be interpreted as a second byte, and their second byte will be interpreted as a first byte.

Now let's see what happens with the same character string, but this time EUC encoded:

	Graphic Representation	EUC Representation			
Original String	漢字辞書	漢	字	辞	書
		B4C1	BBFA	BCAD	BDF1
Correctly Deleted	漢字辞	漢	字	辞	
		B4C1	BBFA	BCAD	

	Graphic Representation	EUC Representation			
Character Added	漢字辞典	漢 B4C1	字 BBFA	辞 BCAD	典 **C5B5**
Incorrectly Deleted	漢字辞	漢 B4C1	字 BBFA	辞 BCAD	 BD
Character Added	漢字辞重	漢 B4C1	字 BBFA	辞 BCAD	重 BD**C5**　**B5**

This problem is fixed by keeping track of the characters at the insertion point—whether they are represented by one or more bytes. If a byte happens to be the second byte of a two-byte character, both bytes must be deleted with a single keystroke. In the case of three-byte characters (for example, characters from EUC code set 3—JIS X 0212-1990 characters), three bytes must be deleted.

Character Insertion

Inserting characters is problematic only when the insertion point (that is, the cursor) is between the two bytes that represent a two-byte character. This then splits the two-byte character, and results in data loss. This section, as you may have expected, relates to cursor movement.

Let's now look at some examples of inserting characters between the two bytes of a two-byte character. The example string is 仮名漢字, and the character と is mistakenly inserted between the two bytes of the character 名—ideally, it should be added between the two *characters* 名 and 漢. The example below is Shift-JIS encoded, and the byte values for the inserted character are highlighted.

	Graphic Representation	Shift-JIS Representation					
Original String	仮名漢字	仮 89BC	名 96BC	漢 8ABF	字 8E9A		
Correctly Inserted	仮名と漢字	仮 89BC	名 96BC	と **82C6**	漢 8ABF	字 8E9A	
Incorrectly Inserted	仮魔ﾆｼ漢字	仮 89BC	魔 96**82**	ﾆ **C6**	ｼ BC	漢 8ABF	字 8E9A

Notice how the two-byte character 名 is split right down the middle, and that unexpected characters have resulted, two of which are interpreted as half-width katakana. Now you can see why incorrect character insertion must never be allowed to happen—it leads to corruption and data loss. Integrity is retained only with proper handling of two-byte characters.

Let's look at this same example, but now EUC encoded. Notice how different characters result from incorrect insertion—an expected 名と string becomes 未半.

	Graphic Representation	EUC Representation				
Original String	仮名漢字	仮 B2BE	名 CCBE	漢 B4C1	字 BBFA	
Correctly Inserted	仮名と漢字	仮 B2BE	名 CCBE	と **A4C8**	漢 B4C1	字 BBFA
Incorrectly Inserted	仮未半漢字	仮 B2BE	未 CC**A4**	半 **C8**BE	漢 B4C1	字 BBFA

The solution to this problem is simply to have the cursor move one or more bytes—the number of bytes to move corresponds to the number of bytes used to represent the current character.

Character Searching

grep is one of the most commonly used utilities on UNIX—short for *Global Regular Expression Printer.** **grep** performs a search based on pattern matching. The standard UNIX version of **grep**, unfortunately, does not recognize two bytes as a single unit. Some versions of UNIX, such as AIX, include versions of **grep** that recognize multiple-byte characters.

So, you may ask, what problem does this cause? Well, take, for instance, a case when you are searching for the kanji 剣 in a large Japanese file. Assuming Shift-JIS encoding, you may encounter matches in quite unexpected places. In fact, some lines for which a match is reported may not even contain the kanji 剣 because searching is normally done one byte at a time. This means that one byte is compared to another. In the case of a search pattern that contains two-byte characters, the following conditions must be met:

- Two bytes of the search string must be compared with two bytes in the document being searched.

- The current index point into the document being searched must advance either one or two bytes depending on whether the character at that index point is represented by one or two bytes. This simply means that the index point must advance one character, which is not always one byte.

The current index into a file must either advance one or two bytes depending on whether the current position is for a one- or two-byte character. This means that matches can be

---

*Or **grep** may be short for something else, depending on the source of information—jokingly, one source even suggested that it represents the first letters of its authors' last names, namely Gregior, Ritchie, Ebersole, and Pike.

made with the second byte of one two-byte character plus the first byte of the next. This, of course, produces totally undesirable results. Let's look at an example using the character 剣 as the search string in a Shift-JIS encoded file (the codes of matches are highlighted):

	Characters	Shift-JIS Codes
Search String	剣	剣 8C95
Correct Match	剣道	剣 道 **8C95** 93B9
Incorrect Match	白血病	白 血 病 9492 8C**8C** **95**61

Note how the example of a bad match spans two characters, namely the second byte of one and the first byte of the next character. The bad match was made by treating every byte as a single character—the one byte equals one character barrier must be overcome in order to handle Japanese text properly.

I created a solution: a simple **grep**-like tool that handles two-byte characters properly. This tool is able to detect whether the current character in the text to be searched is represented by one or two bytes, and advances the insertion point one or two bytes. This program is called `jgrep.c`, and is available (along with its source code) through anonymous FTP. This tool, in its current form, allows for only literal text searching—no support for regular expressions (yet). I consider it to be still in the development stage.

Character Sorting

You can sort English text in a multitude of ways—low to high, high to low, dictionary, numeric—the possibilities are almost endless. Japanese has even more possibilities for sorting text. In English, despite all the possible variations, there are really only two basic ways to sort text. The first is case-insensitive, namely that lowercase and uppercase Roman characters are sorted as though they were the same. The other is an ASCII sort which sorts by increasing value of the byte which represents each character, which has an effect of separating lowercase and uppercase Roman characters whereby uppercase is sorted first.

Japanese has the equivalent of an ASCII sort, namely, characters are ordered by the value of the byte used to represent them. This is often called a *JIS sort*. In Chapter 3 you learned that JIS Level 1 kanji are arranged by pronunciation and that JIS Level 2 kanji are arranged by radical then total number of strokes. Consequently, a JIS sort produces a list of characters sorted in that way. And although they represent the same set of sounds, hiragana and katakana are separated by a JIS sort.

The *iroha* order is another collation sequence in addition to the 50 Sounds order. The name of this ordering comes from its first three sounds, namely *i*, *ro*, and *ha*, the Japanese analogy to *a*, *b*, and *c*. The iroha collation sequence is not very common, but does exist.

Other types of sorts include by radical, by total number of strokes, and by pronunciation. Yes, these were listed above in the JIS sort, but I am referring to the coverage of *all* kanji. For example, a sort by radical should include JIS Level 1 kanji, too. The implementation of these various sorting methods is limited to the database of information you have. Hiragana and katakana can also be sorted together just like a case-insensitive sort of Roman characters, but some dictionaries sort hiragana separate from katakana.

Line Breaking

Many text processing programs allow users to break long lines into shorter ones, usually by specifying a maximum number of columns per line. As you can expect, breaking a line between the bytes of a two-byte character can result in a loss of information, and ends up corrupting surrounding characters.

Let's look at what may happen when JIS, Shift-JIS, and EUC strings are broken into two lines. In the example below a line break is inserted between the two bytes that represent the katakana character サ. Note how that character is apparently lost, and how some characters after the line break become scrambled. Some Japanese telecommunications software programs (such as ASLTelnet) insert their own one-byte character escape sequences at the end of each line to ensure that no errors take place. This means when a line is broken, the software automatically inserts a one-byte character escape sequence. However, when the line is broken in this fashion, the lack of an additional two-byte character escape sequence causes the line following to be interpreted as one-byte-per-character. Here is the original string and one example of JIS encoded text:

Original String	カキクケコサシスセソタチツテト
Broken JIS	カキクケコ
	5%7%9%;%=%?%A%D%F%H

Here is another example of JIS encoding. This time the software (in this case, NinjaTerm) does not automatically insert one-byte character escape sequences at the ends of lines. The second byte of the split character サ is now treated as the first byte for the following two-byte character, which causes a lack of synch. Also note how the following line does not start on the left margin.

Original String	カキクケコサシスセソタチツテト
Broken JIS	カキクケコ
	汽彎好札愁織船張膳

Here is a Shift-JIS example. This time there is no lack of synch. The only character that is lost is the one that was split. The first byte, since it is in the eight-bit range, is invisible, and since the second byte (at least for this particular character) falls into the seven-bit range, it is not treated as the first byte of a two-byte character.

Original String	カキクケコサシスセソタチツテト
Broken Shift-JIS	カキクケコ
	ₜシスセソタチツテト

Finally, here is an EUC example. You should see the lack of synch problem here again. The first byte is invisible, and the second byte is now treated as the first byte of a two-byte character.

Original String	カキクケコサシスセソタチツテト
Broken EUC	カキクケコ
	汽彎好札愁織船張膳

As you can see from these examples, this problem varies in intensity depending on the encoding method, and even on the software you are using (compare the two types of output you get for JIS encoding, using different software). Some encodings require slightly more overhead than simplistically treating two-byte characters as an inseparable unit. For example, when dealing with JIS encoding, you must also remember to insert and perhaps even delete escape sequences.

Character Attribute Detection

A useful function often supported in Japanese text processing programs (or for that matter in most text processing systems) is the ability to determine the attributes of characters within a file. For example, it is often convenient to obtain a listing of the numbers of kanji, kana, and other characters in a file. One can even break those categories down further, such as katakana and hiragana, JIS Levels 1 and 2 kanji, etc.

The C programming language has a useful macro facility which allows programmers to specify simple commands that can be used often within a program. Macros are similar in concept to functions, but require less work (but more thought).

As an example, several C macro definitions for detecting the attributes of Japanese characters are provided. They all assume KUTEN values as input. How you implement this depends on the purpose of the program you are writing. You simply need to convert the

Japanese code of each character to KUTEN values right before executing each of these macros. The macros are as follows:

```
#define ISLEVEL1(A)        (A >= 16 && A <= 47)
#define ISLEVEL2(A)        (A >= 48 && A <= 84)
#define ISKANJI(A)         (ISLEVEL1(A) || ISLEVEL2(A))
#define ISHIRAGANA(A)      (A == 4)
#define ISKATAKANA(A)      (A == 5)
#define ISKANA(A)          (ISKATAKANA(A) || ISHIRAGANA(A))
#define ISKANAKANJI(A)     (ISKANA(A) || ISKANJI(A))
```

Seasoned C programmers should be able to recognize what each of these macro definitions does.

The first two macros:

```
#define ISLEVEL1(A)        (A >= 16 && A <= 47)
#define ISLEVEL2(A)        (A >= 48 && A <= 84)
```

use the first byte (row) value to determine if a character is in JIS Level 1 or 2 kanji. You may recall that in JIS X 0208-1990 the kanji are contained in two ranges—rows 16 through 47, and rows 47 through 84—exactly what the macro checks for.

The next macro:

```
#define ISKANJI(A)         (ISLEVEL1(A) || ISLEVEL2(A))
```

combines the first two macros. Quite often you won't care whether a kanji is in JIS Level 1 or 2 kanji, but rather if it is a kanji at all. Again, it is sufficient to use only the first byte as input to this macro.

The next three macros:

```
#define ISHIRAGANA(A)      (A == 4)
#define ISKATAKANA(A)      (A == 5)
#define ISKANA(A)          (ISHIRAGANA(A) || ISKATAKANA(A))
```

do the same as the first three macros, but with kana. The first two detect whether a character is a hiragana or katakana, and the last one combines them. Like before, only the first byte is used for this.

The last macro:

```
#define ISKANAKANJI(A)     (ISKANA(A) || ISKANJI(A))
```

checks for a larger set of characters, kana and kanji.

Writing such macro definitions can be carried to almost any extreme, and is a very useful tool in the hands of a programmer. Of course, these macros could have been implemented as C functions, or written in yet other programming languages.

Japanese Code Processing Tools

Below you will find brief descriptions of and the help page for three Japanese code processing tools I have written and maintained over a period of several years: jconv.c, jchar.c, and jcode.c. This section also includes some context in which these tools may be useful to your work. The latest source code for these tools are available through anonymous FTP (see Appendix K for more details).

These tools are written in ANSI C, and they are portable on compilers that conform to this standard. This means that the source code, without any modifications, should compile on multiple platforms, and this has been confirmed by their many users. The same source code was written for compilation on the Macintosh using THINK C Version 5.0 or later, and Macintosh ports of these tools, called JConv, JChar, and JCode, are also available through anonymous FTP. Each of these tools displays its help page by using the -h option on the command line. These same help pages are listed below, and are given to show the full potential of the tools' functionality.

Japanese Code Conversion

The most basic Japanese text processing requirement is a tool that converts Japanese text from one encoding to another. This is most important when moving Japanese text from one platform to another, and when receiving e-mail messages or news articles. All in all, such a tool is a general workhorse tool; I use it often.

This tool, called jconv.c, implements the routines for converting from one Japanese encoding to another. The main features of jconv.c are that it:

- Supports the JIS X 0208-1990 character set

- Handles JIS, Shift-JIS, and EUC encodings

- Lists code specifications for Japanese encoding methods

- Filters half-width katakana by converting them to their full-width counterparts

- Repairs damaged JIS encoded files

- Can pre-damage JIS encoded files (so they can be restored later with the repair option)

- Lets one check files for their encoding without actually performing any conversion

- Includes a verbose mode option that displays more information about what the tool is doing

Many of the algorithms and routines listed and explained earlier in this chapter are used in this code processing tool. I plan to modify this tool in the future, so you can expect even more functionality later. Future enhancements may include the ability to handle additional encoding methods or character sets.

Here is this tool's help page:

```
** jconv v3.0 (July 1, 1993) **

Written by Ken R. Lunde, Adobe Systems Incorporated
lunde@mv.us.adobe.com

Usage: jconv [-options] [infile] [outfile]
```

Tool description: This tool is a utility for converting the Japanese code of textfiles, and supports Shift-JIS, EUC, New-JIS, Old-JIS, and NEC-JIS for both input and output. It can also display a file's input code, repair damaged Old- or New-JIS files, and display the specifications for any of the handled codes.

Options include:

-c	Displays the detected input code, then exits -- the types reported include EUC, Shift-JIS, New-JIS, Old-JIS, NEC-JIS, ASCII (no Japanese), ambiguous (Shift-JIS or EUC), and unknown (note that this option overrides "-iCODE")
-f	Converts half-width katakana to their full-width equivalents (this option is forced when output code is New-, Old-, or NEC-JIS)
-h	Displays this help page, then exits
-iCODE	Forces input code to be recognized as CODE
-o[CODE]	Output code set to CODE (default is Shift-JIS if this option is not specified, or if the specified CODE is invalid)
-r[CODE]	Repairs damaged New- and Old-JIS encoded files by restoring lost escape characters, then converts it to the CODE specified (the default is to convert the file to New-JIS if CODE is not specified -- cannot be used in conjunction with "-s")
-s[f]	Removes escape characters from valid escape sequences of New- and Old-JIS encoded files -- "f" will force all escape characters to be removed (default extension is .rem -- cannot be used in conjunction with "-r")
-t[CODE]	Prints a table listing the specifications for the specified CODE, then exits (all code tables will be displayed if CODE is not specified, or if CODE is invalid)
-v	Verbose mode -- displays information such as automatically generated file names, detected input code, number of escape characters restored/removed, etc.

NOTE: CODE has five possible values (and default outfile extensions):
      "e" = EUC (.euc); "s" = Shift-JIS (.sjs); "j" = New-JIS (.new);
      "o" = Old-JIS (.old); and "n" = NEC-JIS (.nec)

Generating Japanese Character Sets

Another general Japanese code processing need is the ability to generate a listing of Japanese character sets. Generating a file that contains a complete electronically encoded Japanese character set can be done most effectively with the use of loops found in most programming languages. After all, who wants to manually input several thousand characters? Generating the electronically encoded character sets is trivial, as loops do all the work for you. The problem is when you want to generate a list containing only the characters in a non-electronic character set, such as Jôyô Kanji. There is no algorithm you can use since the necessary kanji are scattered throughout JIS Level 1 kanji of JIS X 0208-1990. The only way to handle such a task is to key them in manually, and then to be sure to save your work!

I have written a tool, called `jchar.c`, that generates these problematic character sets (and non-problematic ones, too!). Listings of these non-electronic character set standards, generated by `jchar.c`, can be found in Appendixes D through F.

The tool `jchar.c` has many features and options that you will find useful at some time or another—the main ones are that it:

- Supports the JIS X 0208-1990, ASCII/JIS-Roman, half-width katakana, Jôyô Kanji, Gakushû Kanji, and Jinmei-yô Kanji character sets

- Outputs data in JIS, Shift-JIS, or EUC encoding

- Wraps output lines at *n* columns

- Suppresses header information

Algorithms used in this tool are primarily loops (for the electronically encoded character sets) and data structures (for the non-electronically encoded character sets). The use of encoding range bounds are used, though, to generate the whole character encoding space, and not just the cells that contain characters. For example, when choosing to generate the JIS X 0208-1990 list, it does not generate 6,879 code positions, but 8,836 code positions, which is what you get from a complete 94-row-by-94-cell matrix.

Here is this tool's help page:

```
** jchar v3.0 (July 1, 1993) **

Written by Ken R. Lunde, Adobe Systems Incorporated
lunde@mv.us.adobe.com

Usage: jchar [-options] [outfile]

Tool description: This tool is a utility for generating various Japanese
character sets in any code. This includes all the characters specified in
JIS X 0208-1990, half-width katakana (EUC and Shift-JIS output only), the
```

```
94 printable ASCII/JIS-Roman characters, the 1945 Joyo Kanji, the 284
Jinmei-yo Kanji, and the 1006 Gakushu Kanji.

Options include:

  -a         Builds an ASCII/JIS-Roman list (printable characters only)
  -g         Builds the Gakushu Kanji list
  -h         Displays this help page, then exits
  -j         Builds the Joyo Kanji list
  -k         Builds the JIS X 0208-1990 list
  -o[CODE]   Builds lists in CODE format (default is Shift-JIS if this option
             is not specified, if CODE is not specified, or if CODE is invalid)
  -p         Builds the Jinmei-yo Kanji list
  -s         Suppresses headers and row number information
  -w[NUM]    Wraps output lines at NUM columns (if NUM is not specified, 78
             is used as the default value)

NOTE: CODE has six possible values: "e" = EUC; "s" = Shift-JIS;
      "j" = New-JIS; "o" = Old-JIS; and "n" = NEC-JIS
```

Examining Japanese Text Files

Every programmer (or even non-programmer types with enough interest) may occasionally like to take a closer peek at Japanese codes, and how they relate to each other. The non-Japanese analogy is a hex dump of a file. However, since most Japanese characters consist of two bytes, a normal hex dump may not be very useful. Such a tool designed for use with Japanese text should treat two-byte characters as single entities. It should also make use of all the routines for converting between the various encoding methods, but instead of converting characters, it lists each character along with its associated value in a variety of encodings.

A tool I wrote, called jcode.c, fills this gap, and offers two basic functions. It:

• Accepts actual encoded Japanese characters in a variety of encodings, then performs the equivalent of a hex dump

• Accepts four- and five-digit codes, one per line, that represent the encoded value of a character (for instance, JIS 0x3021 for the kanji 亜), then performs the equivalent of a hex dump.

Using a hex dump as the non-Japanese analogy to this tool is not entirely correct. The tool jcode.c also allows you to perform an octal or decimal dump, depending on what notation you want (the default is to use hexadecimal notation).

Now it's time to see some sample output of `jcode.c`. First, you will see how this tool can handle actual Japanese text. Note that the file cannot be of a mixed encoding (that is, Shift-JIS plus EUC, and so on). These four characters are the input to `jcode.c`:

かな漢字

They are pronounced *ka na kan ji* (meaning "kana [and] kanji"). The resulting output is as follows:

Character	Shift-JIS	EUC	JIS	ASCII	KUTEN
か	82-A9	A4-AB	24-2B	$+	04-11
な	82-C8	A4-CA	24-4A	$J	04-42
漢	8A-BF	B4-C1	34-41	4A	20-33
字	8E-9A	BB-FA	3B-7A	;z	27-90

Next, you will see how this tool can handle four- and five-digit codes. To automatically detect all the main encodings, you must add a prefix before EUC and KUTEN values, and require hexadecimal notation for JIS, Shift-JIS, and EUC encodings. Here is the input I used:

```
82A9
xa4cA
3441
k2790
```

The first line is a hexadecimal Shift-JIS code, the second line is a hexadecimal EUC code (note the "x" prefix), the third line is a hexadecimal JIS code, and the last line is a KUTEN code (note the "k" prefix). Now for the output:

Character	Shift-JIS	EUC	JIS	ASCII	KUTEN
か	**82-A9**	A4-AB	24-2B	$+	04-11
な	82-C8	**A4-CA**	24-4A	$J	04-42
漢	8A-BF	B4-C1	**34-41**	4A	20-33
字	8E-9A	BB-FA	3B-7A	;z	**27-90**

As you can see, a different set of input produced the same output. Also note how the handling of the four- and five-digit codes is not case-sensitive, and how each line can use a different encoding.

This tool has other options, most of which allow you to better format the output. It:

- Supports octal, decimal, and hexadecimal notations for output (the default is hexadecimal)
- Pads columns with spaces or a tab (the default is padding with spaces)
- Shows control characters

- Includes a verbose mode that provides more information, such as which Japanese code was detected

This tool, as you might expect, uses many of the code conversion algorithms and routines described earlier in this chapter. The remainder is just fancy formatting of the output.

Now for its help page:

```
** jcode v3.0 (July 1, 1993) **

Written by Ken R. Lunde, Adobe Systems Incorporated
lunde@mv.us.adobe.com

Usage: jcode [-options] [infile] [outfile]

Tool description: This tool is a utility for displaying the electronic values
of Japanese characters within textfiles, and supports Shift-JIS, EUC, New-JIS,
Old-JIS, and NEC-JIS for both input and output.
Options include:

  -c[DATA]      Reads codes, one per line, rather than characters as input --
                if DATA is specified, only that code is treated, then exits
                (KUTEN codes must be prefixed with "k," and EUC codes with
                "x" -- EUC, JIS, and Shift-JIS codes must be hexadecimal)
  -h            Displays this help page, then exits
  -iCODE        Forces input code to be recognized as CODE
  -n[NOTATION]  Output notation set to NOTATION (default is hexadecimal if this
                option is not specified, if NOTATION is not specified, or if
                the specified NOTATION is invalid)
  -o[CODE]      Output code set to CODE (default is Shift-JIS if this option
                is not specified, if CODE is not specified, or if the
                specified CODE is invalid)
  -p[CHOICE]    Pads the columns with CHOICE whereby CHOICE can be either "t"
                for tabs or "s" for spaces (default is spaces if this option
                is not specified, if CHOICE is not specified, or if the
                specified CHOICE is invalid)
  -s            Shows control characters (except escape sequences)
  -v            Verbose mode -- displays information such as automatically
                generated file names, detected input code, etc.

NOTE: CODE has five possible values:
      "e" = EUC; "s" = Shift-JIS; "j" = New-JIS; "o" = Old-JIS;
      and "n" = NEC-JIS

NOTE: NOTATION has three possible values:
      "o" = octal; "d" = decimal; and "h" = hexadecimal
```

8

Japanese Text Processing Tools

The Japanese code processing tools described at the end of Chapter 7 are relatively specialized programmers' tools I developed. In this chapter I discuss computer system software components others have developed, which, when properly integrated and configured, provide the ability to create, format, read, print, send, or receive Japanese text electronically. Figure 8-1 illustrates how these Japanese text processing tools interact with each other.

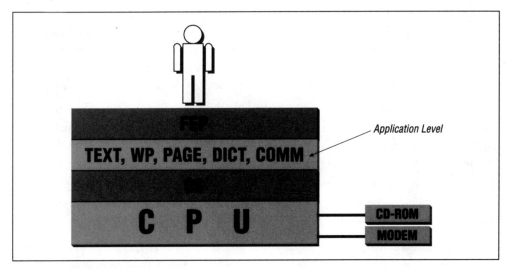

Figure 8-1: The interaction of Japanese text processing tools

The goal of this chapter is to give you a basic knowledge of the types of Japanese text processing tools available, and what capabilities to expect from each. The capabilities of these types of tools range from the most basic to very complex functions. With all of their differences, they share one common feature: they all are multiple-byte aware. That is, they treat multiple-byte characters as a single unit.

The software listed as examples consists of FreeWare, ShareWare, and commercial software. Consult Appendix K for contact information for sources. This chapter will provide you with a basic working knowledge of what functions to expect, but stops short of providing *all* the information about this software. If you are interested in a particular package, I encourage you to obtain more detailed information on it from its creator, manufacturer, or distributor.

I try to describe at least one tool for each of the eight categories listed on the first page of this chapter for the following hardware platforms: IBM PC (and compatibles), Macintosh, and UNIX. The NeXT hardware platform will be mentioned less frequently. NeXT gave up their hardware business—software only now. There are, of course, other hardware platforms, such as Amiga—you will find some coverage here, and some Amiga software sources in Appendix K.

Note that Microsoft Windows in addition to MS-DOS may be required to install and run certain programs described below.

Operating Systems and Operating System Extensions

Many of the text processing tools listed in sections that follow may require that you either have a Japanese operating system or else add Japanese language support to your computer's operating system. This may involve replacing your operating system entirely with a Japanese version, or may involve adding extensions to your current one.

Japanese-capable operating systems usually provide two main benefits. First, they provide multiple-byte handling at the system level—this often (but not always) makes non-Japanese software able to handle multiple-byte characters. Second, they provide menus and dialogs written in Japanese—this is more of a convenience for Japanese users.

This section will specify what hardware or software environments are required for such operating systems or operating system extensions. This material lays the foundation for the discussions that follow this section.

There are too many operating systems and operating system extensions to describe in this section. Others include SweetJAM (Macintosh) by A & A Company, JLE (UNIX) by Sun Microsystems, and Solaris by Sun Microsystems. What is described below is how to add Japanese language support to machines not necessarily intended for the Japanese market. What is *not* described below are PCs manufactured specifically for the Japanese market. These are equipped with a Japanese operating system, and most have special ROMs that contain Japanese font data.

IBM DOS J/V (IBM PC and Compatibles)

Prior to the release of this software, you had to purchase an MS-DOS computer with special ROMs that contained Japanese fonts and Japanese handling routines. This usually meant that you were forced to buy a computer made in Japan, and when you took it out of Japan, you had no reliable way to service it when problems arose. Well, that day is over. IBM DOS J/V allows anyone to install a Japanese operating system onto non-Japanese IBM PC and compatible computers. IBM DOS J/V processes Shift-JIS code internally.

Here are the hardware requirements for IBM DOS J/V:

- PS/55, PC/AT compatible, or PS/2 computer
- VGA, XGA, or PS/55 display adaptor
- 80286 CPU or greater
- 1MB of RAM (4MB is recommended)

There is a public domain version of the keyboard driver required for IBM DOS J/V if you plan to use a non-Japanese keyboard. It is located in the FLEFO (Foreign Language Forum) on CompuServe as the file called NBCC.ZIP. Japanese documentation describes the proper installation procedures. CompuServe's FLEFO has a lot of discussion about IBM DOS J/V.

Note that many text processing tools described below do not require a Japanese operating system—they create their own Japanese environment within themselves, and run under MS-DOS. However, a wider variety of Japanese software is available if you choose to run a Japanese operating system.

Note that I will use IBM DOS J/V in a very generic sense in the sections to follow. It will refer to versions of DOS that have Japanese language support. This usually means Japanese PCs, such as the NEC PC-9800 or PC-9801 series. MS-DOS refers to a non-Japanese operating system.

Microsoft Windows-J (IBM DOS J/V)

The Japanese version of Microsoft Windows is an operating system extension that adds graphics and windowing support for IBM DOS J/V. All applications that run under Microsoft Windows will run under Microsoft Windows-J (but not necessarily with Japanese language support). Microsoft Windows-J comes with a Japanese input program called

IME, and two TrueType Japanese fonts (a gothic and a mincho face). A minimum of 4MB of RAM is required for Microsoft Windows-J.

Microsoft is currently developing Microsoft Windows NT. This new windowing software uses Unicode as its base character set, and thus provides a multilingual environment.

KanjiTalk and WorldScript II (Macintosh)

The developers of the Apple Macintosh computer have always been committed to making Macintosh a multilingual platform. Development of a localized Japanese version of its operating system, called *KanjiTalk* (漢字Talk), began early on. This operating system processes Shift-JIS encoding internally.

The most current version of this operating system is called KanjiTalk 7.1. It provides a complete Japanese environment, and includes seven Japanese outline fonts (TrueType format). Expect this system to consume approximately 50MB of hard disk space if you install all seven fonts. At least 4MB of RAM is recommended when running this operating system. KanjiTalk 7.1 also comes with an excellent Japanese input system called ことえ り (*kotoeri*)—discussed in greater detail later in this chapter. KanjiTalk Version 6.0.7 included a Japanese input system called 2.1変換, and earlier versions of KanjiTalk included one called 2.0変換.

The cost of obtaining this Japanese operating system can range from a couple to several hundred dollars, depending on your KanjiTalk registration status. It is, of course, included with newly purchased Macintosh computers in Japan, and is available as a large set of floppy disks or on a single CD-ROM. Luckily, obtaining KanjiTalk 7.1 is not the only way to process Japanese on Macintosh computers.

Beginning with System 7.1, Apple also introduced operating system extensions called *WorldScript I* and *WorldScript II*. WorldScript I handles non-Roman one-byte encoded scripts, such as Hebrew, Arabic, and Thai; and WorldScript II handles non-Roman two-byte encoded scripts, such as Japanese, Chinese, and Korean. These system extensions allow you to add multilingual processing to System 7.1 (that is, *not* KanjiTalk 7.1). This really makes KanjiTalk 7.1 unnecessary for those who do not need localized Japanese menus. Apple offers the Japanese Language Kit (based on WorldScript II) for System 7.1 users who need to process Japanese, but do not want localized menus and dialog boxes. It provides all the system extensions necessary for processing Japanese on Macintosh computers, such as Japanese fonts, Japanese input software, and so on.

However, you must be warned that adding Japanese language support to your Macintosh using KanjiTalk or WorldScript II does not automatically make all of your English-language applications handle Japanese text. It is best to check with the application vendor before you buy. One of the first applications to be WorldScript II compatible is the word processor called Nisus by Nisus Software. Nisus is described later in this chapter.

GomTalk7 (Macintosh)

There was a gap of almost two years between the release of the English version of System 7 and the Japanese version (KanjiTalk 7.1). Japanese users had the hard choice of staying with KanjiTalk 6.0.7 or switching to System 7 (and losing the ability to handle Japanese text!). Fortunately, a very creative individual, Masashi Gomyo (五明正史), developed a FreeWare software package called GomTalk7. It requires KanjiTalk 6.0.7 and System 7.0/7.0.1. It is able to combine these two operating systems into one that is true System 7 and has the ability to process Japanese text. Like KanjiTalk, GomTalk7 processes Shift-JIS code internally.

I used this operating system for well over a year until KanjiTalk 7.1 was released. The latest release was Version 1.3, and now that KanjiTalk 7.1 has been released by Apple, Version 1.3 may have been the last release.

Those who are not able to obtain KanjiTalk 7.1 may find GomTalk7 a suitable operating system environment. You will need three things:

- The GomTalk7 distribution
- KanjiTalk 6.0.7 disks
- System 7.0 or 7.0.1 disks

I would like to take this opportunity to personally thank Masashi Gomyo for taking the time and effort to develop GomTalk7. It filled a gap during a time of need. I know that many GomTalk7 users share this feeling of gratitude.

Wherever I indicate that a particular program runs under KanjiTalk (except those specifically stating KanjiTalk 7.1), it can usually run under GomTalk7, too.

AIX (RISC System/6000)

AIX (Advanced Interactive Executive) is a fully internationalized UNIX operating system developed by IBM. Japanese language support was added beginning with Version 3.2.* Support for other Asian languages, such as Korean and Chinese, was added beginning with Version 3.2.3.

Being fully internationalized means that AIX can handle multiple-byte characters in almost all library functions, kernel routines, commands, utilities, and so on. Tools such as **vi**, **sed**, **awk**, **grep**, **diff**, **sdiff**, **cat**, **more**, and so on function correctly. Command line arguments, filenames, and the like can also use multiple-byte characters.

AIX internationalization is based on the XPG4 locale model (the locale model was briefly described in the beginning of Chapter 7). This means that character classification and

---

*AIX Version 3.1.5 required a system extension for Japanese language support.

case conversion (CTYPE), collation order (COLLATE), date and time formats (TIME), numeric and non-monetary formatting (NUMERIC), monetary formatting (MONETARY), and the language to be used for informative and diagnostic messages and interactive responses (MESSAGES) are all controlled by the user-selected locale. Changing locales is usually as simple as the following command line:

```
% export LANG=Ja_JP
```

This sets the current locale to handle Japanese characters and cultural aspects of Japan. If you the list all the locale categories along with their associated values, you may see the following:

```
% locale
LANG=Ja_JP
LC_COLLATE="Ja_JP"
LC_CTYPE="Ja_JP"
LC_MONETARY="Ja_JP"
LC_NUMERIC="Ja_JP"
LC_TIME="Ja_JP"
LC_MESSAGES="Ja_JP"
LC_ALL=
```

The following command line sets the current locale to English and cultural aspects of the U.S.:

```
% export LANG=En_US
```

Displaying Japanese text under AIX still requires that you run X Windows. The following command line opens a Japanese-capable window:

```
% aixterm -lang Ja_JP
```

There are actually two Japanese locales: `Ja_JP` and `ja_JP`. The difference is in the encoding method supported by each. The locale `Ja_JP` supports Shift-JIS encoding, and the locale `ja_JP` supports EUC encoding.

For more information on AIX, contact IBM directly, or else obtain *AIX Version 3.2 for RISC System/6000: Internationalization of AIX Software—A Programmer's Guide* (see Bibliography).

Irix (SGI Workstations)

Irix is the name of the operating system for all Silicon Graphics' workstations. International support based on the locale model began with Version 5.0. The locale name for Japanese is `ja_JP.EUC` (EUC encoding), but there is support for JIS encoding for processes such as e-mail and network news posting. EUC remains the internally processed code.

Versions of Irix in Japan prior to Version 5.0 include the Japanese Language System (JLS)—this consisted of adding Japanese language support to the operating system, and included Japanese versions of many of the utilities. Irix Version 5.0 in Japan comes bundled with JLS Version 3.0. JLS 3.0 is available elsewhere as an option. Switching to Japanese under Irix Version 5.0 is a simple matter of changing the locale to `ja_JP.EUC` (if JLS is installed).

There are plans to support Chinese and Korean locales in future releases of Irix. Contact Silicon Graphics for more information on Irix.

PenPoint

GO Corporation has developed the PenPoint operating system. PenPoint is unique in that it provides pen input and OCR technology as a key part of the user interface. The Japanese version comes with a full Japanese environment to include Japanese input software, two Japanese outline fonts, and Unicode support. In fact, it is the first commercially available operating system that uses Unicode as its base character set.

Notice how I did not list the hardware required for PenPoint. GO Corporation currently has PenPoint running on computers equipped with a 80386 processor. There are plans for making PenPoint run on a much wider range of architectures.

Developer kits and information are available. Contact GO Corporation for more information on the PenPoint operating system.

Plan 9 (UNIX)

Plan 9 is a multilingual UNIX operating system under development at AT&T Bell Laboratories. Plan 9 is not based on the locale model, but instead uses Unicode as its character set. No switching between code sets is necessary because all the characters necessary for many cultures or regions are included within the Unicode character set.

The encoding specified by Unicode is a fixed-width 16-bit representation. This is unsuitable for UNIX systems whose text processing functions come in the form of tools and pipes. Plan 9 makes use of UTF, a method of encoding Unicode text such that it can be handled more reliably through text streams.

Information on Plan 9 is available through anonymous FTP in the form of PostScript files. You simply need to spool the file to a PostScript printer to get the documentation. See Appendix K for more information on obtaining Plan 9 documentation.

X11R5 (UNIX)

X11R5 (X Window System, Version 11, Release 5), developed by the MIT X Consortium, is a graphical user interface (GUI), windowing system, and general multilingual environment with support for Japanese. Usually, it runs on top of a UNIX operating system, but is now available for Macintosh and MS-DOS as well.

The UNIX operating system comes in many versions. Each UNIX workstation manufacturer offers their own proprietary UNIX variant with manufacturer-specific enhancements. In addition, there are various "free" and copylefted versions of UNIX around—some are more robust than others.

Each UNIX has taken its own path towards Japanization. Many require that the operating system be language-localized: a language variable fixes the language used on the machine. Other UNIX variants, like OSF/1, are adopting Unicode as their standard for internationalization.

The locales defined in X11R5 are somewhat different from those you learned about in the description of AIX above. For example, the following are possible locales for Japanese under X11R5:

Locale	Japanese Encoding Method
ja_JP.jis7	JIS7
ja_JP.jis8	JIS8
ja_JP.mscode	Shift-JIS
ja_JP.pjis	JIS
ja_JP.ujis	EUC

Some of the most advanced work in this area is coming from Japan itself. There is an effort at Waseda University (早稲田大学) to internationalize, rather than localize, both UNIX and the X Window System. Supported by NTT and Omron, it is an attempt to create a fully internationalized workstation environment which will allow for multiple languages to be used simultaneously with a minimum of overhead.

Here's how it works: one additional locale is defined called wr_WR.ct. This locale contains information for 22 character sets, such as Japanese, Korean, Chinese, and many for Western languages. The encodings are based on the escape sequences defined in ISO 2022-1993 (or JIS X 0202-1991, which is the Japanese equivalent). You learned in Chapter 4 that Japanese, Korean, and Chinese all can be encoded with escape sequences. While this is usually used for information interchange purposes, the locale wr_WR.ct takes advantage of this to provide a multilingual environment. For more information, contact Yutaka Kataoka (片岡裕) at the following e-mail address:

```
kataoka@cfi.waseda.ac.jp
```

For more information on X11R5 in general, I suggest getting one or more volumes from the X Window System Series, published by O'Reilly & Associates, and published in Japanese by Softbank.

NeXTSTEP-J (NeXT)

NeXTSTEP-J is the Japanese version of NeXTSTEP, the operating system and GUI for NeXT computers. There are versions of NeXTSTEP that run on 80486-based computers (called *NeXTSTEP for Intel Processors*). NeXTSTEP-J currently runs only on NeXT hardware. NeXTSTEP-J processes EUC internally, but also has routines for supporting conversion to and from Shift-JIS and JIS encodings.

NeXTSTEP-J (and NeXTSTEP) use Display PostScript (DPS) as part of its GUI, and comes with two PostScript Japanese fonts, Ryumin-Light and GothicBBB-Medium. These are used for both screen display and printer output.

Contact NeXT or Canon for more information on NeXTSTEP-J.

ANS (Amiga)

Amiga computers distributed in Japan come bundled with ANS (Amiga Nihongo System), which is an operating system extension that supports Japanese. ANS is also available for Amiga computers outside of Japan. ANS was originally developed by TECNODE and is now marketed by MIQ Japan.

The ANS distribution consists of several utility programs, Japanese input software (JINPUT), Japanese terminal software (PCJ), Japanese code conversion software (EUC2SJIS and SJIS2EUC), Japanese text editing software (XED-Mini), Japanese fonts, Japanese printer drivers, and dictionary files. ANS processes EUC code internally.

There are currently efforts underway to port several useful programs to ANS. This includes a Japanese version of GNU Emacs and XJDIC (both of these are described in more detail below). The best way to keep up with such developments is to join the Kanji-Amiga Mailing List. See Appendix L for more information on this mailing list.

For additional information on ANS, contact MIQ Japan. See Appendix K for contact information.

Input Software

Japanese front-end processors (FEPs) are the software programs that perform the actual Japanese input. They make use of one or more conversion dictionaries, and often use special rules to more effectively convert input strings into a mixture of kana and kanji. The actual mechanics of Japanese input were described in detail in Chapter 5.

Here you will learn a little bit about a select few FEPs. Under most environments these programs are separate modules from the text editing or word processing software they are used with. This allows them to be used with a variety of applications. Some of these programs are dedicated for use within a specific application. For example, SKK is the dedicated FEP for Emacs.Mule.

Almost all FEPs have a facility that allows the user to add entries to the conversion dictionary (either to the main conversion dictionary or to a special *user* conversion dictionary). This allows users to create entries for hard-to-convert kanji or kanji compounds. This also lets adventurous users create specialized or field-specific conversion dictionaries. Adding entries to a conversion dictionary is sometimes a simple task of providing a key in the form of a kana string followed by one or more names that will act as candidates when the key is encountered during the conversion process. More complex FEPs require additional grammatical information, such as part of speech (noun, verb, and so on) or other information to assist in the conversion process.

Some FEPs, such as VJE, have been ported to multiple platforms, which often means you can exchange their conversion dictionaries among platforms.

There are, of course, other Japanese input programs available. These include EGBridge (IBM DOS J/V or KanjiTalk) by Ergosoft, ATOK (IBM DOS J/V) by JustSystem, Katana (IBM DOS J/V or KanjiTalk) by SomethingGood, kinput2 (UNIX), and so on.

Kotoeri (KanjiTalk 7.1)

Kotoeri (ことえり) is the name of the front-end processor included with KanjiTalk 7.1 (and System 7.1 running WorldScript II). Its name during development was Akiko (*Apple's kana in kanji out*). Kotoeri literally means "word selector" (こと means "word," and えり means "select"). It is much improved over the FEP included with earlier versions of KanjiTalk (2.1変換).

The features of kotoeri are impressive—its quality and features place it among the best FEPs. A character palette allows you to input characters by their encoded value (with the use of a graphic code table—KUTEN, JIS, and Shift-JIS codes are supported), by their classification (for non-kanji), and by their radical (even JIS Level 1 kanji are listed by radical!).

User-specific entries are entered into a special user conversion dictionary. The main conversion dictionary is fixed.

VJE-γ (IBM DOS J/V or NeXTSTEP-J)
MacVJE-γ (KanjiTalk 7.1)

VJE-γ (gamma) is a commercial Japanese input program that has been adapted for a variety of operating systems. VJE-γ is available for Japanese PCs and NeXTSTEP-J, and MacVJE-γ is available for KanjiTalk 7.1 (KanjiTalk 6.0.7 and earlier requires MacVJE, not MacVJE-γ). VJE-γ was developed by VACS, and MacVJE-γ was developed by Dynaware.

All versions of VJE-γ come with utilities for exchanging conversion dictionaries among operating systems. This is useful if you have more than one version of VJE-γ, or want to send someone your conversion dictionary.

I am most familiar with MacVJE-γ, so the descriptions that follow will be based on that version. You can expect VJE-γ to have similar, if not identical, features.

MacVJE-γ comes with two conversion dictionaries. The main conversion dictionary contains approximately 80,000 entries. The other dictionary contains Japanese postal codes along with candidate place names associated with those postal codes. Only one dictionary can be used at a time, but utilities are included for merging dictionaries. The main conversion dictionary can also be decompiled (that is, converted into a large text file for viewing individual entries) with the same utility—this is a feature that many other Japanese input programs do not have. User-specific entries are added directly to the main conversion dictionary.

In my experience, MacVJE-γ requires less RAM compared with other Japanese input programs (at least on the Macintosh). If RAM is at a premium in your environment, MacVJE-γ may be the best choice. Earlier versions of KanjiTalk used MacVJE. MacVJE-γ is often bundled with Japanese word processing software, such as MacWORD by Dynaware and MacWriteII-J by Claris.

Wnn (UNIX or KanjiTalk)

Wnn, which is an abbreviated romanized form of the Japanese sentence 私の名前は中野 です (*Watashi-no Namae-ha Nakano-desu*, which means "my name is Nakano"), is a freely available Japanese input program for UNIX systems developed by the Wnn Consortium. One of the early goals of the Wnn project was to properly parse the above Japanese sentence.

Wnn is actually the name of the conversion program that provides a consistent interface between **jserver** (a Japanese multi-client server) and actual Japanese input methods. Wnn also provides a set of conversion dictionaries. The Japanese input method that is provided with Wnn is called **uum**—this represents the word *wnn* rotated 180 degrees. **Uum** is the client program that is invoked by the user for Japanese input, and defines the keystroke combinations necessary for Japanese input. Wnn, on the other hand, refers to the entire collection of software included in its distribution.

The conversion dictionaries included with Wnn consist of a main dictionary (about 55,000 entries), single kanji dictionary, personal name dictionary, place name dictionary, grammatical dictionaries, and several field-specific conversion dictionaries (for computer science and biological terms, for example). All these dictionaries are used in the conversion process.

The Ministry of Software (a company, not a government body in Japan) adapted Wnn for use with KanjiTalk. Contact the Wnn Consortium for more information on Wnn. See Appendix K for contact information.

SKK (Mule, Nemacs, or Demacs)

SKK, which stands for Simple Kana-to-Kanji converter, is a freely available Japanese input system intended for use with the Japanese versions of a text editor called Emacs (such as Mule, Nemacs, and Demacs, which are described later in this chapter). This means that Japanese input under SKK is restricted to using Japanese Emacs. Many people use Emacs as their working environment—various tasks, such as sending and receiving e-mail, reading Usenet News, writing and compiling programs, and so on can be done from within Emacs.

SKK comes with three conversion dictionaries. There is no need to install all three since they are inclusive of each other (that is, the large conversion dictionary contains all the entries of the medium one). There is also an interactive tutorial, invoked from within Japanese Emacs, that is useful for learning the SKK Japanese input method.

SKK and its associated files have been adapted for use with non-UNIX systems. For example, MOKE, a commercial Japanese text editor for MS-DOS systems, makes use of the SKK conversion dictionary format for its own Japanese text entry system.

The development of SKK is being managed by Masahiko Sato (佐藤雅彦). He can be reached through e-mail at the following address:

```
masahiko@sato.riec.tohoku.ac.jp
```

Appendix K lists FTP sites that have SKK. You can also get the complete latest package of SKK by e-mail. Send a request to the following e-mail address:

```
skk-source@sato.riec.tohoku.ac.jp
```

Include the following subject line:

```
Subject: all
```

Canna (UNIX)

Canna (かんな) is the name of a Japanese input system under development by Akira Kon (今昭) and several others at NEC which offers features and a set of conversion dictionaries similar to Wnn, described above. It is easily customized by the user, and comes with additional utilities for performing tasks such as conversion dictionary maintenance. Much of the customizing is done with LISP-like commands. Canna is unique in that it is the first freely available UNIX Japanese input system that uses automatic conversion, and that it provides a unified user interface.

For more information on Canna, I suggest that you obtain the distribution at an anonymous FTP site (see Appendix K for anonymous FTP site information). Canna comes with extensive documentation. You can also contact the author through the following e-mail address:

```
kon@d1.bs2.mt.nec.co.jp
```

Tcode (Mule, Nemacs, Demacs, or KanjiTalk)

Tcode is a freely available Japanese input method developed at Yamada Laboratory at Tokyo University. Tcode has been adapted to run under a variety of platforms, and uses a two-stroke input method. Each kanji is input by two arbitrary key strokes (this is the opposite of input by association, which was described in Chapter 5).

Tcode is available through anonymous FTP, and through an e-mail distribution service. To receive Tcode distribution through e-mail, send an e-mail message to the following address:

```
tcode-info@lsi-j.co.jp
```

Include the following text in the message body to receive information on how the e-mail distribution service works (no subject is necessary):

```
# help
```

For additional information on Tcode, send an e-mail message to the following address:

```
tcode-ml@lsi-j.co.jp
```

Include the following text in the message body to receive a text file containing the Tcode guide (no subject is necessary):

```
# guide
```

Text Editors

The most basic Japanese text processing tool is a text editor. This tool allows you to input and save Japanese text. The functions are very basic, but, believe it or not, there are cases when you would choose a text editor over a word processor. One such circumstance is if you are composing Japanese text for transmission by e-mail—special formatting such as you would expect from a word processor does not travel well over e-mail. The characters and formatting that you are limited to with text editors is precisely what usually travels well through e-mail.

The features found in text editors are limited, yet useful. Most of them come with search and replace functions, and some even allow the user to write complex macros. Limitations sometimes include lack of word wrap, font limitations, font size limitations, and font style limitations.

Other text editors not covered in this section include YooEdit, MacEdit by Dynaware (bundled with MacVJE and MacVJE-γ), and FlashWriter by Catena. All of these run under KanjiTalk.

MOKE (MS-DOS)

MOKE (short for *Mark's Own Kanji Editor*) was written by Mark Edwards, and is rather inexpensive commercial software with full technical support. MOKE is useful in that it does not require that you have Japanese system software installed on your computer: it will run under standard MS-DOS. MOKE comes with its own set of fonts (and a way to print with them) and its own dedicated Japanese input software. Here is a list of hardware and software requirements for MOKE:

- IBM PC (XT, AT (80286), 80386, PS/2, or compatible)

- MS-DOS Version 3.1 or later

- 512K of RAM

- Hercules, CGA, EGA, or VGA graphics adapter

- Minimum 4MB of hard disk space

MOKE was originally designed and developed for non-Japanese speakers of Japanese since they often require special tools for inputting Japanese text. In addition to the typical Japanese input by pronunciation, MOKE also supports the following special input modes:

- By English meaning (that is, translation)

- By radical

- Of kanji compounds when only one of its kanji is known by the user

- Of katakana words by their corresponding English word

- By hexadecimal JIS code

For Japanese users the benefit is that it is an inexpensive way to enter Japanese on a non-Japanese PC (and without the use of IBM DOS J/V). Japanese users might like the ability of MOKE to obtain translations of Japanese words while entering Japanese text. Japanese users may also like the ability to look up kanji by their radicals, or use the kanji guess feature to look up kanji words when they remember only one of the kanji, or possibly to double-check personal or place names (do not confuse the kanji guess feature with Kanji Guess, which is a Japanese vocabulary learning program also developed by Mark Edwards).

MOKE comes with several utilities, such as a Japanese code converter, a Japanese text viewer, and a tool for searching multiple files for a Japanese word or phrase.

An earlier version of MOKE (specifically, Version 1.1) was FreeWare, which is still available on a number of anonymous FTP sites. However, I recommend the latest version, which is commercial software.

The author can be contacted through KiCompWare. See Appendix K for more information.

ASLEdit+ (KanjiTalk)

The Japanese text editor called ASLEdit+, written by Hiroo Yamada (山田浩大), is one of the most stable and reliable text editors I have used. This FreeWare was designed as a Macintosh text editor for use with compilers (the programs used to transform source code written in a programming language, such as C, into an executable program). You see, most compilers come with editors that are not able to process Japanese well (that is, cannot recognize two-bytes as a single character), and ASLEdit+ was designed to be used as a replacement. ASLEdit+ is distributed as both an application and a desk accessory. KanjiTalk is required to handle Japanese text—otherwise it behaves like a normal English text editor.

ASLEdit+ does not really have any special Japanese features other than being able to handle two-byte characters correctly. Many times, this is all that is necessary, especially for a text editor. It does have a very powerful search and replace function, including pattern matching.

The name ASLEdit+ comes from the author's amateur radio call sign, which is JK1ASL. The author has written other FreeWare Macintosh software such as ASLTelnet, a Japanese communications program, which is described later in this chapter. The author can be contacted at the following e-mail address:

```
76414.372@compuserve.com
```

The author asks that you do not contact him regarding basic questions that are best answered by reading the manuals, or to get a copy of the latest versions—he is just too busy.

Emacs and GNU Emacs Variants

Described in this section are several freely available variants of Emacs and GNU Emacs. Emacs is a text editor which has been ported to many platforms. If you have more than one working environment, you can use the software described below to have similar text editing features and functions.

All of these Emacs and GNU Emacs variants depend on a Japanese environment for displaying Japanese characters to the screen—they handle only the internal manipulation of Japanese codes.

The author of Jstevie can be contacted through the following e-mail address:

    ohta@src.ricoh.co.jp

jelvis (UNIX or IBM DOS J/V)

Another Japanese-capable vi clone is called jelvis, and is based on elvis written by Steve Kirkendall. This software was written by Jun-ichiro Itoh (伊藤純一郎), and is freely available. Like Jstevie, JIS, Shift-JIS, and EUC encodings are supported, but the user does not need to choose one at compile time—Japanese encodings can be set from the command line or from within jelvis.

The author of jelvis can be contacted through the following e-mail address:

    itojun@foretune.co.jp

Word Processors

Word processors (ワードプロセッサ or ワープロ) are the next step up from text editors. Supported features usually include multiple fonts, a wide selection of font styles, word wrap, justification (English and Japanese types), Japanese hyphenation, multiple point sizes, multiple font styles, somewhat complex formatting capabilities, multiple tab styles, and a basic graphics interface. Some even rival the features of page layout software.

There are many other Japanese word processors on the market, such as EGWord (KanjiTalk) by Ergosoft, MacWriteII-J (KanjiTalk) by Claris, MacWORD (KanjiTalk) by Dynaware, WaltzWord (KanjiTalk) by SomethingGood, WordPerfect (IBM DOS J/V, Windows-J, UNIX, and KanjiTalk) by WordPerfect, TurboWriter (KanjiTalk) by TransPac Software, the ByWord series (KanjiTalk) by The Ministry of Software, EW+ (MS-DOS) by Information Technology Laboratory, Ichitaro (IBM DOS J/V) by JustSystem, Yukara (MS-DOS) by Kureo Technology, and Pinecoast Japanese Word Processor (MS-DOS) by Pinecoast Software.

JWP (Microsoft Windows)

Stephen Chung developed a FreeWare Japanese word processor that runs under Microsoft Windows. It is distributed under the GNU General Public License. JWP requires the following environment:

- Microsoft Windows Version 3.0 or later (Version 3.1 is recommended)
- 80286 CPU (80386 or higher is recommended)
- 2MB of RAM (4MB is recommended)

JWP is rich in features, and rivals commercial products with its capabilities.

The author is constantly adding new features to JWP, and accepts suggestions for changes and improvements. He can be contacted through the following e-mail address:

```
schung@kilroy.jpl.nasa.gov
```

NJStar (MS-DOS)

NJStar, a ShareWare program written by Ni Hongbo, was originally designed as a Chinese word processor, but was modified to handle Japanese. It supports JIS and EUC encodings, and also includes Japanese input software. Its interface includes pulldown menus and mouse support, and handles a 19-line EGA or 25-line VGA display. It also has rich editing functions to include multiple file editing, undo, two-way fast search, flexible replace, and extensive block manipulations. NJStar does not require a Japanese operating system since it establishes its own Japanese environment.

Nisus/Solo Writer (KanjiTalk)

Solo Writer began as the word processor called Nisus. Nisus was one of the very few word processors that could handle Japanese adequately although it was not designed for Japanese handling *per se*. An effort began to localize Nisus to the Japanese market, and to add extra features specific to Japanese text handling. Mercury Software and Nisus Software have been continuing to develop this software, and now it is considered one of the top-rated Japanese word processors.

Many of Solo Writer's most notable features are not necessarily specific to handling Japanese. Beginning with Version 3.4, Nisus became identical to Solo Writer. This makes it one of the easiest Japanese word processors to obtain outside of Japan—most Macintosh mail order companies carry Nisus.

There are also *light* versions of these programs: Solo PowerLite and Nisus Compact. They have slightly fewer features than Solo Writer and Nisus, and thus require less RAM to run effectively. They were designed with the Apple Macintosh PowerBook series laptop computers in mind—RAM and hard disk space are at a premium on those computers. Additional features for Solo Power Lite and Nisus Compact are available as add-on modules.

This software was used to produce the manuscript for this book. A free demo version of Solo Writer (and Nisus) is available. This demo version is fully functional except that it will not permit you to save documents. See Appendix K for information on obtaining this demo. Contact Mercury Software or Nisus Software for more information on Solo Writer or Nisus.

Dedicated Japanese Word Processors

The Japanese word processors described in the previous section are software that you can purchase, install, and run on various platforms. There are, however, systems that have Japanese word processing software built in. These are called dedicated Japanese word processors (ワープロ専用機). Their Japanese word processing software is usually fixed (that is, not upgradable).

These machines may be ideal for those who do not wish to invest in a computer system. The features offered on some of these machines are often impressive, and many come with file exchange facilities (that is, they can read and write MS-DOS disks) and telecommunication software (and sometimes even a modem!). There are even some with Lotus 1-2-3 (a very popular spreadsheet program) built in. Most of these machines now have built in outline fonts, and their printers (usually built in) produce very good quality output.

Almost every major Japanese computer manufacturer produces a series of these machines. There is a periodical, published quarterly, called 最新ワープロ大百科 (meaning "The Latest Word Processor Encyclopedia"), that does a good job at providing a current listing of dedicated Japanese word processors. This periodical usually highlights some of the latest models. Full specifications of all current models are listed at the end of each issue.

Page Layout Software

Page layout software constitutes the most complex Japanese text processing tool available, and allows one to set text in a variety of ways and with much greater precision than the above text processing tools. There are many dedicated Japanese page layout systems, but these normally are very expensive and not easily upgraded.

Most page layout systems are not very efficient for text entry. It is usually desirable to first enter the text using word processing software, then import the text into the page layout software. Many times filters are available which allow you to retain attributes of the text during importing, such as the fonts used (names, point sizes, and so on), tab settings, and line spacing. Some page layout systems, such as FrameMaker-J, can also be used effectively for text entry.

You can expect to find features such as vertical setting of Japanese text, multiple columns on a single page, more control over character, word, and line spacing, and a graphics interface. FlashWriter, a rather simplistic Japanese word processor developed by Catena, supports vertical setting of Japanese text, both for input and output.

Some other Japanese page layout programs that exist, but are not covered here, include Quark XPress-J (KanjiTalk) by Quark, EGBook (KanjiTalk) by Ergosoft, Solo Publisher

(KanjiTalk) by Mercury Software, and the different flavors of Japanese TEX. Aldus Free-Hand-J (KanjiTalk) by Aldus is a graphics program that can also be used for page layout purposes to some extent.

Aldus PageMaker-J (Microsoft Windows-J or KanjiTalk)

Aldus has a very popular page layout program called Aldus PageMaker, which has been enhanced to handle Japanese text in a Japanese version called Aldus PageMaker-J. One of the main additions to this program, besides the obvious handling of two-byte characters, is the ability to set Japanese text vertically. Another feature special for Japanese text is the ability to insert *ruby* characters. These characters are usually very small kana, and appear above (or beside, in the case of vertically set Japanese text) one or more kanji. They are used to annotate kanji or kanji compounds with pronunciations. Ruby characters are described in Chapter 6.

Aldus PageMaker includes a very rich set of page layout features, which are also available in the Japanese version.

The latest version of Aldus PageMaker-J provides better text manipulation tools, such as a search and replace function. Aldus PageMaker-J was used to typeset this book.

Adobe Illustrator-J (KanjiTalk)

One of the most famous graphics programs is Adobe Illustrator. It allows precise layout of text and graphics objects within a page. While it does not really constitute a full page layout system, it is useful for short works, such as page advertisements and such. Many of the diagrams and illustrations used in the production of this book, for example, were made with Adobe Illustrator-J.

Adobe Illustrator-J provides both horizontal and vertical text setting for Japanese and English text. This program is much like having the whole PostScript language at your disposal. Almost every attribute can be modified. You can even set text along a curve, and convert text into editable outlines.

FrameMaker-J (UNIX)

FrameMaker is a very popular page layout software system, and has been ported to many platforms such as UNIX and the Macintosh. It is really designed for complex page layout, but can also serve well as a word processor. FrameMaker-J, the Japanese version of FrameMaker, currently runs only under the UNIX environment, but I have heard of plans to eventually port it to the Macintosh.

FrameMaker-J does not require a Japanese operating system—it provides its own Japanese environment. This may be an important factor for those who do not have the resources to set up such an environment on their own.

Online Dictionaries

Online dictionary software is a very useful resource for computer users. Such software allows you to look up individual characters, words, and even phrases. This software usually comes in two parts: the actual dictionary, which is machine-readable text in a database format, and software that accesses the information and displays it to the screen. Sometimes software packages include both parts.

A recent market trend is to store dictionaries on a single CD-ROM. CD-ROMs can store several hundred megabytes of data, and make an excellent media for large distributions of software (and music!). Most of these have been designed to be interfaced using the Sony Data Discman. These are commonly referred to as *electronic books* (電子ブック). Creative people and companies have written software that allow you to read these CD-ROMs on platforms such as the Macintosh using standard CD-ROM drives. The following is a short list of currently available Japanese-related electronic books:

- 広辞苑 by 岩波書店 (YRRS-7 1)
- 大辞林 by 三省堂 (YRRS-082)
- 新英和・和英中辞典 by 研究社 (YRRS-9 1)
- 漢字源 by 学研 (YRRS-050)
- 辞書パック10 by 三省堂
- 科学技術用語大辞典 by 日外アソシエーツ
- 25万語医学用語大辞典 by 日外アソシエーツ
- コンピュータ用語辞典 by 日外アソシエーツ

These and other electronic books can usually be ordered through Kinokuniya bookstores in the U.S. and Japan (see Appendix K for more information). They may even have certain titles in stock now that they are becoming more popular. Prices usually begin at about $50 (U.S.). Note that these are usually 8cm CD-ROMs—most CD-ROM drives accept 12cm CD-ROMs. Most music stores sell adapters that let you play 8cm CD-ROMs in 12cm CD-ROM drives.

Although not described here, there is an online dictionary program called KanjiSama (KanjiTalk) by SANBI Software. There is a demo version of KanjiSama available through anonymous FTP. See Appendix K for more information.

JDIC (MS-DOS)

The only Japanese dictionary software I know of which runs in the MS-DOS environment was written by Jim Breen. He has coordinated EDICT (a public domain Japanese-English dictionary file) and KANJIDIC (a public domain kanji dictionary), and has created two useful programs, called JDIC and JREADER, that use both dictionaries. All four are FreeWare. The following are descriptions of each.

EDICT is a public domain Japanese-English dictionary in machine-readable form. It was intended initially for use with MOKE (described previously in the text editor section) and related software such as JDIC. However, it has the potential to be used in a large number of situations. At present, it is in the public domain, but consideration is being given to placing it under GNU or copyleft protection, mainly to prevent the work of its many contributors from being exploited by commercial software developers. EDICT is in the EDICT format specified by MOKE, and uses EUC encoding for the Japanese portions. It is a text file with one entry per line. Here are a few examples of EDICT entries:

```
英和 [えいわ] /English-Japanese (e.g. dictionary)/
教科書 [きょうかしょ] /text book/
字体 [じたい] /type/font/lettering/
辞書 [じしょ] /dictionary/
辞典 [じてん] /dictionary/
電子計算機 [でんしけいさんき] /computer/
日本 [にっぽん] /Japan/
日本 [にほん] /Japan/
日本語 [にほんご] /Japanese language/
和英辞典 [わえいじてん] /Japanese-English dictionary/
```

EDICT is now over 67,000 entries, and is similar in size to a good quality commercial dictionary. Of these entries, about 15,000 are commonly used place names, given names, and family names. The edict.doc file distributed with EDICT describes its history, and lexographical principles, and lists its many contributors.

KANJIDIC is simply a kanji database file. There are 6,353 entries, one per line, and one for each of the kanji in JIS X 0208-1983. The first two fields of each entry are always the kanji itself (EUC encoded) followed by its hexadecimal JIS code. The remaining fields correspond to additional information. Table 8-1 lists the prefixes and the information their values present (some may not mean much unless you have a particular dictionary handy).

Table 8-1: Explanations of KANJIDIC Fields

Field	Meaning
B	Radical number assigned by Nelson's kanji dictionary (from a set of 214)
C	Classical radical number (from a set of 214) when assigned different from Nelson's kanji dictionary
F	Frequency-of-use ranking, if present (applies only to 2,135 kanji)
G	Jôyô Kanji/Gakushû Kanji/Jinmei-yô Kanji field (a value of 1 to 6 indicates the grade level for Gakushû Kanji; a value of 8 indicates Jôyô Kanji; and a value of 9 indicates Jinmei-yô Kanji)
H	Halpern's dictionary number, if present
N	Nelson's dictionary number, if present
P	SKIP pattern code[1]
S	Number of strokes (more than one such field is acceptable in the case of kanji with varying stroke counts)
U	Hexadecimal Unicode value

[1]SKIP (System of Kanji Indexing by Patterns) is a method for indexing kanji that divides it geometrically—supposedly allowing you to find any kanji in less than 30 seconds.

The final fields are one or more pronunciations written in kana and English meanings. English meanings are enclosed in curly braces. The `kanjidic.doc` file included with KANJIDIC explains these fields in greater detail.

The following are some sample lines taken from KANJIDIC. Compare the information to the listing given above.

```
和 4f42 U548c N3268 B115 S8 G3 H1130 F166 P1-5-3 ワ オ やわ.らぐ
やわ.らげる なご.む なご.やか {harmony} {Japanese style} {peace}
{soften}
剣 3775 U5263 N696 B18 S10 G8 H1672 F1177 P1-8-2 ケン つるぎ
{sabre} {sword} {blade} {clock hand}
漢 3441 U6f22 N2662 B85 S13 G3 H657 F1393 P1-3-10 カン {Sino-}
{China}
```

JDIC selects and displays entries from EDICT and KANJIDIC. Entries can be selected by either Roman or kana keys, and the display is in either alphabetical or 50 Sounds order. Kanji can be selected by radical, total number of strokes, pronunciation, hexadecimal JIS code, and so on. After display of a selected kanji, there can be a display of all compounds in EDICT containing that kanji. JDIC's operating environment is similar to MOKE's.

JREADER is a reader for text files containing Japanese characters, with the option of looking up displayed words in EDICT or in a kana-to-kanji conversion dictionary. The Japanese text can be JIS, Shift-JIS, or EUC encoded. Single kanji can also be looked up in KANJIDIC. Extracts can be logged to another file along with annotations for later analysis.

The EDICT and KANJIDIC online dictionary projects are continuing, and contributions are always welcome. Jim Breen is managing their development, and he can be contacted through the following e-mail address:

```
j.breen@rdt.monash.edu.au
```

MacJDic (KanjiTalk)

Dan Crevier ported XJDIC (based on JDIC, which is described later in this section) to the Macintosh, and called it MacJDic. Like JDIC, MacJDic is FreeWare, and makes use the EDICT and KANJIDIC dictionary files. It provides a Macintosh interface, and allows the user to change the Japanese font used in each of the various display windows.

MacJDic requires KanjiTalk—it does not establish its own Japanese environment as does JDIC on MS-DOS. The author of MacJDic can be contacted through the following e-mail address:

```
crevier@husc8.harvard.edu
```

rSTONE (KanjiTalk)

The rSTONE (from *Rosetta Stone*) series Japanese dictionaries, produced by A.I. Technology, consist of several interesting types. Japanese-English (called rSTONE.JE), English-Japanese (called rSTONE), and kanji code (called rSTONE.KC) dictionaries are available. These take the form of desk accessories, and require KanjiTalk or its equivalent. I have heard of plans to consolidate all three dictionaries into a single application.

The three rSTONE dictionary programs are commercial software. If you are on a budget, it is obvious that MacJDic is a better alternative, but you may find that the rSTONE dictionaries fill a need that MacJDic cannot. I have used all three rSTONE dictionaries and MacJDic, and my preference is MacJDic since it is upgraded quite often (well, an upgrade may be minor—an updated EDICT or KANJIDIC file), and these upgrades can be obtained through anonymous FTP.

Syokendai (KanjiTalk)

Syokendai (書見台) is freely available software that lets you display the contents of and search for text in several electronic books designed for Sony's Data Discman. Syokendai was written by Naritoshi Yoshinaga (吉永成利), and the routines for accessing CD-ROMs were borrowed from source code written by Shigeo Suwa (諏訪茂男) and Nobuhiro Miyatake (宮武伸裕).

Using Syokendai is the most economical way to interface with CD-ROM dictionaries. The only expenses that you need to worry about are the cost of the actual CD-ROM dictionaries and the cost of a standard CD-ROM drive (if you do not currently own one).

XJDIC (UNIX)

Also written by Jim Breen, XJDIC is a freely available UNIX version of JDIC. He calls it XJDIC since he designed it to run under the X Window System, but I have found that it can be used under a non-windowing UNIX environment (with some compromises, of course) as well. XJDIC depends on a Japanese environment to display Japanese text to the screen.

Like JDIC, XJDIC uses the EDICT and KANJIDIC dictionary files. There is also talk of porting XJDIC to the Amiga to run under ANS.

edict.el (Mule or Nemacs)

Per Hammarlund and Robert Kerns have written a program for accessing Jim Breen's EDICT dictionary file from within Mule or Nemacs. This program is called edict.el, and is available under the terms of the GNU Public License. Many people use Mule or Nemacs as their working environment, so edict.el is useful in that they can gain access to EDICT without leaving their work. This program has been written to enable easy reading of Japanese newsgroups or for doing translation work. It offers functionality beyond just accessing EDICT, such as the ability to "clean up" the search string in various ways such as converting Japanese verbs and adjectives to their plain form. It can help you to maintain a local EDICT file—there is a mode for inserting new entries.

For more information on edict.el, get the distribution through anonymous FTP, or contact the authors directly. The authors can be contacted by e-mail using the following addresses:

```
perham@nada.kth.se
rwk@world.std.com
```

Quick Viewer (IBM DOS J/V or KanjiTalk)

HAL Kenkyujo has developed software for viewing electronic books designed for use with Sony's Data Discman. Quick Viewer is available for a variety of platforms, and requires that you have Sony's electronic book drive called the Data Discman (DD-DR1).

Translator's Apprentice (NeXTSTEP)

The Translator's Apprentice is a commercial online dictionary tool ideal for translators and students of Japanese. It features an easy and effective way to access a growing collection of online dictionaries and glossaries. A wide assortment of Japanese-to-English and English-to-Japanese dictionaries are available for the Translator's Apprentice, covering a broad range from general to highly technical references. Its many innovative and unique features like the KanjiInspector, compound search, and browse functions combine to make it a powerful translation and learning aid for those involved in Japanese.

The Translator's Apprentice includes the Spahn & Hadamitzky Japanese Character Dictionary as a convenient built-in reference. Its open-ended interface is also compatible with many CD-ROM dictionaries providing easy expansion as more dictionaries become available. User glossaries are also supported through the system's GlossaryBuilder.

The Translator's Apprentice is available for NeXTSTEP computers including PCs and compatibles running the NeXTSTEP operating system. NeXTSTEP-J is not required since the Translator's Apprentice establishes its own Japanese environment. Contact Language Automation for more detailed information on the Translator's Apprentice.

Machine Translation Software

Machine translation (機械翻訳) software is a bit different from online dictionaries since they handle not only single characters, words, and phrases, but whole sentences. Such software actually performs the first pass translation, thus reducing the translation burden for humans. The state of machine translation is not yet to the point where human intervention is not required. These programs are really machine-*aided* translation software—they merely assist you in translating text faster.

Because these programs do not do a perfect translation, pre- and post-editing functions are usually available. Pre-editing is a form of massaging input text so that the translation software does a better job. Post-editing is the process of correcting errors in translation made by the software.

All the programs described in this section are commercial software. Their prices start at approximately $1,000 (U.S.).

PC-Transer (IBM DOS J/V)

PC-Transer is a machine translation system being marketed in the U.S. by Azuma Lander International. PC-Transer comes in two versions: a Japanese-to-English version, and an English-to-Japanese version. Both versions have technical dictionaries available, such as computer science, economics, engineering, medicine, and biotechnology—these technical dictionaries assist with translation when the topic of the material is one of these fields. You can also register up to 50,000 words in a user dictionary using the optional dictionary compiler. The basic dictionary it uses for translation purposes contains approximately 50,000 entries.

PC-Transer supports pre- and post-editing functions that can improve the translations by massaging the text before and after the software processes the original text. Translation can be done to whole documents, sentences, or individual words—this feature is user-selectable.

PC-Transer requires a 32-bit computer, at least 6MB of RAM, and at least 20MB of hard disk space (more hard disk space is required when you are using technical dictionaries).

EZ JapaneseWriter (MS-DOS)

EZ JapaneseWriter, marketed by EJ Bilingual, is a tool for writing Japanese text by first inputting the equivalent English sentence, then letting the program translate it into Japanese. It is sort of an on-the-fly translation program. A demo version of EZ JapaneseWriter, called JapaneseWriter, is available at a reduced price.

EZ JapaneseWriter establishes its own Japanese environment, but does require VGA, at least 3MB of hard disk space, 640K of RAM, and 260K of XMS (Extended Memory Specification).

TheTranslator (KanjiTalk)

Catena Corporation (カテナ株式会社) in Japan developed an English-to-Japanese machine translation program called TheTranslator. The basic dictionary it uses for translation purposes contains approximately 57,000 entries. It also uses approximately 3,000 grammatical rules. For what it's worth, it uses the *syntactic transfer* method of translation. Specialized dictionaries are available, such as computer science and information processing terms (approximately 35,000 entries).

This software has several translation modes, from individual words up to whole documents. There is no processing of whole paragraphs as a single unit—such text blocks are broken up into sentences, then translated.

TheTranslator supports pre- and post-editing functions. When the time comes to output the translated material to a text file, you are given the option to include the Japanese text, English text, or both.

An included tool allows you to make your own translation dictionaries (both dictionary compilation and decompilation are possible).

TheTranslator requires at least 4MB of RAM and approximately 25MB or hard disk space.

Terminal Software

Terminal software allows you to communicate with a host computer for accessing higher-level functions, such as reading Usenet News or sending and receiving e-mail.

These are usually more complex than other telecommunications software you may have used in that they must be able to handle multiple Japanese encodings on-the-fly. There are some, however, that can handle only a single Japanese encoding, such as Shift-JIS.

With MS-DOS and Macintosh platforms, it is often necessary to connect to a mainframe computer, by modem or network, in order to access an e-mail facility. This is when terminal emulation software is required.

Other Japanese terminal software that I do not cover in this section includes hterm (MS-DOS), KD (MS-DOS), NCSA Telnet-J (KanjiTalk), Eudora-J (KanjiTalk), and EGTalk (KanjiTalk) by Ergosoft. Of these, only EGTalk is commercial software.

YKH (MS-DOS)

YKH is a freely available Japanese DEC VT-320 terminal emulator developed by Bryan McNett for MS-DOS. YKH supports the display and entry of Japanese text in JIS, Shift-JIS, and EUC codes, and is able to make a connection through modems on com1 or com2 ports, and over some local area networks (for instance, using DECNET LAT and DECNET CTERM network terminal protocols). YKH stands for *Yaki Kemono Hosuto*, and in Japanese is written 焼き獣ホスト. The original non-Japanese version was called RBH, which stands for *Roastie-beastie Host*—Yaki Kemono Hosuto is the Japanese equivalent.

One unique feature of YKH is that it is able to fix and display Japanese text that has been mangled by newsreader software (such as **rn**). Without such a feature, those who wish to read Japanese text on Usenet News must either compile a special Japanese-aware version of their newsreading software (usually in the form of a patch), or else save the article to a file then view it later.

YKH requires about 64K of RAM and a VGA graphics adapter. YKH is available through anonymous FTP, and under the terms of the GNU general public license, the full source code for YKH is available free of charge—contact the author at the following e-mail address for a copy of the full source code:

```
u94_bmcnett@vaxc.stevens-tech.edu
```

KCom² (MS-DOS)

Developed by Kureo Technology Limited in Canada, KCom² is a combination Japanese text editor and Japanese terminal emulation software rolled into a single commercial software package. It does not require a Japanese environment, such as IBM DOS J/V, but instead establishes its own. It comes with its own set of bitmapped Japanese fonts which can be used for printing Japanese text to a variety of printers.

KCom² supports VT-100 terminal emulation, and handles JIS, Shift-JIS, and EUC codes. There is also the ability to send facsimiles (that is, if you have a modem that supports the sending of facsimiles), and quite a few file transfer protocols to choose from, such as X-Modem, Y-Modem, Z-Modem, Kermit, and so on.

KCom² is copy protected commercial software, and permits only up to four installations.

ASLTelnet (KanjiTalk)

ASLTelnet was written by the same author as the ASLEdit+ text editor described earlier, and like ASLEdit+, is freely available. ASLTelnet is used to connect to a mainframe host computer, such as a UNIX system, through a network connection.

Multiple connections can be established, which can provide a multi-windowing environment for those with a large enough monitor. Each connection provides Japanese display capability. Supported Japanese codes include JIS, Shift-JIS, EUC, and DEC Kanji. While it is possible to support only a single encoding for transmitting Japanese text, ASLTelnet can support multiple encodings for receiving text. Certain combinations are not possible, such as Shift-JIS plus EUC (their encoding space overlaps too much). However, useful combinations such as JIS plus EUC or JIS plus Shift-JIS are possible—their encoding space does not overlap at all.

ASLTelnet is based on NCSATelnet 2.3 by NCSA group. There are no English manuals for ASLTelnet at this time, so it is recommended that you use the documents included with the NCSATelnet 2.3 distribution. If you are using a Quadra, you must also be using MacTCP Version 1.1.1 or later.

NinjaTerm (KanjiTalk)

If you need to use modems to connect to a mainframe host computer for e-mail purposes, NinjaTerm, written by Michiharu Ariza (有座道春), is an older, yet still useful, freely available Japanese telecommunications program. NinjaTerm supports Shift-JIS, JIS, and EUC encodings, but does not support more than one at a time like ASLTelnet can. It has a buffering system that keeps a log of your communications session. This log file is both a text file (that can be opened by text editors for retrieving data) and a settings file for NinjaTerm itself. The only supported file transfer protocol is X-Modem.

NinjaTerm, unfortunately, is no longer being maintained by its author. In fact, the last release was all the way back in 1988 (Version 0.962)! With the introduction of newer operating systems, such as KanjiTalk 7.1, compatibility problems have crept in, the most notable of which is the lack of 32-bit mode compatibility. A patched version that remedies this problem is available.

Terminal-J (KanjiTalk)

Terminal-J is another freely available Japanese telecommunications program. Terminal-J is based on Terminal, written by Erny Tontlinger. A version that was previously available recognized only Shift-JIS encoded material. This made it useful for tasks such as connecting to a Japanese BBS (most of them run on PCs, and thus use Shift-JIS encoding). However, a more diverse choice of encodings is desirable when dealing with other host computers and e-mail systems. Fortunately, a second flavor of Terminal-J has been released, and can user-selectably change the encoding method. Choices include JIS, Shift-JIS, and EUC.

Terminal-J offers a wide variety of file transfer protocols, such as Y-Modem and Z-Modem. These are more modern protocols, and are much faster than those such as X-Modem.

Terminal-J was developed by Minoru Yoshida (吉田稔) and Masashi Oka (岡昌志).

kterm/exterm (UNIX)

It is not really enough to have X11R5 running on your system if you want to display Japanese text. You need to have windows that support the display of Japanese text. The program called kterm, which is the Japanese version of xterm, is such software, and is freely available. The functionality of kterm is nearly identical to xterm—with added support for Japanese text.

Kterm allows you to configure which Japanese code to use for display. Most of what you will encounter while running a UNIX-based system will be in JIS or EUC codes. JIS and EUC codes can be recognized simultaneously—they occupy different encoding spaces. Shift-JIS is available as an optionally recognized code.

X11R5 includes exterm (internationalized xterm), which is intended to be the replacement for kterm. However, kterm is still widely used.

The function of kterm is simply to *display* Japanese text. Japanese input programs, described earlier in this chapter, are used to input Japanese text.

9

Using Japanese E-mail and News

This chapter describes methods for handling Japanese text in electronic media such as e-mail. To some extent, these discussions also apply to accessing Japanese databases.

The handling of Japanese text within e-mail systems falls into the realm of *information interchange* (情報交換) whereby data are sent from one computer to another without, one hopes, any loss of data. How Japanese text is handled internally by a single computer system is not necessarily the same as the external handling of the same data. Here we can make a distinction between an *internal* and *external* code. An internal code is one which is most efficiently processed directly on a computer system. Examples of internal codes include the Shift-JIS and EUC encoding methods. An external code, however, is used somewhat as a machine-independent code which allows the transfer of data from one encoding to another—an external code is also called an *information interchange* code. An example of an external code is the JIS encoding method—it can be transmitted quite reliably through most e-mail networks.

Let's look at an example of information interchange in action. Figure 9-1 shows how Japanese data are moved from a system processing Shift-JIS to one processing EUC.

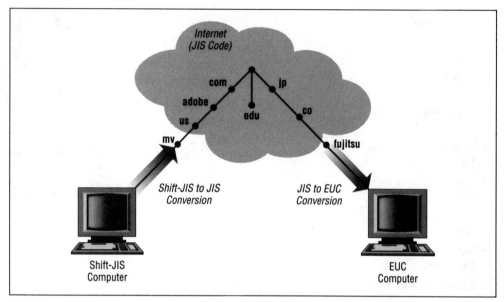

Figure 9-1: Information interchange

Note how JIS encoding is used as the information interchange code. The JIS encoding step may be bypassed if the Japanese data are being moved by other means, such as by a direct connection or by floppy disk.

True information interchange is achieved when data is moved from one platform to another (and perhaps even from one encoding to another) with no loss of information. Information interchange is usually a simple affair when using the ASCII character set, but in the case of Japanese there are more problems, such as different encoding methods (JIS, Shift-JIS, and EUC) and different character sets. Not all encodings support all the character sets. An example is the Shift-JIS lack of support for the JIS X 0212-1990 character set standard. These factors must be taken into consideration when deciding how to implement information interchange in your working environment.

Sending Japanese E-mail

There are different environments under which users can send Japanese text from their computer to a mainframe computer for subsequent transmission through e-mail. Many of these environments are specific to particular types of mainframe computers or electronic services. The algorithms and a tool for converting between Japanese encodings are covered in Chapter 7; the techniques for doing this are described in Chapter 4.

You must make a few preparations before a Japanese text file can be reliably transmitted, especially through e-mail networks. I suggest that these guidelines be followed as closely as possible:

- Break long lines to fewer than 80 columns (75 columns or fewer is preferred).*

- Compose the document using a monospaced font (most communication software uses monospaced fonts for display purposes).

- Do not include any half-width katakana characters since they are not fully supported in all environments.

- Convert the Japanese text file to JIS encoding with escape sequences (JIS C 6226-1978 or JIS X 0208-1983).

Jun Murai, Erik van der Poel, and Mark Crispin have written RFC (Request For Comments) 1468, *Japanese Character Encoding for Internet Messages*. This RFC describes how Japanese is encoded for use in e-mail systems.† The name ISO-2022-JP is assigned to the encoding format used in Japanese networks, which basically follows the recommendations in the above list.

Information on how to obtain RFC and Internet Draft documents can be found in Appendix K.

If the Japanese text is not composed on the system which is running the e-mail software, you must first transfer it to such a system. The most reliable method is to upload the file with a standard file transfer protocol (for example, X-Modem, Kermit, FTP, and so on), then send it as an included file in an e-mail message (check your e-mail documentation to find out how to do this). The file's Japanese code can be converted either before or after transferring to the computer with the e-mail system, depending on where the code conversion software is available.

Some e-mail networks, such as Bitnet, occasionally strip escape characters from e-mail messages. In my experience, Bitnet can handle eight-bit characters much more reliably than escape characters—this may make sending Japanese text files in Shift-JIS or EUC code more reliable! The JIS encoding repair tool and algorithm, discussed in Chapter 7, can help remedy this problem.

---

*Bear in mind that one column is equal to the display width of a single half-width character. This means that a single full-width character is equal to the display width of two columns. 80 columns would then mean 40 full-width characters.

†For those interested in Korean information processing, there is a similar document called *Korean Character Encoding for Internet Messages*, written by Kilnam Chon, Hyun Je Park, and Uhhyung Choi. This document is currently an Internet Draft, but is soon to become an RFC. The name ISO-2022-KR is assigned to the encoding format used in Korean networks.

As a last resort, if you are using a UNIX system, you can **uuencode** the Japanese text file before sending it in an e-mail message.* The file can then be **uudecode**d when it is received. This method, however, assumes that the receiving party has **uudecode** available. Sending Japanese text as a binary file is generally not recommended.

Posting Japanese News

Many of the same techniques recommended for sending Japanese e-mail are also applicable when posting news articles containing Japanese text. Refer to the bulleted items in the previous section. Most of the problems that you will encounter will relate to displaying Japanese news—this topic is covered later in this chapter.

The transmission of news from one site to another usually follows the same paths as e-mail messages. Some of these paths are not friendly to eight-bit data, which is why JIS encoding is also recommended for Japanese news articles.

Appendix L describes how to use e-mail to post articles to Japanese newsgroups.

Receiving Japanese E-mail

Receiving Japanese text is considerably easier than sending it, as you will soon learn below. Whether or not Japanese text is displayed properly online depends heavily on whether your computer, terminal, or communication software has the ability to display Japanese. CompuServe and most UNIX e-mail software seem to permit escape characters to function properly, so users should be able to view Japanese text online just like normal English text. That is, as long as their terminal emulation software allows Japanese to be displayed. A mainframe computer, if acting as a host, simply stores the electronic codes, and your computer, if acting as a Japanese terminal, simply interprets these electronic codes accordingly. The other problem you may encounter is when receiving a file that is in a Japanese code not supported by your displaying software. This requires conversion from one Japanese encoding to one that is supported by your software. Later in this chapter we discuss methods for converting from one Japanese code to another.

Some e-mail systems, such as those used under VMS systems, do not allow control characters to function (that is, if they didn't just strip them out!). This has the effect of rendering Japanese text unreadable within the mail system even if you are using Japanese terminal emulation software. For example, you may sometimes see some text that looks like this:

```
$B$3$1$OOBJ8$NJ8>O$NNc$G!"$=$1$O(JEnglish$B$NJ8>O$NNc$G$9!#(J
```

---

*There are versions of **uuencode** and **uudecode** available for other platforms.

There sure are a lot of $ characters—those happen to represent the first byte of hiragana characters. This should tell you that something has gone wrong.

You may be able to trick your e-mail software into permitting those characters to perform their proper functions. For example, on VMS systems, you can often use the `extract` command followed by `tt:` to accomplish this. Here is an example command line within the VMS e-mail subsystem:

```
Mail> extract tt:
```

If this works, and if the Japanese text has not been damaged, the above text should display properly as a mixture of Japanese and English text, such as the following:

これは和文の文章の例で、それはEnglishの文章の例です。

If there is no method with which you can coerce your e-mail software into displaying Japanese text, you are then forced to save the message to a file, exit the e-mail system, and then attempt to view the message by other means. The most likely method involves saving the e-mail message as a file outside your e-mail program, then, if necessary, downloading the file to your computer. UNIX newsreaders often have a similar problem—to display an article, save the article to a text file, then view it.

For those who must view Japanese text offline due to hardware or software limitations, some type of file transfer protocol (for example, X-Modem, Kermit, FTP, and so on) must be used to move the file to a place where it can be viewed. If your viewer requires the file to be in Shift-JIS or some other Japanese encoding, you may need to convert the file to the appropriate encoding for viewing (if the file originated from an e-mail system, it is most likely in JIS code).

Displaying Japanese News

If you are on a system that allows you to read news off the network, you most likely have access to Usenet News and Japanese newsgroups. The Usenet News newsgroup `sci.lang.japan` often has articles with Japanese text. In the case of Japanese newsgroups—whose names all begin with the two letters *fj* (meaning "from Japan")— most articles are in nothing but Japanese text. Japanese text that is included within these news articles is typically JIS encoded. As you learned in Chapter 4, JIS encoding makes use of the escape character. Most news reading programs do not allow these control characters to pass, thus making Japanese text display improperly.

Displaying Japanese text using news reading software, such as **rn**, can often be problematic. Many of these programs do not allow control characters such as the escape characters to pass. There are ways around these problems, usually in the form of programs or patches.

There are newer news reading programs that do allow escape characters to pass. These include C News and INN. If your system administrator has been keeping up with the latest news reading programs, you may be able to use these programs right now to read Japanese news.

Programs such as **rn** and Bnews require a patch to pass escape characters—these patches are available through anonymous FTP (see Appendix K for more information). One of the best Japanese patches is called **krn**, which is the Japanese patch for **rn**. It not only patches **rn** to pass escape characters, but also has all menus, error messages, and prompts written in Japanese. Other such programs include **knn**, **ktin**, and **ktrn**.

If you do not wish to replace or patch your news reading programs, there are still ways to display Japanese news. A simple trick is to pipe the article through the standard UNIX commands **cat**, **page**, or **more**. The following is an example of a prompt you may see at the end of a news article along with a piped command:

```
End of article 1 (of 1)--what next? [npq] | more
```

Another more severe problem you may encounter is lost escape characters. Some news posting programs actually strip out control characters in a particular range. Neither patching your news reading program nor UNIX pipes can help you here. You must save the article to a file, then use a tool to reinsert the lost escape characters. A tool for performing this type of repair is described in Chapter 7.

E-mail Addressing Templates

Although this section does not relate to Japanese information processing *per se*, it is useful in case a correspondent happens to use an e-mail service other than your own. Because Internet is probably the most widely used network, addressing templates revolve around how to send e-mail to and from Internet. The Internet address used in some of the examples should reply back with a confirmation of receipt. I encourage you to test these examples.

For more information on e-mail networks and e-mail addressing techniques in general, I suggest obtaining one or both of the following:

The Whole Internet User's Guide and Catalog by Ed Krol

!%@:: A Directory of Electronic Mail Addressing & Networks by Donnalyn Frey & Rick Adams

Both books are published by O'Reilly & Associates. For more information consult the Bibliography at the end of this book.

Internet and Aegis

Aegis, short for All English General Information System, is an electronic information service based in Tokyo, Japan, founded by The Aegis Society. Aegis sponsors, protects, and furthers the study of and communication in any language—by electronic means. The term *aegis* originally meant the shield of Zeus, supreme deity of the ancient Greeks, and that of his daughter Athena, the goddess of wisdom, and has come to mean protection or sponsorship. Aegis went online in November 1985. If someone on Aegis wishes to send e-mail to someone on Internet, the following addressing template must be used:

Internet address:	`test-japan@ora.com`
Template on Aegis:	`test-japan@ora.com`

The reverse addressing template is as follows:

Aegis user ID:	*user-id*
Template on Internet:	*user-id*`@aegis.org`

See Appendix K for information on how to contact The Aegis Society. They offer several levels of membership.

Internet and America Online

America Online (AOL) is a relatively new electronic information service which serves primarily Macintosh computer users. A gateway has been established between AOL and Internet. AOL users who wish to send e-mail to Internet users should use the following addressing template:

Internet address:	`test-japan@ora.com`
Template on AOL:	`inet@test-japan@ora.com`

Sending e-mail to an AOL user requires the following addressing template:

AOL user ID:	*user-id*
Template on Internet:	*user-id*`@aol.com`

Internet and AppleLink

AppleLink, an electronic service offered by Apple Computer, has special addressing requirements. If someone on AppleLink wishes to send e-mail to someone on Internet, the following addressing template must be used:

Internet address: `test-japan@ora.com`

Template on AppleLink: `test-japan@ora.com@internet#`

Note that two @ characters are required in the addressing template when going from AppleLink to Internet. The reverse addressing template is as follows:

AppleLink user ID: *user-id*

Template on Internet: *user-id*`@applelink.apple.com`

AppleLink users cannot receive files larger than 32K in size (such files should be segmented before sending), and they may have to pay a surcharge for messages received through the Internet gateway (currently $0.50 per message).

Bitnet and AppleLink

This last section on addressing templates goes beyond the Internet, and shows how one may send e-mail between Bitnet and AppleLink. The following addressing template is required to send from AppleLink to Bitnet (since my e-mail address is not a Bitnet one, I use my old, but still active e-mail address at the University of Wisconsin-Madison—any e-mail directed there is forwarded to my current address):

Bitnet address: `klunde@wiscmacc`

Template on AppleLink: `klunde@wiscmacc.bitnet@internet#`

The reverse addressing template is as follows:

AppleLink user ID: *user-id*

Template on Bitnet: `xb.das@stanford.bitnet`
                              At the `Subject:` prompt: *user-id*`@applelink`

Internet and Bitnet

The first set of addressing templates we cover is for Bitnet. Bitnet users must use the following template to send to an Internet address:

Internet address:	`test-japan@ora.com`
Template on Bitnet:	`test-japan@ora.com`

Internet users must use the following template to send to a Bitnet address. Note the conversion of @ to %, and the additional @—this is how one goes about using a relay.

Bitnet address:	`klunde@wiscmacc`
Template on Internet::	`klunde%wiscmacc@cunyvm.cuny.edu`

Internet and CompuServe

CompuServe users can send e-mail to Internet addresses, and Internet users can send e-mail to CompuServe addresses. CompuServe users must use the following template to send to an Internet address:

Internet address:	`test-japan@ora.com`
Template on CompuServe:	`>INTERNET:test-japan@ora.com`

Internet users must use the following template to send to a CompuServe address (note the conversion of the comma to a period!):

CompuServe user ID:	*12345,6789*
Template on Internet:	*12345.6789*`@compuserve.com`

In addition, the maximum file size which CompuServe users can receive is currently 50K. If you send anything larger, it must be segmented into smaller parts—this is not done automatically.

Internet and Fidonet

Fidonet, founded in 1984 by Tom Jennings, is an amateur e-mail network whose thousands of nodes are typically a BBS (Bulletin Board System). Fidonet is important because it offers a gateway to the Internet for more worldwide connectivity. Since its birth, Fidonet has grown internationally.

Sending e-mail from Fidonet to Internet is rather straightforward, as shown in the following addressing template:

Internet address:	`test-japan@ora.com`
Template on Fidonet:	`test-japan@ora.com`

Fidonet uses Internet addressing templates for sending e-mail to Internet. However, sending e-mail to a Fidonet user requires more complexity, as is shown in the following addressing template:

Fidonet user ID:	*firstname lastname* **at** *1:2/3.4*
Template on Internet:	*firstname.lastname***@p***4***.f***3***.n***2***.z***1***.fidonet.org**

Internet and MCIMail

MCI, a telecommunications company, has established its own e-mail service called MCIMail. The following addressing template should be used to send e-mail from MCIMail to the Internet (note that there is some complexity involved, namely multiple prompts):

Internet address:	**test-japan@ora.com**	
Template on MCIMail:	At the To: prompt:	**Ken Lunde (ems)**
	At the EMS: prompt:	**internet**
	At the MBX: prompt:	**test-japan@ora.com**

Sending e-mail from Internet to MCIMail is a bit easier, and the following addressing template is required:

MCIMail user ID:	*1234567*
Templates on Internet:	*1234567***@mcimail.com**
	*firstname_lastname***@mcimail.com**
	*firstname_lastname/1234567***@mcimail.com**

As you can see, MCIMail users can have more than one user ID. One is usually a series of digits, but the other can be their full name (first and last name separated by the underline character). You can even include both in the e-mail addressing template. Either one can be used, but I suggest using the login ID that takes the form of a number since it uniquely identifies the person you wish to contact.

Internet and NIFTY-Serve

NIFTY-Serve, a Japanese electronic information service, has a newly opened gateway to the outside world. This gateway currently has only limited service (for example, no e-mail is currently accepted from outside Japan), but sources claim that this will change in the future. The following addressing templates may not currently work, but they should in the future.

If someone on NIFTY-Serve wishes to send e-mail to someone on Internet, the following addressing template must be used:

Internet address: **test-japan@ora.com**

Template on NIFTY-Serve: **test-japan@ora.com**

The reverse addressing template is as follows:

NIFTY-Serve user ID: *user-id*

Template on Internet: *user-id***@niftyserve.or.jp**

NIFTY-Serve user IDs are made up of three letters followed by five numbers. For example, abc12345 is a valid (but fictitious) NIFTY-Serve user ID.

Any questions regarding this gateway between Internet and NIFTY-Serve should be directed to the following e-mail address:

wpnc-query@wide.ad.jp

Internet and PC-VAN

PC-VAN (Personal Computer Value Added Network) is a Japanese electronic information service offered and maintained by NEC. PC-VAN, like NIFTY-Serve, has a newly opened, but not yet fully implemented, gateway to the outside world.

If someone on PC-VAN wishes to send e-mail to someone on Internet, the following addressing template and instructions must be used:

Internet address: **test-japan@ora.com**

Template on PC-VAN: At the 宛先コード (destination code) prompt:
MHSX400
Type a subject line, and then on the next line:
TO:INET#test-japan(a)ora.com
Type a blank line, then the message

Note that TO: may need to be typed as part of the address string. Also note how @ is replaced by (a). The reverse addressing template is as follows:

PC-VAN user ID: *user-id*

Template on Internet: *user-id***@pcvan.or.jp**

Internet and TWICS

TWICS is an e-mail and computer conferencing system based in Tokyo, Japan, and is operated as a commercial service. TWICS stands for Two-way Information Communication System. TWICS first went online in 1984, became globally accessible through public packet switched data networks in 1986, and joined the world of inter-system inter-network e-mail in 1987. Here is how to get e-mail from TWICS to the Internet:

Internet address:	**test-japan@ora.com**
Template on TWICS:	**test-japan@ora.com**

The reverse addressing template is as follows:

TWICS user ID:	*user-id*
Template on Internet:	*user-id***@twics.co.jp**

E-mail Troubles & Tricks

Most of the problems you will encounter when sending Japanese text through e-mail will most likely relate to encodings becoming damaged, or else to using the wrong encoding method (for instance, sending Japanese text in Shift-JIS encoding—eight-bit encodings do not survive through most network paths). These problems have already been addressed earlier in this chapter, but there is a bit more to cover.

There are times when the escape sequences become scrambled in Japanese text for one reason or another. This might be due to poorly written telecommunication software, or just a problem with the integrity of the Japanese text, such as it ending in two-byte-per-character mode. This can leave you stuck in two-byte-per-character mode—text such as your system prompt will be interpreted as two bytes per character, and will make no sense at all. A solution to this is to create a short script with an embedded one-byte character escape sequence. The following two lines can be added to your `.cshrc` file (if you are using the C shell on a UNIX system):

```
set e = "`echo x | /bin/tr x \\033`"
alias ko 'echo "${e}(J"; echo "*** FORCED KANJI-OUT ***"'
```

The first line sets the value of the variable `e` to be the same as the escape character. This variable is then used in the second line to complete the one-byte character escape sequence. It is not wise to directly use an escape character in this sort of settings file—it may be detected as a redundant escape sequence by certain Japanese text editors, and subsequently deleted. When invoked, the alias `ko` outputs two lines to the terminal: the first is a valid one-byte character escape sequence, and the second is just a line that tells you that you have successfully returned to the one-byte-per-character mode.

Mail delivery problems can also be quite common. These can happen whether or not the e-mail message contains Japanese text. The two types of mail delivery problems that you may encounter are outlined below:

- Your mail software does not recognize the e-mail address
- Other mail software, such as a gateway, does not permit your e-mail to pass

You may also experience a combination of both problems.

When your mail software does not recognize the e-mail address, the solution is to use a relay. In the early days of the Japanese network, the use of relays was required so that e-mail could be sent from the U.S. to Japan. Fortunately, this is no longer the case for the majority of Japanese sites.

Relays are actually an extension of an e-mail address, and some special syntax is required. Some relays that have seen usage include `uunet.uu.net`, `sh.wide.ad.jp`, and `kyoto-u.ac.jp`. Table 9-1 lists some e-mail addresses as they would appear when using a relay. Note that this information in no way infers that these Japanese sites require a relay—they are used just as examples.

Table 9-1: Example Usages of Relays

E-mail Address	E-mail Address with Relay
`ken@keio.ac.jp`	`ken%keio.ac.jp@uunet.uu.net`
`ken@hokudai.ac.jp`	`ken%hokudai.ac.jp@sh.wide.ad.jp`
`ken@ntt.jp`	`ken%ntt.jp@kyoto-u.ac.jp`

Note the use of the `%` and `@` characters within the e-mail addresses that use a relay. These play an important role in the transmission process. Let's take the address `ken%keio.ac.jp@uunet.uu.net` as an example. The e-mail first travels to the site on the right of the address, namely `uunet.uu.net`. The `@uunet.uu.net` portion of the address is dropped, and the `%` is converted into `@`, thus reverting the address to its original form, namely `ken@keio.ac.jp`. At one time, `relay.cs.net` was a useful relay, but now it no longer exists.

Now we discuss what to do when your e-mail is refused passage. Electronic information services in Japan, such as NIFTY-Serve and PC-VAN, have the ability to exchange e-mail with Internet. However, these gateways may sometimes limit usage to those sites that are physically located in Japan. This restriction is due to the lack of an international communication license required by Japanese law. This makes it quite impossible to send e-mail from the U.S. to someone on NIFTY-Serve. This behavior should change once these services obtain an international communication license.

Japan Network Domains

Two primary e-mail networks/subdomains are currently used in Japan: the JP domain, which is the domain covering Japan;* and Bitnet (also known as *CREN*), which is a network that has nodes in Japan. There are other computer networks in Japan, such as JAIN (*Japanese Academic InterNetwork*), JUICE, TISN (*Todai International Science Network*), and WIDE Internet (*Wide network project*). Most of these networks use Internet-style addresses. More information on these and other Japanese networks can be found in Appendix G of the Japanese translation of *Using UUCP and Usenet* by Grace Todino and Dale Dougherty, published by ASCII Corporation (the English edition, which does not currently include this appendix, is published by O'Reilly & Associates). See the Bibliography for more information.

Soon there will be a new network called IIJ (*Internet Initiative Japan*) which will make common Internet services such as **ftp** and **telnet** available to many in Japan. This can be thought of as a public access UNIX system—they are common in the U.S., but seem to be just springing up in other parts of the world.

The networking environment in Japan (and throughout the world for that matter) is ever changing and improving. Changes that occur since the latest edition of this book, and that are reported to me, will be documented in JAPAN.INF. I limit my discussions to the JP domain and Bitnet.

The JP Domain

The JP domain is by far the most active e-mail network in Japan. There are five subdomains within JP, namely AC (*academic*), GO (*government*), OR (*organization*), AD (*administration*), and CO (*commercial*). As of this writing there are nearly 1,000 entities connected to these five JP subdomains.

These five Japanese subdomains are roughly equivalent to the domains commonly used in the U.S. AC relates to EDU, GO relates to GOV, OR relates to ORG, AD relates to NET, and CO relates to COM. There is no Japanese equivalent to the MIL (*military*) domain in the U.S.

So, how can you send e-mail to someone whose address is in the JP domain? First, each JP subdomain must be specified within the e-mail address. Some entities, such as NTT, belong to the JP domain itself. Table 9-2 lists several entities connected to a JP subdomain or to the JP domain itself:

---

*Once referred to as JUNET, which stands for *Japan UNIX Network*.

Table 9-2: Example JP Sites and Addresses

Entity Name	Subdomain	Site Name	Sample E-mail Address
keio	AC	keio.ac.jp	ken@keio.ac.jp
hokudai	AC	hokudai.ac.jp	ken@hokudai.ac.jp
ntt	...	ntt.jp	ken@ntt.jp
nec	CO	nec.co.jp	ken@nec.co.jp

To see a copy of the most current listing of entities within the five subdomains of the JP domain, please refer to JAPAN.INF, the online companion to this book. The current listing can also be obtained from the anonymous FTP nic.ad.jp (192.41.197.14) in the pub/jpnic directory. The names of the files to look for are domain-list.txt and domain-list-e.txt (the "e" in the latter refers to English language text—the other is in Japanese).

Contact the Japan Network Information Center for more information on the JP domain. Their address and other contact information are listed in Appendix K.

Bitnet Sites in Japan

There are approximately 100 Bitnet nodes in Japan. Besides the JP domain and the now developing Japanese IP internet, there is still an increasing demand for membership in Bitnet, especially within the Japanese academic community.

I have experienced some problems with sending or receiving e-mail with Japanese text to Bitnet addresses. Sending to JP domains is much more reliable. The main problem with Bitnet is that, all too often, it strips out (from e-mail and other messages) the non-printing ASCII escape characters necessary for encoding Japanese text. I have, however, discovered that escape characters do survive when the file is sent as a network file (network files are not considered to be e-mail messages since there is no header; it is much like UUCP (UNIX-to-UNIX copy) on UNIX systems). To send a Japanese network file from a Bitnet host to another Bitnet host, use the following command line:

```
send/file/binary/translate/printer filename bitnet_address
```

A real-life example can look like:

```
send/file/binary/translate/printer file.txt klunde@wiscmacc
```

The printer option is usually required when sending files whose lines are longer than 80 columns. Remember that escape sequences add data to a line although they are invisible when displayed—lines with English and Japanese heavily mixed can become very long data-wise, but not display-wise. Lines may wrap at unexpected places if the `printer` option is omitted from the command line. The other options—`binary`, `file`, and `translate`—are useful to ensure that the data remains intact during transmission.

I have observed that Bitnet appears to handle eight-bit characters within e-mail messages much more reliably than the Internet does. A professor I knew at the University of Wisconsin-Madison was able to send Big Five encoded e-mail messages to Bitnet sites in Taiwan. Big Five is an encoding that makes generous use of eight-bit characters. By a stroke of luck, the network path between UW-Madison and Taiwan permitted transmission of eight-bit characters. I suggest that you experiment with the Bitnet site you wish to contact in order to determine which Japanese encoding works best for you.

Bitnet addresses in Japan look the same as they do in the United States and other countries. Bitnet site names can have up to eight letters. The first two or three letters often indicate the country of the site. For example, Japanese Bitnet sites always begin with the three letters `jpn`. Table 9-3 lists a few example Japanese Bitnet addresses:

Table 9-3: Example Japanese Bitnet Sites and Addresses

Site Name	Example Bitnet Address
jpntsuku	kobayashi@jpntsuku
jpnkyoto	kobayashi@jpnkyoto
jpnwas00	kobayashi@jpnwas00
jpnsut20	kobayashi@jpnsut20

Contact the Japan Bitnet Association for more information on the use of Bitnet in Japan. Their address and other contact information are listed in Appendix K.

Getting Connected

This chapter ends with a few suggestions on how to get connected to an e-mail service. I hope most of you are already connected to some such service, but for those who are not, please read on. Being connected will bring to you a wide variety of information and software, most of which is free.* If you are an employee at a corporation or if you are a student or faculty member at an educational institution, there is probably an e-mail service you can obtain access to. Contact the computing services department to see what is available; in many cases access may be free.

You may have heard many different things about information services such as Prodigy, CompuServe, MCIMail, GEnie, and so on. Some of these information services do not offer much beyond their own environment (that is, a way to send and receive e-mail outside of their realm). I recommend joining CompuServe, MCIMail, or others only as a last resort,

---

*Sometimes being connected is not free, but what you can get from being connected usually is.

and only if they offer a gateway to the outside world. For those in Japan, TWICS or Aegis may turn out to be inexpensive alternatives to NIFTY-Serve, PC-VAN, or CompuServe. TWICS is planning on adding FTP and telnet capability soon. IIJ is another consideration. Contact information for these electronic information services are listed in Appendix K.

But, before you go knocking down CompuServe's door, I suggest that you pick up a copy of *The Whole Internet User's Guide & Catalog* by Ed Krol. Appendix A, *Getting Connected to the Internet*, lists a number of online services that offer more worldwide connectivity. You may find an e-mail service nearby. Unless you want to incur long-distance telephone charges, select one that is close to where you live. Actually, one of CompuServe's virtues is that there is most likely a local access number. For some of you, this may be a deciding factor in making a choice.

Japanese Code Conversion Table

This table is useful when dealing with large amounts of material indexed by the various Japanese encoding methods.

All of these columns are fairly self-explanatory, except for the two Shift-JIS columns. Confusion may occur when you try to convert the first Shift-JIS byte to another code, or when you try to convert the second byte of another code to Shift-JIS. The following two sets rules should help:

KUTEN/JIS/EUC to Shift-JIS

1) The first byte converts using the code conversion table—find the first byte value in KUTEN/JIS/EUC code, then simply slide over to the *Shift-JIS 1st Byte* column.

2) The second byte is a bit tricky. If the first byte (yes, the *first* byte!) of the KUTEN/JIS/EUC code is odd (the hexadecimal digits B, D, and F are odd), select the left-hand value in the *Shift-JIS 2nd Byte* column. Otherwise, select the right-hand value.

Shift-JIS to KUTEN/JIS/EUC

1) If the second Shift-JIS byte is the left-hand entry in the *Shift-JIS 2nd Byte* column, use the first occurrence of the first Shift-JIS byte to determine the first byte value of another code. Otherwise, use the second occurrence of the first Shift-JIS byte.

2) The second Shift-JIS byte converts unambiguously using the code conversion table.

KUTEN	JIS	EUC	Shift-JIS 1st Byte	Shift-JIS 2nd Byte	
01	21	A1	81	40	9F
02	22	A2	81	41	A0
03	23	A3	82	42	A1
04	24	A4	82	43	A2
05	25	A5	83	44	A3
06	26	A6	83	45	A4
07	27	A7	84	46	A5
08	28	A8	84	47	A6
09	29	A9	85	48	A7
10	2A	AA	85	49	A8
11	2B	AB	86	4A	A9
12	2C	AC	86	4B	AA
13	2D	AD	87	4C	AB
14	2E	AE	87	4D	AC
15	2F	AF	88	4E	AD
16	30	B0	88	4F	AE
17	31	B1	89	50	AF
18	32	B2	89	51	B0
19	33	B3	8A	52	B1
20	34	B4	8A	53	B2
21	35	B5	8B	54	B3
22	36	B6	8B	55	B4
23	37	B7	8C	56	B5
24	38	B8	8C	57	B6
25	39	B9	8D	58	B7
26	3A	BA	8D	59	B8
27	3B	BB	8E	5A	B9
28	3C	BC	8E	5B	BA
29	3D	BD	8F	5C	BB
30	3E	BE	8F	5D	BC
31	3F	BF	90	5E	BD
32	40	C0	90	5F	BE
33	41	C1	91	60	BF
34	42	C2	91	61	C0
35	43	C3	92	62	C1
36	44	C4	92	63	C2
37	45	C5	93	64	C3
38	46	C6	93	65	C4
39	47	C7	94	66	C5
40	48	C8	94	67	C6
41	49	C9	95	68	C7
42	4A	CA	95	69	C8
43	4B	CB	96	6A	C9
44	4C	CC	96	6B	CA
45	4D	CD	97	6C	CB
46	4E	CE	97	6D	CC
47	4F	CF	98	6E	CD

KUTEN	JIS	EUC	Shift-JIS 1st Byte	Shift-JIS 2nd Byte	
48	50	D0	98	6F	CE
49	51	D1	99	70	CF
50	52	D2	99	71	D0
51	53	D3	9A	72	D1
52	54	D4	9A	73	D2
53	55	D5	9B	74	D3
54	56	D6	9B	75	D4
55	57	D7	9C	76	D5
56	58	D8	9C	77	D6
57	59	D9	9D	78	D7
58	5A	DA	9D	79	D8
59	5B	DB	9E	7A	D9
60	5C	DC	9E	7B	DA
61	5D	DD	9F	7C	DB
62	5E	DE	9F	7D	DC
63	5F	DF	E0	7E	DD
64	60	E0	E0	80	DE
65	61	E1	E1	81	DF
66	62	E2	E1	82	E0
67	63	E3	E2	83	E1
68	64	E4	E2	84	E2
69	65	E5	E3	85	E3
70	66	E6	E3	86	E4
71	67	E7	E4	87	E5
72	68	E8	E4	88	E6
73	69	E9	E5	89	E7
74	6A	EA	E5	8A	E8
75	6B	EB	E6	8B	E9
76	6C	EC	E6	8C	EA
77	6D	ED	E7	8D	EB
78	6E	EE	E7	8E	EC
79	6F	EF	E8	8F	ED
80	70	F0	E8	90	EE
81	71	F1	E9	91	EF
82	72	F2	E9	92	F0
83	73	F3	EA	93	F1
84	74	F4	EA	94	F2
85	75	F5	EB	95	F3
86	76	F6	EB	96	F4
87	77	F7	EC	97	F5
88	78	F8	EC	98	F6
89	79	F9	ED	99	F7
90	7A	FA	ED	9A	F8
91	7B	FB	EE	9B	F9
92	7C	FC	EE	9C	FA
93	7D	FD	EF	9D	FB
94	7E	FE	EF	9E	FC

JIS X 0208-1990 Table

The following pages constitute a table for the characters of JIS X 0208-1990. They are indexed by KUTEN value. Here is a description of how to determine KUTEN code. The example uses the character A in row 3. First, the row number, 3, is used for the KU portion of the KUTEN code (a zero is prepended since two digits are required):

```
KU   =   03
TEN  =   --
```

Next, within row 3 are subrows. Find the subrow (20) which contains the character A. You then find the column heading (13) directly above the character. Add these two numbers, 20 and 13, to determine the TEN portion of the KUTEN code:

```
KU   =   03
TEN  =   33
```

The correct KUTEN value 0333 is simply the concatenation of these two values.

Note that KUTEN 0101 is a full-width space character.

Row 1   01 02 03 04 05 06 07 08 09 10 11 12 13 14 15 16 17 18 19

00	(SP)	、	。	，	．	・	：	；	？	！	゛	゜	´	`	¨	^	￣	＿	ヽ
20	ヾ	ゝ	ゞ	〃	仝	々	〆	○	―	―	‐	／	＼	～	‖	｜	…	‥	' '
40	" "		（ ）		〔 〕		［ ］		｛ ｝		〈 〉		《 》		「 」		『 』		【 】
60	＋	－	±	×	÷	＝	≠	＜	＞	≦	≧	∞	∴	♂	♀	°	′	″	℃ ¥
80	＄	¢	£	％	＃	＆	＊	＠	§	☆	★	○	●	◎	◇				

Row 2

	01	02	03	04	05	06	07	08	09	10	11	12	13	14	15	16	17	18	19
00		◆	□	■	△	▲	▽	▼	※	〒	→	←	↑	↓		〓			
20						∈	∋	⊆	⊇	⊂	⊃	∪	∩						
40		∧	∨	¬	⇒	⇔	∀	∃											
60		∠	⊥	⌒	∂	∇	≡	≒	≪	≫	√	∞	∝	∴	∫	∬			
80		Å	‰	♯	♭	♪	†	‡	¶					○					

Row 3

	01	02	03	04	05	06	07	08	09	10	11	12	13	14	15	16	17	18	19
00																0	1	2	3
20	4	5	6	7	8	9						A	B	C	D	E	F	G	
40	H	I	J	K	L	M	N	O	P	Q	R	S	T	U	V	W	X	Y	Z
60						a	b	c	d	e	f	g	h	i	j	k	l	m	n	o
80	p	q	r	s	t	u	v	w	x	y	z								

Note: Row 3, line 60 has values a–o across 05–19.

Row 4

	01	02	03	04	05	06	07	08	09	10	11	12	13	14	15	16	17	18	19
00			ぁ	あ	ぃ	い	ぅ	う	ぇ	え	ぉ	お	か	が	き	ぎ	く	ぐ	け	げ
20	こ	ご	さ	ざ	し	じ	す	ず	せ	ぜ	そ	ぞ	た	だ	ち	ぢ	っ	つ	づ	て
40	で	と	ど	な	に	ぬ	ね	の	は	ば	ぱ	ひ	び	ぴ	ふ	ぶ	ぷ	へ	べ	ぺ	ほ
60	ぼ	ぽ	ま	み	む	め	も	ゃ	や	ゅ	ゆ	ょ	よ	ら	り	る	れ	ろ	ゎ	わ
80	ゐ	ゑ	を	ん															

Row 5

	01	02	03	04	05	06	07	08	09	10	11	12	13	14	15	16	17	18	19
00		ァ	ア	ィ	イ	ゥ	ウ	ェ	エ	ォ	オ	カ	ガ	キ	ギ	ク	グ	ケ	ゲ	コ
20	ゴ	サ	ザ	シ	ジ	ス	ズ	セ	ゼ	ソ	ゾ	タ	ダ	チ	ヂ	ッ	ツ	ヅ	テ	デ
40	ト	ド	ナ	ニ	ヌ	ネ	ノ	ハ	バ	パ	ヒ	ビ	ピ	フ	ブ	プ	ヘ	ベ	ペ	ホ
60	ボ	ポ	マ	ミ	ム	メ	モ	ャ	ヤ	ュ	ユ	ョ	ヨ	ラ	リ	ル	レ	ロ	ワ	ワ
80	ヰ	ヱ	ヲ	ン	ヴ	ヵ	ヶ												

Row 6

	01	02	03	04	05	06	07	08	09	10	11	12	13	14	15	16	17	18	19
00		A	B	Γ	Δ	E	Z	H	Θ	I	K	Λ	M	N	Ξ	O	Π	P	Σ	T
20	Υ	Φ	X	Ψ	Ω							α	β	γ	δ	ε	ζ	η		
40	θ	ι	κ	λ	μ	ν	ξ	ο	π	ρ	σ	τ	υ	φ	χ	ψ	ω		
60																			
80																			

Row 7

	01	02	03	04	05	06	07	08	09	10	11	12	13	14	15	16	17	18	19
00		А	Б	В	Г	Д	Е	Ё	Ж	З	И	Й	К	Л	М	Н	О	П	Р	С
20	Т	У	Ф	Х	Ц	Ч	Ш	Щ	Ъ	Ы	Ь	Э	Ю	Я					
40							а	б	в	г	д	е	ё	ж	з	и	й		
60	к	л	м	н	о	п	р	с	т	у	ф	х	ц	ч	ш	щ	ъ	ы	ь	э
80	ю	я																	

Row 8 01 02 03 04 05 06 07 08 09 10 11 12 13 14 15 16 17 18 19

00   ─ │ ┌ ┐ ┘ └ ├ ┬ ┤ ┴ ┼ ━ ┃ ┏ ┓ ┛ ┗ ┣ ┳

20   ┫ ┻ ╋ ┠ ┯ ┨ ┷ ┿ ┝ ┰ ┥ ┸ ┒

40

60

80

Rows 9–15 Unassigned

Row 16 01 02 03 04 05 06 07 08 09 10 11 12 13 14 15 16 17 18 19

00   亜 唖 娃 阿 哀 愛 挨 姶 逢 葵 茜 穐 悪 握 渥 旭 葦 芦 鯵

20   梓 圧 斡 扱 宛 姐 虻 飴 絢 綾 鮎 或 粟 袷 安 庵 按 暗 案 闇

40   鞍 杏 以 伊 位 依 偉 囲 夷 委 威 尉 惟 意 慰 易 椅 為 畏 異

60   移 維 緯 胃 萎 衣 謂 違 遺 医 井 亥 域 育 郁 磯 一 壱 溢 逸

80   稲 茨 芋 鰯 允 印 咽 員 因 姻 引 飲 淫 胤 蔭

Row 17 01 02 03 04 05 06 07 08 09 10 11 12 13 14 15 16 17 18 19

00   院 陰 隠 韻 吋 右 宇 烏 羽 迂 雨 卯 鵜 窺 丑 碓 臼 渦 嘘

20   唄 欝 蔚 鰻 姥 厩 浦 瓜 閏 噂 云 運 雲 荏 餌 叡 営 嬰 影 映

40   曳 栄 永 泳 洩 瑛 盈 穎 頴 英 衛 詠 鋭 液 疫 益 駅 悦 謁 越

60   閲 榎 厭 円 園 堰 奄 宴 延 怨 掩 援 沿 演 炎 焔 煙 燕 猿 縁

80   艶 苑 薗 遠 鉛 鴛 塩 於 汚 甥 凹 央 奥 往 応

Row 18 01 02 03 04 05 06 07 08 09 10 11 12 13 14 15 16 17 18 19

00   押 旺 横 欧 殴 王 翁 襖 鴬 鴎 黄 岡 沖 荻 億 屋 憶 臆 桶

20   牡 乙 俺 卸 恩 温 穏 音 下 化 仮 何 伽 価 佳 加 可 嘉 夏 嫁

40   家 寡 科 暇 果 架 歌 河 火 珂 禍 禾 稼 箇 花 苛 茄 荷 華 菓

60   蝦 課 嘩 貨 迦 過 霞 蚊 俄 峨 我 牙 画 臥 芽 蛾 賀 雅 餓 駕

80   介 会 解 回 塊 壊 廻 快 怪 悔 恢 懐 戒 拐 改

Row 19 01 02 03 04 05 06 07 08 09 10 11 12 13 14 15 16 17 18 19

00   魁 晦 械 海 灰 界 皆 絵 芥 蟹 開 階 貝 凱 劾 外 咳 害 崖

20   慨 概 涯 碍 蓋 街 該 鎧 骸 浬 馨 蛙 垣 柿 蛎 鈎 劃 嚇 各 廓

40   拡 撹 格 核 殻 獲 確 穫 覚 角 赫 較 郭 閣 隔 革 学 岳 楽 額

60   顎 掛 笠 樫 橿 梶 鰍 潟 割 喝 恰 括 活 渇 滑 葛 褐 轄 且 鰹

80   叶 椛 樺 鞄 株 兜 竃 蒲 釜 鎌 噛 鴨 栢 茅 萱

Row 20 01 02 03 04 05 06 07 08 09 10 11 12 13 14 15 16 17 18 19

00		粥	刈	苅	瓦	乾	侃	冠	寒	刊	勘	勧	巻	喚	堪	姦	完	官	寛	干
20	幹	患	感	慣	憾	換	敢	柑	桓	棺	款	歓	汗	漢	澗	潅	環	甘	監	看
40	竿	管	簡	緩	缶	翰	肝	艦	莞	観	諌	貫	還	鑑	間	閑	関	陥	韓	館
60	舘	丸	含	岸	巌	玩	癌	眼	岩	翫	贋	雁	頑	顔	願	企	伎	危	喜	器
80	基	奇	嬉	寄	岐	希	幾	忌	揮	机	旗	既	期	棋	棄

Row 21 01 02 03 04 05 06 07 08 09 10 11 12 13 14 15 16 17 18 19

00		機	帰	毅	気	汽	畿	祈	季	稀	紀	徽	規	記	貴	起	軌	輝	飢	騎
20	鬼	亀	偽	儀	妓	宜	戯	技	擬	欺	犠	疑	祇	義	蟻	誼	議	掬	菊	鞠
40	吉	吃	喫	桔	橘	詰	砧	杵	黍	却	客	脚	虐	逆	丘	久	仇	休	及	吸
60	宮	弓	急	救	朽	求	汲	泣	灸	球	究	窮	笈	級	糾	給	旧	牛	去	居
80	巨	拒	拠	挙	渠	虚	許	距	鋸	漁	禦	魚	亨	享	京

Row 22 01 02 03 04 05 06 07 08 09 10 11 12 13 14 15 16 17 18 19

00		供	侠	僑	兇	競	共	凶	協	匡	卿	叫	喬	境	峡	強	彊	怯	恐	恭
20	挟	教	橋	況	狂	狭	矯	胸	脅	興	蕎	郷	鏡	響	饗	驚	仰	凝	尭	暁
40	業	局	曲	極	玉	桐	粁	僅	勤	均	巾	錦	斤	欣	欽	琴	禁	禽	筋	緊
60	芹	菌	衿	襟	謹	近	金	吟	銀	九	倶	句	区	狗	玖	矩	苦	躯	駆	駈
80	駒	具	愚	虞	喰	空	偶	寓	遇	隅	串	櫛	釧	屑	屈

Row 23 01 02 03 04 05 06 07 08 09 10 11 12 13 14 15 16 17 18 19

00		掘	窟	沓	靴	轡	窪	熊	隈	粂	栗	繰	桑	鍬	勲	君	薫	訓	群	軍
20	郡	卦	袈	祁	係	傾	刑	兄	啓	圭	珪	型	契	形	径	恵	慶	慧	憩	掲
40	携	敬	景	桂	渓	畦	稽	系	経	継	繋	罫	茎	荊	蛍	計	詣	警	軽	頚
60	鶏	芸	迎	鯨	劇	戟	撃	激	隙	桁	傑	欠	決	潔	穴	結	血	訣	月	件
80	倹	倦	健	兼	券	剣	喧	圏	堅	嫌	建	憲	懸	拳	捲

Row 24 01 02 03 04 05 06 07 08 09 10 11 12 13 14 15 16 17 18 19

00		検	権	牽	犬	献	研	硯	絹	県	肩	見	謙	賢	軒	遣	鍵	険	顕	験
20	鹸	元	原	厳	幻	弦	減	源	玄	現	絃	舷	言	諺	限	乎	個	古	呼	固
40	姑	孤	己	庫	弧	戸	故	枯	湖	狐	糊	袴	股	胡	菰	虎	誇	跨	鈷	雇
60	顧	鼓	五	互	伍	午	呉	吾	娯	後	御	悟	梧	檎	瑚	碁	語	誤	護	醐
80	乞	鯉	交	佼	侯	候	倖	光	公	功	効	勾	厚	口	向

Row 25 01 02 03 04 05 06 07 08 09 10 11 12 13 14 15 16 17 18 19

00		后	喉	坑	垢	好	孔	孝	宏	工	巧	巷	幸	広	庚	康	弘	恒	慌	抗
20	拘	控	攻	昂	晃	更	杭	校	梗	構	江	洪	浩	港	溝	甲	皇	硬	稿	糠
40	紅	紘	絞	綱	耕	考	肯	肱	腔	膏	航	荒	行	衡	講	貢	購	郊	酵	鉱
60	砿	鋼	閣	降	項	香	高	鴻	剛	劫	号	合	壕	拷	濠	豪	轟	麹	克	刻
80	告	国	穀	酷	鵠	黒	獄	漉	腰	甑	忽	惚	骨	狛	込

Row 26 01 02 03 04 05 06 07 08 09 10 11 12 13 14 15 16 17 18 19

	01	02	03	04	05	06	07	08	09	10	11	12	13	14	15	16	17	18	19
00		此	頃	今	困	坤	墾	婚	恨	懇	昏	昆	根	梱	混	痕	紺	艮	魂	些
20	佐	叉	唆	嵯	左	差	査	沙	瑳	砂	詐	鎖	裟	坐	座	挫	債	催	再	最
40	哉	塞	妻	宰	彩	才	採	栽	歳	済	災	采	犀	砕	砦	祭	斎	細	菜	裁
60	載	際	剤	在	材	罪	財	冴	坂	阪	堺	榊	肴	咲	崎	埼	碕	鷺	作	削
80	咋	搾	昨	朔	柵	窄	策	索	錯	桜	鮭	笹	匙	冊	刷					

Row 27 01 02 03 04 05 06 07 08 09 10 11 12 13 14 15 16 17 18 19

	01	02	03	04	05	06	07	08	09	10	11	12	13	14	15	16	17	18	19
00		察	拶	撮	擦	札	殺	薩	雑	皐	鯖	捌	錆	鮫	皿	晒	三	傘	参	山
20	惨	撒	散	桟	燦	珊	産	算	纂	蚕	讃	賛	酸	餐	斬	暫	残	仕	仔	伺
40	使	刺	司	史	嗣	四	士	始	姉	姿	子	屍	市	師	志	思	指	支	孜	斯
60	施	旨	枝	止	死	氏	獅	祉	私	糸	紙	紫	肢	脂	至	視	詞	詩	試	誌
80	諮	資	賜	雌	飼	歯	事	似	侍	児	字	寺	慈	持	時					

Row 28 01 02 03 04 05 06 07 08 09 10 11 12 13 14 15 16 17 18 19

	01	02	03	04	05	06	07	08	09	10	11	12	13	14	15	16	17	18	19
00		次	滋	治	爾	璽	痔	磁	示	而	耳	自	蒔	辞	汐	鹿	式	識	鴫	竺
20	軸	宍	雫	七	叱	執	失	嫉	室	悉	湿	漆	疾	質	実	蔀	篠	偲	柴	芝
40	屡	蕊	縞	舎	写	射	捨	赦	斜	煮	社	紗	者	謝	車	遮	蛇	邪	借	勺
60	尺	杓	灼	爵	酌	釈	錫	若	寂	弱	惹	主	取	守	手	朱	殊	狩	珠	種
80	腫	趣	酒	首	儒	受	呪	寿	授	樹	綬	需	囚	収	周					

Row 29 01 02 03 04 05 06 07 08 09 10 11 12 13 14 15 16 17 18 19

	01	02	03	04	05	06	07	08	09	10	11	12	13	14	15	16	17	18	19
00		宗	就	州	修	愁	拾	洲	秀	秋	終	繍	習	臭	舟	蒐	衆	襲	讐	蹴
20	輯	週	酋	酬	集	醜	什	住	充	十	従	戎	柔	汁	渋	獣	縦	重	銃	叔
40	夙	宿	淑	祝	縮	粛	塾	熟	出	術	述	俊	峻	春	瞬	竣	舜	駿	准	循
60	旬	楯	殉	淳	準	潤	盾	純	巡	遵	醇	順	処	初	所	暑	曙	渚	庶	緒
80	署	書	薯	藷	諸	助	叙	女	序	徐	恕	鋤	除	傷	償					

Row 30 01 02 03 04 05 06 07 08 09 10 11 12 13 14 15 16 17 18 19

	01	02	03	04	05	06	07	08	09	10	11	12	13	14	15	16	17	18	19
00		勝	匠	升	召	哨	商	唱	嘗	奨	妾	娼	宵	将	小	少	尚	庄	床	廠
20	彰	承	抄	招	掌	捷	昇	昌	昭	晶	松	梢	樟	樵	沼	消	渉	湘	焼	焦
40	照	症	省	硝	礁	祥	称	章	笑	粧	紹	肖	菖	蒋	蕉	衝	裳	訟	証	詔
60	詳	象	賞	醤	鉦	鍾	鐘	障	鞘	上	丈	丞	乗	冗	剰	城	場	壌	嬢	常
80	情	擾	条	杖	浄	状	畳	穣	蒸	譲	醸	錠	嘱	埴	飾					

Row 31 01 02 03 04 05 06 07 08 09 10 11 12 13 14 15 16 17 18 19

	01	02	03	04	05	06	07	08	09	10	11	12	13	14	15	16	17	18	19
00		拭	植	殖	燭	織	職	色	触	食	蝕	辱	尻	伸	信	侵	唇	娠	寝	審
20	心	慎	振	新	晋	森	榛	浸	深	申	疹	真	神	秦	紳	臣	芯	薪	親	診
40	身	辛	進	針	震	人	仁	刃	塵	壬	尋	甚	尽	腎	訊	迅	陣	靭	笥	諏
60	須	酢	図	厨	逗	吹	垂	帥	推	水	炊	睡	粋	翠	衰	遂	酔	錐	錘	随
80	瑞	髄	崇	嵩	数	枢	趨	雛	据	杉	椙	菅	頗	雀	裾					

Row 32 01 02 03 04 05 06 07 08 09 10 11 12 13 14 15 16 17 18 19

00 　澄 摺 寸 世 瀬 畝 是 凄 制 勢 姓 征 性 成 政 整 星 晴 棲
20 栖 正 清 牲 生 盛 精 聖 声 製 西 誠 誓 請 逝 醒 青 静 斉 税
40 脆 隻 席 惜 戚 斥 昔 析 石 積 籍 績 脊 責 赤 跡 蹟 碩 切 拙
60 接 摂 折 設 窃 節 説 雪 絶 舌 蝉 仙 先 千 占 宣 専 尖 川 戦
80 扇 撰 栓 栴 泉 浅 洗 染 潜 煎 煽 旋 穿 箭 線

Row 33 01 02 03 04 05 06 07 08 09 10 11 12 13 14 15 16 17 18 19

00 　繊 羨 腺 舛 船 薦 詮 賎 践 選 遷 銭 銑 閃 鮮 前 善 漸 然
20 全 禅 繕 膳 糎 噌 塑 岨 措 曾 曽 楚 狙 疏 疎 礎 祖 租 粗 素
40 組 蘇 訴 阻 遡 鼠 僧 創 双 叢 倉 喪 壮 奏 爽 宋 層 匝 惣 想
60 捜 掃 挿 掻 操 早 曹 巣 槍 槽 漕 燥 争 痩 相 窓 糟 総 綜 聡
80 草 荘 葬 蒼 藻 装 走 送 遭 鎗 霜 騒 像 増 憎

Row 34 01 02 03 04 05 06 07 08 09 10 11 12 13 14 15 16 17 18 19

00 　臓 蔵 贈 造 促 側 則 即 息 捉 束 測 足 速 俗 属 賊 族 続
20 卒 袖 其 揃 存 孫 尊 損 村 遜 他 多 太 汰 詑 唾 堕 妥 惰 打
40 柁 舵 楕 陀 駄 騨 体 堆 対 耐 岱 帯 待 怠 態 戴 替 泰 滞 胎
60 腿 苔 袋 貸 退 逮 隊 黛 鯛 代 台 大 第 醍 題 鷹 滝 瀧 卓 啄
80 宅 托 択 拓 沢 濯 琢 託 鐸 濁 諾 茸 凧 蛸 只

Row 35 01 02 03 04 05 06 07 08 09 10 11 12 13 14 15 16 17 18 19

00 　叩 但 達 辰 奪 脱 巽 竪 辿 棚 谷 狸 鱈 樽 誰 丹 単 嘆 坦
20 担 探 旦 歎 淡 湛 炭 短 端 箪 綻 耽 胆 蛋 誕 鍛 団 壇 弾 断
40 暖 檀 段 男 談 値 知 地 弛 恥 智 池 痴 稚 置 致 蜘 遅 馳 築
60 畜 竹 筑 蓄 逐 秩 窒 茶 嫡 着 中 仲 宙 忠 抽 昼 柱 注 虫 衷
80 註 酎 鋳 駐 樗 瀦 猪 苧 著 貯 丁 兆 凋 喋 寵

Row 36 01 02 03 04 05 06 07 08 09 10 11 12 13 14 15 16 17 18 19

00 　帖 帳 庁 弔 張 彫 徴 懲 挑 暢 朝 潮 牒 町 眺 聴 脹 腸 蝶
20 調 諜 超 跳 銚 長 頂 鳥 勅 捗 直 朕 沈 珍 賃 鎮 陳 津 墜 椎
40 槌 追 鎚 痛 通 塚 栂 掴 槻 佃 漬 柘 辻 蔦 綴 鍔 椿 潰 坪 壷
60 嬬 紬 爪 吊 釣 鶴 亭 低 停 偵 剃 貞 呈 堤 定 帝 底 庭 廷 弟
80 悌 抵 挺 提 梯 汀 碇 禎 程 締 艇 訂 諦 蹄 逓

Row 37 01 02 03 04 05 06 07 08 09 10 11 12 13 14 15 16 17 18 19

00 　邸 鄭 釘 鼎 泥 摘 擢 敵 滴 的 笛 適 鏑 溺 哲 徹 撤 轍 迭
20 鉄 典 填 天 展 店 添 纏 甜 貼 転 顛 点 伝 殿 澱 田 電 兎 吐
40 堵 塗 妬 屠 徒 斗 杜 渡 登 菟 賭 途 都 鍍 砥 砺 努 度 土 奴
60 怒 倒 党 冬 凍 刀 唐 塔 塘 套 宕 島 嶋 悼 投 搭 東 桃 梼 棟
80 盗 淘 湯 涛 灯 燈 当 痘 祷 等 答 筒 糖 統 到

Row 38

	01	02	03	04	05	06	07	08	09	10	11	12	13	14	15	16	17	18	19
00		董	蕩	藤	討	謄	豆	踏	逃	透	鐙	陶	頭	騰	闘	働	動	同	堂	導
20	憧	撞	洞	瞳	童	胴	萄	道	銅	峠	鴇	匿	得	徳	涜	特	督	禿	篤	毒
40	独	読	栃	橡	凸	突	椴	届	鳶	苫	寅	酉	瀞	噸	屯	惇	敦	沌	豚	遁
60	頓	呑	曇	鈍	奈	那	内	乍	凪	薙	謎	灘	捺	鍋	楢	馴	縄	畷	南	楠
80	軟	難	汝	二	尼	弐	迩	匂	賑	肉	虹	廿	日	乳	入					

Row 39

	01	02	03	04	05	06	07	08	09	10	11	12	13	14	15	16	17	18	19
00		如	尿	韮	任	妊	忍	認	濡	禰	祢	寧	葱	猫	熱	年	念	捻	撚	燃
20	粘	乃	廼	之	埜	嚢	悩	濃	納	能	脳	膿	農	覗	蚤	巴	把	播	覇	杷
40	波	派	琶	破	婆	罵	芭	馬	俳	廃	拝	排	敗	杯	盃	牌	背	肺	輩	配
60	倍	培	媒	梅	楳	煤	狽	買	売	賠	陪	這	蝿	秤	矧	萩	伯	剥	博	拍
80	柏	泊	白	箔	粕	舶	薄	迫	曝	漠	爆	縛	莫	駁	麦					

Row 40

	01	02	03	04	05	06	07	08	09	10	11	12	13	14	15	16	17	18	19
00		函	箱	硲	箸	肇	筈	櫨	幡	肌	畑	畠	八	鉢	溌	発	醗	髪	伐	罰
20	抜	筏	閥	鳩	噺	塙	蛤	隼	伴	判	半	反	叛	帆	搬	斑	板	氾	汎	版
40	犯	班	畔	繁	般	藩	販	範	釆	煩	頒	飯	挽	晩	番	盤	磐	蕃	蛮	匪
60	卑	否	妃	庇	彼	悲	扉	批	披	斐	比	泌	疲	皮	碑	秘	緋	罷	肥	被
80	誹	費	避	非	飛	樋	簸	備	尾	微	枇	毘	琵	眉	美					

Row 41

	01	02	03	04	05	06	07	08	09	10	11	12	13	14	15	16	17	18	19
00		鼻	柊	稗	匹	疋	髭	彦	膝	菱	肘	弼	必	畢	筆	逼	桧	姫	媛	紐
20	百	謬	俵	彪	標	氷	漂	瓢	票	表	評	豹	廟	描	病	秒	苗	錨	鋲	蒜
40	蛭	鰭	品	彬	斌	浜	瀕	貧	賓	頻	敏	瓶	不	付	埠	夫	婦	富	冨	布
60	府	怖	扶	敷	斧	普	浮	父	符	腐	膚	芙	譜	負	賦	赴	阜	附	侮	撫
80	武	舞	葡	蕪	部	封	楓	風	葺	蕗	伏	副	復	幅	服					

Row 42

	01	02	03	04	05	06	07	08	09	10	11	12	13	14	15	16	17	18	19
00		福	腹	複	覆	淵	弗	払	沸	仏	物	鮒	分	吻	噴	墳	憤	扮	焚	奮
20	粉	糞	紛	雰	文	聞	丙	併	兵	塀	幣	平	弊	柄	並	蔽	閉	陛	米	頁
40	僻	壁	癖	碧	別	瞥	蔑	箆	偏	変	片	篇	編	辺	返	遍	便	勉	娩	弁
60	鞭	保	舗	鋪	圃	捕	歩	甫	補	輔	穂	募	墓	慕	戊	暮	母	簿	菩	倣
80	俸	包	呆	報	奉	宝	峰	峯	崩	庖	抱	捧	放	方	朋					

Row 43

	01	02	03	04	05	06	07	08	09	10	11	12	13	14	15	16	17	18	19
00		法	泡	烹	砲	縫	胞	芳	萌	蓬	蜂	褒	訪	豊	邦	鋒	飽	鳳	鵬	乏
20	亡	傍	剖	坊	妨	帽	忘	忙	房	暴	望	某	棒	冒	紡	肪	膨	謀	貌	貿
40	鉾	防	吠	頬	北	僕	卜	墨	撲	朴	牧	睦	穆	釦	勃	没	殆	堀	幌	奔
60	本	翻	凡	盆	摩	磨	魔	麻	埋	妹	昧	枚	毎	哩	槙	幕	膜	枕	鮪	柾
80	鱒	桝	亦	俣	又	抹	末	沫	迄	侭	繭	麿	万	慢	満					

Row 44 01 02 03 04 05 06 07 08 09 10 11 12 13 14 15 16 17 18 19

	01	02	03	04	05	06	07	08	09	10	11	12	13	14	15	16	17	18	19
00		漫	蔓	味	未	魅	巳	箕	岬	密	蜜	湊	蓑	稔	脈	妙	粍	民	眠	務
20	夢	無	牟	矛	霧	鵡	椋	婿	娘	冥	名	命	明	盟	迷	銘	鳴	姪	牝	滅
40	免	棉	綿	緬	面	麺	摸	模	茂	妄	孟	毛	猛	盲	網	耗	蒙	儲	木	黙
60	目	杢	勿	餅	尤	戻	籾	貰	問	悶	紋	門	匁	也	冶	夜	爺	耶	野	弥
80	矢	厄	役	約	薬	訳	躍	靖	柳	薮	鑓	愉	愈	油	癒					

Row 45 01 02 03 04 05 06 07 08 09 10 11 12 13 14 15 16 17 18 19

	01	02	03	04	05	06	07	08	09	10	11	12	13	14	15	16	17	18	19
00		諭	輸	唯	佑	優	勇	友	宥	幽	悠	憂	揖	有	柚	湧	涌	猶	猷	由
20	祐	裕	誘	遊	邑	郵	雄	融	夕	予	余	与	誉	輿	預	傭	幼	妖	容	庸
40	揚	揺	擁	曜	楊	様	洋	溶	熔	用	窯	羊	耀	葉	蓉	要	謡	踊	遥	陽
60	養	慾	抑	欲	沃	浴	翌	翼	淀	羅	螺	裸	来	莱	頼	雷	洛	絡	落	酪
80	乱	卵	嵐	欄	濫	藍	蘭	覧	利	吏	履	李	梨	理	璃					

Row 46 01 02 03 04 05 06 07 08 09 10 11 12 13 14 15 16 17 18 19

	01	02	03	04	05	06	07	08	09	10	11	12	13	14	15	16	17	18	19
00		痢	裏	裡	里	離	陸	律	率	立	葎	掠	略	劉	流	溜	琉	留	硫	粒
20	隆	竜	龍	侶	慮	旅	虜	了	亮	僚	両	凌	寮	料	梁	涼	猟	療	瞭	稜
40	糧	良	諒	遼	量	陵	領	力	緑	倫	厘	林	淋	燐	琳	臨	輪	隣	鱗	麟
60	瑠	塁	涙	累	類	令	伶	例	冷	励	嶺	怜	玲	礼	苓	鈴	隷	零	霊	麗
80	齢	暦	歴	列	劣	烈	裂	廉	恋	憐	漣	煉	簾	練	聯					

Row 47 01 02 03 04 05 06 07 08 09 10 11 12 13 14 15 16 17 18 19

	01	02	03	04	05	06	07	08	09	10	11	12	13	14	15	16	17	18	19
00		蓮	連	錬	呂	魯	櫓	炉	賂	路	露	労	婁	廊	弄	朗	楼	榔	浪	漏
20	牢	狼	篭	老	聾	蝋	郎	六	麓	禄	肋	録	論	倭	和	話	歪	賄	脇	惑
40	枠	鷲	亙	亘	鰐	詫	藁	蕨	椀	湾	碗	腕								
60																				
80																				

Row 48 01 02 03 04 05 06 07 08 09 10 11 12 13 14 15 16 17 18 19

	01	02	03	04	05	06	07	08	09	10	11	12	13	14	15	16	17	18	19
00		弌	丐	丕	个	丱	丶	丼	丿	乂	乖	乘	亂	亅	豫	亊	舒	弍	于	亞
20	亟	亠	亢	亰	亳	亶	从	仍	仄	仆	仂	仗	仞	仭	仟	价	伉	佚	估	佛
40	佝	佗	佇	佶	侈	侏	侘	佻	佩	佰	侑	佯	來	侖	儘	俔	俟	俎	俘	俛
60	俑	俚	俐	俤	俥	倚	倨	倔	倪	倥	倅	伜	俶	倡	倩	倬	俾	俯	們	倆
80	偃	假	會	偕	偐	偈	做	偖	偬	偸	傀	傚	傅	傴	傲					

Row 49 01 02 03 04 05 06 07 08 09 10 11 12 13 14 15 16 17 18 19

	01	02	03	04	05	06	07	08	09	10	11	12	13	14	15	16	17	18	19
00		僉	僊	傳	僂	僖	僞	僥	僭	僣	僮	價	僵	儉	儁	儂	儖	儕	儔	儚
20	儡	儺	儷	儼	儻	儿	兀	兒	兌	兔	兢	竸	兩	兪	兮	冀	冂	囘	册	冉
40	冏	冑	冓	冕	冖	冤	冦	冢	冩	冪	冫	决	冱	冲	冰	况	冽	凅	凉	凛
60	几	處	凩	凭	凰	凵	凾	刄	刋	刔	刎	刧	刪	刮	刳	刹	剏	剄	剋	剌
80	剞	剔	剪	剴	剩	剳	剿	剽	劍	劔	劔	劒	剱	劈	劑	辨				

Row 50

	01	02	03	04	05	06	07	08	09	10	11	12	13	14	15	16	17	18	19
00		辨	劻	劭	劫	券	劲	勀	晜	劳	勈	飭	勠	勣	勱	勸	勹	匆	匈
20	甸	匍	匐	匏	匕	匚	匣	匱	匸	匚	區	卆	卅	世	卉	卍	準	卞	卩
40	卮	夘	卻	卷	厂	厖	厠	厦	厥	厮	厰	厶	參	簒	雙	叟	曼	燮	叮	叨
60	叭	叺	吁	吽	呀	听	吭	吼	吮	吶	吩	吝	呎	咏	呵	咎	呟	呱	呷	呰
80	咒	呻	咀	呶	咄	咐	咆	哇	咢	咸	咥	咬	哄	哈	咨				

Row 51

	01	02	03	04	05	06	07	08	09	10	11	12	13	14	15	16	17	18	19
00		咫	哂	咤	咾	咼	哘	哥	哦	唏	唔	哽	哮	哭	哺	哢	唹	啀	啣	啌
20	售	啜	啅	啖	啗	唸	唳	啝	喙	喀	咯	喊	喟	啻	啾	喘	喞	單	啼	喃
40	喩	喇	喨	嗚	嗅	嗟	嗄	嗜	嗤	嗔	嘔	嗷	嘖	嗾	嗽	嘛	嗹	噎	噐	營
60	嘴	嘶	嘲	嘸	噫	噤	嘯	噬	噪	嚆	嚀	嚊	嚠	嚔	嚏	嚥	嚮	嚶	嚴	囂
80	嚼	囁	囃	囀	囈	囎	囑	囓	囗	囮	囹	圀	囿	圄	圉				

Row 52

	01	02	03	04	05	06	07	08	09	10	11	12	13	14	15	16	17	18	19
00		圈	國	圍	圓	團	圖	嗇	圜	圦	圷	圸	坎	圻	址	坏	坩	垂	坿	坡
20	坿	垉	垓	垠	垳	垤	垪	垰	埃	埆	埔	埒	埓	堊	埖	埣	堋	堙	堝	塲
40	堡	塢	塋	塰	毀	塒	堽	塹	墅	墹	墟	墫	墺	壞	墻	墸	墮	壅	壓	壑
60	壗	壙	壘	壥	壜	壤	壟	壯	壺	壹	壻	壼	壽	夂	夊	夐	夛	梦	夥	夬
80	夭	本	夸	夾	竒	奕	奐	奎	奚	奘	奢	奠	奧	獎	奩				

Row 53

	01	02	03	04	05	06	07	08	09	10	11	12	13	14	15	16	17	18	19
00		奸	妁	妝	佞	侫	妣	妲	姆	姨	姜	妍	姙	姚	娥	娟	娑	娜	娉	娚
20	婀	婬	婉	娵	娶	婢	婪	媚	媼	媾	嫋	嫂	媽	嫣	嫗	嫦	嫩	嫖	嫺	嫻
40	嬌	嬋	嬖	嬲	嫐	嬪	嬶	嬾	孃	孅	孀	子	孕	孚	孛	孥	孩	孰	孳	孵
60	學	斈	孺	宀	它	宦	宸	寃	寇	寉	寔	寐	寤	實	寢	寞	寥	寫	寰	寶
80	寶	尅	將	專	對	尓	尠	尢	尨	尸	尹	屁	屆	屎	屓				

Row 54

	01	02	03	04	05	06	07	08	09	10	11	12	13	14	15	16	17	18	19
00		屐	屏	孱	屬	屮	乢	屶	屹	岌	岑	岔	妛	岫	岻	岶	岼	岷	峅	岾
20	峇	峙	峩	峽	峺	峭	嶌	峪	崋	崕	崗	嵜	崟	崛	崑	崔	崢	崚	崙	崘
40	嵌	嵒	嵎	嵋	嵬	嵳	嵶	嶇	嶄	嶂	嶢	嶝	嶬	嶮	嶽	嶐	嶷	嶼	巉	巍
60	巓	巒	巖	巛	巫	已	巵	帋	帚	帙	帑	帛	帶	帷	幄	幃	幀	幎	幗	幔
80	幟	幢	幣	幇	开	并	幺	麼	广	庠	廁	廂	廈	廐	廏				

Row 55

	01	02	03	04	05	06	07	08	09	10	11	12	13	14	15	16	17	18	19
00		廖	廣	廝	廚	廛	廢	廡	廨	廩	廬	廱	廳	廰	廴	廸	廾	弁	弉	彝
20	彜	弋	弑	弓	弩	弭	弸	彁	彌	彎	弯	彑	彖	彗	彙	彡	彭	彳	彷
40	徃	徂	彿	徊	很	徑	徇	從	徙	徘	徠	徨	徭	徼	忖	忻	忤	忸	忱	忝
60	悳	忿	怡	恠	怙	怐	怩	怎	怱	怛	怕	怫	怦	快	怺	恚	恁	恪	恷	恟
80	恊	恆	恍	恣	恃	恤	恂	恬	恫	恙	悁	悍	惧	悃	悚				

Row 56　01 02 03 04 05 06 07 08 09 10 11 12 13 14 15 16 17 18 19

00　　悄 俊 悖 俛 悒 俐 恪 惡 悴 惠 悁 悴 忰 悽 惆 悵 惘 慍 愕
20　　愆 惶 惷 愀 惴 惺 愃 惚 惻 惱 愍 愎 慇 愾 愨 愧 慊 愿 愼 愬
40　　愴 愽 愾 愬 慳 慘 慙 慚 慫 慴 慯 慱 慟 慝 慓 慵 憙 憖
60　　憇 憬 憔 憚 憊 憑 憫 憮 懌 懊 應 懷 懈 懃 懆 憺 懋 罹 懍 懦
80　　懣 懶 懺 懴 懿 懽 懼 儡 戀 戈 戉 戍 戌 戔 戛

Row 57　01 02 03 04 05 06 07 08 09 10 11 12 13 14 15 16 17 18 19

00　　戞 戡 截 戮 戰 戲 戳 扁 扎 扞 扣 扛 扠 扨 扼 抂 找 抒
20　　抓 抖 拔 抃 抔 拗 拑 抻 拏 拿 拆 擔 拈 拜 拌 拊 拂 拇 抛 拉
40　　挌 拮 拱 挧 挂 挈 拯 拵 捐 挾 捍 搜 捏 掖 掎 掀 掫 捶 掣 掏
60　　掉 掟 掵 捫 捩 掾 揩 揀 揆 揣 揉 插 揶 揄 搖 搴 搆 搓 搦 搶
80　　攝 搗 搨 搏 摧 摯 摶 摎 攪 撕 撓 撥 撩 撈 撼

Row 58　01 02 03 04 05 06 07 08 09 10 11 12 13 14 15 16 17 18 19

00　　據 擒 擅 擇 撻 擘 擂 擱 擧 舉 擠 擡 抬 擣 擯 攬 擶 擴 擲
20　　擺 攀 擽 攙 攘 攜 攅 攤 攣 攫 攴 攵 攷 收 攸 畋 效 敖 敕 敍
40　　敫 敨 敲 數 斂 斃 變 斛 斟 斫 斷 旃 旆 旁 旄 旌 旒 旛 旙 无
60　　旡 旱 杲 昊 昃 旻 杳 昵 昶 昴 昜 晏 晄 晉 晁 晞 晝 晤 晧 晨
80　　晟 晢 晰 暃 暈 暎 暉 暄 暘 暝 曁 暹 曉 暾 暼

Row 59　01 02 03 04 05 06 07 08 09 10 11 12 13 14 15 16 17 18 19

00　　曄 暸 曖 曚 曠 昿 曦 曩 曰 曵 曷 朏 朖 朞 朦 朧 霸 朮 朿
20　　朶 杁 朸 朷 杆 杞 杠 杙 杣 杤 枉 杰 枩 杼 杪 枌 枋 枦 枡 枅
40　　枷 柯 枴 柬 枳 柩 枸 柤 柞 柝 柢 柮 枹 柎 柆 柧 檜 栞 框 栩
60　　桀 桍 栲 桎 梳 栫 桙 档 桷 桿 梟 梏 梭 梔 條 梛 梃 檮 梹 桴
80　　梵 梠 梺 椏 梍 桾 椁 棊 椈 棘 椢 椦 棡 椌 棍

Row 60　01 02 03 04 05 06 07 08 09 10 11 12 13 14 15 16 17 18 19

00　　棔 棧 棕 椶 椒 椄 棗 棣 椥 棹 棠 棯 椨 椪 椚 椣 椡 棆 楹
20　　楷 楜 楸 楫 楔 楾 楮 椹 楴 椽 楙 椰 楡 楞 楝 榁 楪 榲 榮 槐
40　　榿 槁 槓 榾 槎 寨 槊 槝 榻 槃 榧 樮 榑 榠 榜 榕 榴 槞 槨 樂
60　　樛 槿 權 槹 槲 槧 樅 榱 樞 槭 樔 槫 樊 樒 櫁 樣 樓 橄 樌 橲
80　　樶 橸 橇 橢 橙 橦 橈 樸 樢 檐 檍 檠 檄 檢 檣

Row 61　01 02 03 04 05 06 07 08 09 10 11 12 13 14 15 16 17 18 19

00　　檗 蘗 檻 櫃 櫂 檸 檳 檬 櫞 檪 檪 欄 檻 櫑 櫚 櫛 櫓 櫏 欒
20　　欖 欝 欙 欠 欣 盜 欬 欷 盜 欸 欷 欹 飮 歇 歃 歉 歐 歙 歔 歛
40　　歟 歡 歸 歹 歿 殀 殄 殃 殍 殘 殕 殞 殤 殪 殫 殯 殲 殱 殳 殷
60　　毬 毫 毳 毯 麾 氈 氓 气 氛 氤 氣 汞 汕 汢 汪 沂 沍 沔 沘 沛
80　　汾 汨 汳 沒 沐 泄 泱 泓 沽 泗 泅 泝 沮 沱 沾

Row 62 01 02 03 04 05 06 07 08 09 10 11 12 13 14 15 16 17 18 19

00		沺	泛	泯	泙	泪	洟	衍	洶	洫	洽	洸	洙	洵	洳	洒	洌	浣	涓	浤
20	浚	浹	浙	涎	涕	濤	涅	淹	渕	渊	涵	淇	淦	涸	淆	淬	淞	淌	淨	淒
40	淅	淺	淙	淤	淕	淪	淮	渭	湮	渮	渙	湲	湟	渾	渣	湫	渫	湶	湍	渟
60	湃	渺	湎	渤	滿	渝	游	溂	溪	溘	滉	溷	滓	溽	溯	滄	溲	滔	滕	溏
80	溥	滂	溟	潁	漑	灌	滬	滸	滾	漿	滲	漱	滯	漲	滌

Row 63 01 02 03 04 05 06 07 08 09 10 11 12 13 14 15 16 17 18 19

00		漾	漓	滷	澆	潺	潸	澁	澌	潯	潛	濳	潭	澂	潼	潘	澎	澑	濂	潦
20	澳	澣	澡	澤	澹	濆	澪	濟	濕	濬	濔	濘	濱	濮	濛	瀉	瀋	濺	瀑	瀁
40	瀏	濾	瀛	瀚	潴	瀝	瀘	瀟	瀰	瀾	瀲	灑	灣	炙	炒	炯	烱	炬	炸	炳
60	炮	烟	烋	烝	烙	焉	烽	焜	焙	煥	熙	熙	煦	煢	煌	煖	煬	熏	燻	熄
80	熕	熨	熬	燗	熹	熾	燒	燉	燔	燎	燠	燬	燧	燵	爐

Row 64 01 02 03 04 05 06 07 08 09 10 11 12 13 14 15 16 17 18 19

00		燹	燿	爍	爐	爛	爨	爭	爬	爰	爲	爻	爼	爿	牀	牆	牋	牘	牴	牾
20	犂	犁	犇	犒	犖	犢	犧	犹	犲	狃	狆	狄	狎	狒	狢	狠	狡	狹	狷	倏
40	猗	猊	猜	猖	猝	猴	猯	猩	猥	猾	獎	獏	默	獗	獪	獨	獰	獸	獵	獻
60	獺	珈	玳	珎	玻	珀	珥	珮	珞	璢	琅	瑯	琥	珸	琲	琺	瑕	琿	瑟	瑙
80	瑁	瑜	瑩	瑰	瑣	瑪	瑤	瑾	璋	璞	璧	瓊	瓏	瓔	珱

Row 65 01 02 03 04 05 06 07 08 09 10 11 12 13 14 15 16 17 18 19

00		瓠	瓣	瓧	瓩	瓮	瓲	瓰	瓸	瓷	甄	甃	甅	甌	甎	甍	甕	甓	甞
20	甦	甬	甼	畄	畍	畊	畉	畛	畆	畚	畩	畤	畧	畫	畭	畸	當	疆	疇	畴
40	疊	疉	疂	疔	疚	疝	疥	疣	痂	疳	痃	疵	疽	疽	疼	疱	痍	痊	痒	痙
60	痣	痞	痾	痿	痼	瘁	痰	痺	痲	痳	瘋	瘍	瘉	瘟	瘧	瘠	瘡	瘢	瘤	瘴
80	瘰	瘻	癇	癈	癆	癜	癘	癡	癢	癨	癩	癪	癧	癬	癰

Row 66 01 02 03 04 05 06 07 08 09 10 11 12 13 14 15 16 17 18 19

00		癲	癶	癸	發	皀	皃	皈	皋	皎	皖	皓	皙	皚	皰	皴	皸	皹	皺	盂
20	盍	盖	盒	盞	盡	盥	盧	盪	蘯	盻	眈	眇	眄	眩	眤	眞	眥	眦	眛	眷
40	眸	睇	睚	睨	睫	睛	睥	睿	睾	睹	瞎	瞋	瞑	瞠	瞞	瞰	瞶	瞹	瞿	瞼
60	瞽	瞻	矇	矍	矗	矚	矜	矣	矮	矼	砌	砒	礦	砠	礪	硅	碎	硴	碆	硼
80	碚	碌	碣	碵	碪	碯	磑	磆	磋	磔	碾	碼	磅	磊	磬

Row 67 01 02 03 04 05 06 07 08 09 10 11 12 13 14 15 16 17 18 19

00		磧	磚	磽	磴	礇	礒	礑	礙	礬	礫	祀	祠	祗	崇	祚	祕	祓	祺	祿
20	禊	禝	禧	齋	禪	禮	禳	禹	禺	秉	秕	秧	秬	秡	秣	稈	稍	稘	稙	稠
40	稟	禀	稱	稻	稾	稷	穃	穗	穉	穑	穢	穩	龝	穰	穹	穽	窈	窗	窕	窘
60	窖	窩	竈	窰	窶	竅	竄	窿	邃	竇	竊	竍	竏	竕	竓	站	竚	竝	竡	竢
80	竦	竭	竰	笂	笏	笊	笆	笳	笘	笙	笞	笵	笨	笑	筐

Row 68

	01	02	03	04	05	06	07	08	09	10	11	12	13	14	15	16	17	18	19
00		筐	笄	筍	笋	筌	笅	筵	筥	笰	筧	筰	筱	筬	筮	箌	箝	箘	箟	箜
20	箏	筝	箒	箏	筝	箙	篋	篁	篌	篏	箴	篆	篝	篩	簀	簣	箟	簗	簍	篶
40	簇	簓	篳	篷	簗	簍	篶	簣	簧	簪	簟	簷	簫	簽	簒	籃	籔	簾	籀	籐
60	籐	籟	籤	籖	籥	籬	籵	粃	粐	粤	粭	粢	粫	粡	粨	粳	粲	粱	粮	粹
80	粽	糀	糅	糂	糘	糒	糜	糢	鬻	糯	糲	糴	糶	糺	紆					

Row 69

	01	02	03	04	05	06	07	08	09	10	11	12	13	14	15	16	17	18	19
00		紂	紜	紕	紊	絅	絋	紮	紲	紿	紵	絆	絳	絖	絎	絲	絨	絮	絏	絣
20	經	綉	絛	綏	絽	綛	綺	綮	綣	綵	緇	綽	綫	總	綢	綯	緜	綸	綟	綰
40	緘	緝	緤	緞	緻	緲	緡	縅	縊	縣	縡	縒	縱	縟	縉	縋	縢	繆	繦	縻
60	縵	縹	繃	縷	縲	縺	繧	繝	繞	繙	繚	繹	繪	繩	繼	繻	纃	緕	繽	辮
80	辮	繿	纈	纉	續	纒	纐	纓	纔	纖	纎	纛	纜	缸	缺					

Row 70

	01	02	03	04	05	06	07	08	09	10	11	12	13	14	15	16	17	18	19
00		罅	罌	罍	罎	罐	网	罕	罔	罘	罟	罠	罨	罩	罧	罸	羂	羆	羃	羈
20	羇	羌	羔	羞	羝	羚	羣	羯	羲	羹	羮	羶	羸	譱	翅	翆	翊	翕	翔	翡
40	翦	翩	翳	翹	飜	耆	耄	耋	耒	耘	耙	耜	耡	耨	耿	耻	聊	聆	聒	聘
60	聚	聟	聢	聨	聳	聲	聰	聶	聹	聽	聿	肄	肆	肅	肛	肓	肚	肭	冐	肬
80	胛	胥	胙	胝	胄	胚	胖	脉	胯	胱	脛	脩	脣	脯	腋					

Row 71

	01	02	03	04	05	06	07	08	09	10	11	12	13	14	15	16	17	18	19
00		隋	腆	脾	腓	腑	胼	腱	腮	腥	腦	腴	膃	膈	膊	膀	膂	膠	膕	膤
20	膣	腟	膓	膩	膰	膵	膾	膸	膽	臀	臂	膺	臉	臍	臑	臙	臘	臈	臚	臟
40	臠	臧	臺	臻	臾	舁	舂	舅	與	舊	舍	舐	舖	舩	舫	舸	舳	艀	艙	艘
60	艝	艚	艟	艤	艢	艨	艪	艫	舮	艱	艷	艸	艾	芍	芒	芫	芟	芻	芬	苡
80	苣	苟	苒	苴	苳	苺	莓	范	苻	苹	苞	茆	苜	茉	苙					

Row 72

	01	02	03	04	05	06	07	08	09	10	11	12	13	14	15	16	17	18	19
00		茵	茴	茖	茲	茱	荀	茹	荐	荅	茯	茫	茗	茘	莅	莚	莪	莟	莢	莖
20	茣	莎	莇	莊	荼	莵	荳	荵	莠	莉	莨	菴	萓	菫	菎	菽	萃	菘	萋	菁
40	菷	萇	菠	菲	萍	萢	萠	莽	萸	蔆	菻	葭	萪	萼	蕚	蔻	葷	葫	蒭	葮
60	蒂	葩	葆	萬	葯	葹	萵	蓊	葢	蒹	蒿	蒟	蓙	蓍	蒻	蓚	蓐	蓁	蓆	蓖
80	蒡	蔡	蓿	蓴	蔗	蔘	蔬	蔟	蔕	蔔	蓼	蕀	蕣	蕘	蕈					

Row 73

	01	02	03	04	05	06	07	08	09	10	11	12	13	14	15	16	17	18	19
00		蕁	蘂	蕋	蕕	薀	薤	薈	薑	薊	薨	蕭	薔	薛	藪	薇	薜	蕷	蕾	薐
20	藉	薺	藏	薹	藐	藕	藝	藥	藜	藹	蘊	蘓	蘋	藾	藺	蘆	蘢	蘚	蘰	蘿
40	虍	乕	虔	號	虧	虱	蚓	蚣	蚩	蚪	蚋	蚌	蚶	蚯	蛄	蛆	蚰	蛉	蠣	蚫
60	蛔	蛞	蛩	蛬	蛟	蛛	蛯	蜒	蜆	蜈	蜀	蜃	蛻	蜑	蜉	蜍	蛹	蜊	蜴	蜿
80	蜷	蜻	蜥	蜩	蜚	蝠	蝟	蝸	蝌	蝎	蝴	蝗	蝨	蝮	蝙					

Row 74		01	02	03	04	05	06	07	08	09	10	11	12	13	14	15	16	17	18	19
00		蝓	蝣	蝪	蠅	螢	螟	螂	螯	蟋	螽	蟀	蟐	雖	螫	蟄	螳	蟇	蟆	螻
20	蟯	蟲	蟠	蠏	蠍	蟾	蟶	蟷	蠎	蟒	蠑	蠖	蠕	蠢	蠡	蠱	蠶	蠹	蠧	蠻
40	衄	衂	衒	衙	衞	衢	衫	袁	衾	袞	衵	衽	袵	衲	袂	袗	袒	袮	袙	袢
60	袍	袤	袰	袿	袱	裃	裄	裔	裘	裙	裝	裹	褂	裼	裴	裨	裲	褄	褌	褊
80	褓	襃	褞	褥	褪	褫	襁	襄	褻	褶	褸	襌	褝	襠	襞					

Row 75		01	02	03	04	05	06	07	08	09	10	11	12	13	14	15	16	17	18	19
00		襦	襤	襭	襪	襯	襴	襷	襾	覃	覈	覊	覓	覘	覡	覩	覦	覬	覯	覲
20	覺	覽	覿	觀	觚	觜	觝	觧	觴	觸	訃	訖	訐	訌	訛	訝	訥	訶	詁	詛
40	詒	詆	詈	詼	詭	詬	詢	誅	誂	誄	誨	誡	誑	誥	誦	誚	誣	諄	諍	諂
60	諚	諫	諳	諧	諤	諱	謔	諠	諢	諷	諞	諛	謌	謇	謚	諡	謖	謐	謗	謠
80	謳	鞫	謦	謫	謾	謨	譁	譌	譏	譎	證	譖	譛	譚	譫					

Row 76		01	02	03	04	05	06	07	08	09	10	11	12	13	14	15	16	17	18	19
00		譟	譬	譯	譴	譽	讀	讌	讎	讒	讓	讖	讙	讚	谺	豁	谿	豈	豌	豎
20	豐	豕	豢	豬	豸	豺	貂	貉	貅	貊	貍	貎	貔	豼	貘	戝	貭	貪	貽	貲
40	貳	貮	貶	賈	賁	賤	賣	賚	賽	賺	賻	贄	贅	贊	贇	贏	贍	贐	齎	贓
60	賍	贔	贖	赧	赭	赱	赳	趁	趙	跂	趾	趺	跏	跚	跖	跌	跛	跋	跪	跫
80	跟	跣	跼	踈	踉	跿	踝	踞	踐	踟	蹂	踵	踰	踴	蹊					

Row 77		01	02	03	04	05	06	07	08	09	10	11	12	13	14	15	16	17	18	19
00		蹇	蹉	蹌	蹐	蹈	蹙	蹤	蹠	踪	蹣	蹕	蹶	蹲	蹼	躁	躇	躅	躄	躋
20	躊	躓	躑	躔	躙	躪	躡	躬	躰	軆	躱	躾	軅	軈	軋	軛	軣	軼	軻	軫
40	軾	輊	輅	輕	輒	輙	輓	輜	輟	輛	輌	輦	輳	輻	輹	轅	轂	輾	轌	轉
60	轆	轎	轗	轜	轢	轣	轤	辜	辟	辣	辭	辯	辷	迚	迥	迢	迪	迯	邇	迴
80	逅	迹	迺	逑	逕	逡	逍	逞	逖	逋	逧	逶	逵	逹	迸					

Row 78		01	02	03	04	05	06	07	08	09	10	11	12	13	14	15	16	17	18	19
00		遏	遐	遑	遒	逎	遉	逾	遖	遘	遞	遨	遯	遶	隨	遲	邂	遽	邁	邀
20	邊	邉	邏	邨	邯	邱	邵	郢	郤	扈	郛	鄂	鄒	鄙	鄲	鄰	酊	酖	酘	酣
40	酥	酩	酳	酲	醋	醉	醂	醢	醫	醯	醪	醵	醴	醺	釀	釁	釉	釋	釐	釖
60	釟	釡	釛	釼	釵	釶	鈞	釿	鈔	鈬	鈕	鈑	鉞	鉗	鉅	鉉	鉤	鉈	銕	鈿
80	鉋	鉐	銜	銖	銓	銛	鉚	鋏	銹	銷	鋩	錏	鋺	鍄	錮					

Row 79		01	02	03	04	05	06	07	08	09	10	11	12	13	14	15	16	17	18	19
00		錙	錢	錚	錣	錺	錵	錻	鍜	鍠	鍼	鍮	鍖	鎰	鎬	鎭	鎔	鎹	鏖	鏗
20	鏨	鏥	鏘	鏃	鏝	鏐	鏈	鏤	鐚	鐔	鐓	鐃	鐇	鐐	鐶	鐫	鐵	鐡	鐺	鑁
40	鑒	鑄	鑛	鑠	鑢	鑞	鑪	鈩	鑰	鑵	鑷	鑽	鑚	鑼	鑾	钁	鑿	閂	閇	閊
60	閔	閖	閘	閙	閠	閨	閧	閭	閼	閻	閹	閾	闊	濶	闃	闍	闌	闕	闔	闖
80	關	闡	闥	闢	阡	阨	阮	阯	陂	陌	陏	陋	陷	陜	陞					

Row 80 01 02 03 04 05 06 07 08 09 10 11 12 13 14 15 16 17 18 19

00		陜	陟	陦	陲	阪	隍	隘	隕	隗	險	隧	隱	隲	隰	隴	隸	隷	佳	睢
20	雋	雉	雍	襍	雜	霍	雕	雹	霄	霆	霈	霓	霎	霑	霏	霖	霙	霤	霪	霰
40	霹	霽	霾	靄	靆	靈	靂	靉	靜	靠	靤	靦	靨	勒	靫	靱	靹	鞅	靼	鞁
60	靺	鞆	鞋	鞏	鞐	鞜	鞨	鞦	鞣	鞳	鞴	韃	韆	韈	韋	韜	韭	齏	韲	竟
80	韶	韵	頏	頌	頸	頤	頡	頷	頽	顆	顏	顋	顫	顯	顰					

Row 81 01 02 03 04 05 06 07 08 09 10 11 12 13 14 15 16 17 18 19

00		顱	顴	顳	颪	颯	颱	颶	飄	飃	飆	飩	飫	餃	餉	餒	餔	餘	餡	餝
20	餞	餤	餠	餬	餮	餽	餾	饂	饉	饅	饐	饋	饑	饒	饌	饕	馗	馘	馥	馭
40	馮	馼	駟	駛	駝	駘	駑	駭	駮	駱	駲	駻	駸	騁	騏	騅	駢	騙	騫	騷
60	驅	驂	驀	驃	騾	驕	驍	驛	驗	驟	驢	驥	驤	驩	驫	驪	骭	骰	骼	髀
80	髏	髑	髓	體	髞	髟	髢	髣	髦	髯	髫	髮	髴	髱	髷					

Row 82 01 02 03 04 05 06 07 08 09 10 11 12 13 14 15 16 17 18 19

00		髻	鬆	鬘	鬚	鬟	鬢	鬣	鬥	鬧	鬨	鬩	鬪	鬮	鬯	鬲	魄	魃	魏	魍
20	魎	魑	魘	魴	鮓	鮃	鮑	鮖	鮗	鮟	鮠	鮨	鮴	鯀	鯊	鮹	鯆	鯏	鯑	鯒
40	鯣	鯢	鯤	鯔	鯡	鰺	鯲	鯱	鯰	鰕	鰔	鰉	鰓	鰌	鰆	鰈	鰒	鰊	鰄	鰮
60	鰛	鰥	鰤	鰡	鰰	鱇	鰲	鱆	鰾	鱚	鱠	鱧	鱶	鱸	鳧	鳬	鳰	鴉	鴈	鳫
80	鴃	鴆	鴪	鴦	鶯	鴣	鴟	鵄	鴕	鴒	鵁	鴿	鴾	鵆	鵈					

Row 83 01 02 03 04 05 06 07 08 09 10 11 12 13 14 15 16 17 18 19

00		鵝	鵞	鵤	鵑	鵐	鵙	鵲	鶉	鶇	鶫	鵯	鵺	鶚	鶤	鶩	鶲	鷄	鷁	鶻
20	鶸	鶺	鷆	鷏	鷂	鷙	鷓	鷸	鷦	鷭	鷯	鷽	鸚	鸛	鸞	鹵	鹹	鹽	麁	麈
40	麋	麌	麒	麕	麑	麝	麥	麩	麸	麺	麭	靡	黌	黎	黏	黐	黔	黜	點	黝
60	黠	黥	黨	黯	黴	黶	黷	黹	黻	黼	黽	鼇	鼈	皷	鼕	鼡	鼬	鼾	齊	齒
80	齔	齣	齟	齠	齡	齦	齧	齬	齪	齷	齲	齶	龕	龜	龠					

Row 84 01 02 03 04 05 06 07.08 09 10 11 12 13 14 15 16 17 18 19

00		堯	槇	遙	瑤	凜	熙													
20																				
40																				
60																				
80																				

Rows 85–94 Unassigned

C

JIS X 0212-1990
Table

The following pages constitute a table for the characters of JIS X 0212-1990. They are indexed by KUTEN value. Here is a description of how to determine KUTEN code. The example uses the character © in row 2. First, the row number, 2, is used for the KU portion of the KUTEN code (a zero is prepended since two digits are required):

```
KU   =   02
TEN  =   --
```

Next, within row 2 are subrows. Find the subrow (60) which contains the character ©. You then find the column heading (17) directly above the character. Add these two numbers, 60 and 17, to determine the TEN portion of the KUTEN code:

```
KU   =   02
TEN  =   77
```

The correct KUTEN value 0277 is simply the concatenation of these two values.

Note how row 5 includes characters—it contains four additional katakana characters that may be added to this character set in the future. These four characters were discussed in Chapter 3.

Row 1 Unassigned

Row 2   01 02 03 04 05 06 07 08 09 10 11 12 13 14 15 16 17 18 19

```
                                                    ˘  ˘      •  ″
00
                ‾   ˳   ˚  ~  ʼ  ∴                i  ¦  ¿
20
40 ·
                                                    º  ª  ©  ®  ™
60
80      ¤  №
```

Rows 3–4 Unassigned

Row 5   01 02 03 04 05 06 07 08 09 10 11 12 13 14 15 16 17 18 19

```
00
20
40
60
80            ヷ ヸ ヹ ヺ*
```

Row 6   01 02 03 04 05 06 07 08 09 10 11 12 13 14 15 16 17 18 19

```
00
20
40
60              Ά Έ Ή Ί Ϊ   Ό   Ύ Ϋ   Ώ
80      ά έ ή ί ϊ ό ς ύ ϋ ΰ ώ
```

Row 7   01 02 03 04 05 06 07 08 09 10 11 12 13 14 15 16 17 18 19

```
00
                                              Ђ Ѓ Є Ѕ І Ї
20
40      Ј Љ Њ Ћ Ќ Ў Џ
60
80      ђ ѓ є ѕ і ї ј љ њ ћ ќ ў џ
```

Row 8 Unassigned

Row 9   01 02 03 04 05 06 07 08 09 10 11 12 13 14 15 16 17 18 19

```
00      Æ Đ  Ħ  Ĳ  Ŀ Ł   Ŋ Ø Œ  Ŧ Þ
20                              æ đ ð ħ ı ĳ ĸ
40      ŀ ł ʼn ŋ ø œ ß ŧ þ
60 ·
80
```

---

*Note that these four katakana characters have not yet been formally accepted into this standard.

Row 10 01 02 03 04 05 06 07 08 09 10 11 12 13 14 15 16 17 18 19

00	Á À Ä Â Ã Ă Ā Ą Å Ã Ć Ĉ Č Ç Ċ Ď É È Ë
20	Ê Ě Ė Ē Ę Ĝ Ğ Ġ Ģ Ĥ Í Ì Ï Î Ĭ Ī Į Ĩ
40	Ĵ Ķ Ĺ Ľ Ļ Ń Ň Ņ Ñ Ó Ò Ö Ô Ŏ Ő Ō Õ Ŕ Ř Ŗ
60	Ś Ŝ Š Ş Ť Ţ Ú Ù Ü Û Ŭ Ŭ Ű Ū Ų Ů Ũ Ú Ù
80	Ŭ Ŵ Ý Ÿ Ŷ Ź Ž Ż

Row 11 01 02 03 04 05 06 07 08 09 10 11 12 13 14 15 16 17 18 19

00	á à ä â ă ă ā ą å ã ć ĉ č ç ċ ď é è ë
20	ê ě ė ē ę ĝ ğ ğ ġ ĥ í ì ï î ĭ ī į ĩ
40	ĵ ķ ĺ ľ ļ ń ň ņ ñ ó ò ö ô ŏ ő ō õ ŕ ř ŗ
60	ś ŝ š ş ť ţ ú ù ü û ŭ ŭ ű ū ų ů ũ ú ù ŭ
80	ŭ ŵ ý ÿ ŷ ź ž ż

Rows 12–15 Unassigned

Row 16 01 02 03 04 05 06 07 08 09 10 11 12 13 14 15 16 17 18 19

00	丂 丄 丅 开 刃 丟 丣 两 丨 丫 丮 丯 丰 举 乀 乁 乂 乇
20	乚 乜 乣 乩 乴 乵 乶 乷 亍 三 亖 亝 亯 亹 仃 仐 仚 仛
40	仡 仢 仨 仯 仱 仳 仵 份 仾 仿 伀 伂 伈 伋 伌 伒 伔 众
60	伙 伮 伲 你 伷 伵 伸 伹 伻 伾 佀 佂 佈 佉 佋 佌 佤 佥 佘
80	佟 佣 個 佬 佮 佥 佷 佸 佹 佺 佽 佾 侁 侂 侄

Row 17 01 02 03 04 05 06 07 08 09 10 11 12 13 14 15 16 17 18 19

00	侅 侉 侊 侌 侎 侐 侒 侓 侚 侜 侞 侟 侲 侭 侰 侱 侲 侳
20	侷 侼 俊 俁 俅 徐 俉 俇 俋 俌 俍 俒 俓 俔 俕 俙 俛 俠
40	俢 俍 俐 俒 俖 俵 俇 俴 俅 倘 倛 俻 俽 俿 倎 倓 倕 倰
60	倲 倳 倵 倷 倸 倶 倻 偁 偄 偅 偊 偟 偣 偡 偤 偨 偩 倍
80	偭 偰 偱 偲 偼 偐 偰 傁 傃 傄 傆 傇 傊 傌

Row 18 01 02 03 04 05 06 07 08 09 10 11 12 13 14 15 16 17 18 19

00	傒 偏 傔 傖 傛 傜 傝 傟 傠 傢 傣 傯 傫 傮 傪 傓 僃 備
20	僄 僇 僌 僎 僐 債 僔 僘 僜 僝 僟 僤 僨 僩 僯 僱 僪 傼
40	僰 僵 僶 償 儈 儋 傲 儍 儎 儐 儓 儖 儗 儘 儜 儞 儠 質
60	儩 儬 儭 儴 儵 儷 儸 價 先 兇 厇 尣 兜 兟 祪 尧 牂 兦 兾
80	冃 冄 冋 冎 尤 冝 冡 冣 冭 冸 冺 冼 冾 冿 凁

Row 19		01	02	03	04	05	06	07	08	09	10	11	12	13	14	15	16	17	18	19
00		凈	减	凑	凒	凓	凕	凘	凚	凢	凥	凮	凲	凳	凴	凷	刁	刂	刅	划
20	刌	刕	刖	刘	刢	刨	刱	刲	刵	刼	剅	剉	剕	剗	剘	剚	剜	剟	剠	剡
40	剦	剮	剷	剸	剹	劀	劂	劅	劊	劌	劓	劕	劖	劗	劘	劚	劜	劤	劥	劦
60	劧	劯	劰	劶	劷	劸	劺	劻	劽	勀	勄	勆	勈	勌	勏	勑	勔	勖	勛	勜
80	勡	勥	勨	勩	勪	勬	勰	勱	勴	勶	勷	匀	勼	匊	匋					

Row 20		01	02	03	04	05	06	07	08	09	10	11	12	13	14	15	16	17	18	19
00		匌	匑	匓	匘	匛	匜	匞	匟	匢	匧	匨	匩	匫	匬	匭	匰	匲	匵	匼
20	匽	匾	卂	卌	卋	卙	卛	卡	卣	卥	卬	卭	卲	卹	卾	厃	厇	厈	厎	厓
40	厔	厙	厝	厡	厤	厪	厫	厯	厲	厴	厵	厷	厸	厺	厽	叀	叅	叏	叒	叓
60	叕	叚	叝	叞	叠	另	叧	叵	吂	吓	吚	吡	吧	吨	吪	启	吱	吴	吵	呃
80	呄	呇	呍	呏	呞	呢	呤	呦	呧	呩	呫	呭	呮	呴	呿					

Row 21		01	02	03	04	05	06	07	08	09	10	11	12	13	14	15	16	17	18	19
00		咁	咃	咅	咈	咉	咍	咑	咕	咖	咜	咟	咠	咦	咧	咩	咪	咭	咮	咱
20	咷	咹	咺	咻	咿	哆	哊	响	哎	哠	哪	哬	哯	哶	哼	哾	哿	唀	唁	唅
40	唈	唉	唌	唍	唎	唕	唪	唫	唲	唵	唶	唻	唼	唽	啁	啇	啉	啊	啍	啐
60	啑	啘	啚	啛	啞	啠	啡	啤	啦	啿	喁	喂	喆	喈	喎	喏	喑	喒	喓	喔
80	喗	喣	喤	喭	喲	喿	嗁	嗃	嗆	嗉	嗋	嗌	嗎	嗑	嗒					

Row 22		01	02	03	04	05	06	07	08	09	10	11	12	13	14	15	16	17	18	19
00		嗓	嗗	嗘	嗛	嗞	嗢	嗩	嗶	嗿	嘅	嘈	嘊	嘍	嘎	嘏	嘐	嘑	嘒	嘙
20	嘬	嘰	嘳	嘵	嘷	嘹	嘻	嘼	嘽	嘿	噀	噁	噃	噄	噆	噉	噋	噍	噏	噔
40	噞	噠	噡	噢	噣	噦	噩	噭	噯	噱	噲	噵	嚄	嚅	嚈	嚋	嚌	嚕	嚙	嚚
60	嚝	嚞	嚟	嚦	嚧	嚨	嚩	嚫	嚬	嚭	嚱	嚳	嚷	嚾	囅	囉	囊	囋	囏	囐
80	囌	囍	囙	囜	囝	囟	囡	囤	囥	囦	囧	囨	囱	囫	园					

Row 23		01	02	03	04	05	06	07	08	09	10	11	12	13	14	15	16	17	18	19
00		囶	囷	圁	圂	圇	圊	圌	圑	圕	圚	圛	圝	圠	圢	圣	圤	圥	圩	圪
20	圬	圮	圯	圳	圴	圽	圾	圿	坅	坆	坌	坍	坒	坢	坥	坧	坨	坫	坭	坮
40	坯	坰	坱	坳	坴	坵	坷	坹	坺	坻	坼	坾	垁	垃	垌	垔	垗	垙	垚	垜
60	垝	垞	垟	垡	垕	垧	垨	垩	垬	垸	垽	埇	埈	埌	埏	埕	埝	埞	埤	埦
80	埧	埩	埭	埰	埵	埶	埸	埽	埾	埿	堃	堄	堈	堉	埡					

Row 24		01	02	03	04	05	06	07	08	09	10	11	12	13	14	15	16	17	18	19
00		堌	堍	堛	堞	堟	堠	堦	堧	堭	堲	堹	堿	塉	塌	塍	塏	塐	塕	塟
20	塡	塤	塧	塨	塸	塼	塿	墀	墁	墇	墈	墉	墊	墌	墍	墏	墐	墔	墖	墝
40	墠	墡	墢	墦	墩	墱	墲	墴	墼	壂	壈	壍	壎	壐	壒	壔	壖	壚	壝	壡
60	壢	壨	壳	夅	夆	夋	夌	夒	夓	夔	夔	夝	夡	夣	夤	夨	夰	夳	夵	夽
80	夶	奀	奃	奆	奒	奓	奙	奛	奝	奞	奟	奡	奣	奫	奭					

Row 25		01	02	03	04	05	06	07	08	09	10	11	12	13	14	15	16	17	18	19
00		奱	奲	奵	奶	她	奻	奼	妋	妌	妎	妒	妕	妗	妟	妤	妧	妭	妮	妯
20	妰	妳	妷	妺	妼	姁	姃	姄	姈	姊	姍	姒	姝	姞	姟	姣	姤	姧	姮	姯
40	姱	姲	姴	姷	娀	娄	娌	娍	娎	娒	娓	娞	娣	娤	娧	娨	娪	娭	娰	婄
60	婅	婇	婈	婌	婐	婕	婞	婣	婥	婧	婭	婷	婺	婻	婾	媋	媐	媓	媖	媙
80	媜	媞	媟	媠	媢	媧	媬	媱	媲	媳	媵	媸	媺	媻	媿					

Row 26		01	02	03	04	05	06	07	08	09	10	11	12	13	14	15	16	17	18	19
00		嫄	嫆	嫈	嫏	嫚	嫜	嫠	嫥	嫪	嫮	嫵	嫶	嫽	嬀	嬁	嬈	嬗	嬴	嬙
20	嬛	嬝	嬡	嬥	嬭	嬸	孁	孋	孌	孒	孖	孞	孨	孮	孯	孼	孽	孾	孿	宁
40	宄	宆	宊	宎	宐	宑	宓	宔	宖	宨	宩	宬	宭	宯	宱	宲	宷	宺	宼	寀
60	寁	寍	寏	寖	寗	寘	寙	寚	寠	寯	寱	寴	寽	尌	尗	尞	尟	尣	尦	尩
80	尪	尮	尯	尰	尲	尵	尶	屙	屚	屜	屢	屣	屧	屨	屩					

Row 27		01	02	03	04	05	06	07	08	09	10	11	12	13	14	15	16	17	18	19
00		屭	屰	屲	屵	屺	屻	屼	屽	岇	岈	岊	岏	岒	岝	岟	岠	岢	岣	岦
20	岪	岲	岴	岵	岺	峉	峋	峒	峝	峗	峮	峱	峲	峴	峷	崆	崍	崒	崫	崣
40	崤	崦	崧	崱	崴	崹	崽	崿	嵂	嵃	嵆	嵈	嵕	嵑	嵙	嵊	嵟	嵠	嵡	嵢
60	嵤	嵪	嵭	嵰	嵹	嵺	嵾	嵿	嶁	嶃	嶈	嶊	嶒	嶓	嶔	嶕	嶙	嶛	嶟	嶠
80	嶧	嶫	嶰	嶴	嶸	嶹	巃	巇	巋	巐	巎	巘	巙	巠	巤					

Row 28		01	02	03	04	05	06	07	08	09	10	11	12	13	14	15	16	17	18	19
00		巩	巸	巹	帀	帇	帍	帒	帔	帕	帘	帟	帠	帮	帨	帲	帵	帾	幋	幐
20	幉	幑	幖	幘	幛	幜	幞	幨	幪	幫	幬	幭	幮	幰	庀	庋	庎	庢	庤	庥
40	庨	庪	庬	庱	庳	庽	庾	庿	廆	廌	廋	廎	廑	廒	廔	廕	廜	廞	廥	廫
60	异	弆	弇	弈	弎	弙	弜	弝	弡	弢	弣	弤	弨	弫	弬	弮	弰	弴	弶	弻
80	弽	弿	彀	彄	彅	彇	彍	彐	彔	彘	彛	彟	彣	彤	彧					

Row 29		01	02	03	04	05	06	07	08	09	10	11	12	13	14	15	16	17	18	19
00		彯	彲	彴	彵	彸	彺	彽	彾	徉	徍	徏	徖	徜	徝	徢	徧	徫	徤	徬
20	徯	徰	徱	徸	忄	忇	忈	忉	忋	忐	忑	忒	忓	忔	忞	忡	忢	忨	忩	忪
40	忬	忭	忮	忯	忲	忳	忶	忺	忼	怇	怊	怍	怓	怔	怗	怘	怚	怟	怤	怭
60	怳	怵	恀	恇	恈	恉	恌	恑	恔	恖	恗	恝	恡	恧	恱	恾	恿	悂	悆	悈
80	悊	悎	悑	悓	悕	悘	悝	悞	悢	悤	悥	您	悰	悱	悷					

Row 30		01	02	03	04	05	06	07	08	09	10	11	12	13	14	15	16	17	18	19
00		悻	悾	惂	惄	惈	惉	惊	惋	惎	惏	惔	惕	惙	惛	惝	惞	惢	惥	惲
20	惵	惸	惼	惽	愂	愇	愊	愌	愐	愑	愒	愓	愔	愖	愗	愙	愜	愞	愢	愪
40	愫	愰	愱	愵	愶	愷	愹	慁	慅	慆	慉	慞	慠	慬	慲	慸	慻	慼	慿	憀
60	憁	憃	憄	憋	憍	憒	憓	憗	憘	憜	憝	憟	憠	憥	憨	憪	憭	憸	憹	憼
80	懀	懁	懂	懎	懏	懕	懜	懝	懞	懟	懡	懢	懧	懩	懥					

Row 31

	01	02	03	04	05	06	07	08	09	10	11	12	13	14	15	16	17	18	19
00		懬	懭	懯	戁	戃	戄	戅	戓	戕	或	戠	戢	戣	戧	戩	戫	戹	戽	扂
20	扄	扃	扆	扌	扐	扑	扒	扔	扖	扚	扜	扤	扭	扯	扳	扺	抆	抍	抎	抏
40	抐	抦	抨	抳	抶	抷	抺	抾	抿	拄	拎	拕	拖	拚	拪	拲	拴	拼	拽	挃
60	挄	挊	挋	挍	挐	挓	挖	挘	挩	挪	挭	挵	挶	挹	挼	捁	捂	捃	捄	捆
80	捊	捋	捎	捒	捓	捔	捘	捛	捥	捦	捬	捭	捱	捴	捵					

Row 32

	01	02	03	04	05	06	07	08	09	10	11	12	13	14	15	16	17	18	19
00		捸	捼	捽	捿	掂	掄	掇	掊	掐	掔	掕	掙	掚	掞	掤	掦	掭	掮	掯
20	掽	揁	揅	揈	揎	揑	揓	揔	揕	揜	揠	揥	揪	揬	揲	揳	揵	揸	揹	搉
40	搊	搐	搒	搔	搘	搞	搠	搢	搤	搥	搩	搪	搯	搰	搵	搽	搿	摋	摏	摑
60	摒	摓	摔	摚	摛	摜	摝	摟	摠	摡	摣	摭	摳	摴	摻	摽	撅	撇	撏	撐
80	撑	撘	撙	撛	撝	撟	撡	撣	撦	撨	撬	撳	撽	撾	撿					

Row 33

	01	02	03	04	05	06	07	08	09	10	11	12	13	14	15	16	17	18	19
00		擄	擉	擊	擋	擌	擎	擐	擑	擕	擗	擤	擥	擩	擪	擭	擰	擵	擷	擻
20	擿	攁	攄	攈	攉	攊	攏	攓	攔	攖	攙	攛	攞	攟	攢	攦	攩	攮	攱	攺
40	攼	攽	敃	敇	敉	敐	敒	敔	敟	敠	敧	敫	敺	敽	斁	斅	斊	斒	斕	斘
60	斝	斠	斣	斦	斮	斲	斳	斴	斿	旂	旈	旉	旎	旐	旔	旖	旘	旟	旰	旲
80	旴	旵	旹	旾	旿	昀	昄	昈	昉	昍	昑	昒	昕	昖	昝					

Row 34

	01	02	03	04	05	06	07	08	09	10	11	12	13	14	15	16	17	18	19
00		昞	昡	昢	昣	昤	昦	昩	昪	昫	昬	昮	昰	昱	昳	昹	昷	晀	晅	晆
20	晊	晌	晑	晎	晗	晘	晙	晛	晜	晠	晡	曻	晪	晫	晬	晾	晳	晵	晿	晷
40	晸	晹	晻	暀	晼	暋	暌	暍	暐	暒	暙	暚	暛	暜	暟	暠	暤	暭	暱	暲
60	暵	暻	暿	曀	曂	曃	曈	曌	曎	曏	曔	曛	曟	曨	曫	曬	曮	曺	朅	朇
80	朎	朓	朙	朜	朠	朢	朳	朾	杅	杇	杈	杌	杔	杕	杝					

Row 35

	01	02	03	04	05	06	07	08	09	10	11	12	13	14	15	16	17	18	19
00		杦	杬	杮	杴	杶	杻	极	构	枎	枏	枑	枓	枖	枘	枙	枛	枰	枱	枲
20	枵	枻	枼	枽	柹	柀	柂	柃	柅	柈	柉	柒	柗	柙	柜	柡	柦	柰	柲	柶
40	柷	桒	栔	栙	栝	栟	栨	栧	栬	栭	栯	栰	栱	栳	栻	栿	桄	桅	桊	桌
60	桕	桗	桘	桛	桫	桮	桯	桰	桱	桲	桵	桹	桺	桻	桼	梂	梄	梆	梈	梖
80	梘	梚	梜	梡	梣	梥	梩	梪	梮	梲	梻	棅	棈	棌	棏					

Row 36

	01	02	03	04	05	06	07	08	09	10	11	12	13	14	15	16	17	18	19
00		棐	棑	棓	棖	棙	棜	棝	棥	棨	棪	棫	棬	棭	棰	棱	棵	棶	棻	棼
20	棽	椆	椉	椊	椐	椑	椓	椖	椗	椱	椳	椵	椸	椻	楂	楅	楉	楎	楗	楛
40	楣	楤	楥	楦	楨	楩	楬	楰	楱	楲	楺	楻	楿	榀	榍	榒	榖	榘	榡	榥
60	榦	榨	榫	榭	榯	榷	榸	榺	榼	槅	槈	槑	槖	槗	槢	槥	槮	槯	槱	槳
80	槵	槾	樀	樁	樃	樏	樑	樕	樚	樝	樠	樤	樨	樰	樲					

Row 37

	01	02	03	04	05	06	07	08	09	10	11	12	13	14	15	16	17	18	19
00		檶	橻	槇	樾	樺	橆	槑	橉	椑	播	橐	橑	橒	樽	橖	橛	橤	檜	燃
20	橱	橼	橾	橺	橃	樹	橋	樫	權	橿	檛	橄	橫	檟	橤	橬	檀	橍	橲	橖
40	橆	橤	橜	橀	橱	橈	橒	橰	橱	橫	橲	橡	橎	橱	橫	橳	橡	橔	橱
60	橤	橎	橇	橖	橲	橱	橤	橤	橫	橫	橐	欼	欵	欽	欸	欹	欶	欷	欻
80	欿	歁	歆	歅	歃	歈	歠	歓	歔	歧	歫	歮	歰	歱	歿				

Row 38

	01	02	03	04	05	06	07	08	09	10	11	12	13	14	15	16	17	18	19
00		殀	殂	殄	殈	殌	殑	殥	殫	殖	殪	殬	殮	殭	殮	殰	殸	殴	殳	殶
20	殷	殼	毉	毌	毖	毚	毡	毤	毦	毧	毮	毸	毺	毻	毼	氂	氈	氉	氊
40	氋	氏	氒	氞	氟	氜	氧	氩	氫	氮	氳	氵	承	氷	氻	氿	汉	汋	汍	汏
60	汒	汔	汗	汛	汜	汫	汭	汯	汴	汶	汸	汹	汻	沅	沆	沈	沉	沔	沕	泰
80	沘	沜	沟	沰	泡	沴	泂	洗	本	泏	泐	泑	泒	泔	泖				

Row 39

	01	02	03	04	05	06	07	08	09	10	11	12	13	14	15	16	17	18	19
00		泚	泜	泠	泧	泩	泫	泬	泮	沛	盂	洄	洇	洊	泊	洏	洑	涑	泽	洦
20	洧	洨	汧	洮	挈	洱	洹	洼	洿	浗	浞	浟	浲	浘	涅	浯	涍	涘	涂	涇
40	涑	涒	涔	涖	涗	涘	涪	涬	涴	涷	湊	湛	渚	淄	渥	淊	湊	淏	淖	淛
60	淝	淟	淠	淢	淥	淩	淯	淰	淴	淶	淼	渀	渄	渏	渧	渨	渲	渢	渶	淲
80	渼	湄	湅	湈	湉	湋	湏	湑	湒	湓	湔	湗	湜	湝	湞				

Row 40

	01	02	03	04	05	06	07	08	09	10	11	12	13	14	15	16	17	18	19
00		湢	湣	湨	湳	湻	淄	湼	溓	溔	溠	溧	溨	溮	溱	溳	溻	溿	滀	滁
20	滃	滇	滈	滊	滍	滎	滏	滫	滭	滮	滱	滶	滹	滻	漷	漮	漪	漰	漵	滑
40	漚	漆	漦	漩	漪	漯	漰	漳	漶	漻	潅	潆	潒	潓	潑	潗	潚	潢	潶	潏
60	潞	潡	潢	潦	潭	潽	潾	澃	澇	澈	澋	澌	澍	澐	澒	澔	澕	澖	澗	澟
80	澠	澥	澦	澧	澨	澮	澰	澱	澲	澶	澼	濅	濇	濈	濊				

Row 41

	01	02	03	04	05	06	07	08	09	10	11	12	13	14	15	16	17	18	19
00		濋	濌	濎	濩	濱	濹	濼	濽	濿	瀀	瀇	瀍	瀌	瀒	瀓	瀔	瀕	瀘	瀄
20	瀗	瀙	瀜	瀞	瀤	瀥	瀨	瀬	瀲	瀴	瀶	瀹	瀺	瀻	瀼	瀽	蠢	灬	灹	灵	灶
40	灾	炁	炅	炆	炔	炕	炖	炈	炘	炟	炤	炫	炰	炱	炴	炷	烊	姚	烓	烔
60	烕	烖	烘	烜	烤	烺	烻	焄	焅	焆	焇	焋	焌	焏	焞	焠	焢	焭	焯	焰
80	焱	焸	煁	煅	煆	煇	煊	煋	煐	煒	煖	煗	煜	煞	煠				

Row 42

	01	02	03	04	05	06	07	08	09	10	11	12	13	14	15	16	17	18	19
00		煨	煫	煴	煶	煏	煙	熒	煇	熛	熠	熢	熯	熰	熲	熳	熺	熿	熼	燁
20	燄	燋	燌	燓	燖	燙	燚	燜	燸	燾	燀	燫	燶	燾	爀	爈	爉	爓	爐	爛
40	爫	爯	甌	爸	爹	阿	牂	牒	牖	牚	牏	牐	牕	掌	牛	牞	牠	牣	切
60	牥	牫	牟	牯	牁	牷	牸	牻	牼	牾	犄	犉	犍	犇	犆	犛	犨	犭	犮	犰
80	犴	狀	犹	狄	狂	狉	狊	狋	狘	狟	狗	狳	狴	狺	狻				

Row 43　01 02 03 04 05 06 07 08 09 10 11 12 13 14 15 16 17 18 19

00		猅 猣 猭 猵 猺 猼 猻 獀 獂 猲 猭 猺 猻 獆 獇 獈 獉 獊 獋
20	猵 猺 猻 獌 獍 獎 獏 獐 獑 猺 獒 獓 獔 獕 獖 獗 獘 獙 獚 獛
40	獜 獝 獞 獟 彌 玀 玁 玅 玆 玎 玐 玑 玒 玕 玗 玘 玙 玟 玞 玠
60	玢 玥 玦 玲 玫 玭 玵 玷 玹 玼 玿 珀 珂 珆 珉 珋 珌 珏 珒 珓
80	珖 珙 珝 珡 珣 珦 珧 珩 珫 珬 珮 珹 珺 珽

Row 44　01 02 03 04 05 06 07 08 09 10 11 12 13 14 15 16 17 18 19

00		珵 珶 珸 珹 琇 琊 琑 琚 琛 琤 琦 琨 琪 琫 琬 琭 琮 琯 琱 琲
20	琰 琲 琹 琺 琿 瑀 瑃 瑋 瑍 瑑 瑗 瑝 瑢 瑪 瑨 瑬 瑭 瑮 瑱 瑭
40	瑱 瑱 瑲 瑳 瓁 璆 璇 璉 璚 璐 璑 璒 璘 璙 璚 璜 璟 璠 璡 璢
60	璣 璦 璨 璩 璪 璫 璯 璲 璵 璹 璻 璿 瓈 瓉 瓊 瓏 瓐 瓑 瓘 瓔
80	瓚 瓛 瓞 瓟 瓠 瓡 瓢 瓮 瓯 瓰 瓱 瓲 瓳 瓵

Row 45　01 02 03 04 05 06 07 08 09 10 11 12 13 14 15 16 17 18 19

00		瓼 甖 甗 甠 甡 甤 甥 甩 甬 甯 甶 甽 界 甿 畂 畇 畈 販
20	畎 畐 畒 畗 畞 畟 畯 畱 畹 畺 畼 畽 畾 疁 疄 疅 疊 广 疒
40	疕 疙 疘 疚 疤 疴 疢 疿 痀 痁 痄 痆 痌 痎 痏 痗 痚 痟 痛
60	痤 痧 瘍 痕 痘 痱 痺 瘀 痙 瘇 瘈 瘉 瘊 瘌 瘏 瘐 瘓 瘕 瘖
80	瘙 瘛 瘜 瘝 瘥 瘞 瘢 瘦 瘩 瘰 瘳 瘵 瘲 瘷

Row 46　01 02 03 04 05 06 07 08 09 10 11 12 13 14 15 16 17 18 19

00		瘺 瘻 瘼 癀 癁 療 癄 癅 癆 癈 癊 癋 癌 癎 癏 癐 癑 癒 癜
20	癟 皁 皅 皉 皋 皌 皍 皏 皐 皒 皕 皜 皝 皞 皡 皣 皤 皥 皦
40	皨 盇 盋 盌 盎 盐 盒 盡 盦 盨 盬 盰 盱 盳 盵 盻 盽 眀 盰
60	眊 眅 眈 眔 眕 眗 眙 眚 眜 眢 眫 眨 眭 眮 眴 眵 眶 眹 眾
80	眷 眽 睆 睊 睍 睎 睏 睒 睖 睗 睜 睟 睠 睢

Row 47　01 02 03 04 05 06 07 08 09 10 11 12 13 14 15 16 17 18 19

00		睤 睧 睪 睬 睰 睲 睳 睴 睺 睻 督 瞇 瞌 瞍 瞔 瞕 瞖 瞤 瞟
20	瞢 瞧 瞪 瞰 瞱 瞵 瞷 瞸 瞺 矑 矒 彎 矔 矞 矟 矠 矤 矦 矧
40	矬 矰 矱 矴 矸 矹 砅 砆 砉 砍 砎 砑 砓 砡 碎 砒 砝 砨 砮 砱
60	砷 砼 硃 硇 硌 硌 硎 硒 硜 硤 硨 硫 硯 硭 硻 硾 确 硺 硾 碊
80	碏 碔 碘 碖 碗 碙 碟 碤 碨 碬 碭 碰 碱 碲 碳

Row 48　01 02 03 04 05 06 07 08 09 10 11 12 13 14 15 16 17 18 19

00		碻 碩 碽 磇 磈 磉 磌 磎 磏 磑 磓 磖 磗 磘 磚 磛 磜 磠 磡
20	磥 磦 磪 磧 磷 磺 磻 曆 礆 礇 磬 礉 礊 礋 礍 礎 礏 礐 礑 礒
40	礔 磚 礔 礻 礽 礿 衦 祆 祊 祋 役 祐 袟 衬 祙 祛 祜 祧 祩 袷
60	祲 祹 裋 裸 祾 禋 禌 禑 祼 禔 禕 禖 禘 禛 禜 禝 禡 禨 禩 禮
80	禱 禴 内 离 禿 秊 秖 秗 季 耗 秅 秖 秒 秞 秥 秎 袖

Row 49

	01	02	03	04	05	06	07	08	09	10	11	12	13	14	15	16	17	18	19
00		秠	秢	秥	秖	秫	秮	稐	秸	株	稂	稦	稇	稘	稙	稑	稒	稕	稢	稛
20	稡	稷	稫	稭	稯	稰	稴	稵	稶	稸	稹	稺	穄	穌	穕	穖	穙	穘	穜
40	穚	穟	禮	秧	穧	穫	穵	穸	突	窀	牢	窅	窆	窊	窋	窐	窑	窔	窞
60	窠	窣	窬	窳	窵	窿	窹	窬	竉	凱	竎	竑	竛	竚	竝	竩	竫	竴	竱
80	笂	竿	笆	笇	笔	笊	笽	筂	笩	笫	第	等	筚	笭	筮				

Row 50

	01	02	03	04	05	06	07	08	09	10	11	12	13	14	15	16	17	18	19
00		筠	筢	筦	筨	筤	笛	筰	筎	符	筠	箕	�	莆	筐	筸	筋	筲	筳	筷
20	箄	�	箘	箐	箑	箖	箍	箞	筺	篧	箺	箪	筦	箷	箾	箷	箸	篁	箽
40	簹	篠	篰	濱	篔	篣	篗	篙	篞	篛	篪	篲	篸	篵	篒	篘	篔	篼	篾
60	篢	篿	簃	簊	簏	簉	簌	簥	簎	簙	簦	簨	簺	籆	簵	簧	簸	籇	簆
80	簾	簹	簒	籔	籗	籀	籑	籓	籍	籚	籙	錢	籜	籝	籞				

Row 51

	01	02	03	04	05	06	07	08	09	10	11	12	13	14	15	16	17	18	19
00		籤	籣	籧	籩	籭	籮	籯	籲	粎	粏	籽	粆	粍	粌	粔	粞	粠	粦	粰
20	粮	粷	粺	粻	粼	粿	糂	糃	糈	糉	糄	糋	糕	糗	糙	糚	糝	糦	糵
40	糷	糩	糢	糾	紇	紈	紉	紏	紒	紓	紖	紝	紞	紟	紦	紪	紭	紱	紼
60	紽	紾	絀	絁	絇	絈	絍	絑	絓	絗	絚	絙	絜	絝	絥	絧	絪	絰	絺
80	絻	絿	綁	綄	綅	綆	綇	綈	綋	綌	綍	綑	綒	綗	綝				

Row 52

	01	02	03	04	05	06	07	08	09	10	11	12	13	14	15	16	17	18	19
00		綞	綦	綧	綪	綳	綶	綷	綹	綾	緃	緄	緅	緆	緌	緍	緎	緗	緙	緦
20	緢	緥	緫	緭	緫	絹	緱	緮	緵	緹	緺	縐	縑	縕	縗	縝	縞	縠	縋
40	縍	縔	縓	縜	縛	縶	縷	緊	縲	縼	然	縴	繪	繢	繦	繡	繩	繥	繮
60	繯	繳	繸	繾	繻	繿	纇	纈	纍	纑	纕	纘	纚	纝	纞	飲	瓪	缽	缾	缿
80	罃	罄	罇	罏	罒	罓	眾	罘	置	罜	罡	罪	冐	罦	罭				

Row 53

	01	02	03	04	05	06	07	08	09	10	11	12	13	14	15	16	17	18	19
00		罱	罶	罾	罿	羀	羋	羍	羏	羑	羐	殺	羍	羜	羋	羢	羭	羖	羪	羨
20	羉	羿	翀	翃	翄	翎	翏	翛	翟	翠	翥	翨	翬	翦	翩	翮	翱	翳	翾
40	耇	耈	耊	耎	耏	耔	耑	耖	耤	耬	耡	耜	耤	耨	耩	耪	耰	耴	耻
60	耵	耷	聇	耾	聃	聆	戝	聍	聑	聤	聦	聭	聱	聴	肁	肇	肎	肜	肶	肦
80	肧	肫	肸	肹	肢	肭	肺	肶	肸	肘	胗	胘	胠	胭	胮				

Row 54

	01	02	03	04	05	06	07	08	09	10	11	12	13	14	15	16	17	18	19
00		胰	胲	胳	胶	胹	胺	胾	胞	脅	脖	脃	脘	脗	脞	脡	脤	脧	脵	脰
20	脤	脺	脪	脧	腰	腊	腌	腒	脾	腠	腷	腧	腨	腩	腭	腯	腷	腐	臍	腹
40	膅	膁	脊	膆	膇	膘	腔	膊	膢	膮	膲	膴	膻	臋	臃	膄	臊	臋	臏	臕
60	臇	臃	臝	臞	臟	臤	臩	臬	臱	臻	臹	臿	舋	舋	臽	舌	舀	舄	刮
80	舓	舔	舚	舚	舝	舡	舢	舨	舲	舴	舺	艃	艄	艅	艆				

Row 55

	01	02	03	04	05	06	07	08	09	10	11	12	13	14	15	16	17	18	19
00		艋	艎	艏	艑	艖	艕	艗	艖	艜	艒	艐	芀	芁	芀	芀	尤	芁	芄	芇
20	芉	芊	芎	芑	屮	芙	芡	芭	芧	芰	芡	芣	芤	芋	芨	芩	芪	芮	芰	苍
40	芴	芷	芙	芼	芾	苈	苊	苐	苖	甫	苠	苣	苤	苞	芮	芶	苯	茶	苷	苽
60	苾	莆	茁	茇	茈	苣	茋	荔	茛	茝	茵	筆	荂	荊	茬	荄	茅	萸	汪	茂
80	茢	茼	苹	芎	荃	荄	荇	菽	茎	黄	肪	耄	茂	柱	莩				

Row 56

	01	02	03	04	05	06	07	08	09	10	11	12	13	14	15	16	17	18	19
00		荽	荿	莀	荊	黄	莆	莱	莒	茴	荅	莘	莙	莛	莜	莝	莟	覓	莩	莬
20	莽	莉	菀	菇	眾	菏	美	菑	菔	菝	拜	萎	菪	菹	菼	其	萆	萊		
40	菩	萑	菁	萩	葤	萯	萹	菹	蒸	萲	萻	萍	葑	葒	葵	葍	葙	甚	葜	
60	葚	葤	葡	葓	莉	葰	葳	葴	葶	蕙	葽	葽	迷	蒅	蒔	蒢	蒕	蒞	蒦	蒧
80	葯	蒪	蒯	蒲	蒴	蒺	蒽	蒾	蓀	蓂	蓄	蓇	蓉	蓓					

Row 57

	01	02	03	04	05	06	07	08	09	10	11	12	13	14	15	16	17	18	19
00		蓜	蓧	蓪	蓯	蓰	湃	蓱	蓷	蔻	蓺	蓻	蓽	蔂	蓪	蔰	蔑	蔇	蔀	蔋
20	蔓	蔖	蔣	蔤	蔥	蔧	蔪	蔫	蒲	蔴	蔶	蔿	蒪	蕚	蕅	蕓	蕒	蕓	蕚
40	蕙	蕜	蕝	蕞	蕟	蕣	蕡	蕤	蕫	蕯	蕹	蕺	蕻	蕽	蕷	蕸	薁	薆	薈
60	薉	薌	薏	薐	薘	薝	薟	薜	薢	薤	薧	薪	薫	薬	薭	薱	薲	薳	薴
80	薵	薶	薷	薸	薭	薺	薻	薼	薽	薾	薿	藂	藃						

Row 58

	01	02	03	04	05	06	07	08	09	10	11	12	13	14	15	16	17	18	19
00		藋	藌	藎	藑	藒	藔	藖	藙	藚	藛	藝	藬	藭	藳	藶	藷	藺	藹	藼
20	藾	蘀	蘁	蘂	蘃	虎	虓	虖	虘	虙	虝	虠	號	虩	虪	虫	虬	虮	虯
40	虰	虲	虳	虴	虵	虷	虸	虹	虺	蚃	蚄	蚅	蚆	蚇	蚈	蚉	蚊	蚋	蚍
60	蚎	蚏	蚐	蚑	蚔	蚖	蚗	蚘	蚙	蚚	蚛	蚜	蚝	蚞	蚟	蚠	蚡	蚢	蚣
80	蚤	蚥	蚦	蚧	蚨	蚩	蚪	蚫	蚭	蚮	蚯	蚰	蚱	蚲	蚳				

Row 59

	01	02	03	04	05	06	07	08	09	10	11	12	13	14	15	16	17	18	19
00		蚵	蚶	蚷	蚸	蚹	蚺	蚻	蚼	蚽	蚾	蚿	蛀	蛁	蛂	蛃	蛄	蛅	蛆	蛇
20	蛈	蛉	蛊	蛋	蛌	蛍	蛎	蛏	蛐	蛑	蛒	蛓	蛔	蛕	蛖	蛗	蛘	蛙	蛚
40	蛛	蛜	蛝	蛞	蛟	蛠	蛡	蛢	蛣	蛤	蛥	蛦	蛧	蛨	蛩	蛪	蛫	蛬	蛭
60	蛮	蛯	蛰	蛱	蛲	蛳	蛴	蛵	蛶	蛷	蛸	蛹	蛺	蛻	蛼	蛽	蛾	蛿	蜀
80	蜁	蜂	蜃	蜄	蜅	蜆	蜇	蜈	蜉	蜊	蜋	蜌	蜍						

Row 60

	01	02	03	04	05	06	07	08	09	10	11	12	13	14	15	16	17	18	19
00		蜎	蜏	蜐	蜑	蜒	蜓	蜔	蜕	衍	衎	衒	衖	街	衘	衙	衚	衝	衤
20	衩	衪	衯	衱	衳	衵	衶	衹	衺	袀	袂	袗	袘	袚	袙	袢	袠	袑	袣
40	袦	袧	袨	袩	袪	袬	袮	袯	袰	袴	袵	袶	袸	袹	袺	袻	袽	袾	袿
60	褀	褂	褃	褄	褅	褆	褈	褉	褋	褌	褍	褎	褏	褐	褑	褒	褓	褔	褕
80	褖	褗	褘	褙	褚	褛	褜	褝	褞	褟	褠	褢	褣	褤					

Row 61

	01	02	03	04	05	06	07	08	09	10	11	12	13	14	15	16	17	18	19
00		襂	襼	襷	襽	覍	覎	覔	覛	覝	覞	覟	覰	覤	覥	覨	覩	覬	覭	覯
20	觔	觕	觖	觝	觗	觘	觫	觭	觱	觳	觶	觹	觽	觾	訄	訅	訇	訏	訑
40	訒	訔	訕	訞	訠	訢	訤	訦	訫	訬	訯	訵	訽	訾	詀	詅	詇	詉	詋
60	詌	詎	詓	詖	詗	詘	詜	詝	詡	詥	詧	詵	詶	詷	詹	詺	詻	詾	詿
80	誃	誆	誋	誏	誐	誒	誖	誗	誙	誛	誧	誩	誷	誻	誾				

Row 62

	01	02	03	04	05	06	07	08	09	10	11	12	13	14	15	16	17	18	19
00		諀	諂	諐	諑	諓	諔	諙	諝	諞	諴	諵	諶	諿	謅	謆	謍	謑	謜
20	謞	謤	謦	謪	謰	謱	謲	謵	謶	謷	謸	謯	謺	謼	謾	譁	譆	譈	譊
40	譀	譒	譓	譔	譙	譍	譞	譣	譭	譶	譸	譹	譼	譾	譿	讁	讄	讅	讆
60	讋	讌	讍	讎	讑	衁	衂	衃	衆	衇	衈	衉	衊	衋	衎	衏	衐	衒	衕
80	衖	衘	衚	衜	衟	衠	衤	衦	衧	衪	衭	衯	衱						

Row 63

	01	02	03	04	05	06	07	08	09	10	11	12	13	14	15	16	17	18	19
00		狼	猂	貐	貒	貓	貙	貛	貜	貤	貹	貺	賅	賆	賉	賍	賏	賖	賕	賙
20	賝	賡	賨	賬	賯	賰	賲	賵	賶	賷	賸	賻	賾	賿	贄	赦	艶
40	赬	赮	趂	趄	趐	趒	趔	趖	趚	趛	趜	趡	趦	趫	趮	趯	趲	趵	趷
60	趹	趻	趽	跀	跁	跅	跈	跊	跎	跑	跔	跕	跗	跙	跤	跥	跧	跬	跰
80	跱	跲	跴	跽	踁	踄	踅	踆	踋	踑	踔		踖	踠					

Row 64

	01	02	03	04	05	06	07	08	09	10	11	12	13	14	15	16	17	18	19
00		踣	踦	踧	踱	踳	踶	踷	踸	踹	踽	蹀	蹁	蹋	蹍	蹎	蹔	蹖	蹚
20	蹜	蹝	蹟	蹠	蹣	蹬	蹭	蹯	蹰	蹱	蹺	蹻	蹾	躀	躂	躃	躄	躅	躆
40	躈	躋	躌	躎	躐	躑	躭	躮	躯	躰	軀	躳	躴	軄	軃	軆	軏	軑	軔
60	軜	軨	軮	軰	軱	軷	軹	軺	軭	軶	軒	軤	軥	軩	軫	軧	軨	軭	軭
80	軺	軻	軼	軿	輀	輇	輏	輐	輑	輖	輗	輘	輚						

Row 65

	01	02	03	04	05	06	07	08	09	10	11	12	13	14	15	16	17	18	19
00		輳	輴	輵	輶	輷	轔	轕	轗	轚	轞	轠	辝	辠	辡	辤	辥	辦	辵
20	辷	辺	达	辿	迀	池	迆	迃	迤	迉	迊	迋	迌	迍	迒	迓	迕	迖	迥
40	迣	迯	迥	适	逄	迴	逈	逌	逎	逓	逤	逦	逧	逭	逬	逳	逴	逷	逺
60	逽	遀	遃	遄	遌	遺	達	遬	遰	遴	遹	遻	邀	邂	邅	邋	邑	邒	邗
80	邙	邛	邝	加	邢	邟	邰	邲	邳	邴	邶	邦	邽	邾	邿				

Row 66

	01	02	03	04	05	06	07	08	09	10	11	12	13	14	15	16	17	18	19
00		郀	郅	郇	郈	郕	郗	郘	郙	郜	郝	郊	郥	郒	郶	郫	郯	耶	郴	郾
20	鄅	郿	鄧	鄒	鄆	郊	鄍	鄎	鄔	鄖	鄗	廓	鄚	鄜	鄞	鄂	鄠	鄢	鄧
40	鄣	鄤	鄦	鄩	鄫	鄬	鄲	鄹	鄻	鄾	鄿	酅	酆	酓	酑	酔	酖	酘	酕
60	酡	酤	酔	酦	酴	酹	酺	醀	醁	醃	醅	醆	醊	醍	醐	醑	醓	醔	醖
80	醘	醙	醞	醤	醭	醮	醰	醱	醲	醳	醶	醻	醼	醽	醾				

Row 67

	01	02	03	04	05	06	07	08	09	10	11	12	13	14	15	16	17	18	19
00		醺	醴	釀	釚	釞	釗	釛	釢	釱	釵	釻	釩	釪	釫	釭	釴	釶	�	釱
20	釷	釹	釻	釽	鈀	鈁	鈄	鈅	鈆	鈇	鈉	鈊	鈌	鈐	鈒	鈺	鈖	鈙	鈜	鈝
40	鈣	鈤	鈥	鈦	鈧	鈮	鈯	鈰	鈳	鈶	鈸	鈹	鈺	鈼	鈾	鈽	鉀	鉂	鉄	鉆
60	鉋	鉌	鉍	鉏	鉐	鉑	鉘	鉙	鉝	鉦	鉗	鉥	鉧	鉨	鉩	鉾	鉃	鉶	銅	鉬
80	鉰	鉷	鉸	鉹	鉻	鉼	鉽	鉿	銈	銉	銊	銍	銎	銒	銔				

Row 68

	01	02	03	04	05	06	07	08	09	10	11	12	13	14	15	16	17	18	19
00		銕	銗	銘	銙	銚	銛	銜	銝	銟	銠	銡	鑒	銤	銦	銧	銨	銩	銪	銫
20	銬	銀	鋅	銯	銰	銱	銲	銴	銵	銶	銸	銹	銺	鋓	語	鋆	鋊	鋉	鋜
40	鋐	鋑	鋀	銳	鋨	鋹	鋮	鋰	鋓	鋝	鋱	錂	鋷	鋻	鋟	鋶	錕	鋡	綜
60	錞	錖	錡	錤	錥	錧	錩	錪	錳	錴	錶	錸	錯	錸	錵	鏺	鍐	鍒	鍗
80	錻	錫	鎮	鍂	鍁	鍆	鍏	鍒	錰	鍐	鍖	鑒	鍴	鍶					

Row 69

	01	02	03	04	05	06	07	08	09	10	11	12	13	14	15	16	17	18	19
00		鍺	鍽	鎦	鍮	鎃	鎈	鎉	鍺	鎓	鎏	鎐	鎑	鎘	鎚	鎛	鎜	鎝	鎞
20	鎟	鎨	鎹	鎸	鎵	鎶	鎺	鍛	鎤	鎿	鏀	鏇	鍬	鏊	鏏	鏌	鏍	鏐	鏈
40	鏜	鏞	鏂	鏢	鏦	鏗	鏆	鏰	鏺	鏻	鏽	鏸	鏶	鏽	鏰	鏫	鏬	鏵	鐏
60	鐥	鐡	鐦	鐕	鐩	鐦	鐧	鐯	鐘	鐝	鐪	鐫	鐷	鐬	鐶	鐴	鐭	鐵	鐯
80	鑌	鑽	鑼	鑾	鑢	鑫	鑭	鑮	鑯	鑵	鑲	鑴	鑭	镸	臥				

Row 70

	01	02	03	04	05	06	07	08	09	10	11	12	13	14	15	16	17	18	19
00		钁	閂	閇	閊	閉	閔	閣	開	閟	閠	閡	閨	閩	閫	閬	閶	閣	闇	閿
20	闊	闌	闈	闋	闉	闐	闑	團	闓	關	闕	闔	闐	闍	闓	闞	阝	防	阮	阯
40	陂	阢	阮	阱	阳	阺	阮	陆	阺	阼	阽	陁	陒	陔	陵	陟	陘	陡	陮	陣
60	陲	陼	陻	陾	隄	陰	隃	隄	陞	隖	隈	陽	陳	隕	隥	隣	隩	隮	隯
80	隳	崔	雉	雒	嵩	雘	雚	雝	雞	雟	雯	雯	雰	雱	霂				

Row 71

	01	02	03	04	05	06	07	08	09	10	11	12	13	14	15	16	17	18	19
00		霈	霎	霉	霍	霐	霑	霒	霕	霟	霚	霢	霤	霨	霩	霪	霭	靖	靚
20	艶	靦	靝	面	靨	靫	靭	靳	靷	靸	靻	靽	靾	靿	鞁	鞂	鞃	鞌	鞀
40	鞁	鞾	鞸	鞢	鞮	鞱	鞲	鞵	鞶	鞸	鞹	鞺	鞾	鞿	韁	韃	韆	韈	韇
60	韉	韊	韌	韍	韎	韐	韑	韔	韗	韙	韛	韞	韟	韠	韡	韣	載	鐵	師
80	鮎	韭	韮	頏	頊	頙	頵	頌	頉	頎	領	頗	頖	頤	頮				

Row 72

	01	02	03	04	05	06	07	08	09	10	11	12	13	14	15	16	17	18	19
00		頰	頩	頮	頫	頯	頲	頳	頣	鼌	顑	頼	顂	顅	顧	顠	顡	顢	頚	顛
20	顢	顧	顥	顬	顤	顟	颬	颭	颮	颩	颲	颴	颺	颶	颸	颻	颼	颾	飀
40	飡	飣	飥	飦	飧	飪	飳	飶	飸	飼	養	飿	餕	餗	餚	餛	餜	餧	餬
60	餞	餟	餫	餱	餲	餳	餷	餺	餻	餼	餽	餾	餿	饁	饃	饄	饅	饇	饕
80	饈	饉	饊	饍	饎	饐	饘	馘	馣	馞	馦	馵	馼	駁	駃				

Row 73 01 02 03 04 05 06 07 08 09 10 11 12 13 14 15 16 17 18 19

```
00      駻 馼 罼 馿 駃 駉 駈 駌 駔 駛 駞 駟 駠 駣 駤 駥 駦 駧
20   駩 駪 駫 駬 駭 騃 騄 騂 騑 騖 騠 騍 騵 騩 騶 騷 騸 騿 驪
40   驉 驊 騙 騭 驁 騘 騻 騼 騹 騮 驑 驐 驌 驝 骩 骬 骮 骯 骲 骴
60   骵 骶 骹 骻 骾 骿 髃 髆 髈 髉 髐 髑 髕 髖 骱 髎 髟 髠 髡
80   髢 髣 髦 髫 髮 髯 髹 髷 髻 髺 髼 髽 髾 鬁 鬆
```

Row 74 01 02 03 04 05 06 07 08 09 10 11 12 13 14 15 16 17 18 19

```
00      鬈 鬃 鬏 鬌 鬍 鬐 鬑 鬒 鬓 鬖 鬗 鬘 鬚 鬜 鬠 鬦 鬫 鬭
20   鬴 鬵 鬶 鬷 鬺 彪 魌 魋 魊 魖 魗 魝 魞 魠 魡 魦 魣 魥 魨
40   魭 魬 魟 魴 魵 魲 魳 魶 鮀 鮦 鮒 鮐 鮓 鮄 鮊 鮋 鮑 鮍 鮏
60   鮒 鮖 鮘 鮥 鮧 鮦 鮨 鮩 鮪 鮫 鮬 鮭 鮮 鮯 鮰 鮱 鮳 鮴
80   鮵 鮶 鮷 鮸 鮹 鮺 鮻 鮼 鮽 鮾 鮿 鯀 鯁
```

Row 75 01 02 03 04 05 06 07 08 09 10 11 12 13 14 15 16 17 18 19

```
00      鯃 鯄 鯅 鯆 鯇 鯈 鯉 鯊 鯋 鯌 鯍 鯎 鯏 鯐 鯑 鯒 鯓 鯔
20   鯕 鯖 鯗 鯘 鯙 鯚 鯛 鯜 鯝 鯞 鯟 鯠 鯡 鯢 鯣 鯤 鯥 鯦 鯧
40   鯨 鯩 鯪 鯫 鯬 鯭 鯮 鯯 鯰 鯱 鯲 鯳 鯴 鯵 鯶 鳬 鳭 鳮
60   鳱 鳲 鳳 鳴 鳵 鳶 鳷 鳸 鳹 鳺 鳻 鳼 鳽 鳾 鳿 鴀 鴁 鴂
80   鴃 鴄 鴅 鴆 鴇 鴈 鴉 鴊 鴋 鴌 鴍 鴎 鴏 鴐
```

Row 76 01 02 03 04 05 06 07 08 09 10 11 12 13 14 15 16 17 18 19

```
00      鴑 鴒 鴓 鴔 鴕 鴖 鴗 鴘 鴙 鴚 鴛 鴜 鴝 鴞 鴟 鴠 鴡 鴢
20   鴣 鴤 鴥 鴦 鴧 鴨 鴩 鴪 鴫 鴬 鴭 鴮 鴯 鴰 鴱 鴲 鴳 鴴 鴵
40   鴶 鴷 鴸 鴹 鴺 鴻 鴼 鴽 鴾 鴿 鵀 鵁 鵂 鵃 鵄 鵅 鵆 鵇 鵈
60   麀 麂 麃 麄 麅 麆 麇 麈 麉 麊 麋 麌 麍 麎 麏 麐 麑 麒 麘
80   麵 麶 麷 麸 麹 麺 麻 麼 麽 麾 黀 黁 黂 黃
```

Row 77 01 02 03 04 05 06 07 08 09 10 11 12 13 14 15 16 17 18 19

```
00      鼄 鼅 鼆 鼇 鼈 鼉 鼊 鼋 鼓 鼔 鼕 鼖 鼗 鼘 鼙 鼚 鼛 鼜
20   鼝 鼞 鼟 鼠 鼡 鼢 鼣 鼤 鼥 鼦 鼧 鼨 鼩 鼪 鼫 鼬 鼭 鼮 鼯
40   鼰 鼱 鼲 鼳 鼴 鼵 鼶 鼷 鼸 鼹 鼺 鼻 鼼 鼽 鼾 鼿 齀 齁 齂
60   齃 齄 齅 齆 齇 齈 齉 齊
```
80

Rows 78–94 Unassigned

D

JIS Code Table Supplements

This appendix includes material that may help you to locate kanji in Appendixes B and C. The information here is similar to what you would find in the manuals for JIS X 0208-1990 and JIS X 0212-1990. You will find more complete pronunciation and radical indexes in the specialized Japanese dictionaries described at the end of Chapter 5.

Pronunciation Index

The following table is a pronunciation index for JIS X 0208-1990 which covers only JIS Level 1 kanji (JIS Level 2 kanji are arranged by radical then total number of strokes). A KUTEN range is provided for each basic sound of the 50 Sounds Table. Each sound is written in hiragana and also romanized.

Sound		KUTEN Range		Sound		KUTEN Range
あ	A	1601–1641		そ	SO	3325–3429
い	I	1642–1705		た	TA	3430–3544
う	U	1706–1732		ち	CHI	3545–3636
え	E	1733–1786		つ	TSU	3637–3665
お	O	1787–1827		て	TE	3666–3737
か	KA	1828–2074		と	TO	3738–3863
き	KI	2075–2268		な	NA	3864–3882
く	KU	2269–2320		に	NI	3883–3907
け	KE	2321–2434		ぬ	NU	3908
こ	KO	2435–2618		ね	NE	3909–3920
さ	SA	2619–2736		の	NO	3921–3934
し	SHI	2737–3157		は	HA	3935–4058
す	SU	3158–3203		ひ	HI	4059–4151
せ	SE	3204–3324		ふ	FU	4152–4225

Sound		KUTEN Range		Sound		KUTEN Range
へ	HE	4226–4260		ゆ	YU	4491–4528
ほ	HO	4261–4363		よ	YO	4529–4568
ま	MA	4364–4402		ら	RA	4569–4587
み	MI	4403–4418		り	RI	4588–4659
む	MU	4419–4428		る	RU	4660–4664
め	ME	4429–4445		れ	RE	4665–4703
も	MO	4446–4472		ろ	RO	4704–4732
や	YA	4473–4490		わ	WA	4733–4751

Radical Index

The following table is a radical index for JIS X 0208-1990 (covers JIS Level 2 kanji only) and JIS X 0212-1990. For each of the 214 radicals, their number, shape, name, and KUTEN ranges are given. Note that some radicals are not covered by a particular character set standard.

Number	Shape	Name	JIS X 0208-1990	JIS X 0212-1990
1 Stroke				
1	一	いち	4801–4803	1601–1608
2	丨	ぼう	4804–4805	1609–1614
3	丶	てん	4806–4807	…
4	丿	の	4808–4811	1615–1619
5	乙	おつ	4812	1620–1628
6	亅	はねぼう	4813–4816	…
2 Strokes				
7	二	に	4817–4820	1629–1632
8	亠	なべぶた	4821–4825	1633–1634
9	人	ひと	4826–4924	1635–1868
10	儿	ひとあし	4925–4931	1869–1877
11	入	いる	4932–4933	1878
12	八	はち	4934–4935	1879
13	冂	えんがまえ	4936–4943	1880–1883
14	冖	わかんむり	4944–4949	1884–1887
15	冫	にすい	4950–4959	1888–1908
16	几	つくえ	4960–4964	1909–1914
17	凵	うけばこ	4965–4966	1915
18	刀	かたな	4967–5001	1916–1955
19	力	ちから	5002–5016	1956–1990
20	勹	つつみがまえ	5017–5023	1991–2003

Number	Shape	Name	JIS X 0208-1990	JIS X 0212-1990
2 Strokes (continued)				
21	ヒ	さじのひ	5024	2004
22	匚	はこがまえ	5025–5029	2005–2018
23	匚	かくしがまえ	5030–5031	2019–2021
24	十	じゅう	5032–5037	2022–2026
25	卜	ぼくのと	5038	2027–2029
26	卩	ふしづくり	5039–5043	2030–2034
27	厂	がんだれ	5044–5050	2035–2050
28	ム	む	5051–5053	2051–2056
29	又	また	5054–5057	2057–2064
3 Strokes				
30	口	くち	5058–5187	2065–2281
31	囗	くにがまえ	5188–5208	2282–2312
32	土	つち	5209–5266	2313–2461
33	士	さむらい	5267–5272	2462
34	夂	ふゆがしら	5273	2463–2464
35	夂	すいにょう	5274–5275	2465–2470
36	夕	ゆうべ	5276–5278	2471–2474
37	大	だい	5279–5294	2475–2502
38	女	おんな	5301–5350	2503–2628
39	子	こ	5351–5362	2629–2638
40	宀	うかんむり	5363–5380	2639–2671
41	寸	すん	5381–5384	2672–2673
42	小	ちいさい	5385–5386	2674–2676
43	尢	まげあし	5387–5388	2677–2686
44	尸	しかばね	5389–5404	2687–2701
45	屮	てつ	5405	2702
46	山	やま	5406–5462	2703–2792
47	巛	まがりがわ	5463	2793–2794
48	工	たくみ	5464	2801
49	己	おのれ	5465–5466	2802–2803
50	巾	はば	5467–5483	2804–2833
51	干	ほす	5484–5485	…
52	幺	いとがしら	5486–5487	…
53	广	まだれ	5488–5513	2834–2859
54	廴	えんにょう	5514–5515	…
55	廾	にじゅうあし	5516–5520	2860–2863
56	弋	しきがまえ	5521–5522	2864
57	弓	ゆみ	5523–5531	2865–2886

Number	Shape	Name	JIS X 0208-1990	JIS X 0212-1990
3 Strokes (continued)				
58	彑	けいがしら	5532–5535	2887–2891
59	彡	さんづくり	5536–5537	2892–2902
60	彳	ぎょうにんべん	5538–5553	2903–2923
4 Strokes				
61	心	こころ	5554–5688	2924–3107
62	戈	かのほこ	5689–5707	3108–3116
63	戸	とびらのと	5708	3117–3122
64	手	て	5709–5828	3123–3337
65	支	じゅうまた	…	3338
66	攴	とまた	5829–5846	3339–3355
67	文	ぶん	…	3356–3358
68	斗	とます	5847–5848	3359–3362
69	斤	きん	5849–5850	3363–3367
70	方	ほう	5851–5858	3368–3377
71	无	すでのつくり	5859–5860	…
72	日	にち	5861–5908	3378–3476
73	曰	ひらび	5909–5911	3477–3479
74	月	つき	5912–5917	3480–3485
75	木	き	5918–6122	3486–3771
76	欠	かける	6123–6136	3772–3788
77	止	とめる	6137	3789–3793
78	歹	いちた	6138–6152	3794–3815
79	殳	るまた	6153–6156	3816–3822
80	毋	なかれ	6157–6158	3823
81	比	くらべるひ	…	3824–3825
82	毛	け	6159–6165	3826–3840
83	氏	うじ	6166	3841–3842
84	气	きがまえ	6167–6170	3843–3850
85	水	みず	6171–6352	3851–4135
86	火	ひ	6353–6406	4136–4239
87	爪	つめ	6407–6410	4240–4242
88	父	ちち	…	4243–4244
89	爻	めめ	6411–6412	…
90	爿	しょうへん	6413–6415	4245–4248
91	片	かた	6416–6417	4249–4254
92	牙	きば	…	4255
93	牛	うし	6418–6426	4256–4276
94	犬	いぬ	6427–6460	4277–4347

Number	Shape	Name	JIS X 0208-1990	JIS X 0212-1990
5 Strokes				
95	玄	げん	…	4348–4349
96	玉	たま	6461–6494	4350–4481
97	瓜	うり	6501–6502	4482–4484
98	瓦	かわら	6503–6518	4485–4503
99	甘	あまい	6519	…
100	生	うまれる	6520	4504–4507
101	用	もちいる	6521	4508–4510
102	田	た	6522–6542	4511–4536
103	疋	ひき	…	4537
104	疒	やまいだれ	6543–6601	4538–4620
105	癶	はつがしら	6602–6604	…
106	白	しろ	6605–6613	4621–4639
107	皮	ひのかわ	6614–6618	4640
108	皿	さら	6619–6628	4641–4652
109	目	め	6629–6665	4653–4733
110	矛	むのほこ	6666	4734–4736
111	矢	や	6667–6668	4737–4742
112	石	いし	6669–6710	4743–4842
113	示	しめす	6711–6726	4843–4881
114	禸	ぐうのあし	6727–6728	4882–4883
115	禾	のぎ	6729–6753	4884–4946
116	穴	あな	6754–6770	4947–4969
117	立	たつ	6771–6782	4970–4979
6 Strokes				
118	竹	たけ	6783–6865	4980–5108
119	米	こめ	6866–6892	5109–5142
120	糸	いと	6893–6992	5143–5274
121	缶	ほとぎ	6993–7005	5275–5283
122	网	あみがしら	7006–7020	5284–5305
123	羊	ひつじ	7021–7033	5306–5320
124	羽	はね	7034–7044	5321–5339
125	老	おい	7045–7047	5340–5342
126	而	しかして	…	5343–5346
127	耒	らいすき	7048–7053	5347–5358
128	耳	みみ	7054–7069	5359–5373
129	聿	ふでづくり	7070–7073	5374–5375
130	肉	にく	7074–7140	5376–5464
131	臣	しん	7141	5465

Number	Shape	Name	JIS X 0208-1990	JIS X 0212-1990

6 Strokes (continued)

Number	Shape	Name	JIS X 0208-1990	JIS X 0212-1990
132	自	みずから	…	5466–5470
133	至	いたる	7142–7143	5471–5474
134	臼	うす	7144–7149	5475–5478
135	舌	した	7150–7152	5479–5483
136	舛	ます	…	5484
137	舟	ふね	7153–7168	5485–5510
138	艮	こん	7169	…
139	色	いろ	7170	5511
140	艸	くさ	7171–7339	5512–5824
141	虍	とらがしら	7340–7344	5825–5837
142	虫	むし	7345–7439	5838–6002
143	血	ち	7440–7441	6003–6009
144	行	ぎょう	7442–7445	6010–6018
145	衣	ころも	7446–7507	6019–6103
146	襾	にし	7508–7511	6104

7 Strokes

Number	Shape	Name	JIS X 0208-1990	JIS X 0212-1990
147	見	みる	7512–7523	6105–6119
148	角	つの	7524–7529	6120–6134
149	言	ことば	7530–7613	6135–6265
150	谷	たに	7614–7616	6266–6270
151	豆	まめ	7617–7620	6271–6277
152	豕	いのこ	7621–7623	6278–6291
153	豸	むじな	7624–7634	6292–6308
154	貝	かい	7635–7662	6309–6337
155	赤	あか	7663–7664	6338–6341
156	走	はしる	7665–7668	6342–6357
157	足	あし	7669–7726	6358–6445
158	身	み	7727–7733	6446–6456
159	車	くるま	7734–7766	6457–6512
160	辛	からい	7767–7771	6513–6518
161	辰	しんのたつ	…	…
162	辵	しんにゅう	7772–7822	6519–6576
163	邑	むら	7823–7835	6577–6653
164	酉	さけのとり	7836–7855	6654–6703
165	釆	のごめ	7856–7857	…
166	里	さと	7858	…

Number	Shape	Name	JIS X 0208-1990	JIS X 0212-1990
8 Strokes				
167	金	かね	7859–7956	6704–6992
168	長	ながい	…	6993–7001
169	門	もん	7957–7983	7002–7035
170	阜	ぎふのふ	7984–8015	7036–7080
171	隶	れいづくり	8016–8017	…
172	隹	ふるとり	8018–8026	7081–7089
173	雨	あめ	8027–8047	7090–7117
174	青	あお	8048	7118–7122
175	非	あらず	8049	…
9 Strokes				
176	面	めん	8050–8052	7123–7124
177	革	かくのかわ	8053–8073	7125–7161
178	韋	なめしがわ	8074–8075	7162–7176
179	韭	にら	8076–8078	7177–7178
180	音	おと	8079–8081	7179–7182
181	頁	おおがい	8082–8103	7183–7225
182	風	かぜ	8104–8110	7226–7239
183	飛	とぶ	…	…
184	食	しょく	8111–8135	7240–7286
185	首	くび	8136–8137	…
186	香	においこう	8138	7287–7290
10 Strokes				
187	馬	うま	8139–8175	7291–7353
188	骨	ほね	8176–8183	7354–7375
189	高	たかい	8184	7376–7377
190	髟	かみがしら	8185–8207	7378–7415
191	鬥	とうがまえ	8208–8213	7416–7418
192	鬯	ちょう	8214	…
193	鬲	かく	8215	7419–7424
194	鬼	おに	8216–8222	7425–7431
11 Strokes				
195	魚	うお	8223–8273	7432–7556
196	鳥	とり	8274–8334	7557–7656
197	鹵	ろ	8335–8337	7657–7659
198	鹿	しか	8338–8345	7660–7672
199	麥	むぎ	8346–8350	7673–7680
200	麻	あさ	8351	…

Number	Shape	Name	JIS X 0208-1990	JIS X 0212-1990
12 Strokes				
201	黄	きいろ	8352	7681–7683
202	黍	きび	8353–8355	…
203	黒	くろ	8356–8366	7684–7701
204	黹	ふつ	8367–8369	…
13 Strokes				
205	黽	べん	8370–8372	7702–7705
206	鼎	かなえ	…	7706–7709
207	鼓	つづみ	8373–8374	7710–7716
208	鼠	ねずみ	8375–8376	7717–7727
14 Strokes				
209	鼻	はな	8377	7728–7736
210	齊	せい	8378	…
15 Strokes				
211	歯	は	8379–8391	7737–7755
16 Strokes				
212	龍	りゅう	8392	7756–7762
213	龜	かめ	8393	7763
17 Strokes				
214	龠	やく	8394	7764–7767

E

Jôyô Kanji List

This appendix provides a list of the 1,945 kanji that constitute Jôyô Kanji. They are presented in the order in which they appear in JIS X 0208-1990 (I call this *JIS order*). This Jôyô Kanji list was generated with the `jchar.c` tool (see Chapter 7 for more information). See Chapter 3 for more information on Jôyô Kanji.

亜哀愛悪握圧扱安暗案以位依偉囲委威尉意慰易為異移維緯胃衣違遺
医井域育一壱逸稲芋印員因姻引飲院陰隠韻右宇羽雨渦浦運雲営影映
栄永泳英衛詠鋭液疫益駅悦謁越閲円園宴延援沿演炎煙猿縁遠鉛塩汚
凹央奥往応押横欧殴王翁黄沖億屋憶乙卸恩温穏音下化仮何価佳加可
夏嫁家寡科暇果架歌河火禍稼箇花荷華菓課貨過蚊我画芽賀雅餓介会
解回塊壊快怪悔懐戒拐改械海灰界皆絵開階貝劾外害慨概涯街該垣嚇
各拡格核殻獲確穫覚角較郭閣隔革学岳楽額掛潟割喝括活渇褐轄且
株刈乾冠寒刊勘勧巻喚堪完官寛干幹患感慣憾換敢棺款歓汗漢環甘監
看管簡緩缶肝艦観貫還鑑間閑関陥館丸含岸眼岩頑顔願企危喜器基奇
寄岐希幾忌揮机旗既期棋棄機帰気汽祈季紀規記貴起軌輝飢騎鬼偽儀
宜戯技擬欺犠疑義議菊吉喫詰却客脚虐逆丘久休及吸宮弓急救朽求泣
球究窮級糾給旧牛去居巨拒拠挙虚許距漁魚享京供競共凶協叫境峡強
恐恭挟教橋況狂狭矯胸脅興郷鏡響驚仰凝暁業局曲極玉勤均斤琴禁筋
緊菌襟謹近金吟銀九句区苦駆具愚虞空偶遇隅屈掘靴繰桑勲君薫訓群
軍郡係傾刑兄啓型契形径恵慶憩掲携敬景渓系経継茎蛍計警軽鶏芸迎
鯨劇撃激傑欠決潔穴結血月件倹健兼券剣圏堅嫌建憲懸検権犬献研絹
県肩見謙賢軒遣険顕験元原厳幻弦減源玄現言限個古呼固孤己庫弧戸
故枯湖誇雇顧鼓五互午呉娯後御悟碁語誤護交侯候光公功効厚口向后
坑好孔孝工巧幸広康恒慌抗拘控攻更校構江洪港溝甲皇硬稿紅絞綱耕

287

考肯航荒行衡講貢購郊酵鉱鋼降項香高剛号合拷豪克刻告国穀酷黒獄
腰骨込今困墾婚恨懇昆根混紺魂佐唆左差査砂詐鎖座債催再最妻宰彩
才採栽歳済災砕祭斎細菜裁載際剤在材罪財坂咲崎作削搾昨策索錯桜
冊刷察撮擦札殺雑皿三傘参山惨散桟産算蚕賛酸暫残仕伺使刺司史嗣
四士始姉姿子市師志思指支施旨枝止死氏祉私糸紙紫肢脂至視詞詩試
誌諮資賜雌飼歯事似侍児字寺慈持時次滋治璽磁示耳自辞式識軸七執
失室湿漆疾質実芝舎写射捨赦斜煮社者謝車遮蛇邪借勺尺爵酌釈若寂
弱主取守手朱殊狩珠種趣酒首儒受寿授樹需囚収周宗就州修愁拾秀秋
終習臭舟衆襲週酬集醜住充十従柔汁渋獣縦重銃叔宿淑祝縮粛塾熟出
術述俊春瞬准循旬殉準潤盾純巡遵順処初所暑庶緒署書諸助叙女序徐
除傷償勝匠升召商唱奨宵将小少尚床彰承抄招掌昇昭晶松沼消渉焼焦
照症省硝礁祥称章笑粧紹肖衝訟証詔詳象賞鐘障上丈乗冗剰城場壌嬢
常情条浄状畳蒸譲醸錠嘱飾植殖織職色触食辱伸信侵唇娠寝審心慎振
新森浸深申真神紳臣薪親診身辛進針震人仁刃尋甚尽迅陣酢図吹垂帥
推水炊睡粋衰遂酔錘随髄崇数枢据杉澄寸世瀬畝是制勢姓征性成政整
星晴正清牲生盛精聖声製西誠誓請逝青静斉税隻席惜斥昔析石積籍績
責赤跡切拙接摂折設窃節説雪絶舌仙先千占宣専川戦扇栓泉浅洗染潜
旋線繊船薦践選遷銭銑鮮前善漸然全禅繕塑措疎礎祖租粗素組訴阻僧
創双倉喪壮奏層想捜掃挿操早曹巣槽燥争相窓総草荘葬藻装走送遭霜
騒像増憎臓蔵贈造促側則即息束測足速俗属賊族続卒存孫尊損村他多
太堕妥惰打駄体対耐帯待怠態替泰滞胎袋貸退逮隊代台大第題滝卓宅
択拓沢濯託濁諾但達奪脱棚谷丹単嘆担探淡炭短端胆誕鍛団壇弾断暖
段男談値知地恥池痴稚置致遅築畜竹蓄逐秩窒茶嫡着中仲宙忠抽昼柱
注虫衷鋳駐著貯丁兆帳庁弔張彫徴懲挑朝潮町眺聴脹腸調超跳長頂鳥
勅直朕沈珍賃鎮陳津墜追痛通塚漬坪釣亭低停偵貞呈堤定帝底庭廷弟
抵提程締艇訂逓邸泥摘敵滴的笛適哲徹撤迭鉄典天展店添転点伝殿田
電吐塗徒斗渡登途都努度土奴怒倒党冬凍刀唐塔島悼投搭東桃棟盗湯
灯当痘等答筒糖統到討謄豆踏逃透陶頭騰闘働動同堂導洞童胴道銅峠
匿得徳特督篤毒独読凸突届屯豚曇鈍内縄南軟難二尼弐肉日乳入如尿
任妊忍認寧猫熱年念燃粘悩濃納能脳農把覇波派破婆馬俳廃拝排敗杯
背肺輩配倍培媒梅買売賠陪伯博拍泊白舶薄迫漠爆縛麦箱肌畑八鉢発
髪伐罰抜閥伴判半反帆搬板版犯班畔繁般藩販範煩頒飯晩番盤蛮卑否
妃彼悲扉批披比泌疲皮碑秘罷肥被費避非飛備尾微美鼻匹必筆姫百俵
標氷漂票表評描病秒苗品浜貧賓頻敏瓶不付夫婦富布府怖扶敷普浮父
符腐膚譜負賦赴附侮武舞部封風伏副復幅服福腹複覆払沸仏物分噴墳
憤奮粉紛霧文聞丙併兵塀幣平弊柄並閉陛米壁癖別偏変片編辺返遍便

勉弁保舗捕歩補穂募墓慕暮母簿倣俸包報奉宝峰崩抱放方法泡砲縫胞
芳褒訪豊邦飽乏亡傍剖坊妨帽忘忙房暴望某棒冒紡肪膨謀貿防北僕墨
撲朴牧没堀奔本翻凡盆摩磨魔麻埋妹枚毎幕膜又抹末繭万慢満漫味未
魅岬密脈妙民眠務夢無矛霧婿娘名命明盟迷銘鳴滅免綿面模茂妄毛猛
盲網耗木黙目戻問紋門夕夜野矢厄役約薬訳躍柳愉油癒諭輸唯優勇友
幽悠憂有猶由裕誘遊郵雄融夕予余与誉預幼容庸揚揺擁曜様洋溶用窯
羊葉要謡踊陽養抑欲浴翌翼羅裸来頼雷絡落酪乱卵欄濫覧利吏履理痢
裏里離陸律率立略流留硫粒隆竜慮旅虜了僚両寮料涼猟療糧良量陵領
力緑倫厘林臨輪隣塁涙累類令例冷励礼鈴隷零霊麗齢暦歴列劣烈裂廉
恋練連錬炉路露労廊朗楼浪漏老郎六録論和話賄惑枠湾腕

Gakushû Kanji List

This appendix provides a listing of the 1,006 Gakushû Kanji presented by grade level, and in JIS order within each grade level. These kanji constitute a subset of Jôyô Kanji, which are listed in Appendix E. This Gakushû Kanji list was generated with the `jchar.c` tool (see Chapter 7 for more information). See Chapter 3 for more information on Gakushû Kanji.

Grade Level 1 (80 Kanji)

一右雨円王音下火花貝学気休玉金九空月犬見五口校左三山四子糸字
耳七車手十出女小上森人水正生青石赤先千川早草足村大男竹中虫町
天田土二日入年白八百文本名木目夕立力林六

Grade Level 2 (160 Kanji)

引羽雲園遠黄何夏家科歌画会回海絵外角楽活間丸岩顔帰汽記弓牛魚
京強教近兄形計元原言古戸午後語交光公工広考行高合国黒今才細作
算姉市思止紙寺時自室社弱首秋週春書少場色食心新親図数星晴声西
切雪線船前組走多太体台谷知地池茶昼朝長鳥直通弟店点電冬刀東当
答頭同道読内南肉馬買売麦半番父風分聞米歩母方北妹毎万明鳴毛門
夜野矢友曜用来理里話

Grade Level 3 (200 Kanji)

悪安暗委意医育員飲院運泳駅横屋温化荷界開階寒感漢館岸期起客宮
急球究級去橋業局曲銀区苦具君係軽決血研県庫湖向幸港号根祭坂皿
仕使始指死詩歯事持次式実写者主取守酒受州拾終習集住重宿所暑助
勝商昭消章乗植深申真神身進世整昔全想相送息速族他打対待代第題
炭短談着柱注丁帳調追定庭笛鉄転登都度島投湯等豆動童農波配倍箱

畑発反板悲皮美鼻筆氷表病秒品夫負部服福物平返勉放味命面問役薬
油有由遊予様洋羊葉陽落流旅両緑礼列練路和

Grade Level 4 (200 Kanji)

愛案以位囲胃衣印栄英塩央億加果課貨芽改械害街各覚完官管観関願
喜器希旗機季紀議救求泣給挙漁競共協鏡極訓軍郡型径景芸欠結健建
験固候功好康航告差最菜材昨刷察札殺参散産残司史士氏試児治辞失
借種周祝順初唱松焼照省笑象賞信臣成清静席積折節説戦浅選然倉巣
争側束続卒孫帯隊達単置仲貯兆腸低停底的典伝徒努灯働堂得特毒熱
念敗梅博飯費飛必標票不付府副粉兵別変辺便包法望牧末満未脈民無
約勇要養浴利陸料良量輪類令例冷歴連労老録

Grade Level 5 (185 Kanji)

圧易移因営永衛液益演往応恩仮価可河過賀解快格確額刊幹慣眼基寄
規技義逆久旧居許境興均禁句群経潔件券検険減現限個故護効厚構耕
講鉱混査再妻採災際在罪財桜雑賛酸師志支枝資飼似示識質舎謝授修
術述準序承招証常情条状織職制勢性政精製税績責接設絶舌銭祖素総
像増造則測属損態貸退団断築張提程敵適統導銅徳独任燃能破判版犯
比肥非備俵評貧婦富布武復複仏編弁保墓報豊暴貿防務夢迷綿輸余預
容率略留領

Grade Level 6 (181 Kanji)

異遺域宇映延沿我灰拡閣革割株巻干看簡危揮机貴疑吸供胸郷勤筋敬
系警劇激穴憲権絹厳源呼己誤后孝皇紅鋼降刻穀骨困砂座済裁策冊蚕
姿私至視詞誌磁射捨尺若樹収宗就衆従縦縮熟純処署諸除傷将障城蒸
針仁垂推寸盛聖誠宣専泉洗染善創奏層操窓装臓蔵存尊宅担探誕暖段
値宙忠著庁潮頂賃痛展党糖討届難乳認納脳派俳拝背肺班晩否批秘腹
奮並閉陛片補暮宝訪亡忘棒枚幕密盟模訳優郵幼欲翌乱卵覧裏律臨朗
論

G

Jinmei-yô Kanji List

Listed below are the 284 Jinmei-yô Kanji listed in JIS order. This Jinmei-yô Kanji list was generated with the `jchar.c` tool (see Chapter 7 for more information). See Chapter 3 for more information on Jinmei-yô Kanji.

阿葵茜渥旭梓絢綾鮎杏伊惟亥郁磯允胤卯丑唄叡瑛艶苑於旺伽嘉茄霞
魁凱馨叶樺鎌茅侃莞巖伎嬉毅稀亀誼鞠橘亨匡喬尭桐錦欣欽芹衿玖矩
駒熊栗袈圭慧桂拳絃胡虎伍吾梧瑚鯉倖宏弘昂晃浩紘鴻嵯沙瑳裟哉采
冴朔笹皐燦爾蒔汐鹿偲紗洲峻竣舜駿淳醇曙渚恕庄捷昌梢菖蕉丞穣晋
榛秦須翠瑞嵩雛碩爽惣綜聡蒼汰黛鯛鷹啄琢只辰巽旦檀智猪暢蝶椎槻
蔦椿紬鶴悌汀禎杜藤憧瞳寅酉惇敦奈那凪捺楠虹乃之巴萩肇鳩隼斐緋
眉柊彦媛彪彬芙楓蕗碧甫輔朋萌鳳鵬睦槙柾亦麿巳稔椋孟也冶耶弥靖
佑宥柚湧祐邑楊耀蓉遥嵐藍蘭李梨璃亮凌瞭稜諒遼琳麟瑠伶嶺怜玲蓮
呂禄倭亘侑勁奎峅彗昴晏晨晟暉栞椰毬洸洵滉漱澪燎燿瑶皓眸笙綺綸
翔脩茉莉菫詢諄赳迪頌颯黎凜熙

H

Japanese Corporate Character Set Standards

The material presented in this appendix supplements Chapter 3 by including detailed information on Japanese corporate character set standards. This appendix is primarily intended as reference material in the event that you need to deal with one of the included character set standards. I do not include exhaustive information here, such as complete character set listings. The Bibliography has information on the documentation for most of the corporate character set standards covered below, and Appendix K has information on how to go about ordering them.

Nearly all of the corporate character sets described in this appendix are based on one of the versions of JIS, namely JIS C 6226-1978, JIS X 0208-1983, or JIS X 0208-1990, and include extra symbols within the JIS table, additional kanji outside the JIS table, or both. In addition, you will find that many corporate-specific kanji can be found in the national character set standards, more specifically, in JIS X 0212-1990.

The corporate character set standards covered in this appendix do not represent an exhaustive list—nearly every major computer manufacturer in Japan has developed its own Japanese character set standard. This material shows you not only how diverse such character sets can be, but also how they are totally compatible neither with each other nor with the national character set standards covered in Chapter 3.

Table H-1 summarizes the corporate character set standards covered in this appendix. The first column specifies which Japanese national standard is used as its base set of characters. JIS78 refers to JIS C 6226-1978; JIS83 refers to JIS X 0208-1983; and JIS90 refers to JIS X 0208-1990.

Table H-1: Japanese Corporate Character Set Standards

	Base Set	Additional Kanji	Other Characters	User-defined
JEF	JIS78	4,039	1,010	3,102 [1]
FMR Kanji	JIS83		3	2,444
IBM Kanji	JIS90	360	28	4,370 [2]
DEC78	JIS78			2,914
DEC83	JIS83			2,914
NTT Kanji	JIS78	5,238	261	2,820
NEC Kanji	JIS78	3,382	1,090	2,256 [3]
IKIS	JIS83 [4]		63	376
HP Kanji	JIS83			5,366
Apple83	JIS83		135	2,256
Apple90	JIS90		313	2,256
KEIS78	JIS78	2,042	1,021	3,008
KEIS83	JIS83	2,200	966	3,008

[1] 457 of these have been pre-assigned under some implementations.

[2] IBM DBCS-Host encoding permits up to 4,370 user-defined character, but IBM DBCS-PC encoding permits up to 1,880, and IBM DBCS-EUC encoding permits up to 2,538.

[3] There are 2,256 user-defined characters in the Shift-JIS encoded version of this character set. The JIS encoded version is usually limited to 188 user-defined characters.

[4] That is, JIS X 0208-1983 less 32 line-drawing elements.

JEF

JEF is the Japanese character set standard developed by Fujitsu (富士通). Also known as *Japanese processing Extended Feature*, JEF is primarily used on Fujitsu's mainframe computers (called FACOM) and their OASYS series personal word processors. It contains the JIS C 6226-1978 character set as a subset. It also contains thousands of other characters. Table H-2 lists the characters included in JEF.

Table H-2: The JEF Character Set

Character Type	Number of Characters
JIS C 6226-1978	6,802
JEF Extended kanji	4,039
JEF Extended non-kanji	1,010
User-defined characters	3,102 (457 assigned)

Some implementations of JEF have assigned 457 characters to the 3,102 user-defined character area. These 457 kanji are specified by the Ministry of Labor (労働省).

As you would expect, the JEF Extended characters are arranged into rows of 94 characters. They are assigned KUTEN values beginning from the value 101. Table H-3 shows how JEF Extended characters are allocated to rows.

Table H-3: The JEF Extended Character Set

Row	Number of Characters	Content
101–148	4,039	JEF Extended kanji
149–161	917	JEF Extended non-kanji
162	0	Unused
163	93	JEF Extended non-kanji

For the most part, the 4,039 extended kanji are arranged by radical. However, there is a compatibility zone containing 71 kanji at the end of the JEF Extended kanji set, which are also arranged by radical. The JEF Extended kanji area is not fully used—the block of JEF Extended kanji has many empty character positions scattered throughout. JEF actually predates JIS C 6226-1978, and has undergone modifications such that conversion from JIS is possible.*

I also conducted a study similar to that which I conducted for IBM Kanji whereby I tried to match JIS X 0212-1990 kanji with the 4,039 JEF Extended kanji. This study was not complete, and was simply an exercise to extract an initial mapping table from the Unicode kanji database file. This database file, which is available from the Unicode Consortium, contains about 21,000 lines (one line for each of the approximately 21,000 Unicode kanji), and one of the fields was for mappings to JEF Extended kanji. When I extracted all the lines that had a JEF entry, and then further extracted those lines that had a mapping to JIS X 0212-1990, I found that there were 2,627 such lines. This means that there are at least 2,627 kanji that are common to both JIS X 0212-1990 and JEF Extended kanji. I expect that there are more since the Unicode kanji database contains only 3,144 JEF Extended kanji mappings, but there are 4,039 kanji specified in JEF Extended kanji.

Most implementations of JEF also contain ASCII/JIS-Roman and half-width katakana characters.

FMR Kanji

The Fujitsu FM-R series of personal computers uses a Japanese character set different from JEF. This character set is called FMR Kanji. FMR Kanji contains the characters of JIS

---

*Not round-trip conversion, though, as JEF is a superset of JIS.

X 0208-1983 as its base, but still makes use of many JIS C 6226-1978 glyphs. It also has three additional hiragana characters, as shown in Table H-4.

Table H-4: The Three Extra Hiragana in FMR Kanji

Hiragana	Pronunciation
う	vu
か	ka (small version of か)
け	ke (small version of け)

You may recall from Chapter 3 that there are 83 hiragana and 86 katakana. The difference between these numbers happens to be three characters. The three hiragana characters listed above bring the hiragana set up to 86 characters, like katakana.

Also included in the FMR Kanji character set are the ASCII/JIS-Roman and half-width katakana character set standards, and a user-defined character area that can hold up to 2,444 characters.

IBM Kanji

IBM (アイ・ビー・エム) was one of the first companies to develop a corporate Japanese character set standard. In fact, they have corporate character set standards for Chinese and Korean. This corporate character set standard includes those characters from JIS X 0208-1990 plus an additional 360 kanji and 28 non-kanji specific to IBM Kanji (these are known as IBM select kanji and non-kanji). This character set has followed the JIS X 0208 standard very closely. For example, when JIS X 0208-1990 superseded JIS X 0208-1983, IBM moved quickly to standardize to JIS X 0208-1990.

IBM Kanji does have a peculiar twist, though. There are two encodings for this character set, and although both encoding methods handle the same set of characters, their characters are arranged differently. Table H-5 shows how the characters are defined under one encoding method (DBCS-Host).

Table H-5: The IBM DBCS-Host Character Set

Character Type	Number of Characters
Full-width space	1
Non-kanji	551
Basic kanji	3,226
Extended kanji	3,489
User-defined characters	4,370

Under the other encoding methods (DBCS-PC and DBCS-EUC), you see clearly that the break-down is quite different. Table H-6 illustrates this.

Table H-6: The IBM DBCS-PC and IBM DBCS-EUC Character Set

Character Type	Number of Characters
Non-kanji	524
JIS Level 1 kanji	2,965
JIS Level 2 kanji	3,390
IBM select non-kanji	28
IBM select kanji	360
User-defined characters	1,880 [1]

[1] IBM DBCS-EUC encoding permits up to 2,538 user-defined characters.

With the exception of the number of user-defined characters, the total number of characters is identical, namely 7,267. The current number of IBM select non-kanji happens to be 26. The difference between that number and the number (28) in the above table consists of two characters that were not part of JIS C 6226-1978, but became standard in JIS X 0208-1983. Once IBM standardized to JIS X 0208-1983, these two character were dropped, thus reducing IBM select non-kanji to 26 characters. I will usually refer to 28 IBM select non-kanji for backward compatibility. These two characters are shown in Table H-7 (JIS X 0208-1983/90 lists KUTEN code with hexadecimal JIS in parentheses).

Table H-7: Mappings for Two IBM DBCS-PC Characters

Character	IBM DBCS-PC Code	JIS X 0208-1983/90
¬	FA54	0244 (224C)
∵	FA5B	0272 (2268)

I once conducted a study in which I tried to match the 360 IBM select kanji with kanji from JIS X 0212-1990. The outcome of this study was that 279 kanji within JIS X 0212-1990 matched those in IBM select kanji. There was even one that matched a kanji in JIS X 0208-1990. Approximately 70 of the remaining 80 kanji are common to the JEF character set standard.

IBM Kanji also includes the ASCII/JIS-Roman and half-width katakana character set standards as part of its own character set standard. These fall into what is called SBCS (Single-Byte Character Set). A DBCS (Double-Byte Character Set) and an SBCS (Single-Byte Character Set) together are referred to as an MBCS (Multiple-Byte Character Set).

Other corporations have included IBM select kanji and non-kanji into their products or even into their own character set standards. As an example, some of NEC's PC-9800 computer systems include all 360 IBM select kanji in rows 89 through 92 of the JIS table, and 14 of the 28 IBM select non-kanji in row 92 of the JIS table.* As another example,

---

*The remaining 14 IBM select non-kanji are not found here since they are already part of NEC Kanji, NEC's Japanese character set standard.

you learned in Chapter 3 that Xerox's XCCS character set standard includes IBM select kanji as a subset.

DEC Kanji

Digital Equipment Corporation (ディジタルイクイップメント株式会社) developed its own Japanese character set standard. It is made up of the ASCII/JIS-Roman character set, JIS X 0208-1983 plus an extended character set. There are two versions of DEC Kanji: one based on JIS C 6226-1978 (DEC78); the other on JIS X 0208-1983 (DEC83). Appendix J pinpoints differences between these two versions of the Japanese character set—those differences apply here as well.

The actual character space consists of a 94-row-by-94-cell matrix identical to JIS X 0208-1983, and an additional 94-row-by-94-cell matrix for additional characters. Rows 1 through 31 (2,914 cells) of this additional character space are reserved for user-defined characters, and rows 32 through 94 (5,922 cells) are reserved for private DEC use (but are unused). Rows 9 through 15 and rows 85 through 94 of the JIS X 0208-1983 table are also reserved for DEC use (and currently unused).

Table H-8 shows how characters are allocated to the additional 94-row-by-94-cell matrix.

Table H-8: The DEC Extended Character Set

Row	Number of Characters	Content
1–31	0	Unassigned (free)
32–94	0	Unassigned (maintained by DEC)

NTT Kanji

Nippon (Japan) Telegraph and Telephone (日本電信電話) developed a character set which includes a non-kanji portion identical to JIS X 0208-1983, and a kanji portion identical to JIS C 6226-1978. There are 261 NTT-specific symbols in the non-kanji area. These include lowercase and uppercase Roman numerals, additional mathematical symbols, symbols for units of measurement, additional line-drawing characters, and graphic representations for control characters.

NTT Kanji also includes an additional 94-by-94 character space for kanji above and beyond those specified in JIS C 6226-1978. The first 60 rows of this additional character space (5,640 cells) have 5,238 kanji allocated to them, 4,048 of which are kanji found in the book 新字源 (pronounced *shinjigen*, and means "new character origins"), but not in JIS C 6226-1978; the remaining 1,190 kanji are for use in writing person and place names. Within the first 60 rows of this character space, rows 1 through 44 are called Level 1 (contain 4,048 kanji), and rows 45 through 57 are called Level 2 (contain 1,190 kanji).

Rows 61 through 64 (376 cells) are allocated for extended non-kanji, but have yet to have characters assigned to them. Rows 65 through 94 (2,820 cells) are reserved for user-defined characters.

Table H-9 shows how characters are allocated to the additional 94-row-by-94-cell matrix.

Table H-9: The NTT Kanji Character Set

Row	Number of Characters	Content
1–44	4,048	Level 1 kanji
44–60	1,190	Level 2 kanji
61–64	0	Unassigned (reserved for extended non-kanji)
65–94	0	Unassigned (free)

NEC Kanji

Nippon (Japan) Electronics Corporation (日本電気株式会社) developed its own character set for use on its personal computers and dedicated Japanese word processors. This character set is based on JIS C 6226-1978, and also includes JIS-Roman and half-width katakana. Some implementations of NEC Kanji also include the 360 IBM select kanji and 14 of the 28 IBM select non-kanji set into rows 89 through 92. Table H-10 lists the differences between NEC Kanji and JIS X 0208-1990.

Table H-10: The Differences Between JIS X 0208-1990 and NEC Kanji

Row	Number of Characters	Content
2	14	Miscellaneous symbols
8	0	Unassigned (reserved)
9	94	Half-width JIS-Roman characters
10	94	63 standard half-width katakana, 31 additional half-width katakana
11	93	76 half-width line-drawing elements, 17 half-width miscellaneous symbols
12	76	Full-width line-drawing elements
13[1]	83	Circled numerals 1–20, uppercase Roman numerals 1–10, 16 katakana words, 10 abbreviations, 4 two-kanji Japanese era names, 5 circled kanji, 3 parenthesized kanji, 15 miscellaneous symbols
84	0	Unassigned (reserved)

[1]This row initially contained only 82 characters. Sometime after 1989 the two-kanji Japanese era name character ㍻ was added to this row to bring the total up to 83. This character is a compressed form of the kanji compound 平成 (pronounced *heisei*), which stands for the *Heisei Era* (1989–present).

Note the inclusion of half-width characters here, namely the JIS-Roman and half-width katakana character sets. But what do those other characters look like? Table H-11 provides some examples.

Table H-11: Special Characters From NEC Kanji

Character Description	Examples
Circled numerals	① ② ③ ④ ⑤ ⑥ ⑦ ⑧ ⑨ ⑩ ⑪ ⑫ ⑬
Katakana words	㍉ ㌔ ㌢ ㍍ ㌘ ㌧ ㌦ ㌶ ㍑ ㍗ ㌍ ㌦ ㌣
Abbreviations	㎜ ㎝ ㎞ ㎎ kg cc ㎡ No. K.K. TEL
Two-kanji Japanese era names	㍾ ㍽ ㍼ ㍻
Circled kanji	㊤ ㊥ ㊦ ㊧ ㊨
Parenthesized kanji	㈱ ㈲ ㈹

Other character sets to be covered later may use these same types of characters. Now you know what they look like.

NEC Kanji can also include an extended character set. Let's call this NEC Extended Kanji. These characters are arranged into a separate 94-row-by-94-cell matrix, and include 682 non-kanji and 3,382 kanji. Table H-12 lists the contents of this extended character set.

Table H-12: The NEC Kanji Extended Character Set

Row	Number of Characters	Content
1	94	Miscellaneous symbols
2	93	Miscellaneous symbols
3	92	Miscellaneous symbols
4	94	Miscellaneous symbols
5	94	Miscellaneous symbols
6	63	41 katakana words, 20 parenthesized kanji, 2 circled kanji
7–15	0	Unassigned (free)
16–17	152	Cursive kana characters
18–53	3,382	Kanji arranged by radical then stroke count
54–94	0	Unassigned (free)

Many of these 3,382 kanji are common with JIS X 0212-1990. NEC Extended Kanji was developed nearly 10 years before JIS X 0212-1990, and doesn't appear to be in very common use these days.

There seems to be a shift at NEC whereby its character set is becoming compatible with JIS X 0208-1990. Two NEC products released in late 1991 (both dedicated Japanese word processors) boast the JIS X 0208-1990 character set.

IKIS

Nippon (Japan) Data General (日本データゼネラル) developed a character set standard very similar to JIS X 0208-1983, except that it contains the half-width katakana character set within the 94-by-94 character space—these characters are placed in row 8. In addition, only rows 9 through 12 are assigned as a user-defined character space. This character set standard is referred to as IKIS, which stands for Interactive Kanji Information System. Table H-13 illustrates the differences between IKIS and JIS X 0208-1990.

Table H-13: The Differences Between JIS X 0208-1983 and IKIS

Row	Number of Characters	Content
8	63	Half-width katakana
9–12	0	Unassigned (free)
13–15	0	Unassigned (reserved)

HP Kanji

The Japanese character set implemented by Hewlett-Packard consists of the 94 printable ASCII/JIS-Roman characters, the 63 half-width katakana characters, and JIS X 0208-1983. Nothing out of the ordinary here. However, in Appendix I, which discusses HP Kanji's encoding methods, you will see a departure from this apparent lack of ordinariness in that there is a large user-defined character area that can hold up to 5,366 characters.

Apple Kanji

Apple Computer (アップルコンピュータ) developed their own Japanese character set with the introduction of KanjiTalk (漢字Talk), the Japanese operating system for the Macintosh computer. This character set is based on JIS X 0208-1983, but has 82 additional characters in row 13, and 53 vertically-set variants. I call this character set Apple83. This character set is implemented in KanjiTalk prior to Version 7.1. Table H-14 shows the differences between JIS X 0208-1983 and Apple83.

Table H-14: The Differences Between JIS X 0208-1983 and Apple83

Row	Number of Characters	Content
11	31	Vertically-set variants of row 1 (miscellaneous symbols)
13	82	Circled numerals 1–20, uppercase Roman numerals 1–10, 16 katakana words, 10 abbreviations, 3 two-kanji Japanese era names, 5 circled kanji, 3 parenthesized kanji, 15 miscellaneous symbols

Row	Number of Characters	Content
14	10	Vertically-set variants of row 4 (hiragana)
15	12	Vertically-set variants of row 5 (katakana)

One note is that row 13 was actually copied from NEC Kanji. NEC Kanji now defines 83 characters in this row, though. So why the difference? Apple83 does not include the two-kanji Japanese era name character 﨟, which is a recent addition to NEC Kanji.

Apple Computer developed a new Japanese character set with the introduction of KanjiTalk 7.1 in late 1992. This character set is based on JIS X 0208-1990. I call this Japanese character set Apple90. This character set contains ASCII/JIS-Roman, half-width katakana, and JIS X 0208-1990. Rows 9 through 15 of this character set standard contain 260 characters above and beyond JIS X 0208-1990, plus the 53 vertically-set variants described in Apple83. Table H-15 illustrates the differences between JIS X 0208-1990 and Apple90.

Table H-15: The Differences Between JIS X 0208-1990 and Apple90

Row	Number of Characters	Content
9	59	Circled numerals 1–20, parenthesized numerals 1–20, black-circled numerals 1–9, numerals 0–9 with period
10	56	Lowercase and uppercase Roman numerals 1–15, parenthesized lowercase Roman characters
11	34	Abbreviations
12	27	Miscellaneous symbols
13	39	25 parenthesized kanji, 14 circled kanji
14	35	28 katakana words, 4 two-kanji Japanese era names, 3 four-kanji characters
15	10	5 miscellaneous symbols, 1 hiragana, 4 katakana
85	31	Vertically-set variants of row 1 (miscellaneous symbols)
88	10	Vertically-set variants of row 4 (hiragana)
89	12	Vertically-set variants of row 5 (katakana)

What in the world is a four-kanji character? It is a single character that contains four small kanji characters within its graphic space. One is 株式会社, which is a single character that represents the kanji compound 株式会社, and means "stock company" or "Incorporated." Another is 有限会社, which represents the kanji compound 有限会社, and means "limited liability company" or "Limited." The third one is 財団法人, which represents the kanji compound 財団法人, and means "juridical foundation" or "foundation."

There are some characters used in Japanese, mainly punctuation, parentheses, and small versions of kana, that need to be positioned differently within their em-square when set vertically. Vertically-set Japanese text is described in Chapter 6. These characters are found in rows 1, 3, and 4. Rows 85, 88, and 89 in Apple90 contain the vertically-set variants of rows 1, 4, and 5, respectively. Likewise, rows 11, 14, and 15 in Apple83 contain the vertically-set variants of rows 1, 4, and 5, respectively. This difference between Apple83 and Apple90 is not found in the characters contained in these rows, but in the offsets used. Table H-16 details this difference between Apple83 and Apple90.

Table H-16: Vertically-set Character Positions in Apple83 and Apple90

	Row Offset Value	Row 1	Row 4	Row 5
Apple83	10	11	14	15
Apple90	84	85	88	89

You can just imagine what a headache this row offset value change caused developers who produced software that relied on a value of 10 to access the vertically-set variants of those rows. Apple Computer has plans to eventually phase out these vertically-set variants altogether. I don't mean that you will no longer be able to set Japanese vertically on a Macintosh, but that they will be removed from the character set. This may mean that they are stored internally at the same code positions as their horizontally-set counterparts.*

Both Apple83 and Apple90 provide 2,256 user-defined character positions. This is equivalent to 24 rows of 94 characters.

KEIS

Hitachi (日立) developed a character set standard known as KEIS, short for *Kanji processing Extended Information System*. This character set standard comes in two forms: KEIS78 and KEIS83. The former is based heavily on JIS C 6226-1978, and includes 36 additional characters used for print formatting. The latter is based on JIS X 0208-1983. I have a hunch that there is a KEIS90 in the works, based on JIS X 0208-1990.

Under both KEIS78 and KEIS83, JIS Level 1 kanji and JIS non-kanji are in what Hitachi calls the KEIS Basic Character Set. JIS Level 2 kanji in its entirety makes up KEIS Extended Character Set 1. Corporate-defined kanji and non-kanji are in KEIS Extended Character Set 3 (the kanji are arranged by radical then stroke count, just like JIS Level 2 kanji). Oddly enough, there is no mention of a KEIS Extended Character Set 2.† The actual

---

*As you learned in Chapter 6, PostScript Japanese fonts already do this by providing both vertically- and horizontally-set fonts for most character sets.

†This is similar to the lack of Type 2 fonts—there are Type 1 and Type 3 fonts, but no Type 2 fonts. See Chapter 6 for more information.

number of characters differs depending on whether you are dealing with KEIS78 or KEIS83. Table H-17 illustrates this within each subset of KEIS78 and KEIS83.

Table H-17 The KEIS Character Sets

	Basic Character Set	Extended Character Set 1	Extended Character Set 3
KEIS78	3,454[1]	3,384	3,027[2]
KEIS83	3,489	3,388	3,166[3]

[1]This is the same as JIS C 6226-1978 plus 36 formatted printing characters.
[2]This includes 71 JIS non-kanji specific to JIS X 0208-1983, 914 Hitachi non-kanji, and 2,042 kanji.
[3]This includes 966 Hitachi non-kanji and 2,200 kanji.

KEIS78 and KEIS83 also includes a user-defined character range. This area can hold up to 3,008 characters.

I

Japanese Corporate Encoding Methods

The material covered in this appendix supplements Chapter 4 and Appendix H. Like Appendix H, it is intended as reference material in the event that you need to implement a particular Japanese corporate character set. The material here should provide enough information.

Most of the corporate encoding methods share similar encodings with the national character set encodings. This is appropriate since, as you have already learned, most corporate character set standards share many of the same characters with only slight variations. Table I-1 lists these corporate character sets along with the encodings that support them.

Table I-1: Corporate Character Set Standards and Their Encoding Methods

	JIS	Shift-JIS	EUC	Other
JEF	*no*	*no*	*yes*[1]	
FMR Kanji	*no*	*yes*	*no*	
IBM Kanji	*no*	*yes*	*yes*	*IBM-Host*[1]
DEC78	*no*	*no*	*yes*	
DEC83	*no*	*no*	*yes*	
NTT Kanji	*yes*	*no*	*no*	
NEC Kanji	*yes*	*yes*	*yes*	
IKIS	*no*	*no*	*yes*	
HP Kanji	*no*	*yes*	*yes*	
Apple83	*no*	*yes*	*no*	
Apple90	*no*	*yes*	*no*	
KEIS78	*no*	*no*	*yes*[1]	
KEIS83	*no*	*no*	*yes*[1]	

[1]This encoding method is modal, namely that special character sequences (or a single character in some cases) are used to switch between one- and two-byte-per-character modes.

In the remainder of this appendix comparisons are drawn between corporate encoding methods and JIS, Shift-JIS, and EUC encodings.

JEF Encoding

JEF encoding is quite unusual. First, it does not use the ASCII/JIS-Roman character set or encoding—it uses EBCDIC/EBCDIK instead. This allows for a quite different encoding structure, yet you will see some similarities with EUC. The first byte's value spans the seven- and eight-bit range. This does not allow such an encoding to make use of the byte's value to determine whether it represents itself, or is part of an expected two-byte sequence. JEF, instead, uses special characters for performing such shifts of state. The code specifications for JEF are listed in Table I-2.

Table I-2: JEF Encoding Specifications

	Decimal	Hexadecimal	Octal
Two-byte characters (JIS C 6226-1978)[1]			
First byte range	161–254	A1–FE	241–376
Second byte range	161–254	A1–FE	241–376
Two-byte characters (JEF Extended characters)			
First byte ranges	65–125, 127	41–7D, 7F	101–175, 177
Second byte range	161–254	A1–FE	241–376
Two-byte characters (user-defined characters)			
First byte range	128–160	80–A0	200–240
Second byte range	161–254	A1–FE	241–376
One-byte characters (EBCDIC/EBCDIK)			
Byte range	65–249	41–F9	101–371
Shifting characters			
Two-byte character	40	28	050
One-byte character	41	29	051
Full-width space character			
First byte	64	40	100
Second byte	64	40	100

[1] 0xA1A1 is not a valid code position.

First, the encoding for the JIS C 6226-1978 character set is identical to EUC code set 1. The remainder is unique to JEF, except for the special encoding for the full-width space, which is shared by IBM Kanji DBCS-Host encoding (this appears later in this appendix).

Figure I-1 shows the JEF encoding space. Note that it is similar to EUC (the JIS C 6226-1978 portion shares the same encoding with EUC code set 1), and that the full-width space character is off by itself within the encoding space.

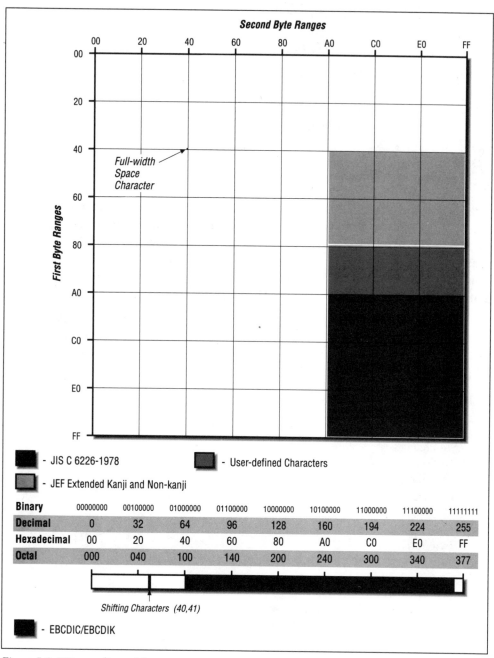

Figure I-1: JEF encoding tables

JEF Encoding Versus EUC Encoding

The JIS C 6226-1978 portion of JEF encoding is identical to that of EUC code set 1. The rest of JEF encoding, as you saw, is quite different.

FMR Kanji Encoding

The FMR Kanji encoding is identical to Shift-JIS encoding. There is not much more to say about it here. See Figure 4-8 for an illustration of Shift-JIS encoding, and Table 4-9 for a listing of its specifications. Also see Table 4-10 for a listing of the user-defined character area. The first byte range for these characters is from 0xF0 to 0xFC.

IBM Kanji Encoding

IBM has defined four basic multiple-byte language-independent encoding methods: DBCS-PC, DBCS-EUC, TBCS-EUC, and DBCS-Host (the acronym DBCS stands for *Double-Byte Character Set*; likewise, the acronym TBCS stands for *Triple-Byte Character Set*). TBCS-EUC is not used to encode Japanese. IBM manufactures and supports a wide variety of computing environments, such as host computers, PCs, and UNIX workstations, and thus requires many encoding methods. You will also learn that most of these IBM encoding methods are specific to a particular environment.

The encoding method used by DBCS-PC is nearly identical to Shift-JIS, contains a user-defined character encoding space, and is widely used on IBM PCs. The data found in Table I-3 is also known as IBM-932, which is a mixture of DBCS-PC, ASCII, and half-width katakana.

Table I-3: IBM DBCS-PC Encoding Specifications

	Decimal	Hexadecimal	Octal
Two-byte characters (JIS X 0208-1990)			
First byte ranges	129–159, 224–239	81–9F, E0–EF	201–237, 340–357
Second byte ranges	64–126, 128–252	40–7E, 80–FC	100–176, 200–374
Two-byte IBM select non-kanji/kanji set			
First byte range	250–252	FA–FC	372–374
Second byte ranges	64–126, 128–252	40–7E, 80–FC	100–176, 200–374
Two-byte user-defined characters			
First byte range	240–249	F0–F9	360–271
Second byte ranges	64–126, 128–252	40–7E, 80–FC	100–176, 200–374

	Decimal	Hexadecimal	Octal
Two-byte reserved character space[1]			
First byte ranges	133–135, 235–239	85–87, EB–EF	205–207, 353–357
Second byte ranges	64–126, 128–252	40–7E, 80–FC	100–176, 200–374
Half-width katakana			
Byte range[2]	161–223	A1–DF	241–337
ASCII/JIS-Roman			
Byte range	33–126	21–7E	041–176

[1] Note that these ranges fall within the JIS X 0208-1990 encoding space.
[2] Sometimes the code position 0xA0 is used for a half-width katakana space.

See Figure I-2 for an illustration of IBM Kanji's DBCS-PC encoding.

The actual definition for DBCS-PC is a bit different. What is listed above is the specific Japanese implementation of DBCS-PC. The main difference is that the first byte range falls between hexadecimal 0x81 and 0xFE. Japanese restricts this range to 0x81–0x9F and 0xE0–0xFC so that half-width katakana, whose encoding range falls in 0xA1–0xDF, could be accommodated. It is important to note that IBM select kanji and non-kanji fall into a code range that does not correspond to valid code positions in JIS or EUC (code set 1)—they fall well outside the 94-row-by-94-cell matrix when run through the normal conversion algorithms. This becomes an issue when you learn about IBM's implementation of EUC, the next topic of discussion.

DBCS-EUC encoding is essentially identical to EUC, which was covered in detail in a previous section. All four code sets are implemented. This encoding is primarily found on the AIX environment, and the Japanese implementation is commonly known as IBM-eucJP. TBCS-EUC is defined by IBM for future standardization, and is currently not specified for handling Japanese.

You may be asking how DBCS-EUC handles IBM select kanji and non-kanji. The answer is that these characters are mapped to JIS X 0208-1990 and JIS X 0212-1990 code positions. Table I-4 summarizes how these characters are mapped.

Table I-4: IBM Select Kanji and Non-kanji Mappings

	Total	JIS X 0208-1990	JIS X 0212-1990	User-defined
IBM Select kanji	360	1	279	80
IBM Select non-kanji	28	2	1	25

25 of the 28 IBM select non-kanji are mapped to row 83 of JIS X 0212-1990, and 80 of the 360 IBM select kanji are mapped to row 84 of JIS X 0212-1990. Table J-4 lists how the 388 IBM select kanji and non-kanji are mapped to JIS X 0208-1990 and JIS X 0212-1990 code

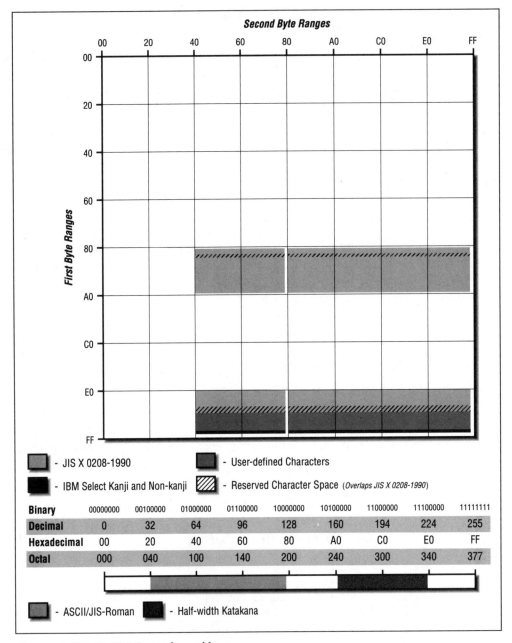

Figure I-2: IBM DBCS-PC encoding tables

positions. The results of this mapping, at least for the 360 IBM select kanji, concur with the findings of my own study that compared them with JIS X 0212-1990.

There are three user-defined character areas defined for IBM's Japanese EUC implementation. They are listed in Table I-5.

Table I-5: IBM DBCS-EUC User-defined Character Encoding Positions

Area	Location	Number of Characters
Primary	Rows 85 through 94 of JIS X 0208-1990	940
Secondary	Rows 85 through 94 of JIS X 0212-1990	940
Tertiary	Rows 78 through 84 of JIS X 0212-1990	658

DBCS-Host encoding, usually found on host computer systems, has a much larger character encoding space than DBCS-PC encoding. This two-byte encoding space can hold up to 36,481 unique characters. It is also used in conjunction with EBCDIC. This encoding method also existed long before any similar national standards existed. It is listed in Table I-6.

Table I-6: IBM DBCS-Host Encoding Specifications

	Decimal	Hexadecimal	Octal
Two-byte characters			
First byte range	65–254	41–FE	101–376
Second byte range	65–254	41–FE	101–376
One-byte characters (EBCDIC/EBCDIK)			
Byte range	65–249	41–F9	101–371
Full-width space character			
First byte	64	40	100
Second byte	64	40	100
Shifting characters			
Two-byte character	14	0E	016
One-byte character	15	0F	017

Figure I-3 illustrates this information.

Converting Japanese text between IBM DBCS-Host and IBM DBCS-PC/EUC requires the use of mapping tables—no code conversion algorithm exists, and every character must be treated as a special case. These mapping tables exist in machine-readable form. Contact IBM for more information on availability.

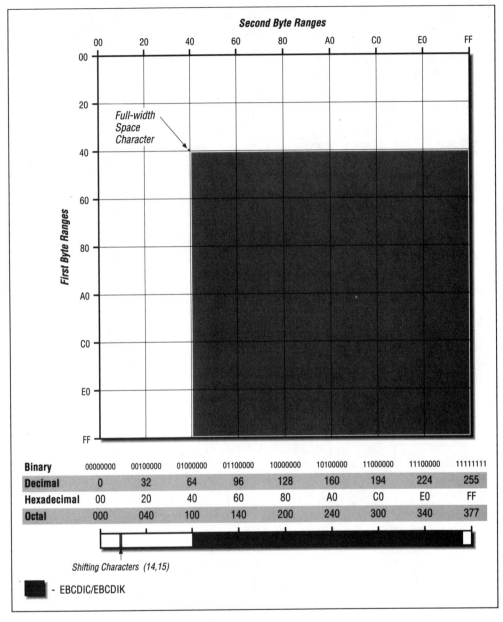

Figure I-3: IBM DBCS-Host encoding tables

IBM Kanji Encoding Versus Shift-JIS and EUC Encodings

DBCS-Host encoding does not correspond to JIS, Shift-JIS, or EUC encoding. DBCS-PC corresponds to Shift-JIS encoding with the addition of a user-defined characters space (this is where the 386 IBM select kanji and non-kanji are encoded). DBCS-EUC corresponds to EUC encoding. You learned how the 386 IBM select kanji and non-kanji are mapped to appropriate positions in DBCS-EUC encoding.

DEC Kanji Encoding

DEC Kanji encoding is very similar to EUC complete two-byte format. The equivalent of EUC code sets 0, 1, and 3 are supported. Note that the ASCII/JIS-Roman portion of DEC Kanji encoding is identical to EUC packed format (that is, one-byte). Also note that the equivalent of EUC code set 2, namely half-width katakana, is not supported. Table I-7 shows the encoding, and Figure I-4 illustrates it.

Table I-7: DEC Kanji Encoding Specifications

	Decimal	Hexadecimal	Octal
Two-byte characters (JIS X 0208-1983)			
First byte range	161–254	A1–FE	241–376
Second byte range	161–254	A1–FE	241–376
Two-byte characters (DEC Extended character set)			
First byte range	161–254	A1–FE	241–376
Second byte range	33–126	21–7E	041–176
ASCII/JIS-Roman			
Byte range	33–126	21–7E	041–176

DEC Kanji Encoding Versus EUC Encoding

DEC Kanji encoding is identical to EUC complete two-byte format without code set 2 (half-width katakana). Also note that the equivalent of EUC code set 3 is not specified to be used for the JIS X 0212-1990 character set.

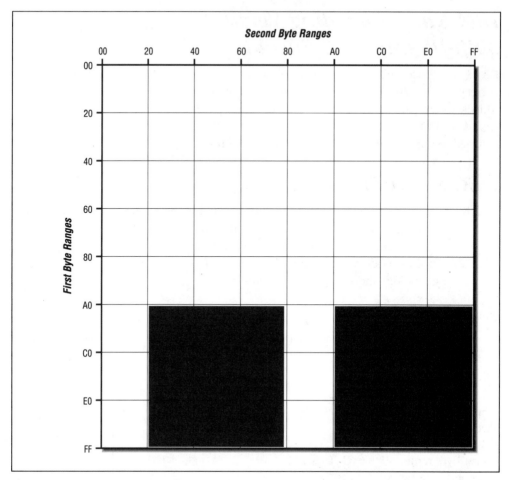

Figure I-4: DEC Kanji encoding table

NTT Kanji Encoding

NTT Kanji encoding is much like JIS encoding, except that there is an additional two-byte character escape sequence defined for extended character set. See Table I-8 for a listing of its encoding specifications.

Table I-8: NTT Kanji Encoding Specifications

	Decimal	Hexadecimal	Octal
Two-byte character escape sequences JIS C 6226-1978[1]	27 36 64	1B 24 40	033 044 100

---
[1]Represented graphically as <ESC> $ @.

	Decimal	Hexadecimal	Octal
NTT Extended[2]	27 36 41 48	1B 24 29 30	033 044 051 060
Two-byte characters			
First byte range	33–126	21–7E	041–176
Second byte range	33–126	21–7E	041–176
One-byte character escape sequence			
JIS-Roman[3]	27 40 74	1B 28 4A	033 050 112
JIS-Roman			
Byte range	33–126	21–7E	041–176

[2]Represented graphically as <ESC> $) 0.
[3]Represented graphically as <ESC> (J.

NTT Kanji Encoding Versus JIS Encoding

NTT Kanji encoding is like JIS plus an additional two-byte character escape sequence for the extended character set. Note that only the JIS C 6226-1978 character set is supported.

NEC Kanji Encoding

NEC Kanji can be encoded similarly to JIS, Shift-JIS, and EUC, depending on the environment. The JIS implementation is sometimes referred to as NEC-JIS. ASCII/JIS-Roman (half-width) and half-width katakana are also in the same encoding space as kanji, and thus can be encoded using two bytes. This can simplify the handling of text streams (no need to have any state shifting between one- and two-byte-per-character modes), but significantly increases the storage requirements for documents not written in Japanese. Table I-9 lists its specifications.

Table I-9: NEC Kanji Encoding Specifications

	Decimal	Hexadecimal	Octal
Two-byte character escape sequence			
JIS C 6226-1978[1]	27 75	1B 4B	033 113
Two-byte characters (JIS C 6226-1978)			
First byte range	33–126	21–7E	041–176
Second byte range	33–126	21–7E	041–176
Two-byte characters (NEC extended character set)			
First byte range	161–254	A1–FE	241–376
Second byte range	161–254	A1–FE	241–376

[1]Represented graphically as <ESC> K.

	Decimal	Hexadecimal	Octal
One-byte character escape sequence JIS-Roman[2]	27 72	1B 48	033 110
JIS8 half-width katakana Byte range	161–223	A1–DF	241–337
JIS-Roman Byte range	33–126	21–7E	041–176

[2]Represented graphically as <ESC> H.

Refer to Tables 4-9 and 4-17 for descriptions of the Shift-JIS and EUC implementations of the NEC Kanji character set. Note that Shift-JIS does not support the NEC extended character set, but sometimes includes the 388 IBM select kanji and non-kanji. I have no information that would suggest support for the NEC extended character set in EUC encoding.

NEC Kanji Encoding Versus JIS Encoding

The escape sequences for NEC Kanji encoding are unique in that they are made up of the escape character followed by only a single printable character. While this makes the escape sequences shorter, it does not leave much context with which you may insert lost escape characters (the insertion of lost escape characters was discussed in Chapter 4 and Chapter 7).

IKIS Encoding

The encoding method for IKIS closely resembles EUC, but lacks two of the codes sets (code set 2 for half-width katakana, and code set 3 for JIS X 0212-1990). Remember from our discussion in Chapter 3 that the half-width katakana character set is included within the JIS X 0208-1983 character space, namely in row 8. Table I-10 illustrates its code specifications.

Table I-10: IKIS Encoding Specifications

	Decimal	Hexadecimal	Octal
ASCII/JIS-Roman Byte range	33–126	21–7E	041–176
Two-byte characters (JIS X 0208-1983)			
First byte range	161–254	A1–FE	241–376
Second byte range	161–254	A1–FE	241–376

IKIS Encoding Versus EUC Encoding

IKIS encoding is identical to the encoding specified in EUC complete two-byte format. Only the equivalent of EUC code sets 0 and 1 are supported by IKIS.

HP Kanji Encoding

Hewlett-Packard developed two Japanese encoding methods called HP-15 and HP-16. Both support the same set of characters. HP-15 is a superset of Shift-JIS encoding, and HP-16 is similar to EUC encoding. These encoding methods are fully compatible, and Hewlett-Packard software is able to convert between them. I have seen the mapping tables, and they are not in a form that can be readily digested.

HP-15 is more or less the same as Shift-JIS—all the standard Shift-JIS code positions fall entirely into the HP-15 code space. Hewlett-Packard defines HP-15 as a series of four encoding blocks, but this can be simplified into two ranges for both bytes. Table I-11 lists the code specifications for HP-15.

Table I-11: HP-15 Encoding Specifications

	Decimal	Hexadecimal	Octal
Two-byte characters			
First byte ranges	128–160, 224–254	80–A0, E0–FE	200–240, 340–376
Second byte ranges	33–126, 128–255	21–7E, 80–FF	041–176, 200–377

These ranges include a user-defined character area that falls at the outskirts of the standard Shift-JIS encoding space. More about this below. Figure I-5 illustrates the encoding space for HP-15.

HP-16—the other Japanese encoding developed by Hewlett-Packard—has an area in its code space that is identical to EUC code set 1. The remaining code space is used for user-defined characters. Hewlett-Packard defines the HP-16 encoding with a series of four encoding blocks. Table I-12 lists the code specifications for HP-16.

Table I-12: HP-16 Encoding Specifications

	Decimal	Hexadecimal	Octal
Two-byte characters			
First byte range	161–254	A1–FE	241–376
Second byte range	161–254	A1–FE	241–376
Two-byte user-defined characters			
First byte range	161–194	A1–C2	241–302
Second byte range	33–126	21–7E	041–176

	Decimal	Hexadecimal	Octal
Two-byte user-defined characters			
First byte range	195–227	C3–E3	303–343
Second byte range	33–63	21–3F	041–077
Two-byte user-defined characters			
First byte range	195–225	C3–E1	303–341
Second byte range	64–100	40–64	100–144

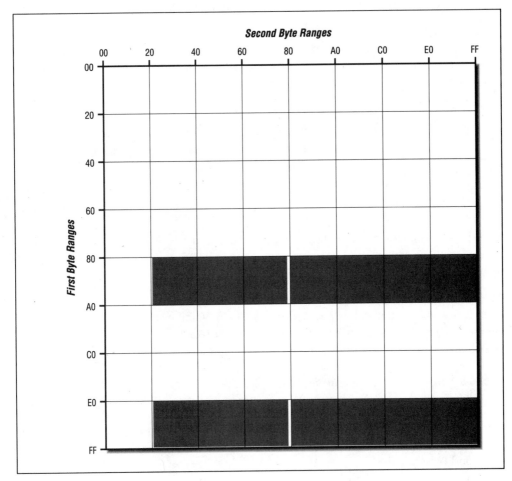

Figure I-5: HP-15 encoding table

HP Kanji Encoding Versus Shift-JIS and EUC Encodings

We really should compare HP Kanji encoding to Shift-JIS and EUC encodings. HP-15, as mentioned before, is a superset of Shift-JIS encoding, and HP-16 is similar to EUC encoding.

Figure I-6 shows the encoding space for HP-16, and Figure I-7 shows how Shift-JIS encoding is a subset of HP-15.

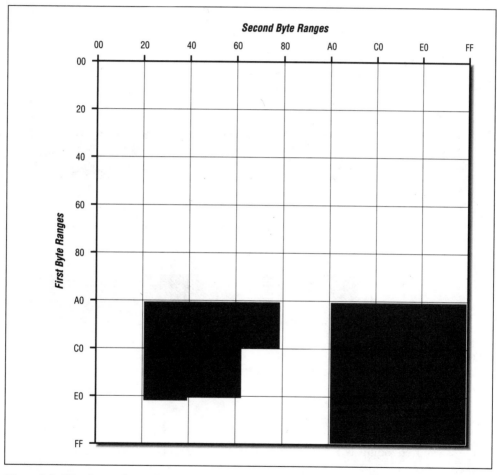

Figure I-6: HP-16 encoding table

EUC code set 1 is the same as the main portion of HP-16. This is the only similarity between EUC and HP-16. Compare Figures 4-11 and I-6 to confirm this.

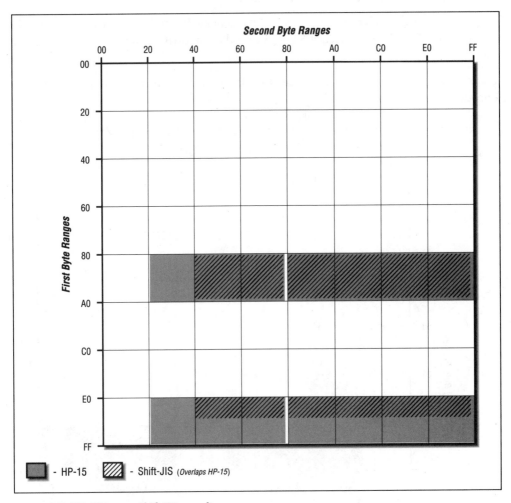

Figure I-7: HP-15 versus Shift-JIS encoding

Apple Kanji Encoding

Apple's Kanji encoding is Shift-JIS plus an additional encoded range for 2,256 user-defined characters equal to 24 extra rows of 94 characters each. This additional encoding range, however, is not compatible with other encodings such as JIS and EUC—they do not convert to valid code points in those encoding methods.

Table I-13 illustrates the encoding space for Apple Kanji.

Table I-13: Apple Kanji Encoding Specifications

	Decimal	Hexadecimal	Octal
Two-byte characters			
First byte ranges	129–159, 224–239	81–9F, E0–EF	201–237, 340–357
Second byte ranges	64–126, 128–252	40–7E, 80–FC	100–176, 200–374
Two-byte user-defined characters			
First byte range	240–251	F0–FB	360–373
Second byte ranges	64–126, 128–252	40–7E, 80–FC	100–176, 200–374
Half-width katakana			
Byte range	161–223	A1–DF	241–337
ASCII/JIS-Roman			
Byte range	33–126	21–7E	041–176

Apple Kanji Encoding Versus Shift-JIS Encoding

The encoding method used by Apple Kanji is more or less identical to Shift-JIS, except that there is an extra user-defined character encoding area. Both Apple Kanji character sets, Apple83 and Apple90, use the same encoding as described above.

KEIS Encoding

The encoding method used for KEIS includes encoding ranges found in parts of EUC encoding, namely EUC code set 1. It also uses shifting sequences to shift between one- and two-byte-per-character modes. KEIS encoding is used in conjunction with EBCDIK.*
The valid code ranges for KEIS are actually quite large, but a large chunk of it is reserved and apparently unused. Table I-14 illustrates this.

You may recall from Appendix H that KEIS Basic Character Set and KEIS Extended Character Set 1 constitute the JIS character set standard.

Table I-14: KEIS Encoding Space

	Decimal	Hexadecimal	Octal
First byte range	65–254	41–FE	101–376
Second byte range	65–254	41–FE	101–376

---

*EBCDIK is similar to EBCDIC, but includes half-width katakana.

Table I-15 lists the encoding specifications for KEIS.

Table I-15: KEIS Encoding Specifications

	Decimal	Hexadecimal	Octal
KEIS Basic Character Set			
First byte range	161–207	A1–CF	241–317
Second byte range	161–254	A1–FE	241–376
KEIS Extended Character Set 1			
First byte range	208–254	D0–FE	320–376
Second byte range	161–254	A1–FE	241–376
KEIS Extended Character Set 3			
First byte range	89–128	59–80	131–200
Second byte range	161–254	A1–FE	241–376
KEIS user-defined characters			
First byte range	129–160	81–A0	201–240
Second byte range	161–254	A1–FE	241–376
Full-width space character[1]			
First byte	64 or 161	40 or A1	100 or 241
Second byte	64 or 161	40 or A1	100 or 241
Shifting characters			
Two-byte character	10 66	0A 42	012 102
One-byte character	10 65	0A 41	012 101

[1]A full-width space can be represented by either 0x4040 or 0xA1A1.

KEIS Encoding Versus EUC Encoding

The encoding for KEIS Basic Character Set and KEIS Extended Character Set 1 is identical to the encoding used for EUC code set 1. The encoding for KEIS Extended Character Set 3 and KEIS user-defined characters departs from what we find in EUC encoding, and does not correspond to JIS or Shift-JIS encodings.

The big difference is that KEIS encoding is modal; it uses shifting sequences to handle one- and two-byte characters.

J

Character Lists and Mapping Tables

This appendix contains long lists that are referred to in earlier parts of this book. These lists are reference material, and contain encoded values for each character (KUTEN followed by hexadecimal JIS in parentheses).

JIS C 6226-1978 Versus JIS X 0208-1983

This section supplements Chapter 3. The differences between JIS C 6226-1978 and JIS X 0208-1983 can be classified into four categories, each of which is described here with complete examples. These differences vary depending on the source of the information. The first three categories are consistently treated the same by all sources I have referenced, but the fourth category gets different treatment depending on the source of the information.

Category 1

Several non-kanji were added to the character set. The first set consists of 39 miscellaneous characters added to row 2, and the second set consists of 32 line-drawing elements added to row 8.

∈ 0226 (223A)	√ 0269 (2265)	⊥ 0810 (282A)
∋ 0227 (223B)	∽ 0270 (2266)	┼ 0811 (282B)
⊆ 0228 (223C)	∝ 0271 (2267)	━ 0812 (282C)
⊇ 0229 (223D)	∵ 0272 (2268)	┃ 0813 (282D)
⊂ 0230 (223E)	∫ 0273 (2269)	┏ 0814 (282E)
⊃ 0231 (223F)	∬ 0274 (226A)	┓ 0815 (282F)
∪ 0232 (2240)	Å 0282 (2272)	┛ 0816 (2830)
∩ 0233 (2241)	‰ 0283 (2273)	┗ 0817 (2831)
∧ 0242 (224A)	♯ 0284 (2274)	┣ 0818 (2832)
∨ 0243 (224B)	♭ 0285 (2275)	┳ 0819 (2833)
¬ 0244 (224C)	♪ 0286 (2276)	┫ 0820 (2834)
⇒ 0245 (224D)	† 0287 (2277)	┻ 0821 (2835)
⇔ 0246 (224E)	‡ 0288 (2278)	╋ 0822 (2836)
∀ 0247 (224F)	¶ 0289 (2279)	┠ 0823 (2837)
∃ 0248 (2250)	◯ 0294 (227E)	┯ 0824 (2838)
∠ 0260 (225C)	─ 0801 (2821)	┨ 0825 (2839)
⊥ 0261 (225D)	│ 0802 (2822)	┷ 0826 (283A)
⌒ 0262 (225E)	┌ 0803 (2823)	┿ 0827 (283B)
∂ 0263 (225F)	┐ 0804 (2824)	┝ 0828 (283C)
∇ 0264 (2260)	┘ 0805 (2825)	┰ 0829 (283D)
≡ 0265 (2261)	└ 0806 (2826)	┥ 0830 (283E)
≒ 0266 (2262)	├ 0807 (2827)	┸ 0831 (283F)
≪ 0267 (2263)	┬ 0808 (2828)	╂ 0832 (2840)
≫ 0268 (2264)	┤ 0809 (2829)	

Category 2

The kanji shape in the original code position had simplified, and the unsimplified kanji was given a new code position after JIS Level 2 kanji. The final result was an addition of four kanji to row 84.

Original Code	Added Code
尭 2238 (3646)	堯 8401 (7421)
槙 4374 (4B6A)	槇 8402 (7422)
遥 4558 (4D5A)	遙 8403 (7423)
瑶 6486 (6076)	瑤 8404 (7424)

Category 3

22 simplified and traditional kanji pairs exchanged code positions between JIS Level 1 kanji and JIS Level 2 kanji (44 affected code points). The table below shows the characters as found in JIS X 0208-1983, so the simplified form is in the JIS Level 1 column, and the traditional form is in the JIS Level 2 column.

JIS Level 1		JIS Level 2		JIS Level 1		JIS Level 2	
鯵	1619 (3033)	鰺	8245 (724D)	賎	3308 (4128)	賤	7645 (6C4D)
鴬	1809 (3229)	鶯	8284 (7274)	壷	3659 (445B)	壺	5268 (5464)
蛎	1934 (3342)	蠣	7358 (695A)	砺	3755 (4557)	礪	6674 (626A)
撹	1941 (3349)	攪	5788 (5978)	梼	3778 (456E)	檮	5977 (5B6D)
竃	1986 (3376)	竈	6762 (635E)	涛	3783 (4573)	濤	6225 (5E39)
潅	2035 (3443)	灌	6285 (5E75)	迩	3886 (4676)	邇	7778 (6D6E)
諌	2050 (3452)	諫	7561 (6B5D)	蝿	3972 (4768)	蠅	7404 (6A24)
頚	2359 (375B)	頸	8084 (7074)	桧	4116 (4930)	檜	5956 (5B58)
砿	2560 (395C)	礦	6672 (6268)	侭	4389 (4B79)	儘	4854 (5056)
蕊	2841 (3C49)	蘂	7302 (6922)	薮	4489 (4C79)	藪	7314 (692E)
靭	3157 (3F59)	靱	8055 (7057)	竜	4722 (4F36)	籠	6838 (6446)

Category 4

The shapes of several kanji were altered. This category of change is quite subjective (that is the nature of glyph changes), and what appears below are 250 such characters. The actual number of affected kanji depends on your source. The source used here is the Adobe Japanese Glyph Set.

1978	1983			1978	1983			1978	1983		
唖	唖	1602 (3022)		澗	澗	2034 (3442)		諺	諺	2433 (3841)	
逢	逢	1609 (3029)		翰	翰	2045 (344D)		巷	巷	2511 (392B)	
芦	芦	1618 (3032)		翫	翫	2069 (3465)		昂	昂	2523 (3937)	
飴	飴	1627 (303B)		徽	徽	2111 (352B)		溝	溝	2534 (3942)	
溢	溢	1678 (306E)		祇	祇	2132 (3540)		麹	麹	2577 (396D)	
鰯	鰯	1683 (3073)		侠	侠	2202 (3622)		鵠	鵠	2584 (3974)	
淫	淫	1692 (307C)		卿	卿	2210 (362A)		甑	甑	2589 (3979)	
迂	迂	1710 (312A)		僅	僅	2247 (364F)		采	采	2651 (3A53)	
欝	欝	1721 (3135)		軀	躯	2277 (366D)		榊	榊	2671 (3A67)	
厩	厩	1725 (3139)		喰	喰	2284 (3674)		柵	柵	2684 (3A74)	
噂	噂	1729 (313D)		櫛	櫛	2291 (367B)		薩	薩	2707 (3B27)	
餌	餌	1734 (3142)		屑	屑	2293 (367D)		鯖	鯖	2710 (3B2A)	
焔	焔	1775 (316B)		靴	靴	2304 (3724)		錆	錆	2712 (3B2C)	
襖	襖	1808 (3228)		祁	祁	2323 (3737)		珊	珊	2725 (3B39)	
鴎	鴎	1810 (322A)		慧	慧	2337 (3745)		屡	屡	2840 (3C48)	
迦	迦	1864 (3260)		稽	稽	2346 (374E)		遮	遮	2855 (3C57)	
恢	恢	1890 (327A)		繋	繋	2350 (3752)		杓	杓	2861 (3C5D)	
拐	拐	1893 (327D)		荊	荊	2353 (3755)		灼	灼	2862 (3C5E)	
晦	晦	1902 (3322)		隙	隙	2368 (3764)		繍	繍	2911 (3D2B)	
喝	喝	1969 (3365)		倦	倦	2381 (3771)		酋	酋	2922 (3D36)	
葛	葛	1975 (336B)		嫌	嫌	2389 (3779)		曙	曙	2976 (3D6C)	
鞄	鞄	1983 (3373)		捲	捲	2394 (377E)		渚	渚	2977 (3D6D)	
嚙	嚙	1990 (337A)		瞼	瞼	2420 (3834)		薯	薯	2982 (3D72)	

1978	1983		1978	1983		1978	1983	
諸	諸	2983 (3D73)	凋	凋	3592 (437C)	柊	柊	4102 (4922)
哨	哨	3005 (3E25)	捗	捗	3629 (443D)	稗	稗	4103 (4923)
廠	廠	3019 (3E33)	槌	槌	3640 (4448)	逼	逼	4115 (492F)
梢	梢	3031 (3E3F)	鎚	鎚	3642 (444A)	媛	媛	4118 (4932)
蒋	蒋	3053 (3E55)	塚	塚	3645 (444D)	謬	謬	4121 (4935)
醤	醤	3063 (3E5F)	摑	摑	3647 (444F)	廟	廟	4132 (4940)
鞘	鞘	3068 (3E64)	辻	辻	3652 (4454)	瀬	瀬	4146 (494E)
蝕	蝕	3110 (3F2A)	鄭	鄭	3702 (4522)	頻	頻	4149 (4951)
靭	靭	3157 (3F59)*	擢	擢	3707 (4527)	蔽	蔽	4235 (4A43)
逗	逗	3164 (3F60)	溺	溺	3714 (452E)	瞥	瞥	4245 (4A4D)
翠	翠	3173 (3F69)	塡	塡	3722 (4536)	娩	娩	4258 (4A5A)
摺	摺	3202 (4022)	顚	顚	3731 (453F)	庖	庖	4289 (4A79)
逝	逝	3234 (4042)	堵	堵	3740 (4548)	泡	泡	4302 (4B22)
蟬	蟬	3270 (4066)	屠	屠	3743 (454B)	蓬	蓬	4309 (4B29)
撰	撰	3281 (4071)	菟	菟	3749 (4551)	頰	頰	4343 (4B4B)
栓	栓	3282 (4072)	賭	賭	3750 (4552)	鱒	鱒	4380 (4B70)
煎	煎	3289 (4079)	塘	塘	3768 (4564)	迄	迄	4388 (4B78)
煽	煽	3290 (407A)	禱	祷	3788 (4578)	麺	麺	4445 (4C4D)
詮	詮	3307 (4127)	鎬	鎬	3830 (463E)	儲	儲	4457 (4C59)
噌	噌	3325 (4139)	潰	洸	3834 (4642)	餅	餅	4463 (4C5F)
遡	遡	3344 (414C)	瀞	瀞	3852 (4654)	籾	籾	4466 (4C62)
創	創	3347 (414F)	噸	噸	3853 (4655)	鑓	鑓	4490 (4C7A)
搔	搔	3363 (415F)	遁	遁	3859 (465B)	愈	愈	4492 (4C7C)
瘦	瘦	3373 (4169)	頓	頓	3860 (465C)	癒	癒	4494 (4C7E)
遜	遜	3429 (423D)	那	那	3865 (4661)	猷	猷	4518 (4D32)
驒	驒	3445 (424D)	謎	謎	3870 (4666)	熔	熔	4548 (4D50)
腿	腿	3460 (425C)	灘	灘	3871 (4667)	耀	耀	4552 (4D54)
黛	黛	3467 (4263)	楢	楢	3874 (466A)	萊	萊	4573 (4D69)
啄	啄	3479 (426F)	襦	襦	3909 (4729)	遼	遼	4643 (4E4B)
濯	濯	3485 (4275)	嚢	嚢	3925 (4739)	漣	漣	4690 (4E7A)
琢	琢	3486 (4276)	牌	牌	3955 (4757)	煉	煉	4691 (4E7B)
蛸	蛸	3493 (427D)	這	這	3971 (4767)	蓮	蓮	4701 (4F21)
巽	巽	3507 (4327)	秤	秤	3973 (4769)	榔	榔	4717 (4F31)
辿	辿	3509 (4329)	剝	剝	3977 (476D)	蠟	蝋	4725 (4F39)
棚	棚	3510 (432A)	箸	箸	4004 (4824)	兔	兔	4929 (513D)
鱈	鱈	3513 (432D)	潑	溌	4014 (482E)	冉	冉	4939 (5147)
樽	樽	3514 (432E)	醱	醗	4016 (4830)	冕	冕	4943 (514B)
簞	簞	3529 (433D)	挽	挽	4052 (4854)	冤	冤	4945 (514D)
註	註	3580 (4370)	扉	扉	4066 (4862)	唹	唹	5116 (5330)
瀦	瀦	3585 (4375)	樋	樋	4085 (4875)	喨	喨	5126 (533A)

---

*This kanji is also listed under Category 3. The kanji in the KUTEN position 3157 had the form 靭 in JIS C 6226-1978, but before it swapped code positions with KUTEN 8055, it transformed into 靭.

1978	1983			1978	1983			1978	1983	
嘲	嘲	5162	(535E)	皓	皓	6611	(622B)	諞	諞	7570	(6B66)
嚥	嚥	5175	(536B)	硼	硼	6679	(626F)	譁	譁	7586	(6B76)
堋	堋	5236	(5444)	稱	稱	6742	(634A)	蹣	蹣	7673	(6C69)
媾	媾	5329	(553D)	穤	穤	6752	(6354)	跟	跟	7684	(6C74)
宛	宛	5367	(5563)	簸	簸	6825	(6439)	輓	輓	7746	(6D4E)
屏	屏	5402	(5622)	籸	籸	6868	(6464)	迪	迪	7776	(6D6C)
悗	悗	5604	(5824)	粮	粮	6878	(646E)	迯	迺	7778	(6D6E)*
捩	捩	5764	(5960)	絅	絅	6925	(6539)	遘	遘	7809	(6E29)
搆	搆	5776	(596C)	綮	綮	6927	(653B)	屢	屢	7829	(6E3D)
攢	攢	5825	(5A39)	緤	緤	6938	(6546)	釁	釁	7855	(6E57)
斃	斃	5845	(5A4D)	翔	翔	7038	(6646)	雷	雷	8037	(7045)
枦	枦	5937	(5B45)	艫	艫	7168	(6764)	靠	靠	8049	(7051)
枴	枴	5942	(5B4A)	芍	芍	7173	(6769)	靭	靱	8055	(7057)
梛	梛	5975	(5B6B)	苒	苒	7182	(6772)	頤	頤	8085	(7075)
棺	棺	5984	(5B74)	莫	莫	7220	(6834)	闌	闌	8213	(722D)
湮	湮	6248	(5E50)	蕊	蕊	7227	(683B)	鮯	鮯	8228	(723C)
爨	爨	6406	(6026)	蔗	蔗	7284	(6874)	鯲	鯲	8246	(724E)
珎	珎	6463	(605F)	蠅	蠅	7407	(6A27)	麭	麭	8349	(7351)
甄	甄	6511	(612B)	蟒	蟒	7429	(6A3D)	龜	龜	8393	(737D)
甕	甕	6516	(6130)	褊	褊	7479	(6A6F)				
甕	甕	6517	(6131)	覿	覿	7518	(6B32)				

JIS X 0208-1983 Versus JIS X 0208-1990

This section also supplements Chapter 3. Changes made to JIS X 0208-1983 to create JIS X 0208-1990 were very minor, and basically consist of two categories. The first category consists of characters added to the character set standard. In the case of JIS X 0208-1990, the following two kanji characters were appended after JIS Level 2 kanji:

凜 8405 (7425)
熙 8406 (7426)

However, there were some very subtle glyph changes introduced with JIS X 0208-1990. These glyph changes can be categorized into approximately six different types. See Table J-1 for several examples of such glyph changes.

---

*This kanji is also listed under Category 3. The kanji in the KUTEN position 7778 had the form 迯 in JIS C 6226-1978, but before it swapped code positions with KUTEN 3886, it transformed into 迺 (a one stroke difference!).

Table J-1: Glyph Change Examples Between JIS X 0208-1983 and JIS X 0208-1990

JIS X 0208-1983	JIS X 0208-1990
帰	帰
公	公
邪	邪
埴	埴
緋	緋
靱	靱

What? You cannot see the differences? This then goes to show just how subtle (and subjective) glyph changes can be. The following is a complete list of the 145 affected kanji.

1983	1990		1983	1990		1983	1990	
偉	偉	1646 (304E)	罪	罪	2665 (3A61)	頒	頒	4050 (4852)
緯	緯	1662 (305E)	使	使	2740 (3B48)	悲	悲	4065 (4861)
違	違	1667 (3063)	史	史	2743 (3B4B)	扉	扉	4066 (4862)
厩	厩	1725 (3139)	邪	邪	2857 (3C59)	斐	斐	4069 (4865)
衛	衛	1750 (3152)	収	収	2893 (3C7D)	緋	緋	4076 (486C)
延	延	1768 (3164)	瞬	瞬	2954 (3D56)	誹	誹	4080 (4870)
沿	沿	1772 (3168)	舜	舜	2956 (3D58)	貧	貧	4147 (494F)
鉛	鉛	1784 (3174)	松	松	3030 (3E3E)	父	父	4167 (4963)
翁	翁	1807 (3227)	訟	訟	3057 (3E59)	分	分	4212 (4A2C)
慨	慨	1920 (3334)	丈	丈	3070 (3E66)	粉	粉	4220 (4A34)
概	概	1921 (3335)	埴	埴	3093 (3E7D)	紛	紛	4222 (4A36)
殻	殻	1944 (334C)	職	職	3106 (3F26)	雰	雰	4223 (4A37)
敢	敢	2026 (343A)	船	船	3305 (4125)	便	便	4256 (4A58)
頑	頑	2072 (3468)	総	総	3377 (416D)	盆	盆	4363 (4B5F)
帰	帰	2102 (3522)	聡	聡	3379 (416F)	桝	桝	4381 (4B71)
窮	窮	2171 (3567)	像	像	3392 (417C)	耶	耶	4477 (4C6D)
均	均	2249 (3651)	誕	誕	3534 (4342)	吏	吏	4589 (4D79)
傑	傑	2370 (3766)	恥	恥	3549 (4351)	隣	隣	4657 (4E59)
穴	穴	2374 (376A)	兆	兆	3591 (437B)	麗	麗	4679 (4E6F)
健	健	2382 (3772)	眺	眺	3615 (442F)	聯	聯	4694 (4E7E)
建	建	2390 (377A)	聴	聴	3616 (4430)	匕	匕	5024 (5238)
交	交	2482 (3872)	跳	跳	3623 (4437)	雙	雙	5054 (5256)
公	公	2488 (3878)	庭	庭	3677 (446D)	喩	喩	5140 (5348)
更	更	2525 (3939)	廷	廷	3678 (446E)	圍	圍	5203 (5423)
校	校	2527 (393B)	艇	艇	3690 (447A)	姚	姚	5313 (552D)
硬	硬	2537 (3945)	桃	桃	3777 (456D)	娶	娶	5324 (5538)
絞	絞	2542 (394A)	逃	逃	3808 (4628)	巉	巉	5458 (565A)
考	考	2545 (394D)	排	排	3951 (4753)	巓	巓	5460 (565C)
降	降	2563 (395F)	輩	輩	3958 (475A)	弖	弖	5525 (5739)
拷	拷	2573 (3969)	班	班	4041 (4849)	徘	徘	5549 (5751)

1983	1990			1983	1990			1983	1990	
悧	悧	5617 (5831)		瓠	瓠	6501 (6121)		襪	襪	7504 (6B24)
扨	扨	5714 (592E)		癲	癲	6601 (6221)		襯	襯	7505 (6B25)
擲	擲	5819 (5A33)		磔	磔	6689 (6279)		訝	訝	7535 (6B43)
敝	敝	5841 (5A49)		窕	窕	6758 (635A)		贅	贅	7652 (6C54)
晟	晟	5880 (5A70)		絹	絹	6941 (6549)		贏	贏	7655 (6C57)
杰	杰	5932 (5B40)		縵	縵	6960 (655C)		蹕	蹕	7722 (6D36)
柧	柧	5955 (5B57)		翡	翡	7039 (6647)		躑	躑	7726 (6D3A)
椰	椰	6031 (5C3F)		聚	聚	7060 (665C)		鐺	鐺	7950 (6F52)
榧	榧	6050 (5C52)		聰	聰	7066 (6662)		隘	隘	8007 (7027)
橄	橄	6077 (5C6D)		聶	聶	7067 (6663)		靠	靠	8049 (7051)
檐	檐	6089 (5C79)		腓	腓	7104 (6724)		靭	靭	8055 (7057)
氈	氈	6165 (5D61)		膵	膵	7125 (6739)		頌	頌	8083 (7073)
渣	渣	6254 (5E56)		菲	菲	7243 (684B)		顳	顳	8103 (7123)
溉	溉	6284 (5E74)		蜚	蜚	7384 (6974)		魍	魍	8219 (7233)
滾	滾	6288 (5E78)		蠶	蠶	7436 (6A44)		鯡	鯡	8244 (724C)
漾	漾	6301 (5F21)		袞	袞	7449 (6A51)		鯢	鯢	8247 (724F)
爥	爥	6402 (6022)		裴	裴	7474 (6A6A)		鶫	鶫	8294 (727E)
珥	珥	6466 (6062)		褫	褫	7485 (6A75)				
琲	琲	6474 (606A)		襞	襞	7488 (6A78)				

JIS X 0212-1990

Table J-2 supplements material in the section about JIS X 0212-1990 in Chapter 3. This table illustrates the 28 kanji that were removed from the JIS X 0208 series in 1983, but were subsequently included in JIS X 0212-1990.

Table J-2: The 28 Kanji from JIS C 6226-1978 in JIS X 0212-1990

JIS C 6226-1978		JIS X 0208-1983/90		JIS X 0212-1990	
俠	2202 (3622)	俠	2202 (3622)	俠	1734 (3142)
啞	1602 (3022)	唖	1602 (3022)	啞	2164 (3560)
噛	1990 (337A)	噛	1990 (337A)	嚙	2258 (365A)
嚢	3925 (4739)	嚢	3925 (4739)	囊	2276 (366C)
填	3722 (4536)	填	3722 (4536)	塡	2420 (3834)
屡	2840 (3C48)	屡	2840 (3C48)	屢	2690 (3A7A)
掻	3363 (415F)	掻	3363 (415F)	搔	3243 (404B)
摑	3647 (444F)	掴	3647 (444F)	摑	3259 (405B)
攢	5825 (5A39)	攅	5825 (5A39)	攢	3334 (4142)
潑	4014 (482E)	溌	4014 (482E)	潑	4053 (4855)
瀆	3834 (4642)	涜	3834 (4642)	瀆	4112 (492C)
焔	1775 (316B)	焔	1775 (316B)	焰	4179 (496F)
痩	3373 (4169)	痩	3373 (4169)	瘦	4587 (4D77)
禱	3788 (4578)	祷	3788 (4578)	禱	4880 (5070)
繡	2911 (3D2B)	繍	2911 (3D2B)	繡	5255 (5457)

JIS C 6226-1978	JIS X 0208-1983/90	JIS X 0212-1990
繋　2350　(3752)	繋　2350　(3752)	繋　5258　(545A)
萊　4573　(4D69)	莱　4573　(4D69)	莱　5639　(5847)
蔣　3053　(3E55)	蒋　3053　(3E55)	蔣　5722　(5936)
蠟　4725　(4F39)	蝋　4725　(4F39)	蠟　5988　(5B78)
軀　2277　(366D)	躯　2277　(366D)	軀　6452　(6054)
醬　3063　(3E5F)	醤　3063　(3E5F)	醬　6683　(6273)
醱　4016　(4830)	醗　4016　(4830)	醱　6687　(6277)
煩　4343　(4B4B)	煩　4343　(4B4B)	煩　7204　(6824)
顚　3731　(453F)	顛　3731　(453F)	顚　7219　(6833)
鷗　1810　(322A)	鴎　1810　(322A)	鷗　7631　(6C3F)
鹸　2420　(3834)	鹸　2420　(3834)	鹼　7659　(6C5B)
麴　2577　(396D)	麹　2577　(396D)	麴　7679　(6C6F)
麵　4445　(4C4D)	麺　4445　(4C4D)	麵　7680　(6C70)

Jôyô Kanji

Table J-3 lists the 95 kanji that were added to Tôyô Kanji in 1981 to form Jôyô Kanji. This brought the total number of kanji from 1,850 to 1,945.

Table J-3: The 95 Kanji Added to Tôyô Kanji to Become Jôyô Kanji

渦　1718　(3132)	昆　2611　(3A2B)	曹　3366　(4162)
猿　1778　(316E)	崎　2674　(3A6A)	槽　3369　(4165)
凹　1790　(317A)	皿　2714　(3B2E)	藻　3384　(4174)
稼　1852　(3254)	傘　2717　(3B31)	駄　3444　(424C)
拐　1893　(327D)	桟　2723　(3B37)	濯　3485　(4275)
涯　1922　(3336)	肢　2772　(3B68)	棚　3510　(432A)
垣　1932　(3340)	遮　2855　(3C57)	挑　3609　(4429)
殻　1944　(334C)	蛇　2856　(3C58)	眺　3615　(442F)
潟　1967　(3363)	酌　2864　(3C60)	塚　3645　(444D)
喝　1969　(3365)	汁　2933　(3D41)	漬　3650　(4452)
褐　1976　(336C)	塾　2946　(3D4E)	釣　3664　(4460)
缶　2044　(344C)	宵　3012　(3E2C)	亭　3666　(4462)
頑　2072　(3468)	尚　3016　(3E30)	偵　3669　(4465)
挟　2220　(3634)	壌　3077　(3E6D)	泥　3705　(4525)
矯　2226　(363A)	唇　3116　(3F30)	搭　3775　(456B)
襟　2263　(365F)	甚　3151　(3F53)	棟　3779　(456F)
隅　2289　(3679)	据　3188　(3F78)	洞　3822　(4636)
靴　2304　(3724)	杉　3189　(3F79)	凸　3844　(464C)
渓　2344　(374C)	逝　3234　(4042)	屯　3854　(4656)
蛍　2354　(3756)	斉　3238　(4046)	縄　3876　(466C)
嫌　2389　(3779)	仙　3271　(4067)	猫　3913　(472D)
洪　2531　(393F)	栓　3282　(4072)	把　3936　(4744)
溝　2534　(3942)	挿　3362　(415E)	覇　3938　(4746)

漠	3989 (4779)		俸	4280 (4A70)		妄	4449 (4C51)
肌	4009 (4829)		泡	4302 (4B22)		戻	4465 (4C61)
鉢	4013 (482D)		褒	4311 (4B2B)		厄	4481 (4C71)
扉	4066 (4862)		僕	4345 (4B4D)		癒	4494 (4C7E)
披	4068 (4864)		朴	4349 (4B51)		悠	4510 (4D2A)
頻	4149 (4951)		堀	4357 (4B59)		羅	4569 (4D65)
瓶	4151 (4953)		磨	4365 (4B61)		竜	4621 (4E35)
雰	4223 (4A37)		抹	4385 (4B75)		枠	4740 (4F48)
塀	4229 (4A3D)		岬	4408 (4C28)			

IBM Kanji

Tables J-4 through J-6 supplement material found in Appendix I. They illustrate how the 388 IBM select kanji and non-kanji are mapped from DBCS-PC encoding to DBCS-EUC encoding. Table J-4 shows how 3 of the IBM select kanji and non-kanji are mapped to JIS X 0208-1990 character positions in DBCS-EUC encoding. Table J-5 shows how 280 IBM select kanji and non-kanji are mapped to JIS X 0212-1990 character positions. Table J-6 shows how the remaining 105 IBM select kanji and non-kanji are mapped to user-defined character positions in the JIS X 0212-1990 code table.

Table J-4: IBM Select Characters Mapping Table (to JIS X 0208-1990 Positions)

Character	DBCS-PC	JIS X 0208-1990
⌐	FA54	0244 (A2CC)
∵	FA5B	0272 (A2E8)
昂	FAD0	2523 (B9B7)

Table J-5: IBM Select Characters Mapping Table (to JIS X 0212-1990 Positions)

Character	DBCS-PC	JIS X 0212-1990	Character	DBCS-PC	JIS X 0212-1990
¦	FA55	0235 (8FA2C3)	仔	FA6C	1652 (8FB0D4)
纉	FA5C	5267 (8FD4E3)	但	FA6D	1667 (8FB0E3)
襃	FA5D	6063 (8FDCDF)	佖	FA6E	1678 (8FB0EE)
鍈	FA5E	6873 (8FE4E9)	安	FA6F	1707 (8FB1A7)
銈	FA5F	6788 (8FE3F8)	侊	FA70	1703 (8FB1A3)
菔	FA60	5701 (8FD9A1)	侚	FA71	1712 (8FB1AC)
唔	FA61	1727 (8FB1BB)	侔	FA72	1709 (8FB1A9)
昱	FA63	3413 (8FC2AD)	俍	FA73	1730 (8FB1BE)
楮	FA64	3592 (8FC3FC)	俠	FA74	1763 (8FB1DF)
銀	FA65	6848 (8FE4D0)	健	FA75	1756 (8FB1D8)
昪	FA66	3431 (8FC2BF)	俿	FA76	1740 (8FB1C8)
弥	FA67	2884 (8FBCF4)	倞	FA77	1755 (8FB1D7)
∣	FA68	1609 (8FB0A9)	倍	FA78	1767 (8FB1E3)
亿	FA69	1640 (8FB0C8)	偰	FA79	1784 (8FB1F4)
仫	FA6B	1650 (8FB0D2)	偸	FA7A	1765 (8FB1E1)

Character	DBCS-PC	JIS X 0212-1990
傔	FA7B	1803 (8FB2A3)
僘	FA7D	1827 (8FB2BB)
兊	FA7E	1870 (8FB2E6)
兤	FA80	1877 (8FB2ED)
冝	FA81	1885 (8FB2F5)
冾	FA82	1892 (8FB2FC)
刕	FA84	1921 (8FB3B5)
劜	FA85	1956 (8FB3D8)
劦	FA86	1959 (8FB3DB)
勀	FA87	1969 (8FB3E5)
勛	FA88	1978 (8FB3EE)
匀	FA89	1991 (8FB3FB)
卲	FA8C	2032 (8FB4C0)
厓	FA8D	2039 (8FB4C7)
厲	FA8E	2048 (8FB4D0)
叝	FA8F	2062 (8FB4DE)
咜	FA91	2110 (8FB5AA)
咩	FA93	2115 (8FB5AF)
哿	FA94	2136 (8FB5C4)
喆	FA95	2172 (8FB5E8)
坥	FA97	2334 (8FB7C2)
垬	FA98	2368 (8FB7E4)
埈	FA99	2372 (8FB7E8)
埇	FA9A	2371 (8FB7E7)
墲	FA9E	2446 (8FB8CE)
夋	FA9F	2465 (8FB8E1)
奓	FAA0	2485 (8FB8F5)
奛	FAA1	2487 (8FB8F7)
奝	FAA2	2488 (8FB8F8)
奣	FAA3	2492 (8FB8FC)
妤	FAA4	2515 (8FB9AF)
妺	FAA5	2523 (8FB9B7)
孖	FAA6	2630 (8FBABE)
寀	FAA7	2659 (8FBADB)
甯	FAA8	4510 (8FCDAA)
寘	FAA9	2665 (8FBAE1)
尞	FAAB	2675 (8FBAEB)
岦	FAAC	2719 (8FBBB3)
岺	FAAD	2724 (8FBBB8)
崧	FAAF	2742 (8FBBCA)
嵂	FAB2	2748 (8FBBD0)
嵭	FAB3	2762 (8FBBDE)
嶸	FAB4	2784 (8FBBF4)
嶹	FAB5	2785 (8FBBF5)
巐	FAB6	2789 (8FBBF9)
弡	FAB7	2868 (8FBCE4)
弴	FAB8	2877 (8FBCED)
彧	FAB9	2894 (8FBCFE)
忞	FABB	2934 (8FBDC2)
恝	FABC	2971 (8FBDE7)
悊	FABE	2980 (8FBDF0)
惞	FABF	3016 (8FBEB0)
惕	FAC0	3012 (8FBEAC)
惲	FAC2	3019 (8FBEB3)
愑	FAC3	3029 (8FBEBD)
愷	FAC4	3045 (8FBECD)
愰	FAC5	3041 (8FBEC9)
憘	FAC6	3068 (8FBEE4)
戓	FAC7	3108 (8FBFA8)
抦	FAC8	3141 (8FBFC9)
揵	FAC9	3236 (8FC0C4)
摠	FACA	3268 (8FC0E4)
撝	FACB	3284 (8FC0F4)
擎	FACC	3306 (8FC1A6)
昀	FACE	3385 (8FC1F5)
昕	FACF	3392 (8FC1FC)
昉	FAD1	3388 (8FC1F8)
昮	FAD2	3411 (8FC2AB)
昞	FAD3	3401 (8FC2A1)
昤	FAD4	3405 (8FC2A5)
晗	FAD6	3424 (8FC2B8)
晙	FAD7	3426 (8FC2BA)
晳	FAD9	3436 (8FC2C4)
暙	FADA	3450 (8FC2D2)
暠	FADB	3455 (8FC2D7)
暲	FADC	3459 (8FC2DB)
暿	FADD	3462 (8FC2DE)
曺	FADE	3477 (8FC2ED)
朎	FADF	3480 (8FC2F0)
杦	FAE1	3501 (8FC3A1)
枻	FAE2	3521 (8FC3B5)
桒	FAE3	3541 (8FC3C9)
柀	FAE4	3525 (8FC3B9)
桄	FAE6	3556 (8FC3D8)
棏	FAE7	3594 (8FC3FE)
楨	FAE9	3644 (8FC4CC)

Character	DBCS-PC	JIS X 0212-1990
榘	FAEB	3657 (8FC4D9)
槢	FAEC	3674 (8FC4EA)
樰	FAED	3693 (8FC4FD)
橆	FAEF	3707 (8FC5A7)
橳	FAF0	3721 (8FC5B5)
橾	FAF1	3722 (8FC5B6)
櫤	FAF3	3753 (8FC5D5)
毖	FAF4	3824 (8FC6B8)
氿	FAF5	3855 (8FC6D7)
汜	FAF6	3864 (8FC6E0)
沆	FAF7	3874 (8FC6EA)
汯	FAF8	3867 (8FC6E3)
泚	FAF9	3901 (8FC7A1)
洄	FAFA	3911 (8FC7AB)
涇	FAFB	3939 (8FC7C7)
浯	FAFC	3935 (8FC7C3)
涖	FB40	3943 (8FC7CB)
涬	FB41	3947 (8FC7CF)
淏	FB42	3957 (8FC7D9)
淼	FB45	3970 (8FC7E6)
渹	FB46	3978 (8FC7EE)
湜	FB47	3992 (8FC7FC)
渧	FB48	3975 (8FC7EB)
渼	FB49	3980 (8FC7F0)
溿	FB4A	4017 (8FC8B1)
澈	FB4B	4069 (8FC8E5)
澵	FB4C	4088 (8FC8F8)
濵	FB4D	4106 (8FC9A6)
瀅	FB4E	4111 (8FC9AB)
瀇	FB4F	4113 (8FC9AD)
炅	FB51	4142 (8FC9CA)
炫	FB52	4151 (8FC9D3)
焏	FB53	4173 (8FC9E9)
焄	FB54	4167 (8FC9E3)
煜	FB55	4192 (8FC9FC)
煆	FB56	4184 (8FC9F4)
煇	FB57	4185 (8FC9F5)
燁	FB59	4219 (8FCAB3)
燾	FB5A	4229 (8FCABD)
犱	FB5B	4279 (8FCAEF)
犾	FB5C	4281 (8FCAF1)
猤	FB5D	4314 (8FCBAE)
獷	FB5F	4342 (8FCBCA)
玽	FB60	4370 (8FCBE6)
珉	FB61	4374 (8FCBEA)
珖	FB62	4380 (8FCBF0)
珣	FB63	4384 (8FCBF4)
珒	FB64	4378 (8FCBEE)
琇	FB65	4405 (8FCCA5)
珵	FB66	4389 (8FCBF9)
琦	FB67	4411 (8FCCAB)
琪	FB68	4414 (8FCCAE)
琩	FB69	4413 (8FCCAD)
琮	FB6A	4418 (8FCCB2)
瑢	FB6B	4434 (8FCCC2)
璉	FB6C	4448 (8FCCD0)
璟	FB6D	4457 (8FCCD9)
畯	FB6F	4527 (8FCDBB)
皜	FB71	4627 (8FCEBB)
皛	FB73	4626 (8FCEBA)
皦	FB74	4635 (8FCEC3)
睆	FB76	4682 (8FCEF2)
劯	FB77	1961 (8FB3DD)
砡	FB78	4753 (8FCFD5)
硎	FB79	4766 (8FCFE2)
硤	FB7A	4773 (8FCFE9)
硺	FB7B	4777 (8FCFED)
禔	FB81	4869 (8FD0E5)
禛	FB83	4873 (8FD0E9)
竑	FB84	4972 (8FD1E8)
竫	FB87	4976 (8FD1EC)
箞	FB88	5027 (8FD2BB)
絈	FB8A	5165 (8FD3E1)
絜	FB8B	5172 (8FD3E8)
綷	FB8C	5207 (8FD4A7)
繒	FB8F	5252 (8FD4D4)
罇	FB90	5282 (8FD4F2)
羡	FB91	5314 (8FD5AE)
茁	FB93	5562 (8FD7DE)
荿	FB95	5602 (8FD8A2)
菇	FB96	5623 (8FD8B7)
菶	FB97	5633 (8FD8C1)
葈	FB98	5649 (8FD8D1)
蒴	FB99	5684 (8FD8F4)
蕓	FB9A	5738 (8FD9C6)
蕙	FB9B	5740 (8FD9C8)

Character	DBCS-PC	JIS X 0212-1990	Character	DBCS-PC	JIS X 0212-1990
董	FB9C	5749 (8FD9D1)	鋐	FBD2	6830 (8FE4BE)
裦	FBA2	6051 (8FDCD3)	銇	FBD4	6832 (8FE4C0)
訒	FBA3	6140 (8FDDC8)	鋠	FBD5	6839 (8FE4C7)
裈	FBA4	6152 (8FDDD4)	銅	FBD6	6831 (8FE4BF)
詹	FBA5	6174 (8FDDEA)	銷	FBD7	6864 (8FE4E0)
誧	FBA6	6190 (8FDDFA)	錡	FBD8	6862 (8FE4DE)
誾	FBA7	6204 (8FDEA4)	鋻	FBD9	6849 (8FE4D1)
諟	FBA8	6216 (8FDEB0)	錞	FBDB	6860 (8FE4DC)
諶	FBAA	6221 (8FDEB5)	鍋	FBDC	6850 (8FE4D2)
譧	FBAB	6243 (8FDECB)	錝	FBDD	6859 (8FE4DB)
瞔	FBAD	6325 (8FDFB9)	錂	FBDE	6852 (8FE4D4)
贒	FBAF	6335 (8FDFC3)	鍰	FBDF	6890 (8FE4FA)
軐	FBB2	6457 (8FE0D9)	鍗	FBE0	6879 (8FE4EF)
達	FBB5	6566 (8FE1E2)	錩	FBE1	6919 (8FE5B3)
鄧	FBB9	6639 (8FE2C7)	鑚	FBE2	6931 (8FE5BF)
釖	FBBA	6708 (8FE3A8)	鏞	FBE3	6941 (8FE5C9)
釗	FBBB	6706 (8FE3A6)	鏸	FBE4	6948 (8FE5D0)
釴	FBBC	6709 (8FE3A9)	鑑	FBE5	6966 (8FE5E2)
釭	FBBD	6715 (8FE3AF)	鑠	FBE6	6974 (8FE5EA)
釸	FBBE	6716 (8FE3B0)	鑭	FBE7	6975 (8FE5EB)
鈏	FBBF	6710 (8FE3AA)	隖	FBEB	7072 (8FE6E8)
鈋	FBC0	6711 (8FE3AB)	隯	FBEC	7079 (8FE6EF)
鈜	FBC1	6728 (8FE3BC)	霆	FBED	7112 (8FE7AC)
鈴	FBC2	6733 (8FE3C1)	霳	FBEF	7114 (8FE7AE)
鈺	FBC3	6731 (8FE3BF)	靉	FBF1	7117 (8FE7B1)
鈺	FBC4	6753 (8FE3D5)	靖	FBF3	7118 (8FE7B2)
鉀	FBC5	6756 (8FE3D8)	顗	FBF4	7217 (8FE8B1)
鉅	FBC6	6754 (8FE3D6)	顥	FBF5	7222 (8FE8B6)
銈	FBC7	6763 (8FE3DF)	餕	FBF8	7261 (8FE8DD)
鉥	FBC8	6767 (8FE3E3)	驎	FBFB	7349 (8FE9D1)
鉑	FBC9	6765 (8FE3E1)	骭	FC40	7377 (8FE9ED)
鉞	FBCA	6752 (8FE3D4)	魵	FC41	7445 (8FEACD)
鉧	FBCB	6773 (8FE3E9)	鮏	FC43	7459 (8FEADB)
銚	FBCC	6806 (8FE4A6)	鮐	FC44	7470 (8FEAE6)
銇	FBCD	6781 (8FE3F1)	鮫	FC45	7474 (8FEAEA)
鉸	FBCE	6782 (8FE3F2)	鰻	FC46	7505 (8FEBA5)
鋧	FBCF	6843 (8FE4CB)	鵰	FC47	7591 (8FEBFB)
銷	FBD0	6833 (8FE4C1)	鶀	FC48	7590 (8FEBFA)
鋙	FBD1	6835 (8FE4C3)	鷉	FC4A	7654 (8FECD6)

Table J-6: IBM Select Characters Mapping Table (to JIS X 0212-1990 User-defined Positions)

Character	DBCS-PC	JIS X 0212-1990	Character	DBCS-PC	JIS X 0212-1990
ⅰ	FA40	8301 (8FF3A1)	悅	FABD	8419 (8FF4B3)
ⅱ	FA41	8302 (8FF3A2)	愠	FAC1	8420 (8FF4B4)
ⅲ	FA42	8303 (8FF3A3)	敎	FACD	8421 (8FF4B5)
ⅳ	FA43	8304 (8FF3A4)	晥	FAD5	8423 (8FF4B7)
ⅴ	FA44	8305 (8FF3A5)	晴	FAD8	8424 (8FF4B8)
ⅵ	FA45	8306 (8FF3A6)	朗	FAE0	8425 (8FF4B9)
ⅶ	FA46	8307 (8FF3A7)	栁	FAE5	8426 (8FF4BA)
ⅷ	FA47	8308 (8FF3A8)	﨓	FAE8	8427 (8FF4BB)
ⅸ	FA48	8309 (8FF3A9)	﨔	FAEA	8428 (8FF4BC)
ⅹ	FA49	8310 (8FF3AA)	橫	FAEE	8429 (8FF4BD)
Ⅰ	FA4A	8311 (8FF3AB)	櫢	FAF2	8430 (8FF4BE)
Ⅱ	FA4B	8312 (8FF3AC)	淸	FB43	8431 (8FF4BF)
Ⅲ	FA4C	8313 (8FF3AD)	淲	FB44	8432 (8FF4C0)
Ⅳ	FA4D	8314 (8FF3AE)	瀨	FB50	8434 (8FF4C2)
Ⅴ	FA4E	8315 (8FF3AF)	凞	FB58	8436 (8FF4C4)
Ⅵ	FA4F	8316 (8FF3B0)	猪	FB5E	8437 (8FF4C5)
Ⅶ	FA50	8317 (8FF3B1)	甁	FB6E	8438 (8FF4C6)
Ⅷ	FA51	8318 (8FF3B2)	皂	FB70	8439 (8FF4C7)
Ⅸ	FA52	8319 (8FF3B3)	皞	FB72	8440 (8FF4C8)
Ⅹ	FA53	8320 (8FF3B4)	益	FB75	8441 (8FF4C9)
＇	FA56	8321 (8FF3B5)	礰	FB7C	8443 (8FF4CB)
＂	FA57	8322 (8FF3B6)	礼	FB7D	8444 (8FF4CC)
㈱	FA58	8323 (8FF3B7)	神	FB7E	8445 (8FF4CD)
№	FA59	8324 (8FF3B8)	祥	FB80	8446 (8FF4CE)
℡	FA5A	8325 (8FF3B9)	福	FB82	8447 (8FF4CF)
炻	FA62	8401 (8FF4A1)	竧	FB85	8448 (8FF4D0)
仼	FA6A	8402 (8FF4A2)	靖	FB86	8449 (8FF4D1)
僴	FA7C	8403 (8FF4A3)	精	FB89	8451 (8FF4D3)
凬	FA83	8404 (8FF4A4)	綠	FB8D	8452 (8FF4D4)
匇	FA8A	8405 (8FF4A5)	緖	FB8E	8453 (8FF4D5)
匤	FA8B	8406 (8FF4A6)	羽	FB92	8454 (8FF4D6)
叝	FA90	8407 (8FF4A7)	荢	FB94	8455 (8FF4D7)
﨎	FA92	8408 (8FF4A8)	﨟	FB9D	8456 (8FF4D8)
坙	FA96	8409 (8FF4A9)	薰	FB9E	8457 (8FF4D9)
埇	FA9B	8410 (8FF4AA)	蘒	FB9F	8458 (8FF4DA)
﨏	FA9C	8411 (8FF4AB)	﨡	FBA0	8459 (8FF4DB)
增	FA9D	8412 (8FF4AC)	蠇	FBA1	8460 (8FF4DC)
寬	FAAA	8414 (8FF4AE)	諸	FBA9	8462 (8FF4DE)
峵	FAAE	8415 (8FF4AF)	譿	FBAC	8463 (8FF4DF)
嵓	FAB0	8416 (8FF4B0)	賴	FBAE	8464 (8FF4E0)
﨑	FAB1	8417 (8FF4B1)	赶	FBB0	8465 (8FF4E1)
德	FABA	8418 (8FF4B2)	﨣	FBB1	8466 (8FF4E2)

Character	DBCS-PC	JIS X 0212-1990
﨤	FBB3	8467 (8FF4E3)
逸	FBB4	8468 (8FF4E4)
郞	FBB6	8469 (8FF4E5)
都	FBB7	8470 (8FF4E6)
鄕	FBB8	8471 (8FF4E7)
鋍	FBD3	8472 (8FF4E8)
﨧	FBDA	8473 (8FF4E9)
閒	FBE8	8474 (8FF4EA)
﨨	FBE9	8475 (8FF4EB)
隝	FBEA	8476 (8FF4EC)
﨩	FBEE	8477 (8FF4ED)
靏	FBF0	8478 (8FF4EE)
靑	FBF2	8479 (8FF4EF)
飯	FBF6	8481 (8FF4F1)
飼	FBF7	8482 (8FF4F2)
館	FBF9	8483 (8FF4F3)
馞	FBFA	8484 (8FF4F4)
髙	FBFC	8485 (8FF4F5)
魲	FC42	8486 (8FF4F6)
鶴	FC49	8487 (8FF4F7)
黑	FC4B	8488 (8FF4F8)

K

Software and Document Sources

Here you will find addresses and other contact information for the authors and vendors of the software and documents described in this book. This information will be divided into two sections: those available through anonymous FTP and those available through commercial distribution. ISBNs and part numbers for documents can be found in the Bibliography.

Whenever I list an anonymous FTP site, I also provide an IP number. There are some times when an IP number works when a site name does not. Please note that IP numbers can change, so when possible, use the site name.

Anonymous FTP

FTP stands for *file transfer protocol*, and is a very convenient way to obtain files and programs from Internet sites worldwide. Using FTP is usually a simple matter of typing the command **ftp** followed by the site name or IP number. Below are some examples:

```
% ftp ftp.ora.com
% ftp 140.186.65.25
```

The site name `ftp.ora.com` and the IP number `140.186.65.25` refer to the same physical site. You may find that your FTP server may sometimes prefer an IP number over a site name. If you supply the site name, the FTP server will then look up the name in a table to obtain the IP address anyway. More often it is easier to remember site names rather than IP numbers.

Anyway, once you initialize an FTP session, you will be greeted with a prompt from the FTP server. This prompt will ask you for a login. The login to use is anonymous (after all, this is *anonymous* FTP). You will then be prompted for a password in the form of your *real* login or e-mail address. This lets the site administrators keep track of anonymous FTP access to their site. Now that you are on, what do you do?

The following list provides some of the basic FTP commands you will use. Examples of their use are also included.

Command	Purpose	Example of Usage
cd *directory*	Change working directory	`cd pub`
cdup	Go one directory up (same as **cd ..**)	`cdup`
dir *<directory>*	List directory (or *directory*) contents	`dir pub/mac`
binary	Binary transfer mode	`binary`
ascii	ASCII (text) transfer mode	`ascii`
get *file*	Copy a file from FTP host	`get japan1.inf`
mget *file*	Copy group of files from FTP host	`mget japan*.inf`
put *file*	Copy a file to FTP host	`put japan1.inf`
mput *file*	Copy group of files to FTP host	`mput japan*.inf`
quit	End the FTP session	`quit`

Quite often you will find a file called `ls-lR.Z` or `ls-lR` (or some other incantation thereof) at the root level of an FTP server. This file contains a complete directory and file listing for the FTP site. If you are not sure where the file is located, you can often use the **get** command to obtain this file, then use **grep** or some other searching mechanism to find where a particular file is located. You can also use Archie, which is described below.

FTP Mail

For those of you who do not have access to FTP, there is a service called FTP Mail. You send a request to an FTP Mail server which then uses FTP to obtain the files, and finally sends them to you as one or more e-mail messages. A very commonly used FTP Mail server is:

    ftpmail@decwrl.dec.com

You can get a help file for FTP Mail by sending an e-mail message to the above address with the word *help* in the message body.

FTP Mail requires a few pieces of information to work properly. They are as follows:

Basic Commands	Example of Usage
connect *host login password*	`connect msi.umn.edu anonymous` `lunde@mv.us.adobe.com`
get *filename*	`get pub/lunde/japan1.inf`
quit	`quit`

It is a good idea to use your complete e-mail address as the password for anonymous FTP—it not only lets system administrators know who has copied files, but also lets them contact such people in case a virus has been discovered in one of the copied programs.

There are also other commands that can be used, such as **binary**, **uuencode**, **compress**, **chunksize**, **dir**, and **chdir**.

The e-mail address for requesting IETF or RFC documents is a bit different, and is as follows:

```
mail-server@nisc.sri.com
```

In the message body include the command **send** followed by the filename you require.

Finding Files

I have tried to list enough anonymous FTP sites so that you should be able to locate a copy of the file or files you want. However, there may be times when you need to find other files. This is when an Archie server becomes useful. An Archie server can be accessed interactively using **telnet**, or through the form of an e-mail request. What I describe below is how to access an Archie server using e-mail.

An Archie server stores complete listings of files from thousands of FTP sites. Accessing an Archie server is much like a database search—you provide it with search criteria, and it returns information that matches that criteria. In the case of an Archie server, you get the FTP site name, IP number, file and directory names that match the search criteria, and the complete path to those files or directories. A very commonly used Archie server is as follows:

```
archie@archie.rutgers.edu
```

You can get a help file for Archie by sending an e-mail message to the above address with the word *help* in the message body. Other Archie servers include the following:

```
archie@archie.au
archie@archie.doc.ic.ac.uk
archie@archie.foretune.co.jp*
archie@archie.funet.fi
archie@archie.kuis.kyoto-u.ac.jp*
archie@archie.mcgill.ca
archie@archie.sura.net
archie@archie.unl.edu
archie@archie.wide.ad.jp
```

---

*These Archie sites contain information for only Japanese FTP sites.

Please note that not all of these Archie servers accept e-mail service, and you must connect directly using **telnet**. In this case, just drop the `archie@` portion of the e-mail addresses listed above. Also, Archie servers are designed to handle requests from locations close to them, so pick one that is close to where you are located.

Archie requires some information to work properly. This information should be placed into the message body—the subject line of the message is ignored. This information is as follows:

Basic Commands	Example of Usage	Meaning
prog *string*	`prog [Jj]apan`	Returns a listing of files and directories whose names contain the string *japan* or *Japan*
list *string*	`list jp`	Returns a list of all FTP servers whose names contain the string *jp*
servers	`servers`	Returns a list of all known Archie servers
quit	`quit`	Processing is terminated

There are also other commands that can be used, but this should be sufficient to begin using Archie. Chapter 9 of *The Whole Internet User's Guide and Catalog* by Ed Krol contains detailed information on using Archie.

You can contact the people who administrate Japanese Archie servers by sending e-mail to the following address:

    jp-archie-admin@wide.ad.jp

Useful Anonymous FTP Sites

There is much more software available from anonymous FTP sites than I could possibly describe in this book. I encourage you to browse several key FTP sites for other new and interesting software packages. Below you will find a list of some useful anonymous FTP sites.

Site Name	IP Address
ahkcus.org	192.55.187.25
azabu.tkl.iis.u-tokyo.ac.jp	157.82.99.7
clover.ucdavis.edu	128.120.57.1
crl.nmsu.edu	128.123.1.33
cs.arizona.edu	192.12.69.5
etlport.etl.go.jp	192.31.197.99
ftp.adobe.com	130.248.1.4
ftp.ae.keio.ac.jp	131.113.36.12
ftp.apple.com	130.43.2.3

Site Name	IP Address
ftp.ascii.co.jp	133.152.1.1
ftp.canon.co.jp	150.61.4.3
ftp.cs.titech.ac.jp	131.112.16.39
ftp.dcl.co.jp	133.143.1.1
ftp.dit.co.jp	133.156.1.1
ftp.foretune.co.jp	133.123.1.2
ftp.funet.fi	128.214.6.100
ftp.ics.es.osaka-u.ac.jp	133.1.12.100
ftp.iij.ad.jp	192.244.176.33
ftp.iis.u-tokyo.ac.jp	157.82.96.67
ftp.join.ad.jp	157.20.1.10
ftp.junet.ad.jp	192.244.176.61
ftp.kaist.ac.kr	143.248.1.201
ftp.kuis.kyoto-u.ac.jp	130.54.20.1
ftp.luth.se	130.240.18.2
ftp.mei.co.jp	132.182.49.2
ftp.ncc.go.jp	160.190.10.1
ftp.nec.co.jp	192.135.93.2
ftp.nic.ad.jp	192.41.192.1
ftp.ora.com	140.186.65.25
ftp.sigmath.es.osaka-u.ac.jp	133.1.136.6
ftp.sra.co.jp	133.137.4.3
ftp.tohoku.ac.jp	130.34.8.9
ftp.u-tokyo.ac.jp	130.69.254.254
ftp.usafa.af.mil	128.236.1.4
ftp.uu.net	192.48.96.9
ftp.uwtc.washington.edu	128.95.202.40
ftp.waseda.ac.jp	133.9.1.32
ftp.omron.co.jp	133.210.4.4
ifcss.org	129.107.1.155
kuso.shef.ac.uk	143.167.25.1
mac.archive.umich.edu	141.211.165.41
miki.cs.titech.ac.jp	131.112.172.15
mindseye.berkeley.edu	128.32.232.19
moe.ipl.t.u-tokyo.ac.jp	130.69.168.19
monu6.cc.monash.edu.au	130.194.1.106
msdos.archive.umich.edu	141.211.164.153
msi.umn.edu	128.101.24.1
nic.ad.jp	192.41.197.14
nic.nm.kr	143.248.1.100

Site Name	IP Address
rhino.cis.vutbr.cz	147.229.3.10
scslwide.sony.co.jp	133.138.199.1
sh.wide.ad.jp	133.4.11.11
sumex-aim.stanford.edu	36.44.0.6
syrinx.kgs.ukans.edu	129.237.140.14
thalamus.sans.kth.se	130.237.219.100
ucdavis.edu	128.120.2.1
utsun.s.u-tokyo.ac.jp	133.11.11.11
weber.ucsd.edu	128.54.16.129
world.std.com	192.203.74.1

FTP Sources

The FreeWare and ShareWare software packages and information sources described in this book are available from one or more anonymous FTP sites. Note that this information changes, so I will try to list more than one site for each software package. You may wish to use an Archie server, described earlier in this section, before accessing these anonymous FTP sites.

I plan to consolidate most of these software packages and information sources at the anonymous FTP site ftp.ora.com (140.186.65.25). This same anonymous FTP site will also contain code fragments, mapping tables, and character lists from this book in machine-readable form.

Note that some software packages, such as Apple Computer's ResEdit and System Software, cannot be transported to other anonymous FTP sites due to license restrictions.

	Site Name	IP Address
Amiga Japanese software	ftp.luth.se	130.240.18.2
ASLEdit+	ftp.tohoku.ac.jp	130.34.8.9
	ftp.uwtc.washington.edu	128.95.202.40
ASLKConvert	ftp.tohoku.ac.jp	130.34.8.9
	ftp.uwtc.washington.edu	128.95.202.40
ASLTelnet	ftp.tohoku.ac.jp	130.34.8.9
	ftp.uwtc.washington.edu	128.95.202.40
Bnews	ftp.uu.net	192.48.96.9
Canna	ftp.nec.co.jp	192.135.93.2
Chinese related material	ahkcus.org	192.55.187.25
	crl.nmsu.edu	128.123.1.33
	ifcss.org	129.107.1.155
C News	ftp.uu.net	192.48.96.9

	Site Name	IP Address
Demacs	`ftp.sigmath.es.osaka-u.ac.jp`	`133.1.136.6`
	`mindseye.berkeley.edu`	`128.32.232.19`
dserver	`sics.se`	`192.16.123.90`
EDICT	`ftp.uwtc.washington.edu`	`128.95.202.40`
	`monu6.cc.monash.edu.au`	`130.194.1.106`
edict.el	`thalamus.sans.kth.se`	`130.237.219.100`
Eudora-J	`ftp.cs.titech.ac.jp`	`131.112.16.39`
GomTalk7	`ftp.foretune.co.jp`	`133.123.1.2`
	`ftp.tohoku.ac.jp`	`130.34.8.9`
	`ftp.uwtc.washington.edu`	`128.95.202.40`
GomTalk7 English manuals	`ftp.uwtc.washington.edu`	`128.95.202.40`
hterm	`azabu.tkl.iis.u-tokyo.ac.jp`	`157.82.99.7`
INN	`ftp.uu.net`	`192.48.96.9`
Internet Drafts	`ftp.nisc.sri.com`	`192.33.33.22`
	`munnari.oz.au`	`128.250.1.21`
	`nic.nordu.net`	`192.36.148.17`
	`nnsc.nsf.net`	`128.89.1.178`
JAPAN.INF	`ftp.ora.com`	`140.186.65.25`
	`ftp.uwtc.washington.edu`	`128.95.202.40`
Japanese bitmapped fonts	`crl.nmsu.edu`	`128.123.1.33`
	`etlport.etl.go.jp`	`192.31.197.99`
	`ftp.tohoku.ac.jp`	`130.34.8.9`
	`ftp.uwtc.washington.edu`	`128.95.202.40`
	`utsun.s.u-tokyo.ac.jp`	`133.11.11.11`
Japanese network info	`nic.ad.jp`	`192.41.197.14`
	`ftp.join.ad.jp`	`157.20.1.10`
	`ftp.nic.ad.jp`	`192.41.192.1`
Japanese TEX	`ftp.ascii.co.jp`	`133.152.32.11`
JChar	`ftp.ora.com`	`140.186.65.25`
jchar.c	`ftp.ora.com`	`140.186.65.25`
JCode	`ftp.ora.com`	`140.186.65.25`
jcode.c	`ftp.ora.com`	`140.186.65.25`
jcode.pl (Perl library file)	`ftp.sra.co.jp`	`133.137.4.3`
JConv	`ftp.ora.com`	`140.186.65.25`
jconv.c	`ftp.ora.com`	`140.186.65.25`
JDIC	`ftp.uwtc.washington.edu`	`128.95.202.40`
	`monu6.cc.monash.edu.au`	`130.194.1.106`
jelvis	`ftp.foretune.co.jp`	`133.123.1.2`
jenscript	`ftp.ascii.co.jp`	`133.152.1.1`
jgrep.c	`ftp.ora.com`	`140.186.65.25`

	Site Name	IP Address
JREADER	ftp.uwtc.washington.edu	128.95.202.40
	monu6.cc.monash.edu.au	130.194.1.106
Jstevie	mindseye.berkeley.edu	128.32.232.19
	utsun.s.u-tokyo.ac.jp	133.11.11.11
JWP	ftp.uwtc.washington.edu	128.95.202.40
	kilroy.jpl.nasa.gov	128.149.1.165
KANJIDIC	ftp.uwtc.washington.edu	128.95.202.40
	monu6.cc.monash.edu.au	130.194.1.106
kanjips	ftp.iis.u-tokyo.ac.jp	157.82.96.67
	ftp.waseda.ac.jp	133.9.1.32
	miki.cs.titech.ac.jp	131.112.172.15
	mindseye.berkeley.edu	128.32.232.19
	utsun.s.u-tokyo.ac.jp	133.11.11.11
KanjiSama demo	ftp.uwtc.washington.edu	128.95.202.40
KanjiTalk related utilities	ftp.foretune.co.jp	133.123.1.2
KD (Kanji Driver)	mindseye.berkeley.edu	128.32.232.19
kinput2	*Included in X11R5*	
knn	ftp.dit.co.jp	133.156.1.1
Korean network info	nic.nm.kr	143.248.1.100
Korean related material	ftp.kaist.ac.kr	143.248.1.201
krn	ftp.dit.co.jp	133.156.1.1
kterm	*Included in X11R5*	
ktin	ftp.dit.co.jp	133.156.1.1
ktrn	ftp.dit.co.jp	133.156.1.1
Macintosh System 7	ftp.apple.com	130.43.2.3
MacJDic	ftp.uwtc.washington.edu	128.95.202.40
	monu6.cc.monash.edu.au	130.194.1.106
MacKc	ftp.uwtc.washington.edu	128.95.202.40
MicroEmacs-J	ftp.ora.com	140.186.65.25
MOKE 1.1	ftp.uwtc.washington.edu	128.95.202.40
	monu6.cc.monash.edu.au	130.194.1.106
Mule	etlport.etl.go.jp	192.31.197.99
	ftp.funet.fi	128.214.6.100
	sh.wide.ad.jp	133.4.11.11
NCSA Telnet-J	ftp.dit.co.jp	133.156.1.1
Nemacs	sh.wide.ad.jp	133.4.11.11
Ng	ftp.iis.u-tokyo.ac.jp	157.82.96.67

	Site Name	IP Address
NinjaTerm	`ftp.uwtc.washington.edu`	`128.95.202.40`
NinjaTerm 32-bit version	`ftp.ora.com`	`140.186.65.25`
Nisus macros	`weber.ucsd.edu`	`128.54.16.129`
	`syrinx.kgs.ukans.edu`	`129.237.140.14`
Nisus demo	`syrinx.kgs.ukans.edu`	`129.237.140.14`
NJStar	`monu6.cc.monash.edu.au`	`130.194.1.106`
nkf	`ftp.uwtc.washington.edu`	`128.95.202.40`
	`utsun.s.u-tokyo.ac.jp`	`133.11.11.11`
pkf	`ftp.sra.co.jp`	`133.137.4.3`
Plan 9 documents	`research.att.com`	`192.20.225.2`
PostScript Japanese fonts	`moe.ipl.t.u-tokyo.ac.jp`	`130.69.168.19`
PostScript material	`ftp.adobe.com`	`130.248.1.4`
ResEdit	`ftp.apple.com`	`130.43.2.3`
RFC documents	`ftp.nisc.sri.com`	`192.33.33.22`
	`munnari.oz.au`	`128.250.1.21`
	`nic.nordu.net`	`192.36.148.17`
	`nnsc.nsf.net`	`128.89.1.178`
romkan.pl (Perl library file)	`ftp.sra.co.jp`	`133.137.4.3`
SKK	`ftp.uwtc.washington.edu`	`128.95.202.40`
	`sail.stanford.edu`	`36.28.0.130`
	`skk.tohoku.ac.jp`	`133.34.200.30`
	`utsun.s.u-tokyo.ac.jp`	`133.11.11.11`
Syokendai	`ftp.foretune.co.jp`	`133.123.1.2`
	`ftp.mei.co.jp`	`132.182.49.2`
Tcode	`utsun.s.u-tokyo.ac.jp`	`133.11.11.11`
Terminal-J	`ftp.foretune.co.jp`	`133.123.1.2`
Unicode material	`metis.com`	`140.186.33.40`
	`unicode.org`	`192.195.185.2`
Wnn	`ftp.omron.co.jp`	`133.210.4.4`
XJDIC	`ftp.uwtc.washington.edu`	`128.95.202.40`
	`monu6.cc.monash.edu.au`	`130.194.1.106`
X11R5	`export.lcs.mit.edu`	`18.24.0.12`
	`ftp.waseda.ac.jp`	`133.9.1.32`
	`utsun.s.u-tokyo.ac.jp`	`133.11.11.11`
YKH	`wuarchive.wustl.edu`	`128.252.135.4`
YooEdit	`ftp.foretune.co.jp`	`133.123.1.2`

Commercial Sources

Below you will find contact information that should help you to find software, hardware, and documents mentioned in this book. I encourage you to contact them for more information, and how to order their products.

Contact Information	Products
A & A Company Limited Takatanobaba Family Building 3-13-3 Takatanobaba Shinjuku-ku, Tokyo 160 JAPAN 03-3360-6531 (phone) 03-3360-6532 (facsimile)	SweetJAM
Adobe Systems Incorporated 1585 Charleston Road Box 7900 Mountain View, CA 94039-7900 USA 800-833-6687 (phone) 415-961-4400 (phone) 415-961-4111 (Adobe Developer Support) 415-961-3769 (facsimile)	Adobe Acrobat Adobe Illustrator-J Adobe Photoshop-J Adobe Type 1 Coprocessor Adobe Type Composer Adobe Type Manager-J *Font & Function* catalog PostScript Japanese typefaces SuperATM
Adobe Systems Japan 4-1-8 Toranomon, Swiss Bank House Minato-ku, Tokyo 105 JAPAN 03-3437-8950 (phone) 03-3437-8968 (facsimile)	See *Adobe Systems Incorporated*
The Aegis Society 1-6 Minami Hirao, Imazato Nagaokakyo-shi, Kyoto-fu 617 JAPAN 075-951-1168 (phone) 075-957-1087 (facsimile) aegis@aegis.org	Aegis
A.I. Technology Corporation 8-8-15-301 Nishi Shinjuku Shinjuku-ku, Tokyo 160 JAPAN 03-5386-7521 (phone) 03-5386-7522 (facsimile)	rSTONE rSTONE.JE rSTONE.KC

Contact Information	Products
AIN Technologies Company, Limited Sanpuku Building 4-13-11 Takadanobaba Shinjuku-ku, Tokyo 169 JAPAN 03-3368-3061 (phone) 03-2268-3080 (facsimile)	Japanese parametric fonts
Aldus Corporation 411 First Avenue South Seattle, WA 98104-2871 USA 800-685-3540 (phone) 206-622-5500 (phone) 206-343-3360 (facsimile)	Aldus PageMaker-J
Altsys Corporation 269 West Renner Road Richardson, TX 75080 USA 214-680-2060 (phone) 214-680-0537 (facsimile) altsys@aol.com d0590@applelink.apple.com 76004.2071@compuserve.com altsys@mcimail.com	Altsys Rollup Fontographer Fontographer-J Metamorphosis Professional
America Online 8619 Roswell Road, Suite 535 Atlanta, GA 30328 USA 800-786-0717 (phone) 404-250-0054 (phone) 404-250-1848 (facsimile)	America Online
ANSI 11 West 42nd Street New York, NY 10036 USA 212-642-4900 (phone) 212-302-1286 (facsimile)	ANSI technical manuals GB technical manuals ISO technical manuals JIS technical manuals KS technical manuals

Contact Information	Products

Apple Computer Incorporated
20525 Mariani Avenue
Cupertino, CA 95014
USA
800-776-2333 (phone)
408-996-1010 (phone)
408-974-6726 (facsimile)
`76666.2045@compuserve.com`
`apda@applelink.apple.com`
	AppleLink
	KanjiTalk 7.1
	Macintosh computers
	PostScript Japanese printers
	System 7.1
	System 7.1 Japanese Language Kit

Apple Japan Incorporated 1-14-1 Sendagaya Shibuya-ku, Tokyo 175 JAPAN 03-5411-8500 (phone)	See *Apple Computer Incorporated*
ASCII Corporation Minami Aoyama Building 3F 6-11-1 Minami Aoyama Minato-ku, Tokyo 107-24 JAPAN 03-3486-1977 (phone) 03-5485-2991 (facsimile)	Japanese books Japanese magazines
Azuma Lander International 250 World Trade Center #251 San Francisco, CA 94111 USA 415-928-7914 (phone)	PC-Transer
Canon, Incorporated 3-11-28 Mita Minato-ku, Tokyo 108 JAPAN 03-3455-9317 (phone)	Bitmapped Japanese fonts Canon WordTank NeXTSTEP-J PostScript Japanese printers
Catena Corporation 2-10-24 Shiomi Koto-ku, Tokyo 135 JAPAN 03-3615-9001 (phone) 03-3615-9060 (facsimile)	FlashWriter TheTranslator

Contact Information	Products
CCIC 605 Addison Street, Suite A Berkeley, CA 94710 USA 510-843-5626 (phone) 510-843-5173 (facsimile) `ccic.usa@applelink.apple.com`	Macintosh software
Cheng & Tsui Company 25 West Street Boston, MA 02111 USA 617-426-6074 (phone) 617-426-3669 (facsimile)	Macintosh software MS-DOS software
CIC Japan, Incorporated RK Building 8F 2-13-10 Shita Meguro Meguro-ku, Tokyo 153 JAPAN 03-5434-6877 (phone)	MacHandwriter II

Claris Corporation
5201 Patrick Henry Drive
Box 58168
Santa Clara, CA 95052
USA
800-544-8554 (phone)
408-987-7000 (phone)
408-987-7440 (facsimile)
`claris@aol.com`
`claris@claris.com`
`76004.1614@compuserve.com`
	MacWriteII-J

Claris Corporation Bancho HY Building 5F 11-5 Nibancho Chiyoda-ku, Tokyo 102 JAPAN 03-5210-9060 (phone) 03-5210-9022 (facsimile)	MacWriteII-J

Contact Information	Products
CompuServe 5000 Arlington Center Boulevard Columbus, OH 43220 USA 800-848-8199 (phone) 614-457-8600 (phone) 614-457-0348 (facsimile) `postmaster@compuserve.com`	CompuServe `NBCC.ZIP` (keyboard driver)
Concord International Incorporated 509 Olive Street Saint Louis, MO 63101 USA 314-241-0101 (phone) 314-241-2222 (facsimile)	*KanjiLink* magazine
Dainippon Screen Corporation SunShine Building 5F 1-1 Nishi-Hanaike-cho, Koyama Kita-ku, Kyoto 603 JAPAN 075-415-3701 (phone)	PostScript Japanese printers
Digital Equipment Corporation 146 Main Street Maynard, MA 01754-2571 USA 800-343-4040 (phone)	PostScript Japanese printers
Digital Equipment Corporation Sunshine Building 55F 3-1-1 Higashi Ikebukuro Toshima-ku, Tokyo 170 JAPAN 03-3989-7212 (phone)	PostScript Japanese printers
Dynaware Corporation 2-2-4 Senba Nishi Minoo-shi, Osaka 562 JAPAN 0727-27-2051 (phone) 0727-27-3011 (facsimile)	MacVJE MacVJE-γ MacWORD
Dynaware USA, Incorporated 950 Tower Lane, Suite 1150 Foster City, CA 94404 USA 415-349-5700 (phone) 415-349-5879 (facsimile)	See *Dynaware Corporation*

Contact Information	Products
EJ Bilingual Incorporated 2463 Torrance Boulevard, Suite 1 Torrance, CA 90501 USA 310-320-8139 (phone) 310-320-3228 (facsimile)	EZ JapaneseWriter
Electronics for Imaging, Incorporated 2855 Campus Drive San Mateo, CA 94403 USA 415-286-8600 (phone)	PostScript Japanese printers
Ergosoft Corporation 3-9-1 Akasaka, Kiyo Building 3F Minato-ku, Tokyo 107 JAPAN 03-3589-4455 (phone) 03-3589-4466 (facsimile)	EGBook EGBridge EGTalk EGWord EGWord Classic
FontWorks Limited Washington Plaza 16F Wanchai HONG KONG 638-5228 (phone) 574-3728 (facsimile)	PostScript Japanese typefaces
Frame Technology Corporation 1010 Rincon Circle San Jose, CA 95131 USA 800-843-7263 (phone) 408-433-3311 (phone) 408-433-1928 (facsimile) `comments@frame.com`	FrameMaker-J
Free Software Foundation 675 Mass Avenue Cambridge, MA 02139 USA `gnu@prep.ai.mit.edu`	GNU General Public License GNU software
Fujitsu Business Systems Shiraishi Dai2 Building, 6F, 1-14 Kanda Chiyoda-ku, Tokyo 101 JAPAN 03-3253-4151 (phone)	Fujitsu technical manuals

Contact Information	Products
GITCO Box 9044 North Berkeley Station Berkeley, CA 94709 USA 800-527-2607 (phone) 510-841-0502 (phone) 510-848-7706 (facsimile)	Canon WordTank SweetJAM
GO Corporation 919 East Hillsdate Boulevard., Suite 400 Foster City, CA 94404 USA 415-345-7400 (phone) 415-345-9833 (facsimile) `gocustomer@go.com`	PenPoint operating system
GO Corporation 2-7-8 Higashi Gotanda Shinagawa-ku, Tokyo 141 JAPAN 03-5421-1721 (phone) 03-5421-1729 (facsimile)	PenPoint operating system
HAL Kenkyujo Corporation 2-6-5 Kanda Suda Machi Chiyoda-ku, Tokyo 101 JAPAN 03-3252-5561 (phone)	Quick Viewer software for DD-DR1
Hello Systems, Incorporated Sphinx Center 2-14-1 Hatakaeki Higashi Fukuoka 812 JAPAN 092-412-5995 (phone) 092-412-6984 (facsimile)	PostScript Japanese typefaces
Hewlett-Packard Department C2MO Box 1145 Roseville, CA 95678 USA 800-227-8164 (phone)	Hewlett-Packard technical manuals HP-UX

Contact Information	Products
Hitachi Corporation Omori Bell Port B, 6-26-2 Minamiooi Shinagawa-ku, Tokyo 140 JAPAN 03-5471-2183 (phone) 03-5471-2947 (facsimile)	Hitachi technical manuals
ICL Company, Limited 5-11-22 Shinjuku Shinjuku-ku, Tokyo 160 JAPAN 03-5379-7470 (phone) 03-5379-7471 (facsimile)	PostScript Japanese typefaces
ITL Incorporated 415 Madison Avenue, 19th Floor New York, NY 10017 USA 212-832-8877 (phone) 212-832-6677 (facsimile)	EW+
International Business Machines Corporation IBM Standards Program Old Orchard Road Armonk, NY 10504 USA 303-924-4807 (phone)	AIX IBM DOS J/V IBM technical manuals
International Standards Organization 1, rue de Varembe Case Postale 56 CH-1211, Geneva 20 SWITZERLAND	ISO technical manuals
International Typeface Corporation 866 Second Avenue New York, NY 10017 USA 800-634-9325 (phone) 212-371-0699 (phone) 212-752-4752 (facsimile)	*U&lc* magazine
Internet Initiative Japan, Incorporated 2-11-2 Nagatacho, Hoshigaoka Building Chiyoda-ku, Tokyo 100 JAPAN 03-3580-3781 (phone) 03-3580-3782 (facsimile) info@iij.ad.jp	IIJ

Contact Information	Products
Japanese Language Services 186 Lincoln Street Boston, MA 02111 USA 800-872-5272 (phone) 617-338-2211 (phone) 617-338-4611 (facsimile)	Macintosh software PC software

Japan Bitnet Association
Science University of Tokyo
1-3 Kagurazaka
Shinjuku-ku, Tokyo 162
JAPAN
03-3260-4271 ext 1721 (phone)
03-3260-2280 (facsimile)
`official@join.ad.jp`
`official@jpn.bitnet`
	Bitnet

Japan Network Information Center (JPNIC) Todai Computer Center 2-11-16 Yayoi Bunkyo-ku, Tokyo 113 JAPAN `info@domain.nic.ad.jp`	Japanese network information
Japanese Standards Association 4-1-24 Akasaka Minato-ku, Tokyo 107 JAPAN 03-3224-9366 (phone) 03-3224-9365 (facsimile)	Heisei typefaces JIS technical manuals
JustSystem Corporation 3-46 Okinohama-higashi Tokushima 770 JAPAN 0886-55-1121 (phone) 0886-25-1291 (facsimile)	ATOK Ichitaro
K Electronics 1581 Webster Street San Francisco, CA 94115 USA 415-346-5964 (phone) 415-346-0764 (facsimile)	Macintosh Software PC software

Contact Information	Products
KiCompWare Box 536 Appleton, WI 54912 USA 612-773-8621 (phone) 612-779-0886 (bbs) `101015.206@compuserve.com`	Kanji Guess MOKE
Kinokuniya Bookstores of America* Japan Center 1581 Webster Street San Francisco, CA 94115-9948 USA 415-567-7625 (phone) 415-567-7626 (phone) 415-567-4109 (facsimile)	Japanese books Japanese CD-ROM dictionaries Japanese magazines これが５万字 poster
Kureo Technology Limited 3700 Gilmore Way, Suite 300 Burnaby BC V5G 4M1 CANADA 604-433-7715 (phone) 604-433-3393 (facsimile)	KCom^2 Yukara AT Yukara ATmini

Language Automation, Incorporated
1806 Parkwood Drive
San Mateo, CA 94403
USA
415-571-7877 (phone)
415-571-6294 (facsimile)
`lai@applelink.apple.com`
`apprentice@lai.com`
	The Translator's Apprentice

LaserMaster Corporation 7156 Shady Oak Road Eden Prairie, MN 55344 USA 800-950-6868 (phone) 612-944-9330 (phone) 612-944-0522 (facsimile)	PostScript Japanese printers

*There are other Kinokuniya locations throughout the U.S. and in Japan, including branch stores in Edgewater, NY; New York, NY; Seattle, WA; San Jose, CA; Costa Mesa, CA; Newport Beach, CA; Torrance, CA; and Los Angeles, CA.

Contact Information	Products

Letraset USA, Incorporated
40 Eisenhower Drive
Paramus, NY 07653
USA
800-343-8973 (phone)
201-845-6100 (phone)
201-845-4708 (facsimile)
`letraset@aol.com`
`d0696@applelink.apple.com`
	FontStudio

Linotype-Hell Corporation Ohtsuka Daiichi Seimei Building 7F 2-32-22 Higashi Ikebukuro Toshima-ku, Tokyo 170 JAPAN 03-5391-6740 (phone)	PostScript Japanese printers
MacSTATION Incorporated Grande Maison Rokubancho #206 6-2 Rokubancho Chiyoda-ku, Tokyo 102 JAPAN 03-5276-7981 (phone) 03-5276-7985 (facsimile) `mstation.dvj@applelink.apple.com`	Macintosh software
MANGAJIN, Incorporated 200 North Cobb Parkway, Suite 421 Marietta, GA 30062 USA 800-552-3206 (phone) 404-634-3874 (phone) 404-634-1799 (facsimile)	*MANGAJIN* (漫画人) magazine
MCI Mail 1111 19th Street NW #500 Washington, DC 20036 USA 800-444-6245 (phone) 202-833-8484 (phone) 202-416-5858 (facsimile) `3248333@mcimail.com`	MCI Mail

Contact Information	Products
Media Drive Laboratory 1-5-2 Chuo-machi Meguro-ku, Tokyo 152 JAPAN 03-3710-4133 (phone) 03-3716-8104 (facsimile)	MacReader plus
Mercury Software Japan, Incorporated Rengezo-cho 20 Shogoin Hassei Building 2F Sakyo-ku, Kyoto 606 JAPAN 075-751-0205 (phone) 075-751-0206 (facsimile) `mercuryj.dvj@applelink.apple.com`	Solo PowerLite Solo Publisher Solo Writer

Microsoft Corporation
One Microsoft Way
Redmond, WA 98052
USA
800-426-9400 (phone)
206-936-8661 (phone)
206-936-7329 (facsimile)
`d0304@applelink.apple.com`
`d0963@applelink.apple.com`
`76146.1244@compuserve.com`
	Microsoft Windows-J
	Microsoft Windows-Pen

The Ministry of Software 5-8-2-506 Sinjuku Shinjuku-ku, Tokyo 160 JAPAN 03-3356-9743 (phone) 03-3356-1395 (facsimile)	ByWord NiBaiWord Wnn for Macintosh ZeroByWord
MIQ Japan, Incorporated SIT Nishi Shinjuku Building 4-7-1 Nishi Shinjuku Shinjuku-ku, Tokyo 160 JAPAN 03-3299-7377 (phone) 03-3299-7371 (facsimile)	ANS
Morisawa & Company, Limited 2-6-25 Shikitsu-Higashi Naniwa-ku, Osaka 556 JAPAN 06-649-2151 (phone) 06-649-2154 (facsimile)	Japanese typefaces PostScript Japanese typefaces

Contact Information	Products
NEC Corporation 1-4-2 Mita Minato-ku, Tokyo 108 JAPAN 03-3455-0333 (phone)	NEC technical manuals
NeXT, Incorporated 900 Chesapeake Drive Redwood City, CA 94063 USA 415-366-0900 (phone) 415-780-3714 (facsimile)	NeXTSTEP-J
NIFTY Corporation Omori Bellport A 26-1-6 Minami-oi Shinagawa-ku, Tokyo 140 JAPAN 03-5471-5800 (phone) 03-5471-5890 (facsimile)	NIFTY-Serve

Nisus Software Incorporated
107 South Cedros Avenue
Solana Beach, CA 92075
USA
800-922-2993 (phone)
619-481-1477 (phone)
619-481-6154 (facsimile)
`nisus.mkts@applelink.apple.com`
`75300.1243@compuserve.com`
`nisus@weber.ucsd.edu`
	MacQWERTY
	Nisus
	Nisus Compact

Oki Electric Corporation 1-17-1 Toranomon Minato-ku, Tokyo 105 JAPAN 03-3501-3351 (phone)	PostScript Japanese printers
O'Reilly & Associates, Incorporated 103 Morris Street, Suite A Sebastopol, CA 95472 USA 800-998-9938 (phone) 707-829-0515 (phone) 707-829-0104 (facsimile) `nuts@ora.com`	Nutshell Handbooks X Window System books

Contact Information	Products
Pacific HiTech 4530 Fortùna Way Salt Lake City, UT 84124 USA 800-765-8369 (phone) 801-278-2042 (phone) 801-278-2666 (facsimile) `71175.3152@compuserve.com`	Info-Mac CD-ROM
Pacific HiTech Tokyo Branch 5-52-6 Yoyogi Shibuya-ku, Tokyo 151 JAPAN 03-3485-3005 (phone) 03-3485-5092 (facsimile) `jcd01660@niftyserve.or.jp`	See *Pacific HiTech*
Pacific Rim Connections 1838 El Camino Real #109 Burlingame, CA 94010 USA 415-697-0911 (phone) 415-697-9439 (facsimile)	Macintosh software PC software
PC-VAN NEC Corporation 5-7-1 Shiba Minato-ku, Tokyo 108-01 JAPAN 03-3454-6909 (phone)	PC-VAN
Pinecoast Software, Incorporated 31 Kirkland Boulevard Kirkland, Quebec H9J 1N2 CANADA 514-694-0456 (phone) 514-694-0405 (facsimile)	Pinecoast Japanese Word Processor
Portal Communications Company 20863 Stevens Creek Boulevard, Suite 200 Cupertino, CA 95014 USA 408-973-9111 (phone) 408-725-1580 (facsimile) `cs@portal.com`	Internet services

Contact Information	Products
Profile Company Limited 1-8-3 Soto Kanda Chiyoda-ku, Tokyo 101 JAPAN 03-3251-0365 (phone) pgb00342@niftyserve.or.jp	最新ワープロ大百科 magazine
Qualitas Trading Company 2029 Durant Street Berkeley, CA 94704 USA 510-848-8080 (phone) 510-848-8009 (facsimile)	Macintosh Software
Quark, Incorporated 1800 Grant Street Denver, CO 80203 USA 800-788-7835 (phone) 303-894-8888 (phone) 303-894-3395 (facsimile) d0605@applelink.apple.com 75140.1137@compuserve.com	Quark XPress-J
Ryobi Imagix Corporation 3-15-1 Soto Kanda Chiyoda-ku, Tokyo 101 JAPAN 03-3257-1211 (phone) 03-3257-1239 (facsimile)	Japanese typefaces
SANBI Software Company 3594 Crowell Avenue Riverside, CA 92504 714-253-0276 (phone/facsimile)	KanjiSama
Seiko Instruments Incorporated 1-8 Nakase Mihama-ku, Chiba 261 JAPAN 043-211-1111 (phone) 043-211-8050 (facsimile)	Electronic dictionaries

Contact Information	Products
Sesame Computer Projects 8 Avenue Road Harrogate, North Yorkshire HG2 7PG ENGLAND 0423-888432 (phone) 0423-883918 (facsimile)	*SESAME Bulletin* journal
Shaken Corporation 2-26-13 Higashi Otsuka Toshima-ku, Tokyo 170 JAPAN 03-3942-2211 (phone)	Japanese typefaces
Silicon Graphics, Incorporated 2011 North Shoreline Boulevard Mt. View, CA 94039-7311 USA 415-960-1980 (phone) 415-961-0595 (facsimile) ird@esd.sgi.com	Irix
Softbank Corporation Softbank Square Building, 5F 3-42-3 Nihonbashi, Hamacho Chuo-ku, Tokyo 103 JAPAN 03-5642-8101 (phone) 03-5641-3424 (facsimile)	Japanese books
SomethingGood Corporation 2-5-20 City Plaza Shinjuku, Daikubo Shinjuku-ku, Tokyo 169 JAPAN 03-3232-0801 (phone) 03-3232-0963 (facsimile)	Katana WaltzWord
Sony Corporation 6-7-35 Kita Shinagawa Shinagawa-ku, Tokyo 141 JAPAN 03-3448-3311 (phone)	DD-DR1 (Data Discman drive) PalmTop computer
Sun Microsystems, Incorporated 2550 Garcia Avenue Mountain View, CA 94043 USA 415-691-4343 (phone) users@sun.com	JLE Solaris SPARC Workstations

Contact Information	Products
SystemSoft Corporation 3-10-30 Tenjin Chuo-ku, Fukuoka 810 JAPAN 092-722-4857 (phone)	Adobe Systems' Japanese products Claris' Japanese products QuarkXPress-J System 7.1 Japanese Language Kit
SystemSoft America, Incorporated 333 17th Street, Suite L Vero Beach, FL 32960 USA 800-882-8856 (phone) 407-770-3371 (phone) 407-569-1937 (facsimile) `kanji.sales@applelink.apple.com`	See SystemSoft Corporation
Taishukan Shoten 3-24 Kanda Nishiki-cho Chiyoda-ku, Tokyo 101 JAPAN 03-3294-2221 (phone)	これが５万字 poster
TransPac Software, Incorporated 4300 Stevens Creek Boulevard, Suite 245 San Jose, CA 95129 USA 408-261-7550 (phone) 408-984-6303 (facsimile)	TurboWriter
TWICS IEC/NichiBei Kaiwa Gakuin 1-21 Yotsuya Shinjuku-ku, Tokyo 160 JAPAN 03-3351-5977 (phone) 03-3353-6096 (facsimile) `twics@twics.co.jp`	TWICS
TypeBank Company, Limited Sendagaya Park Square Building 3F 1-33-5 Sendagaya Shibuya-ku, Tokyo 151 JAPAN 03-3359-6013 (phone) 03-3359-6016 (facsimile)	PostScript Japanese typefaces

Contact Information	Products
Unicode, Incorporated 1965 Charleston Road Mountain View, CA 94043 USA 415-966-0305 (phone) 415-966-1637 (facsimile) unicode-inc@unicode.org	Unicode
URW America 4 Manchester Street Nashua, NH 03060 USA 603-882-7445 (phone) 603-882-7210 (facsimile)	Ikarus M
UUNET Technologies, Incorporated 3110 Fairview Park Drive, Suite 570 Falls Church, VA 22042 USA 800-488-6383 (phone) 703-204-8000 (phone) 703-204-8001 (facsimile) info@uunet.uu.net	UUNET
VACS Corporation Daiichi-Yazawa Building 1-34-10 Morino Machida-shi, Tokyo 194 JAPAN 0427-24-9200 (phone) 0427-28-6864 (facsimile)	VJE-γ
Wnn Consortium Research Institute of Kyoto 17 Kyoto Research Park Chudoji Minami-machi Shimogyo-ku, Kyoto 600 JAPAN 075-315-8653 (phone) 074-315-2897 (facsimile) wnn@astem.or.jp	JIS X 0212-1990 bitmapped fonts Wnn

Contact Information	Products

WordPerfect Corporation
1555 North Technology Way
Orem, UT 84057
USA
800-451-5151 (phone)
801-225-5000 (phone)
801-222-5377 (facsimile)
`wordperfect@aol.com`
`d0069@applelink.apple.com`
	WordPerfect
	WordPerfect-J

Worldwide Publishing Group
Antelope Mountain Road
Box 327
Clark Fork, ID 83811
USA
208-266-1473 (phone)
208-266-1666 (facsimile)
`multilingual@applelink.apple.com`
`71224.1003@compuserve.com`
	Multilingual Computing magazine

X/Open Company Limited Apex Plaza Foxbury Road Reading, Berkshire RG1 1AX ENGLAND `xospecs@xopen.co.uk`	X/Open standards
Xerox Systems Institute 3400 Hillview Avenue Box 10034 Palo Alto, CA 94303 USA 415-813-7839 (phone) 415-813-7811 (facsimile)	XEROX technical manuals
Yinu System, Incorporated Owariya Bldg., Yamabuki-cho 130 Shinjuku-ku, Tokyo 162 JAPAN 03-5261-8587 (phone) 03-5261-8584 (facsimile)	JIS X 0212-1990 bitmapped fonts

L

Mailing Lists

There are many mailing lists which you can, without charge, join to get more information, or better yet, to participate in a discussion on a topic of interest. So, fire up your e-mail system, and start sending those subscription requests!

Joining a mailing list such as I will describe below usually consists of sending an e-mail message to a particular address. The user name that you use is generally either `listserv` or the name of the mailing list plus `-request`. When possible, do not send subscription requests to the actual discussion list as this bothers their participants. This is basic mailing list etiquette.

For more information on mailing lists, I suggest that you get the book entitled *Internet: Mailing Lists*. In its pages you will find detailed information on hundreds, if not thousands, of mailing lists. Also included is information on how to start your own mailing list.

Canna Mailing List

For those who use Canna, the Japanese input software, there is a discussion forum available in the form of a mailing list. To subscribe or unsubscribe to the Canna Mailing List, send a request to the following e-mail address:

    canna-request@astec.co.jp

Once you have joined the Canna Mailing List, submissions can be sent to:

    canna@astec.co.jp

CCNET Mailing List

The CCNET (Chinese Computing Network) Mailing List is a forum for those interested in using Chinese on computer systems. Subscribing to the CCNET Mailing List is accomplished by sending a request to the following e-mail address:

    listserv@uga.uga.edu (or listserv@uga for Bitnet users)

The message body of this request must contain certain information. The following table lists this information along with examples:

Action	Command	Example
Subscribing	`subscribe` *mailing_list name*	`subscribe ccnet-1 Ken Lunde`
Unsubscribing	`signoff` *mailing_list*	`signoff ccnet-1`

Once you have joined the CCNET Mailing List, submissions should be sent to the following e-mail address:

    ccnet-1@uga.uga.edu

INSOFT-L Mailing List

INSOFT-L (Internationalization of Software Discussion List) is a forum for discussing the many aspects of internationalization. This mailing list is also available as the Usenet News newsgroup called `bit.software.international`, and all messages to either are posted to both the mailing list and newsgroup.

The charter of the INSOFT-L Mailing List is to discuss the internationalization and localization of software, and topics of discussion include the following:

- Techniques for developing new software
- Techniques for converting existing software
- Internationalization tools
- Announcements of internationalized public domain software
- Announcements of foreign-language versions of commercial software
- Calls for papers
- Conference announcements
- References to documentation related to the internationalization of software

Subscribing to the INSOFT-L Mailing List is done by sending an e-mail message to the following address:

    listserv@cis.vutbr.cz

The message body of this request must contain certain information. The following table lists this information along with examples:

Action	Command	Example
Subscribing	**subscribe** *mailing_list name*	**subscribe insoft-l Ken Lunde**
Unsubscribing	**signoff** *mailing_list*	**signoff insoft-l**

Posting messages to the INSOFT-L Mailing List is accomplished by sending them to the following e-mail address:

    insoft-l@cis.vutbr.cz

For more information on the INSOFT-L Mailing List, either subscribe to it or send e-mail to Jeffrey Bowyer at the following e-mail address:

    jbowyer@cis.vutbr.cz

ISO 10646 Mailing List

Similar to Unicode, there is also a mailing list for ISO 10646 issues. To subscribe you send e-mail to the following e-mail address:

    listserv@jhuvm.hcf.jhu.edu (or listserv@jhuvm for Bitnet users)

The message body of this request must contain certain information. The following table lists this information along with examples:

Action	Command	Example
Subscribing	**subscribe** *mailing_list name*	**subscribe iso10646 Ken Lunde**
Unsubscribing	**signoff** *mailing_list*	**signoff iso10646**

Submissions to this mailing list are sent to the following e-mail address:

    iso10646@jhuvm.hcf.jhu.edu

Japanese Newsgroup Mailing List

Japanese newsgroups are the Japanese equivalent of Usenet News, and the two letters fj (meaning "from Japan") begin the name of each newsgroup. It is sometimes difficult to get a feed of Japanese newsgroups outside of Japan, and some people do not even have access to news reader software, so it has been made available as a mailing list. The e-mail address for subscribing and unsubscribing to Japanese newsgroups is as follows:

    listserv@ntt-20.ntt.jp

This address can also be used to obtain a current listing of Japanese newsgroups.

The following list shows what you need to include in your message body to subscribe or unsubscribe to newsgroups, and to get a listing of newsgroups:

Action	Command	Example
Subscribing	`subscribe` *newsgroup name*	`subscribe fj.kanji Ken Lunde`
Unsubscribing	`unsubscribe` *newsgroup*	`unsubscribe fj.kanji`
Newsgroup list	`lists`	`lists`

Posting to Japanese newsgroups is performed by sending the article to the following e-mail address:

    post2junet@nttlab.ntt.jp

It is important that the first line of the article (not the subject line!) conforms to the following pattern (this is how the posting software knows which Japanese newsgroup to post the article to):

    Newsgroups: *newsgroup*

A real-life example is as follows:

    Newsgroups: fj.kanji

You then continue your message with the text of the article. The news posting software will remove the line containing `Newsgroups: fj.kanji`, and post the article to the appropriate Japanese newsgroup. A word of caution: although `Newsgroups` is plural, the news posting software recognizes only a single newsgroup name—posting to multiple Japanese newsgroups requires sending multiple e-mail messages.

The list of Japanese newsgroups changes on a regular basis, so it is not very practical to provide a listing here—request a listing by sending an e-mail request as described above. Just to get you started, though, the following is a list of Japanese newsgroups that readers of this book may be interested in:

    fj.binaries.mac
    fj.binaries.misc
    fj.binaries.msdos
    fj.binaries.msdos.d
    fj.binaries.x68000
    fj.comp.printers
    fj.editor.emacs
    fj.editor.misc
    fj.kanakan.misc

```
fj.kanakan.wnn
fj.kanji
fj.lang.c
fj.lang.perl
fj.lang.postscript
fj.sys.ibmpc
fj.sys.mac
fj.sys.next
fj.sys.pc98
fj.sys.rs6000
fj.sys.sun
fj.unix
fj.windows.x
```

Note that this service is being offered through the efforts of people in Japan, and may be discontinued in the future.

Kanji-Amiga Mailing List

The Amiga computer is slowly becoming more widely used as far as processing Japanese text is concerned. The basic Japanese operating system is called ANS (Amiga Nihongo System), and was described in Chapter 8. There is currently an effort to launch the Kanji-Amiga Mailing List, and hopefully it will be active by the time this book is published. The administrator is currently waiting for 100 subscribers before the mailing list is activated.

For more information on the Kanji-Amiga Mailing List, or to subscribe, please send e-mail to Taizo Shiozaki at the following e-mail address:

```
c88660ts@sfc.keio.ac.jp
```

KanjiTalk Mailing List

A mailing list has been established that is dedicated to KanjiTalk (the Japanese operating system for the Macintosh platform) and the software that runs under its environment. The primary language used for communicating is English, but there will be occasional Japanese text.

If you are interested in joining this mailing list, you must send a request in a special format to the following e-mail address:

```
kanjitalk-request@crl.go.jp
```

Several commands are accepted, any that are present must be in the body of the message, and each must begin with the # character:

Command	Action
# help	Sends you a help file
# on	Adds your name and address to the active list
# off	Removes you from the active list
# bye	Removes you from the mailing list
# members	Sends a member list

Articles are then posted by sending them to the following e-mail address:

    kanjitalk@crl.go.jp

If you experience problems with using the crl.go.jp portion of these e-mail addresses, I suggest trying cs15.atr-sw.atr.co.jp instead.

Mule Mailing List

Two mailing lists offer discussions about Mule. They are as follows:

    mule@etl.go.jp (English language discussions)
    mule-jp@etl.go.jp (Japanese language discussions)

The mailing list mule@etl.go.jp is inclusive in mule-jp@etl.go.jp, so by subscribing to mule-jp@etl.go.jp you get everything.

Subscription requests should be sent to the following e-mail address:

    mule-request@etl.go.jp

Be sure to specify which mailing list you wish to join.

NeXT Nihongo Mailing List

Izumi Ohzawa has established a mailing list for those who wish to exchange ideas and information on using Japanese text on NeXT computers.

If you are interested in joining this mailing list, you must send a request to the following e-mail address:

    next-nihongo-request@pinoko.berkeley.edu

Submissions to the NeXT Nihongo Mailing List should be sent to the following e-mail address:

    next-nihongo@pinoko.berkeley.edu

NIHONGO Mailing List

Many Usenet News newsgroups are available in mailing list form. This is designed for those who do not have access to a news reader. The NIHONGO Mailing List is actually the Usenet News newsgroup called `sci.lang.japan`. Discussions are about the Japanese language in general, but also serves as a forum for using Japanese on computers.

To join this mailing list, you must send a request to the following address:

> `listserv@mitvma.mit.edu` (or `listserv@mitvma` for Bitnet users)

The message body of this request must contain certain information. The following table lists this information along with examples:

Action	Command	Example
Subscribing	`subscribe` *mailing_list name*	`subscribe nihongo Ken Lunde`
Unsubscribing	`signoff` *mailing_list*	`signoff nihongo`

To post a message to the NIHONGO Mailing List, send it as an e-mail message to the following e-mail address:

> `nihongo@mitvma.mit.edu`

Your post will then appear on `sci.lang.japan`, and will also be sent to those who have subscribed to the NIHONGO Mailing List. Also be sure to get the FAQ (Frequently Asked Questions) file for `sci.lang.japan`, which is being maintained by Rafael Santos.

Nisus Mailing List

Nisus is the word processor that has been adapted to handle Japanese and other languages. There is also a fully localized Japanese version called Solo Writer—they are functionally identical. To subscribe or unsubscribe to the Nisus Mailing List, send a request to the following e-mail address:

> `listserv@syrinx.kgs.ukans.edu`

The message body of this request must contain certain information. The following table lists this information along with examples:

Action	Command	Example
Subscribing	`subscribe` *mailing_list name*	`subscribe nisus Ken Lunde`
Unsubscribing	`unsubscribe` *mailing_list*	`unsubscribe nisus`

Once you have joined this mailing list, send submissions to the following e-mail address:

> `nisus@syrinx.kgs.ukans.edu`

PenPoint Mailing List

The PenPoint technology developed by GO Corporation has discussion forums which are available as a mailing list, a forum on CompuServe, and a Usenet News newsgroup.

To join this mailing list, send a request to the following e-mail address:

```
penpoint-request@netcom.com
```

To post a message to this mailing list, send it as an e-mail message to the following address:

```
penpoint@netcom.com
```

For those of you who are CompuServe users, there is the CompuServe Pen Technology Forum there. For those of you who have Usenet News access, there is a newsgroup called `comp.sys.pen`.

RES-JAPAN-GROUP Mailing List

Rick Schlichting (`rick@cs.arizona.edu`) has established a mailing list version of the Usenet News newsgroup `comp.research.japan`. Like the NIHONGO Mailing List, it is intended for people who do not have access to Usenet News, and all posts to the mailing list are cross-posted to the Usenet News newsgroup version.

According to the mailing list's charter, the following is appropriate discussion material for this group:

- Information about CS research papers published in Japan, including titles, authors, and (where feasible) abstracts. This includes papers in both English and Japanese.
- Descriptions of current Japanese computing and CS activities, trip reports to Japanese universities and companies, etc.
- Announcements related to computing and CS in Japan, including those related to conferences held in Japan, research opportunities in Japan, funding for research visits to Japan, etc.
- Queries related to computing and CS research underway in Japan.
- General discussions on computing and CS in Japan, both academic and industrial.

To subscribe or unsubscribe to this mailing list, send a request to the following e-mail address:

```
res-japan-group-request@cs.arizona.edu
```

To post an article, send it as an e-mail message to the following address:

```
res-japan-group@cs.arizona.edu
```

SKK Mailing List

The Japanese input software called SKK has an associated mailing list, and allows SKK users to discuss their problems, offer suggestions for improvements, and answer others' questions. Most of the discussions are in Japanese.

To join the SKK Mailing List, send a subscription request to the following e-mail address:

```
skk-join@sato.riec.tohoku.ac.jp
```

To unsubscribe to the SKK Mailing List, send an e-mail message to the following address:

```
skk-leave@sato.riec.tohoku.ac.jp
```

Contributions to the SKK Mailing List should be sent to the following e-mail address:

```
skk@sato.riec.tohoku.ac.jp
```

Tcode Mailing List

There is a mailing list for those who use or are interested in the two-stroke Japanese input method called Tcode. To join the Tcode Mailing List, send a request to the following e-mail address:

```
tcode-admin@is.s.u-tokyo.ac.jp
```

To contribute articles to the Tcode Mailing List, send them to the following e-mail address:

```
tcode-ml@is.s.u-tokyo.ac.jp
```

Unicode Mailing List

Although the Unicode books have been published, Unicode itself is constantly changing. Joining this mailing list will keep you informed of changes made to the Unicode standard.

To join this mailing list, send a request to the following e-mail address:

```
unicode-request@unicode.org
```

To post a message to this mailing list, use the following e-mail address:

```
unicode@unicode.org
```

M

Professional Organizations

There are organizations dedicated to the advancement of processing Japanese on computer systems. If you find one that sparks your interest, I encourage you to join.

Association for the Internationalization of Computing Resources

The Association for the Internationalization of Computing Resources (AICR) is an organization dedicated to issues relating to I18N (internationalization) and L10N (localization). Membership dues include four issues of *I18N*, its quarterly journal. For more complete information, or to join AICR, please write to the following address:

> Jeffrey Bowyer
> Computing Center
> Technical University of Brno
> Udolni 19, 602 00 BRNO
> Czech Republic
> `jbowyer@cis.vutbr.cz`

Chinese Language Computer Society

The Chinese Language Computer Society (CLCS) is an excellent organization to join. Membership dues for individuals are $30.00 (U.S.) per year, and include four issues of *Computer Processing of Chinese & Oriental Languages* (CPCOL), its quarterly journal. For more information, or to join CLCS, please write to the following address:

Professor Yaohan Chu
CLCS Membership Chairman
Department of Computer Science
University of Maryland
College Park, MD 20742
USA
301-405-2719 (phone)
301-405-6707 (facsimile)
ychu@cs.umd.edu

International Macintosh Users Group

If you live in the San Francisco Bay Area, and work with Macintosh, then the International Macintosh Users Group (IMUG) may be of interest to you. IMUG hosts talks in the San Francisco Bay Area on a variety of subjects once a month. Membership dues for individuals are $12.00 (U.S.) per year. Attending IMUG talks is free to members, and non-members are charged $2.00 (U.S.).

IMUG
c/o Yuan Ho
3891 Corina Way
Palo Alto, CA 94303
USA

Glossary

10646.UCS-2	The fixed-width two-byte (16-bit) encoding method for ISO 10646.
10646.UCS-4	The fixed-width four-byte (32-bit) encoding method for ISO 10646.
50 Sounds array	50音配列. The Japanese keyboard array whose keys follow the sequence of the 50 Sounds Table. See *50 Sounds Table*.
50 Sounds order	50音順. A Japanese collation sequence that follows the ordering from the 50 Sounds Table. See *50 Sounds Table*.
50 Sounds Table	50音表. A table made of a five-by-ten matrix whose total number of possible sounds is 50. Kana characters are set into this table.
Aegis	All English General Information System. The name of an electronic information service based in Japan.
AIX	Advanced Interactive Executive. IBM's version of the UNIX operating system.
Algorithmic conversion	A type of conversion that makes use of mathematical operations to change the values of the converted objects. Also see *hard-coded conversion*.
America Online	An electronic information service.
ANK	Alphabet, Numerals, and Katakana.
ANS	Amiga Nihongo System. The Japanese operating system for Amiga computers.

ANSI	American National Standards Institute.
ANSI X3.4-1986	*Coded Character Set—7-bit American National Standard Code for Information Interchange.* The document which describes the ASCII character set standard.
AOL	See *America Online.*
Apple83	Apple Computer's Japanese character set standard. Based largely on JIS X 0208-1983.
Apple90	Apple Computer's latest Japanese character set standard. Based largely on JIS X 0208-1990. Apple90 was introduced with KanjiTalk Version 7.1.
AppleLink	Apple Computer's corporate and dealer electronic network.
ASCII	American Standard Code for Information Interchange.
ATM	Adobe Type Manager.
AT&T JIS	An alternate name for the Japanese implementation of the EUC encoding method.
Basic Multilingual Plane	See *BMP.*
BBS	電子掲示板. Bulletin Board System.
BDF	Bitmap Distribution Format. A popular bitmapped font format developed by Adobe Systems.
Bézier curve	The type of curve used for representing character shape contours in the PostScript page-description language and its supported font formats.
Big Five	The name of the Chinese character set and encoding used extensively in Taiwan. Big Five is not a national standard, though.
Binary	2進. Base two. A number notation that uses two possible values, 0 or 1.
Bit	ビット. Binary digit. The basic units of memory that computers process.
Bitmapped font	A font whose character shapes are defined by arrays of bits. Also see *parametric* and *outline font.*
Bitnet	Because It's Time Network. Also called CREN.

BMP	Basic Multilingual Plane. The plane within ISO 10646 that contains the Unicode character set.
Bopomofo	The name of the symbols used to represent standard pronunciations in Chinese. Its name is derived from the first four sounds in that set of symbols, namely *b*, *p*, *m*, and *f*.
Byte	バイト. Eight bits.
CAE	Common Applications Environment.
Calligraphic	See *cursive*.
Candidate	候補. In Japanese input candidate refers to the *names* that are associated with *keys* in a conversion dictionary. Candidates are usually presented as a list from which you must select. Also see *key* and *name*.
CD	Compact Disk.
CD-ROM	Compact Disk Read Only Memory.
Cell	点. In a two-byte encoding, cell refers to the second byte. In a two-dimensional matrix, cell represents the values along the horizontal axis. Also see *row*.
Character	文字. An abstract notion denoting a class of shapes declared to have the same meaning or form.
Character set	文字集合. A collection of characters.
CharCode	See *Char8Code* and *Char16Code*.
Char8Code	Short for character eight bit code. A term used in XCCS encoding, and refers to the encoded values for characters that follow a CS8Declaration. A Char8Code is a single byte. See *CS8Declaration*.
Char16Code	Short for character 16 bit code. A term used in XCCS encoding, and refers to the encoded values for characters that follow a CS16Declaration. A Char16Code consists of two Char8Codes, or two bytes. See *Char8Code* and *CS16Declaration*.
CharSet	See *CharSet8* and *CharSet16*.
CharSet8	Short for character set eight bit. A term used in XCCS encoding, and refers to the part of a CS8Declaration

	that sets the character set. See *CS8Declaration* and *CSselect*.
CharSet16	Short for character set 16 bit. A term used in XCCS encoding, and refers to the part of a CS16Declaration that sets the character set. See *CS16Declaration* and *CSselect*.
Chinese	中国語. The language spoken in Mainland China and Taiwan.
CIC	Communication Intelligence Corporation.
CNS 11643-1986	The national character set for Taiwan. Very similar to Big Five, but used much less frequently. See *Big Five*.
CS8Declaration	A term used in XCCS encoding, and refers to the combination of one CSselect character plus a CharSet8 indication character. See *CharSet8* and *CSselect*.
CS16Declaration	A term used in XCCS encoding, and refers to the combination of two CSselect characters plus a CharSet16 indication character. See *CharSet16* and *CSselect*.
CJK	Chinese, Japanese, and Korean. Refers to the languages that use kanji as a large part of their writing system.
Code position	The numeric code within an encoding method that is used to refer to a specific character. For two-byte characters, this refers to the row and the cell.
Code space	コード領域. The space in which characters can be encoded according to the specifications of a given encoding method. Code positions outside the code space are considered invalid.
Compound	熟語. A Japanese word consisting of two or more kanji.
CompuServe	An electronic information service.
Control character	制御文字. A character whose purpose is to control printing devices or communication devices as opposed to actually producing visible marks on a screen or printer. Carriage return, for example, is a control character, whereas the letter A is a printing character.

Conversion dictionary	変換辞書. The dictionary that is used by kana-to-kanji conversion software (front-end processor) to convert kana input into a mixture of kana and kanji characters. Each entry in this dictionary is a *key* along with one or more *names* associated with it. The size of such dictionaries are typically in the range of several tens of thousands of entries. Also see *FEP, kana-to-kanji conversion, key,* and *name.*
Corporate-defined character	See *gaiji.*
CPU	中央処理装置. Central Processing Unit. Usually refers to the computer itself.
CREN	See *Bitnet.*
CS	Computer Science.
CSselect	Short for character set select. A term used in XCCS encoding, and refers to the 0xFF character, which is used to indicate a character set or encoding change. See *CharSet.*
Cursive	A smoother, hand-written style of a character. Hiragana is an example of a cursive writing system. Also called calligraphic writing.
Dangling hyphenation	ぶら下がり禁則処理. A method of moving characters up to the previous line in order to prevent prohibited characters for ending or beginning a line. The character or characters that are moved appear to *dangle* outside of the right margin. Also see *Japanese hyphenation, wrap-down hyphenation,* and *wrap-up hyphenation.*
DBCS	Double-Byte Character Set. A character set whose characters are represented by two bytes.
DBCS-EUC	A double-byte character set encoded according to the specification of EUC.
DBCS-Host	A double-byte character set with an encoding method designed for running on host computers.
DBCS-PC	A double-byte character set with an encoding method designed for running on PCs.

DEC   ディジタルイクイップメント株式会社. Digital Equip-
                              ment Corporation.

DEC Kanji   The Japanese character set and encoding defined by
                              DEC. There are two implementations, DEC78 and
                              DEC83. See *DEC78* and *DEC83*.

DEC78   A specific implementation of DEC Kanji which is based
                              largely on the JIS C 6226-1978 character set standard.
                              See *DEC Kanji*.

DEC83   A specific implementation of DEC Kanji which is based
                              largely on the JIS X 0208-1983 character set standard.

Decimal   10進. Base 10. A number notation that uses 10 possible
                              values, ranging from 0 to 9.

Diachronic   A linguistic term that refers to linguistic changes that
                              occur between different periods.

Diacritic mark   A mark that serves to annotate characters with addi-
                              tional information, usually a variant pronunciation.
                              Diacritic marks typically found above or below charac-
                              ters. In the West it is common to see accented charac-
                              ters such as á, à, â, ä, ã, å, and ç. Japanese examples
                              include the hiragana characters ば (*ba*) and ぱ (*pa*),
                              which are derived from the basic hiragana character は
                              (*ha*).

Dialect   A linguistic term that refers to different flavors of a lan-
                              guage that are usually spoken in different regions.

Display PostScript   A special version of PostScript designed for computer
                              monitor output. Used as standard software on the
                              NeXT platform.

DOS   Disk Operating System.

DPI   Dots-per-inch. A measurement for device resolution.

DPS   See *Display PostScript*.

DTP   Desk Top Publishing.

Dvorak array   A Western keyboard array developed by August
                              Dvorak and William Dealey in the 1930s as an im-
                              provement over the QWERTY keyboard array. See
                              QWERTY array.

EBCDIC	Extended Binary-Coded-Decimal Interchange Code. An encoding for the ASCII character set standard developed by IBM for use on IBM-based computers. Used in conjunction with several double-byte character sets and encodings, such as DBCS-Host (IBM), JEF (Fujitsu), and KEIS (Hitachi). Requires eight bits for representation.
EBCDIK	Extended Binary-Coded-Decimal Interchange Kana Code. A Japanese version of EBCDIC that includes uppercase Roman characters, numerals, symbols, half-width katakana, and control characters. See *EBCDIC*.
Em-square	A square space whose height and width roughly corresponds to the width of the letter *M*. Also called a *mutton*.
Encoding	The correspondence between numerical character codes and the final printable glyphs. For instance, 0x41 is the ASCII (JIS-Roman) code for the letter *A*. 0xC1 is the EBCDIC (EBCDIK) code for the letter *A*.
Escape character	The control character (0x1B) that is used as part of an escape sequence. Escape sequences are used in JIS encoding to switch between one- and two-byte-per-character modes. Also see *escape sequence* and *JIS*.
Escape sequence	A string of characters that contains one or more escape characters, and is used to signify a shift in mode of some sort. In the case of the Japanese character set, they are used to shift between one- and two-byte-per-character modes, and to shift between different character sets or different versions of the same character set. Also see *shifting sequence*.
EUC	Extended UNIX Code. There are two versions of EUC that support Japanese: EUC complete two-byte format, which is a fixed-width 16-bit encoding; and EUC packed format, which is a variable-width encoding.
External character	See *gaiji*.
FDPC	文字フォント開発・普及センター. Font Development and Promotion Center. The consortium, which is part

of JSA, that is developing the *Heisei* series of Japanese typefaces.

FEP   Front-end Processor. A common name for Japanese input software, which is so named from the way it captures keyboard strokes before they are sent to the text buffer of the current application. These keyboard strokes are then processed, converted into a mixture of kana and kanji text, and finally sent to the current application's text buffer.

Fidonet   An electronic bulletin board (BBS) service that offers a gateway to the outside world. See *BBS*.

Fixed-width encoding An encoding method whereby every character in the character set is represented by the same number of bytes. Examples include Unicode, 10646.UCS-2, 10646.UCS-2, and EUC complete two-byte format. Actually, ASCII encoding, if used by itself, is fixed-width encoded. Also see *modal encoding* and *non-modal encoding*.

fj   From Japan. The initial two letters found in the names of newsgroups distributed within Japan. These newsgroups are also available outside of Japan.

FM-R   The name of the PC series of computers produced by Fujitsu.

FSF   Free Software Foundation.

FTP   File Transfer Protocol. A common way to move files between host computers, and sometimes between a host computer and a personal computer.

Full-width   全角. A character whose shape occupies a space roughly that of a square. Most Japanese characters are considered to be full-width. Also see *half-width*.

Furigana   振り仮名. See *ruby*.

Gaiji   外字. A user- or corporate-defined character.

Gaiji solution   A solution that makes it possible to interchange documents that contain non-standard characters to systems that do not have such characters installed, and allows such characters to be displayed and printed properly.

Gairaigo	外来語. Means "loan word," but usually refers to loan words written using katakana.
Gakushû Kanji	学習漢字. The 1,006 kanji that are formerly taught in the Japanese educational system during the first six grades.
GB 1988-80	The name of the document that defines GB-Roman, which is the Chinese equivalent of ASCII. See *GB-Roman*.
GB 2312-80	The name of the document that describes the basic Chinese character set as used in Mainland China. It enumerates 7,445 characters.
GB-Roman	The Chinese equivalent of the ASCII character set and encoding. The name of the document that defines this character set is called GB 1988-80.
Gloss	See *ruby*.
Glyph	A specific instance of a character. A classic example is that *f* and *i* are two separate glyphs, but you can fuse these two characters into a single glyph called a ligature: fi. See *ligature*.
GNU	Short for GNU is Not UNIX. A series of UNIX-based software that is provided free of charge. GNU software (and other software that seeks protection) falls under the terms of the GNU General Public License, which protects software from being exploited for commercial uses. It ensures that there will always be a large body of software freely available.
Gothic	ゴシック. The name commonly given to the Japanese typeface style in which horizontal and vertical strokes are of the same relative weight. This is roughly equivalent to the sans serif typeface style in Western typography. See *sans serif*.
grep	Global regular expression printer. The standard pattern-matching utility found on most UNIX systems.
GUI	Graphical User Interface.

Half-width

半角. A character whose shape occupies a space half that of a square. ASCII characters as used in the West are typically considered half-width. Also see *full-width*.

Han Unification

The effort on the part of the Unicode Consortium to collapse the Chinese, Japanese, and Korean versions of kanji* down to a common code set by eliminating duplication.

Hangul

ハングル. The name of the native Korean writing system.

Hankaku

半角. Analogous to half-width. See *half-width*.

Hanja

The Korean word for kanji. See *kanji*.

Hanzi

The Chinese word for kanji. See *kanji*.

Hard-coded conversion

A type of conversion that uses mapping tables for converting objects. Also see *algorithmic conversion*.

Heisei

平成. The name of the current Japanese era, which began in 1989. Also the name of the typefaces being produced by developing members of FDPC. Also see *FDPC*.

Hexadecimal

16進. Base 16. A number notation that uses 16 possible values, 0–9 and A–F. The most common notation used in the computer world.

Hiragana

平仮名. The cursive Japanese syllabic writing system. Together with katakana is collectively called kana. Also see *kana* and *katakana*.

Hojo Kanji

補助漢字. Supplemental kanji. The name given to the kanji contained in JIS X 0212-1990. These kanji are ordered by radical, then by total number of strokes.

HP

Hewlett-Packard.

HP-UX

Hewlett-Packard's version of the UNIX operating system.

I18N

Abbreviation for internationalization. See *internationalization*.

---

*Or *hanzi* or *hanja*, depending on whether you are Chinese or Korean

IBM	アイ・ビー・エム. International Business Machines Corporation.
IBM-eucJP	A specific instance of DBCS-EUC to include ASCII/JIS-Roman and half-width katakana.
IBM-932	A specific instance of DBCS-PC to include ASCII/JIS-Roman and half-width katakana.
IBM Kanji	The name of the Japanese character set as defined by IBM. Some implementations include IBM-eucJP and IBM-932.
ID	Identification. Usually refers to the user's name as used to access an electronic service or host computer.
Ideograph	指事文字. A character which represents an abstract shape. In the case of kanji, this includes characters such as 上 (*up*) and 下 (*down*).
IEEE	Institute of Electrical and Electronics Engineers.
IETF	Internet Engineering Task Force. A volunteer organization that deals with networking issues on the Internet. Also refers to the documents produced by this organization. These are also called Internet Drafts. They are then called RFCs when they are no longer in draft status. See *RFC*.
IIJ	Internet Initiative Japan.
IKIS	Interactive Kanji Information System. The Japanese character set and encoding developed by Nippon Data General.
In-line conversion	インライン変換. The ability to handle Japanese input at the cursor position rather than in a dedicated window.
Indexing	The process of locating the encoded position of a character, thus providing access to it.
Information interchange	情報交換. The process of moving information from one hardware or software configuration to another with no loss of data.
Information processing	情報処理. The process of manipulating electronically encoded information at different levels. Japanese code

and text processing are forms of information processing.

Internationalization

国際化. The process of designing software (or hardware) in a flexible manner such that it becomes an easy task to adapt or *localize* to another country with different languages. Internationalization also makes it possible to use more than one writing system on computers. There are two main implementations of internationalization: the locale model and the multilingual model. See *locale model*, *localization*, and *multilingual model*.

Internet

The name given to the world-wide network of computers.

IP

Internet Protocol.

Iroha

いろは. A Japanese collation sequence based on the same sounds from the 50 Sounds order. See *50 Sounds order*.

ISO

国際標準化機構. International Standards Organization.

ISO 2022-1993

See *JIS X 0202-1991*.

ISO 646-1991

Identical to JIS X 0201-1976 except that it contains the extensions for JIS-Roman and half-width katakana. See *JIS X 0201-1976*.

ISO 8859

A set of nine documents that describe extensions to the ASCII character set to handle other European languages.

ISO 9541-1993

A set of three documents that describe the standard digital font format. Based on the Type 1 font format by Adobe Systems.

ISO 10646

The document that describes the ISO version of the Unicode character set. ISO 10646 specifies 16- and 32-bit representations.

ITC

International Typeface Corporation.

J10N

Abbreviation for Japanization. See *Japanization*.

Jaggies

The uneven effect when bitmapped fonts are scaled to large sizes.

JAIN	Japanese Academic InterNetwork.
Japan	日本. The country in which the Japanese language is spoken.
JAPAN.INF	The name of the electronic document on which this book is based.
Japanese	日本語. The language spoken in Japan.
Japanese hyphenation	禁則処理. The proper handling of Japanese characters at the beginning and at the ends of lines. Punctuation, such as 「, should not terminate a line. Likewise, punctuation, such as 」, should not begin a new line.
Japanese justification	均等割付. A special case of justification that is done on a much smaller scale than in the West. Japanese justification is typically used for lists of names whereby varying numbers of characters per name are made flush to the left and right, but not to the margin of the printed page.
Japanization	日本語化. The localization of software to the Japanese market. See *localization*.
JEF	Japanese processing Extended Feature. A character set and encoding developed by Fujitsu. JIS C 6226-1978 is a subset.
Jinmei-yô Kanji	人名用漢字. The 284 kanji, above and beyond Jôyô Kanji, specified by the Japanese government as appropriate for use in writing personal names. See *Jôyô Kanji*.
JIS	日本工業規格. ㋐. ジス. Japanese Industrial Standard. The name of the standards established by JISC. Also the name of the encoding method used for the JIS X 0208-1990 and JIS X 0212-1990 character set standards. See *JISC*.
JIS78	Short for JIS C 6226-1978. See *JIS C 6226-1978*.
JIS83	Short for JIS X 0208-1983. See *JIS X 0208-1983*.
JIS90	Short for JIS X 0208-1990. See *JIS X 0208-1990*.
JIS array	JIS配列. The most widely used Japanese keyboard array. Specified in the document JIS X 6002-1985. Like

the QWERTY keyboard array in the West, it is also the most inefficient. Also called Old-JIS array.

JISC

日本工業標準調査会. Japanese Industrial Standards Committee. The name of the organization that establishes JIS standards.

JISCII

Japanese Industrial Standard Code for Information Interchange. An improper reference to the Japanese character set standards established by JIS. More correctly known as just JIS. See *JIS*.

JIS C 6220-1976

The original designation of what is now known as JIS X 0201-1976. The name changed on March 1, 1987. See *JIS X 0201-1976*.

JIS C 6226-1978

The first double-byte character set. Developed in 1978 by Japanese Industrial Standards. Two revisions followed, first in 1983, and finally in 1990. See *JIS X 0208-1983* and *JIS X 0208-1990*.

JIS C 6226-1983

The original designation of what is now known as JIS X 0208-1983. The name changed on March 1, 1987. See *JIS X 0208-1983*.

JIS C 6228-1984

The original designation for what is now known as JIS X 0202-1991. The name changed on March 1, 1987. See *JIS X 0202-1991*.

JIS C 6232-1984

The original designation for what is now known as JIS X 9051-1984. The name changed on March 1, 1987. See *JIS X 9051-1984*.

JIS C 6233-1980

The original designation for what is now known as JIS X 6002-1985. The name changed on March 1, 1987. See *JIS X 6002-1985*.

JIS C 6234-1983

The original designation for what is now known as JIS X 9052-1983. The name changed on March 1, 1987. See *JIS X 9052-1983*.

JIS C 6235-1984

The original designation for what is now known as JIS X 6003-1989. The name changed on March 1, 1987. See *JIS X 6003-1989*.

JIS C 6236-1986	The original designation for what is now known as JIS X 6004-1986. The name changed on March 1, 1987. See *JIS X 6004-1986.*
JIS encoding	The most basic Japanese encoding method that uses escape sequences to shift between one- and two-byte-per-character modes. A modal encoding method. See *modal encoding.*
JIS Level 1 kanji	JIS第1水準漢字. The name given to the 2,965 characters that consitute the first set of kanji in JIS X 0208-1990. Ordered by pronunciation (usually ON reading). See *JIS X 0208-1990.*
JIS Level 2 kanji	JIS第2水準漢字. The name given to the 3,390 characters that constitute the second set of kanji in JIS X 0208-1990. The 1978 version (JIS C 6226-1978) had 3,384 such kanji, and the 1983 version (JIS X 0208-1983) had 3,388 such kanji. Ordered by radical, then by total number of strokes. See *JIS X 0208-1990.*
JIS Level 3 kanji	JIS第3水準漢字. A name sometimes given to the kanji in JIS X 0212-1990. A more correct reference is Hojo Kanji. See *Hojo Kanji* and *JIS X 0212-1990.*
JIS order	The order in which characters appear in the Japanese character set standards published by JSA.
JIS sort	A sort done in JIS order. See *JIS order.*
JIS X 0201-1976	The document that describes the JIS-Roman and half-width katakana character sets along with their encodings.
JIS X 0202-1991	The document that details the escape sequences used for encoding Japanese and other languages. The Japanese equivalent of ISO 2022-1993.
JIS X 0208-1983	The 1983 edition of the document that describes the Japanese character set standard, and was originally named JIS C 6226-1983. 6,877 characters are enumerated.
JIS X 0208-1990	The latest version of the document that describes the Japanese character set standard. 6,879 characters are enumerated.

JIS X 0212-1990   The document that describes the supplement to the Japanese character set standard. 6,067 characters are enumerated.

JIS X 4161-1993   The document (part 1 of 4) that describes the standard digital font format. Based on the Type 1 font format by Adobe Systems.

JIS X 4162-1993   The document (part 2 of 4) that describes the standard digital font format. Based on the Type 1 font format by Adobe Systems.

JIS X 4163-1993   The document (part 3 of 4) that describes the standard digital font format. Based on the Type 1 font format by Adobe Systems.

JIS X 4164-1993   The document (part 4 of 4) that describes the standard digital font format. Based on the Type 1 font format by Adobe Systems.

JIS X 6002-1985   The document that spells out the specifications for the JIS keyboard array. See *JIS array*.

JIS X 6003-1989   The document that describes the layout of a kanji tablet, a large input device used to input kanji directly. See *kanji tablet*.

JIS X 6004-1986   The document that describes the New-JIS keyboard array. See *New-JIS array*.

JIS X 9051-1984   The document that illustrates the 16-by-16 dot-matrix patterns for the characters specified in JIS X 0208-1983. See *JIS X 0208-1983*.

JIS X 9052-1983   The document that illustrates the 24-by-24 dot-matrix patterns for the characters specified in JIS X 0208-1983. See *JIS X 0208-1983*.

JIS-Roman   The Japanese equivalent of ASCII.

JIS7   A variation of JIS encoding that encodes half-width katakana using seven bits. See *JIS encoding*.

JIS8   A variation of JIS encoding that encodes half-width katakana using eight bits. See *JIS encoding*.

JLE   Japanese Language Environment. The name of Sun's Japanese operating system.

JLS	Japanese Language System. The Japanese extensions for SGI's Irix operating system.
Jôyô Kanji	常用漢字. The 1,945 kanji designated by the Japanese government as the ones to be used in public documents such as newspapers. Superseded Tôyô Kanji in 1981. See *Tôyô Kanji*.
JP	The name of the top-level Internet domain for Japan. Once called JUNET.
JPNIC	Japan Network Information Center.
JSA	日本規格協会. Japanese Standards Association. The publisher of the JIS standards.
JUNET	Japan UNIX Network. See *JP*.
K	Kilobyte. 1,024 bytes.
Kana	仮名. The term that collectively refers to hiragana and katakana.
Kana-to-kanji conversion	仮名漢字変換. The process of converting kana input into a mixture of kana and kanji characters. The most common method of inputting Japanese text.
Kanji	漢字. The Chinese characters that the Japanese borrowed from the Chinese. These number in the thousands.
Kanji compound	See *compound*.
Kanji tablet	A large tablet containing thousands of individual keys, one for each character. This allows for direct kanji input.
Kanji-in	漢字イン. The name usually given to two-byte character escape sequences as used in JIS encoding. A kanji-in switches the current n-byte-per-character mode into two-byte mode.
Kanji-out	漢字アウト. The name usually given to one-byte character escape sequences as used in JIS encoding. A kanji-out switches the current n-byte-per-character mode into one-byte mode.
KanjiTalk	漢字Talk. The name of the localized Japanese operating system for the Apple Macintosh computer.

Katakana	片仮名. The square-shaped Japanese syllabary. Usually used for writing recent words of foreign origin. Together with hiragana is collectively called kana. Also see *kana* and *hiragana*.
KB	Kilobyte. 1,024 bytes. Usually written as just K.
KEIS	Kanji processing Extended Information System. The Japanese character set and encoding developed by Hitachi.
KEIS78	The version of KEIS which corresponds to JIS C 6226-1978. See *KEIS*.
KEIS83	The version of KEIS which corresponds to JIS X 0208-1983. See *KEIS*.
Kermit	A popular file transfer protocol.
Key	The basic text unit that is used to index into a conversion dictionary in order to obtain the *names* associated with the key. Also see *candidate, conversion dictionary*, and *name*.
Kokuji	国字. Japanese-made kanji.
Korean	韓国語. The language spoken in Korea.
KS C 5601-1992	The name of the document that describes the basic Korean character set. It enumerates 8,224 characters. Previous version were dated 1987 and 1989.
KS C 5861-1992	The name of the document that describes the EUC encoding for Korean text.
KUN reading	訓読み. The name given to the native Japanese pronunciation for a kanji.
KUTEN	区点. Literally means "ward [and] point" (or "row [and] cell"). A machine-independent way of indexing characters in JIS X 0208-1990 and JIS X 0212-1990 (and the corporate character sets derived from them).
Kyôiku Kanji	教育漢字. The 1,006 kanji that are formally taught during the first six years of school in Japan.
L10N	Abbreviation for localization. See *localization*.

Ligature	A character whose glyph consists of two or more characters fused together. An example is *fi*, which is the ligature for the letters *f* and *i*.
Locale model	A model of internationalization that predefines many attributes that are language or country specific, such as the maximum number of bytes per character, date formats, time formats, currency formats, and so on. The actual attributes are located in a library or locale object file that is loaded when required. Also see *internationalization* and *multilingual model*.
Localization	地方化. The process of adapting software (or hardware) such that it conforms to the expectations of a specific country. This often includes rewriting menus and dialogs into the target language, but sometimes involves more complex changes, such as handling special character encoding methods. Other issues to be addressed are time zones, ways of writing dates and times, currency, and others. See *internationalization* and *Japanization*.
Logical compound	会意文字. A kanji character which is built from two or more primitive elements, which may be pictographs or ideographs. See *ideographs* and *pictographs*.
M	Megabyte. 1,048,576 bytes.
Machine(-aided) translation	機械(支援)翻訳. The process of converting text in one language into another language. Most software to date cannot fully perform this task, and pre- or post-editing by a human is usually required in order to obtain acceptable results.
Maru	丸. Literally means "circle," but in this book refers to the circle-like diacritic mark that serves to transform h-based kana characters into their p-based counterparts. For example, katakana *ha* (ハ) is transformed into katakana *pa* (パ). Also called the *semi-voiced mark*. Also see *nigori*.
MB	Megabyte. 1,048,576 bytes.
MBCS	Multiple-Byte Character Set. A character set that contains characters of mixed encoding lengths.

MCI Mail	The name of the electronic information service offered by MCI, a telecommunications company.
Mincho	明朝. The name commonly given to the Japanese typeface style in which vertical strokes are heavy, and horizontal strokes are thin. This is roughly equivalent to the serif typeface style in Western typography. See *serif*.
Ming	See *mincho*.
MITI	通商産業省. Ministry of International Trade and Industry.
Modal encoding	An encoding method that uses special sequences of one or more characters to signal a change in mode. Mode changes can include shifting between one- and two-byte-per-character modes, between different character sets, and between different versions of the same character set. Examples include JIS, JEF, KEIS, IBM DBCS-Host, and XCCS encodings. Also see *fixed-width* and *non-modal encoding*.
Morisawa	モリサワ. A major Japanese type foundry. Also see *Ryobi* and *Shaken*.
M-style array	M式配列. A keyboard array designed by Masasuke Morita for NEC. It not only specifies an ergonomic keyboard design, but an input methods that allows users to select what part converts to kanji, and what part does not.
MS	Microsoft Corporation.
MS-DOS	Microsoft Disk Operating System.
MS Kanji	Another name for Shift-JIS. Stands for Microsoft Kanji. See *Shift-JIS*.
MSB	Most Significant Byte. The initial byte in an expected multiple-byte sequence.
Multilingual model	A model of internationalization that uses a character set whose repertoire contains enough characters to represent most of the world's writing systems. No flipping between character sets is required. Also see *internationalization* and *locale model*.

Multiple-byte character	A character that is represented by more than one byte.
Name	One or more text strings that are associated with a key in a conversion dictionary. These are presented to the user as a list of candidates from which to choose. Also see *candidate, conversion dictionary,* and *key.*
NEC	日本電気株式会社. Nippon Electronics Corporation.
NEC Kanji	The Japanese character set standard and encoding developed by NEC.
NEC-JIS	See *NEC Kanji.*
New-JIS	新JIS. A common name given to the JIS X 0208-1983 character set standard. Usually refers to the two-byte escape sequence used to designate the JIS X 0208-1990 character set in JIS encoding.
New-JIS array	新JIS配列. The Japanese keyboard array that was designed to replace the JIS keyboard array. It departs from the JIS array in that there are two kana characters per key. It failed, and the JIS array is still the most commonly used among the Japanese keyboard arrays.
NIFTY-Serve	A Japanese electronic information service based in Japan.
Nigori	濁り. Refers to the diacritic mark that serve to transform several kana characters into their voiced counterparts. For example, the katakana character *ta* (タ) is transformed into *da* (ダ). Also called the *voiced mark.* Also see *maru.*
NLIO	Native Language Input/Output.
Non-kanji	非漢字. Characters other than kanji, such as Roman characters, hiragana, katakana, and other symbols.
Non-modal encoding	An encoding method that does not use special sequences of characters to switch between one- and two-byte-per-character modes. Also see *fixed-width* and *modal encoding.*
Non-printing character	A character that makes no printable marks on an output device. These include control characters and white space characters, such as a space or tab character.

Notation

A method of representing units. In the world of computers, the most commonly used notations are *binary* (base two), *octal* (base eight), *decimal* (base 10), and *hexadecimal* (base 16). Also see *binary*, *decimal*, *hexadecimal*, and *octal*.

NTT

日本電信電話. Nippon Telegraph and Telephone.

NTT Kanji

The name of the character set and encoding as developed by NTT. See *NTT*.

Numeral

数字. The printed numbers ranging from zero through nine.

OCR

光学的文字認識. Optical Character Recognition. A device that can scan, recognize, and convert printed shapes into meaningful units, such as characters.

Octal

8進. Base eight. A number notation that uses eight possible values, ranging from 0 to 7.

Octet

An array of eight bits represented as a single unit (a byte).

Old-JIS

旧JIS. A common name given to the JIS C 6226-1978 character set standard. See *JIS C 6226-1978*.

Old-JIS array

See *JIS array*.

ON reading

音読み. The name given to the approximated Chinese pronunciation for a kanji.

Orthography

正書法. A linguistic term that refers to the writing system of a language.

OS

Operating System. The software that drives the hardware associated with a computer system.

OSF

Open Software Foundation.

Outline font

A font whose characters are described mathematically in terms of lines and curves. Outline fonts are often referred to as *scalable fonts*, because they can be scan converted on demand to bitmaps of any desired size and orientation.

Parametric font

A font whose shape is described as a series of vectors. This type of font format has scalable properties, but is

	not as high of quality as outline fonts. Also see *bitmapped* and *outline font*.
Particle	助詞. Grammatical markers used in the Japanese language. They are equivalent to prepositions in English, but unlike English, they come after the noun or phrase they modify. Particles are sometimes call postpositions.
PC	パソコン. Personal Computer. Usually refers to machines that run MS-DOS.
PC-VAN	Personal Computer Value Added Network. A Japanese electronic information service based in Japan.
PDF	Portable Document Format. The document format that is generated by Adobe Acrobat technology.
Pen input	ペン入力. An input method that allows the user to enter text and commands with a pen (or stylus) onto a tablet. OCR technology is often used in the process of interpreting hand-written text.
PenPoint	An operating system developed by GO Corporation that supports pen input and the Unicode character set.
Phonetic compound	形声文字. A kanji character constructed from at least two radicals. One radical is used for its pronunciation, and the other used for its meaning. Together they form a unique kanji.
Pictograph	象形文字. A character whose shape reflects the shape of the object which it represents. An example of such a kanji is 山, which means "mountain."
Plan 9	The multilingual UNIX operating system under development at AT&T Bell Laboratories.
Point	ポイント. A unit of measure used in typography. A *printer's point* in the United States is 1/72.27 of an inch. This is usually rounded to 1/72 of an inch.
POSIX	Portable Operating System Interface.
Postposition	See *particle*.
PostScript	The page description language developed by Adobe Systems.

Printable character	A character that makes some sort of mark on an output devices. Also called a *graphic* character.
Pseudo ruby	疑似ルビ. Small characters, usually kanji or Roman characters, that appear above normal size characters, and serve annotate them with a pronunciation or meaning. Similar to ruby characters. Also see *ruby*.
Quadratic spline curve	The type of curve used for representing character shape contours in the TrueType font format.
QWERTY array	The most common keyboard in use today. Its name comes from the first six keys that have 26 letters of the Alphabet imprinted on them.
Radical	部首. The 214 building blocks of kanji. Many character set standards arrange kanji by radical. For example, the kanji of JIS Level 2 are arranged by radical. Radicals are subcomposed of strokes. See *strokes*.
RAM	Random Access Memory.
RFC	Request For Comments. The name given to the more than 1,000 documents that describe the inner workings of the Internet.
RKSJ	Roman, (half-width) Katakana, and Shift-JIS. An encoding used by PostScript Japanese fonts.
ROM	Read Only Memory.
Roman character	ローマ字. The 52 lowercase and uppercase characters of the Alphabet.
Row	区. In a two-byte encoding, row refers to the first byte. In a two-dimensional matrix, row represents the values along the vertical axis. Also see *cell*.
Ruby	ルビ. Small characters, usually kana, that appear above normal size characters, and serve annotate them with a pronunciation or meaning.
Ryobi	リョービ. A major Japanese type foundry. Also see *Morisawa* and *Shaken*.
Sans serif	French for *without serifs*. Sans serif characters do not have little *feet* on them. Helvetica (**this is Helvetica**) is a widely used sans serif typeface. Also see *serif*.

SBCS	Single-Byte Character Set.
Serif	Characters which have little *feet* to act as guide marks. Derives all the way from days when letters were carved in stone—the serifs were added to provide even height. Garamond, which is used as the standard textface in this book, is an example of a serif typeface. Also see *sans serif*.
SGI	Silicon Graphics Incorporated.
Shaken	写研. A major Japanese type foundry. Also see *Morisawa* and *Ryobi*.
Shift-JIS	The most common encoding method used on Japanese PCs. So named from how the first byte range of two-byte characters *shift* around the encoding range of single-byte half-width katakana. Also called MS Kanji.
Shifting sequence	A sequence of one or more characters that are often used to shift between one- and two-byte-per-character modes. Also see *escape sequence*.
Simplified kanji	A modified version of a traditional kanji such that it is written with less strokes. See *traditional kanji*.
SJIS	An abbreviation for Shift-JIS. See *Shift-JIS*.
SKIP	System of Kanji Indexing by Patterns. A method for indexing kanji that divides it geometrically thus allowing you to find any kanji in less than 30 seconds. It is found in a kanji dictionary written by Jack Halpern, and implemented in Jim Breen's KANJIDIC.
SMTP	Simple Mail Transfer Protocol.
SS2	Single Shift 2. A special character (0x8E) used in EUC encoding as a prefix to characters in code set 2.
SS3	Single Shift 3. A special character (0x8F) used in EUC encoding as a prefix to characters in code set 3.
Stroke	画. The basic building blocks of radicals and kanji. A single stroke is defined as an element drawn while a writing utensil is still on the paper. These usually are straight lines, curves, and some angles.
Supplemental kanji	See *hojo kanji*.

Syllabary

A writing system whose characters are composed of syllables. Hiragana and katakana are examples of syllabaries. See *syllable*.

Syllable

A sound sequence consisting of a consonant plus vowel.

Synchronic

A linguistic term that is used to refer to linguistic changes that exist during the same period

T1C

Adobe Type 1 Coprocessor. A computer chip designed by Adobe Systems that significantly reduces the time necessary to render characters to the screen or printer.

TBCS

Triple-Byte Character Set. A character set whose characters are encoded with three bytes.

TBCS-EUC

A Triple-Byte Character Set encoded according to the specification of EUC.

TEX

A popular text setting language for which a Japanese version exists.

Thumb-shift array

親指シフト配列. The Japanese keyboard array developed by Fujitsu.

TISN

Todai (University of Tokyo) International Science Network.

Tôyô Kanji

当用漢字. The 1,850 kanji designated by the Japanese government as the ones to be used in public documents such as newspapers. Superseded by Jôyô Kanji in 1981. See *Jôyô Kanji*.

Traditional kanji

Refers to the original, sometimes complex, shapes of kanji. The opposite of simplified kanji. 國 is an example of a traditional kanji. Its simplified counterpart is 国. Korea and Taiwan use the traditional form of kanji. Japan and Mainland China, in general, uses the simplified forms.

TRON

トロン. The Real-time Operating system Nucleus. A new operating system being developed in Japan. Variations include ITRON (Industrial TRON) and BTRON (Business TRON).

TrueImage

A page-description language developed by Microsoft.

TrueType	An outline font format developed by Apple Computer.
TWICS	Two-way Information Communication System. The name of an electronic information service based in Japan.
Two-stroke input method	2ストローク入力方式. A Japanese input method that associates two key strokes per kanji. In the case of input by association, the two keys have some sort of relationship to the kanji, usually by pronunciation or meaning. There is also input by unassociation, which arbitrarily associates two key strokes per kanji.
Type 0 font	Adobe Systems' *composite font* format. A Type 0 font *contains* other fonts in a hierarchical fashion, providing access to huge character sets, such as those used in Japan.
Type 1 font	Adobe Systems' format for describing outlines or scalable fonts. Type 1 fonts use a very special and limited subset of PostScript, optimized for compactness and speed. See also *ISO 9541-1993*.
Type 3 font	A *user-defined* PostScript font. Type 3 fonts can use all of the PostScript language to obtain effects (gray scale, for instance) not available to Type 1 fonts.
Type 4 font	Adobe Systems' disk-based font format.
Type 5 font	Adobe Systems' ROM-based font format.
Type 42 font	Adobe Systems' font format that provides a wrapper for a TrueType font. This allows a TrueType font to be used in much the same way as a Type 1 font. See *Type 1 font*.
Typeface	A distinctive design for a set of visually related symbols. Examples include Helvetica, Garamond, Ryumin-Light, and Heisei Mincho W3.
UI	UNIX International or User Interface.
UJIS	Short for UNIXized JIS, and is identical to EUC. See *EUC*.
Unicode	The name of the international 16-bit character set and encoding developed by the members of the Unicode Consortium.

UNIX	The name of the operating system that runs on most workstations.
User-defined character	See *gaiji*.
USLP	UNIX System Laboratories Pacific.
UTF	UCS (Universal Character Set) Transformation Format. A method of encoding 16- or 32-bit encodings such that they pass as a stream of ASCII bytes.
UTF-2	The 16-bit version of UTF. Used by Plan 9 for encoding Unicode text as a stream of ASCII bytes. Also see *Plan 9*.
UTF-4	The 32-bit version of UTF.
UUCP	UNIX-to-UNIX Copy.
uudecode	A UNIX utility for decoding a file encoded by **uuencode**. See *uuencode*.
uuencode	A UNIX utility for encoding a file (usually a binary file) such that it can pass through networks within an e-mail message. Decoding is performed by **uudecode**. See *uudecode*.
Vector font	See *parametric font*.
Voice input	音声入力. An input method that is driven by the human voice. Such devices must usually be trained to understand the user's voice.
Ward	See *row*.
White space	Characters that produce empty space, such as the space character or the tab character.
Wide character	A character that consists of a larger than normal byte. A byte typically consists of seven or eight bits. A character represented by 16 bits is considered a wide character.
Word processor	ワープロ. A text processing tool that manipulates text in such a way that it is possible to include multiple fonts in a single document. Sufficient formatting capabilities are also quite common.

Wrap-down hyphenation	追出し禁則処理. A method of moving characters down to the next line in order to prevent prohibited characters for ending or beginning a line. Also see *Japanese hyphenation* and *wrap-up hyphenation*.
Wrap-up hyphenation	追込み禁則処理. A method of moving characters up to the previous line in order to prevent prohibited characters for ending or beginning a line. Also see *Japanese hyphenation* and *wrap-down hyphenation*.
WYSIWYG	ウィジウィグ. What You See Is What You Get.
X-Modem	A popular file transfer protocol.
X Window System	The name of a very popular UNIX windowing system developed at MIT. The last release is called X11R5.
XCCS	Xerox Character Code Standard.
XPG4	X/Open Portability Guide issue 4.
Y-Modem	A popular file transfer protocol.
Z-Modem	A popular file transfer protocol.
Zenkaku	全角. Analogous to full-width. See *full-width*.

O

Code Table

The following table lists all of the 256 encoded values in binary, octal, decimal, and hexadecimal notation. It includes characters that are represented with those values for ASCII, JIS-Roman (includes half-width katakana) EBCDIC, and EBCDIK encodings. Control characters, when defined, appear as abbreviations. Use this table as a guide when dealing with such codes used throughout this book.

ASCII	JIS-Roman	EBCDIC	EBCDIK	Binary	Octal	Decimal	Hexadecimal
<NUL>	<NUL>	<NUL>	<NUL>	00000000	000	0	00
<SOH>	<SOH>	<SOH>	<SOH>	00000001	001	1	01
<STX>	<STX>	<STX>	<STX>	00000010	002	2	02
<ETX>	<ETX>	<ETX>	<ETX>	00000011	003	3	03
<EOT>	<EOT>	<SEL>	<SEL>	00000100	004	4	04
<ENQ>	<ENQ>	<HT>	<HT>	00000101	005	5	05
<ACK>	<ACK>	<RNL>	<RNL>	00000110	006	6	06
<BEL>	<BEL>	<DEL>	<DEL>	00000111	007	7	07
<BS>	<BS>	<GE>	<GE>	00001000	010	8	08
<HT>	<HT>	<SPS>	<SPS>	00001001	011	9	09
<LF>	<LF>	<RPT>	<RPT>	00001010	012	10	0A
<VT>	<VT>	<VT>	<VT>	00001011	013	11	0B
<FF>	<FF>	<FF>	<FF>	00001100	014	12	0C
<CR>	<CR>	<CR>	<CR>	00001101	015	13	0D
<SO>	<SO>	<SO>	<SO>	00001110	016	14	0E
<SI>	<SI>	<SI>	<SI>	00001111	017	15	0F
<DLE>	<DLE>	<DLE>	<DLE>	00010000	020	16	10
<DC1>	<DC1>	<DC1>	<DC1>	00010001	021	17	11
<DC2>	<DC2>	<DC2>	<DC2>	00010010	022	18	12
<DC3>	<DC3>	<DC3>	<DC3>	00010011	023	19	13
<DC4>	<DC4>	<RES>	<RES>	00010100	024	20	14
<NAK>	<NAK>	<NL>	<NL>	00010101	025	21	15
<SYN>	<SYN>	<BS>	<BS>	00010110	026	22	16
<ETB>	<ETB>	<POC>	<POC>	00010111	027	23	17
<CAN>	<CAN>	<CAN>	<CAN>	00011000	030	24	18

ASCII	JIS-Roman	EBCDIC	EBCDIK	Binary	Octal	Decimal	Hexadecimal
\<EM>	\<EM>	\<EM>	\<EM>	00011001	031	25	19
\<SUB>	\<SUB>	\<UBS>	\<UBS>	00011010	032	26	1A
\<ESC>	\<ESC>	\<CU1>	\<CU1>	00011011	033	27	1B
\<FS>	\<FS>	\<IFS>	\<IFS>	00011100	034	28	1C
\<GS>	\<GS>	\<IGS>	\<IGS>	00011101	035	29	1D
\<RS>	\<RS>	\<IRS>	\<IRS>	00011110	036	30	1E
\<US>	\<US>	\<IUS>	\<IUS>	00011111	037	31	1F
\<SP>	\<SP>	\<DS>	\<DS>	00100000	040	32	20
!	!	\<SOS>	\<SOS>	00100001	041	33	21
"	"	\<FS>	\<FS>	00100010	042	34	22
#	#	\<WUS>	\<WUS>	00100011	043	35	23
$	$	\<BYP>	\<BYP>	00100100	044	36	24
%	%	\<LF>	\<LF>	00100101	045	37	25
&	&	\<ETB>	\<ETB>	00100110	046	38	26
'	'	\<ESC>	\<ESC>	00100111	047	39	27
(	(	\<SA>	\<SA>	00101000	050	40	28
)	)	\<SFE>	\<SFE>	00101001	051	41	29
*	*	\<SM>	\<SM>	00101010	052	42	2A
+	+	\<CSP>	\<CSP>	00101011	053	43	2B
,	,	\<MFA>	\<MFA>	00101100	054	44	2C
–	–	\<ENQ>	\<ENQ>	00101101	055	45	2D
.	.	\<ACK>	\<ACK>	00101110	056	46	2E
/	/	\<BEL>	\<BEL>	00101111	057	47	2F
0	0			00110000	060	48	30
1	1			00110001	061	49	31
2	2	\<SYN>	\<SYN>	00110010	062	50	32
3	3	\<IR>	\<IR>	00110011	063	51	33
4	4	\<PP>	\<PP>	00110100	064	52	34
5	5	\<TRN>	\<TRN>	00110101	065	53	35
6	6	\<NBS>	\<NBS>	00110110	066	54	36
7	7	\<EOT>	\<EOT>	00110111	067	55	37
8	8	\<SBS>	\<SBS>	00111000	070	56	38
9	9	\<IT>	\<IT>	00111001	071	57	39
:	:	\<RFF>	\<RFF>	00111010	072	58	3A
;	;	\<CU3>	\<CU3>	00111011	073	59	3B
<	<	\<DC4>	\<DC4>	00111100	074	60	3C
=	=	\<NAK>	\<NAK>	00111101	075	61	3D
>	>			00111110	076	62	3E
?	?	\<SUB>	\<SUB>	00111111	077	63	3F
@	@	\<SP>	\<SP>	01000000	100	64	40
A	A		｡	01000001	101	65	41
B	B		｢	01000010	102	66	42
C	C		｣	01000011	103	67	43
D	D		､	01000100	104	68	44
E	E		･	01000101	105	69	45
F	F		ｦ	01000110	106	70	46
G	G		ｧ	01000111	107	71	47
H	H		ｨ	01001000	110	72	48
I	I		ｩ	01001001	111	73	49
J	J	[	£	01001010	112	74	4A
K	K	.	.	01001011	113	75	4B
L	L	<	<	01001100	114	76	4C

ASCII	JIS-Roman	EBCDIC	EBCDIK	Binary	Octal	Decimal	Hexadecimal
M	M	(	(	01001101	115	77	4D
N	N	+	+	01001110	116	78	4E
O	O	!	|	01001111	117	79	4F
P	P	&	&	01010000	120	80	50
Q	Q		ｪ	01010001	121	81	51
R	R		ｫ	01010010	122	82	52
S	S		ｬ	01010011	123	83	53
T	T		ｭ	01010100	124	84	54
U	U		ｮ	01010101	125	85	55
V	V		ｯ	01010110	126	86	56
W	W			01010111	127	87	57
X	X		ｰ	01011000	130	88	58
Y	Y			01011001	131	89	59
Z	Z	]	!	01011010	132	90	5A
[	[	$	¥	01011011	133	91	5B
\	¥	*	*	01011100	134	92	5C
]	]	)	)	01011101	135	93	5D
^	^	;	;	01011110	136	94	5E
_	_	^	¬	01011111	137	95	5F
`	`	-	-	01100000	140	96	60
a	a	/	/	01100001	141	97	61
b	b			01100010	142	98	62
c	c			01100011	143	99	63
d	d			01100100	144	100	64
e	e			01100101	145	101	65
f	f			01100110	146	102	66
g	g			01100111	147	103	67
h	h			01101000	150	104	68
i	i			01101001	151	105	69
j	j	¦	¦	01101010	152	106	6A
k	k	,	,	01101011	153	107	6B
l	l	%	%	01101100	154	108	6C
m	m	_	_	01101101	155	109	6D
n	n	>	>	01101110	156	110	6E
o	o	?	?	01101111	157	111	6F
p	p			01110000	160	112	70
q	q			01110001	161	113	71
r	r			01110010	162	114	72
s	s			01110011	163	115	73
t	t			01110100	164	116	74
u	u			01110101	165	117	75
v	v			01110110	166	118	76
w	w			01110111	167	119	77
x	x			01111000	170	120	78
y	y	`	`	01111001	171	121	79
z	z	:	:	01111010	172	122	7A
{	{	#	#	01111011	173	123	7B
¦	|	@	@	01111100	174	124	7C
}	}	'	'	01111101	175	125	7D
~	‾	=	=	01111110	176	126	7E
<DEL>	<DEL>	"	"	01111111	177	127	7F
				10000000	200	128	80

ASCII	JIS-Roman	EBCDIC	EBCDIK	Binary	Octal	Decimal	Hexadecimal
		a	ア	10000001	201	129	81
		b	イ	10000010	202	130	82
		c	ウ	10000011	203	131	83
		d	エ	10000100	204	132	84
		e	オ	10000101	205	133	85
		f	カ	10000110	206	134	86
		g	キ	10000111	207	135	87
		h	ク	10001000	210	136	88
		i	ケ	10001001	211	137	89
			コ	10001010	212	138	8A
				10001011	213	139	8B
			サ	10001100	214	140	8C
			シ	10001101	215	141	8D
			ス	10001110	216	142	8E
			セ	10001111	217	143	8F
			ソ	10010000	220	144	90
		j	タ	10010001	221	145	91
		k	チ	10010010	222	146	92
		l	ツ	10010011	223	147	93
		m	テ	10010100	224	148	94
		n	ト	10010101	225	149	95
		o	ナ	10010110	226	150	96
		p	ニ	10010111	227	151	97
		q	ヌ	10011000	230	152	98
		r	ネ	10011001	231	153	99
			ノ	10011010	232	154	9A
				10011011	233	155	9B
				10011100	234	156	9C
			ハ	10011101	235	157	9D
			ヒ	10011110	236	158	9E
			フ	10011111	237	159	9F
			ー	10100000	240	160	A0
。		~	、	10100001	241	161	A1
	「	s	ヘ	10100010	242	162	A2
	」	t	ホ	10100011	243	163	A3
	、	u	マ	10100100	244	164	A4
	・	v	ミ	10100101	245	165	A5
	ヲ	w	ム	10100110	246	166	A6
	ァ	x	メ	10100111	247	167	A7
	ィ	y	モ	10101000	250	168	A8
	ゥ	z	ヤ	10101001	251	169	A9
	ェ		ユ	10101010	252	170	AA
	ォ			10101011	253	171	AB
	ャ		ヨ	10101100	254	172	AC
	ュ		ラ	10101101	255	173	AD
	ョ		リ	10101110	256	174	AE
	ッ		ル	10101111	257	175	AF
	ー			10110000	260	176	B0
	ア			10110001	261	177	B1
	イ			10110010	262	178	B2
	ウ			10110011	263	179	B3
	エ			10110100	264	180	B4

ASCII	JIS-Roman	EBCDIC	EBCDIK	Binary	Octal	Decimal	Hexadecimal
	オ			10110101	265	181	B5
	カ			10110110	266	182	B6
	キ			10110111	267	183	B7
	ク			10111000	270	184	B8
	ケ			10111001	271	185	B9
	コ		レ	10111010	272	186	BA
	サ		ロ	10111011	273	187	BB
	シ		ワ	10111100	274	188	BC
	ス		ン	10111101	275	189	BD
	セ		゛	10111110	276	190	BE
	ソ		゜	10111111	277	191	BF
	タ	{	{	11000000	300	192	C0
	チ	A	A	11000001	301	193	C1
	ツ	B	B	11000010	302	194	C2
	テ	C	C	11000011	303	195	C3
	ト	D	D	11000100	304	196	C4
	ナ	E	E	11000101	305	197	C5
	ニ	F	F	11000110	306	198	C6
	ヌ	G	G	11000111	307	199	C7
	ネ	H	H	11001000	310	200	C8
	ノ	I	I	11001001	311	201	C9
	ハ			11001010	312	202	CA
	ヒ			11001011	313	203	CB
	フ			11001100	314	204	CC
	ヘ			11001101	315	205	CD
	ホ			11001110	316	206	CE
	マ			11001111	317	207	CF
	ミ	}	}	11010000	320	208	D0
	ム	J	J	11010001	321	209	D1
	メ	K	K	11010010	322	210	D2
	モ	L	L	11010011	323	211	D3
	ヤ	M	M	11010100	324	212	D4
	ユ	N	N	11010101	325	213	D5
	ヨ	O	O	11010110	326	214	D6
	ラ	P	P	11010111	327	215	D7
	リ	Q	Q	11011000	330	216	D8
	ル	R	R	11011001	331	217	D9
	レ			11011010	332	218	DA
	ロ			11011011	333	219	DB
	ワ			11011100	334	220	DC
	ン			11011101	335	221	DD
	゛			11011110	336	222	DE
	゜			11011111	337	223	DF
		\	$	11100000	340	224	E0
				11100001	341	225	E1
		S	S	11100010	342	226	E2
		T	T	11100011	343	227	E3
		U	U	11100100	344	228	E4
		V	V	11100101	345	229	E5
		W	W	11100110	346	230	E6
		X	X	11100111	347	231	E7

ASCII	JIS-Roman	EBCDIC	EBCDIK	Binary	Octal	Decimal	Hexadecimal
		Z	Z	11101001	351	233	E9
				11101010	352	234	EA
				11101011	353	235	EB
				11101100	354	236	EC
				11101101	355	237	ED
				11101110	356	238	EE
				11101111	357	239	EF
		0	0	11110000	360	240	F0
		1	1	11110001	361	241	F1
		2	2	11110010	362	242	F2
		3	3	11110011	363	243	F3
		4	4	11110100	364	244	F4
		5	5	11110101	365	245	F5
		6	6	11110110	366	246	F6
		7	7	11110111	367	247	F7
		8	8	11111000	370	248	F8
		9	9	11111001	371	249	F9
				11111010	372	250	FA
				11111011	373	251	FB
				11111100	374	252	FC
				11111101	375	253	FD
				11111110	376	254	FE
				11111111	377	255	FF

Bibliography

Below is a list of some useful reference works I used to write this book. They are separated into books, standards, periodicals, and papers and articles. While they are all useful to some extent, it is not necessary to obtain them all. I find a select few to be very key references. I have included ISBNs, ISSNs, and part numbers so that ordering these references is an easier task. See Appendix K for information on how to order.

Books

Adobe Systems Incorporated. *Adobe Type 1 Font Format*. Version 1.1. Addison-Wesley. 1990. ISBN 0-201-57044-0.

———. *Adobe CMap and CIDFont Files Specification*. Adobe Developer Support. Adobe Systems part number LPS5014.

———. *Glyph Bitmap Distribution Format (BDF) Specification*. Adobe Developer Support. Adobe Systems part number LPS5005.

———. *PostScript Language Tutorial and Cookbook*. Addison-Wesley (English) and ASCII Corporation (Japanese). 1985 (English) and 1989 (Japanese). ISBN 0-201-10179-3 (English) and ISBN 4-7561-0005-8 (Japanese).

———. *PostScript Language Program Design*. Addison-Wesley (English) and ASCII Corporation (Japanese). 1988 (English) and 1990 (Japanese). ISBN 0-201-14396-8 (English) and ISBN 4-7561-0047-3 (Japanese).

———. *PostScript Language Reference Manual*. Second edition. Addison-Wesley (English) and ASCII Corporation (Japanese). 1990 (English) & 1991 (Japanese). ISBN 0-201-18127-4 (English) and ISBN 4-7561-0092-9 (Japanese).

American Electronics Association. *Software Partners: The Directory of Japanese Software Distributors*. 1992.

Ames, Patrick. *Beyond Paper: the official guide to Adobe Acrobat*. Adobe Press. 1993. ISBN 1-56830-050-6.

Apple Computer Japan. Macintosh漢字Talkテクニカル・リファレンス. 技術評論社. 1990. ISBN 4-87408-369-2.

アスキー出版技術部責任編集. 日本語TEXテクニカルブック. ASCII Corporation. 1990. ISBN 4-7561-0405-3.

Bienz, Tim & Richard Cohen. *Portable Document Format Reference Manual*. Addison-Wesley. 1993. ISBN 0-201-62628-4.

Bringhurst, Robert. *The Elements of Typographic Style*. Hartley & Marks. 1992. ISBN 0-88179-033-8.

Cameron, Debra & Bill Rosenblatt. *Learning GNU Emacs*. O'Reilly & Associates, Inc. 1992. ISBN 0-937175-84-6.

張玉書 et al. 康熙字典. 中華書局. 1716. ISBN 962-231-006-0.

Clews, John. *Language Automation Worldwide: The Development of Character Set Standards*. Sesame Computer Projects. 1988. ISBN 1-870095-01-4.

エツコ・オバタ・ライマン. 日本人の作った漢字. 南雲堂. 1990. ISBN 4-523-26156-3.

遠藤紹徳. 早わかり中国簡体字. 国書刊行会. 1986.

Frey, Donnalyn & Rick Adams. *!%@:: A Dictionary of Electronic Mail Addressing & Networks*. Third edition. O'Reilly & Associates, Inc. 1990. ISBN 1-56592-031-7.

Fujitsu Limited. FACOM JEF 文字コード索引辞書. 1987. Fujitsu part number 99FR-0012-3.

古瀬幸広. ネットワーク通信活用ブック. 実業之日本社. 1991. ISBN 4-408-10096-X.

———. 最新ワープロ用語辞典. 実業之日本社. 1991. ISBN 4-408-10095-1.

Halpern, Jack, editor. *New Japanese-English Character Dictionary*. Kenkyusha. 1990. ISBN 4-7674-9040-5.

原田種成. 漢字小百科辞典. 三省堂. 1990. ISBN 4-385-13590-8.

Hardie, Edward T. L. & Vivian Neou, editors. *Internet: Mailing Lists*. Prentice Hall. 1993. ISBN 0-13-327941-3.

Hewlett-Packard. *Japanese Input Method Guide for NLIO 8.0*. 1991. Hewlett-Packard part number B2200-90003.

———. *Kanji Code Book*. 1989. Hewlett-Packard part number 98861-90003.

———. *Native Language I/O Access User's Guide*. 1991. Hewlett-Packard part number B2200-90001 (Japanese) and B2200-90005 (English).

———. *Native Language I/O System Administrator's Guide*. 1991. Hewlett-Packard part number B2200-90002 (Japanese) and B2200-90006 (Japanese).

飛田良文. 国字の字典. 東京堂出版. 1990. ISBN 4-490-10279-8.

Hitachi. HITAC文字コード表(KEIS83). 1989. Hitachi part number 8080-2-100-10.

———. HITAC文字パターン辞書/コードブック(KEIS83拡張文字セット3). 1987. Hitachi part number 8080-2-109.

———. HITAC文字パターン辞書/コードブック(拡張文字セット3). 1984. Hitachi part number 8080-2-074-10.

Huang, Jack & Timothy Huang. *An Introduction to Chinese, Japanese and Korean Computing*. World Scientific Computing. 1989. ISBN 9971-50-664-5.

IBM Corporation. *DBCS Design Guide for DOS/V and MS Windows Programming*. IBM DBCS Technical Coordination Office. 1992. IBM part number DTC 0-0012-0.

———. *AIX Version 3.2 for RISC System/6000: Internationalization of AIX Software — A Programmer's Guide*. Second edition. 1992. IBM part number SC23-2431.

泉均. ワープロ用語図説辞典. 山海堂. 1988. ISBN 4-381-08071-8.

常用漢字表. 大蔵省印刷局. 1987. ISBN 4-17-214500-0.

樺島忠夫 et al., editors. 事典日本の文字. 大修館書店. 1985. ISBN 4-469-01209-2.

鎌田正 & 米山寅太郎. 大漢語林. 大修館書店. 1992. ISBN 4-469-03154-2.

Krol, Ed. *The Whole Internet User's Guide & Catalog*. O'Reilly & Associates, Inc. 1992. ISBN 1-56592-025-2.

McGilton, Henry & Mary Campione. *PostScript by Example*. Addison-Wesley. 1992. ISBN 0-201-63228-4.

森浩孝. パソコン通信ガイドブック. HBJ Publishing. 1986. ISBN 4-8337-8512-9.

森田正典 & 丸山和光. 日本語だから速く入力できる. 日刊工業新聞社. 1988. ISBN 4-526-02310-8.

森田正典. これが日本語に最適なキーボードだ. 日本経済新聞社. 1992. ISBN 4-532-40014-7.

長尾真 et al., editors. 情報科学辞典. 岩波書店. 1990. ISBN 4-00-080074-4.

NEC. 日本電気標準文字セット辞書 基本編. 1983. NEC part number ZBB10-2.

———. 日本電気標準文字セット辞書 拡張編. 1983. NEC part number ZBB11-1.

Nelson, Andrew. *The Modern Reader's Japanese-English Character Dictionary*. Second Revised Edition. Charles E. Tuttle. 1974. ISBN 0-8048-0408-7.

新村出, editor. 広辞苑. Fourth edition. 岩波書店. 1991. ISBN 4-00-080101-5.

小川環樹 et al. 新字源. 角川書店. 1990. ISBN 4-04-010801-9.

Pollack, David, editor. *Soft Landing in Japan: A Market Entry Handbook for U.S. Software Companies*. Version 2.0J. American Electronics Association. 1992.

Reid, Glenn. *Thinking in PostScript*. Addison-Wesley. 1990. ISBN 0-201-52372-8.

佐藤喜代治 et al. 漢字講座: 漢字とは. Volume 1. 大修館書店. 1988. ISBN 4-625-52081-9.

———. 漢字講座: 漢字研究の歩み. Volume 2. 大修館書店. 1989. ISBN 4-625-52082-7.

———. 漢字講座: 漢字と日本語. Volume 3. 大修館書店. 1987. ISBN 4-625-52083-5.

———. 漢字講座: 漢字と仮名. Volume 4. 大修館書店. 1989. ISBN 4-625-52084-3.

———. 漢字講座: 古代の漢字とことば. Volume 5. 大修館書店. 1988. ISBN 4-625-52085-1.

———. 漢字講座: 中世の漢字とことば. Volume 6. 大修館書店. 1988. ISBN 4-625-52086-X.

———. 漢字講座: 近世の漢字とことば. Volume 7. 大修館書店. 1987. ISBN 4-625-52087-8.

———. 漢字講座: 近代日本語と漢字. Volume 8. 大修館書店. 1988. ISBN 4-625-52088-6.

———. 漢字講座: 近代文字と漢字. Volume 9. 大修館書店. 1988. ISBN 4-625-52089-4.

———. 漢字講座: 現代生活と漢字. Volume 10. 大修館書店. 1989. ISBN 4-625-52090-8.

———. 漢字講座: 漢字と国語問題. Volume 11. 大修館書店. 1989. ISBN 4-625-52091-6.

———. 漢字講座: 漢字教育. Volume 12. 大修館書店. 1988. ISBN 4-625-52092-4.

真堂彬 & プロビット. JIS補助漢字. エーアイ出版. 1991. ISBN 4-87193-158-7.

Spahn, Mark & Wolfgang Hadamitzky. *Japanese Character Dictionary with Compound Lookup via Any Kanji.* Nichigai Associates, Inc. 1989. ISBN 4-8169-0828-5.

Spiekermann, Erik & E.M. Ginger. *Stop Stealing Sheep & find out how type works.* Adobe Press. 1993. ISBN 0-672-48543-5.

田嶋一夫. 最新JIS漢字辞典. 講談社. 1990. ISBN 4-06-123264-9.

Todino, Grace & Dale Dougherty. *UUCP入門 (Using UUCP and Usenet)*. ASCII Corporation. 1993. ISBN 4-7561-0280-8.

Tuthill, Bill. *Solaris International Developer's Guide.* SunSoft Press and PTR Prentice Hall. 1993. ISBN 013-031063-9.

上柿力. パソコンワープロ漢字辞典. ナツメ社. 1987. ISBN 4-8163-0696-X.

Unicode Consortium, The. *The Unicode Standard: Worldwide Character Encoding.* Version 1.0, Volume 1. Addison-Wesley. 1991. ISBN 0-201-56788-1.

―――. *The Unicode Standard: Worldwide Character Encoding.* Version 1.0, Volume 2. Addison-Wesley. 1992. ISBN 0-201-60845-6.

Uren, Emmanuel et al. *Software Internationalization and Localization: An Introduction.* Van Nostrand Reinhold. 1993. ISBN 0-442-01498-8.

Standards

American National Standards Institute. *ANSI X3.4-1986 Coded Character Set— 7-bit American National Standard Code for Information Interchange.* 1986.

Fujitsu Limited. 富士通文字コード解説書. 1989. Fujitsu part number 99FR-8010-1.

GB 2312-80 Code of Chinese Graphic Character Set for Information Interchange—Primary Set. Technical Standards Publishing. 1981.

Hitachi. KEIS概説. 1990. Hitachi part number 6180-3-003.

IBM Corporation. *Coded Character Sets: Implementation.* IBM Standards Program. 1991. IBM part number C-S 3-3220-019 1991-10.

―――. *Double-Byte Character Set (DBCS): Terminology and Code Scheme.* IBM Standards Program. 1992. IBM part number C-S 3-3220-102 1992-11.

―――. *Extended BCD Interchange Code: EBCDIC.* IBM Standards Program. 1990. IBM part number C-S 3-3220-002 1990-05.

―――. *IBM Japanese Graphic Character Set, Kanji: DBCS-Host and DBCS-PC.* IBM Standards Program. 1992. IBM part number C-H 3-3220-024 1992-11.

―――. *IBM Japanese Graphic Character Set for Extended UNIX Code (EUC): DBCS-EUC.* IBM Standards Program. 1993. IBM part number C-H 3-3220-127 1993-03.

International Standards Organization. *ISO 646-1991 Information Processing—ISO 7-bit Coded Character Set for Information Interchange.* 1991.

―――. *ISO 2022-1993 Information Processing—ISO 7-bit and 8-bit Coded Character Sets—Code Extension Techniques.* 1993.

————. *ISO 8859 Information Processing—8-bit Single-byte Coded Graphic Character Sets*. Nine parts. 1987-1989.

————. *ISO 9541-1993 Information Technology—Font Information Interchange*. Three parts. 1993.

————. *ISO 10646-1:1993 Information Technology—Universal Multiple-octet Coded Character Set (UCS)*. 1993.

Japanese Industrial Standards Committee. *JIS C 6226-1978 Code of the Japanese Graphic Character Set for Information Interchange* (情報交換用漢字符号). Japanese Standards Association. 1978.

————. *JIS X 0201-1976 Code for Information Interchange* (情報交換用符号). Japanese Standards Association. 1976.

————. *JIS X 0202-1991 Information Processing—ISO 7-bit and 8-bit Coded Character Sets—Code Extension Techniques* (情報交換用符号の拡張法). Japanese Standards Association. 1991.

————. *JIS X 0208-1983 Code of the Japanese Graphic Character Set for Information Interchange* (情報交換用漢字符号). Japanese Standards Association. 1983.

————. *JIS X 0208-1990 Code of the Japanese Graphic Character Set for Information Interchange* (情報交換用漢字符号). Japanese Standards Association. 1990.

————. *JIS X 0212-1990 Code of the Supplementary Japanese Graphic Character Set for Information Interchange* (情報交換用漢字符号ー補助漢字). Japanese Standards Association. 1990.

————. *JIS X 4161-1993 Font Information Interchange—Architecture* (フォント情報交換—体系). Japanese Standards Association. 1993.

————. *JIS X 4162-1993 Font Information Interchange—Interchange Format* (フォント情報交換—交換用式). Japanese Standards Association. 1993.

————. *JIS X 4163-1993 Font Information Interchange—Glyph Shape Representation* (フォント情報交換—グリフ形状表現). Japanese Standards Association. 1993.

————. *JIS X 4164-1993 Font Information Interchange—Application-specific Extensions* (フォント情報交換—応用別拡張). Japanese Standards Association. 1993.

————. *JIS X 6002-1985 Keyboard Layout for Information Processing Using the JIS 7 Bit Coded Character Set* (情報処理系けん盤配列). Japanese Standards Association. 1985

————. *JIS X 6004-1986 Basic Keyboard Layout for Japanese Text Processing Using Kana-Kanji Translation Method* (仮名漢字変換形日本文入力装置用けん盤配列). Japanese Standards Association. 1986.

————. *JIS X 6003-1989 Keyboard Layout for Japanese Text Processing* (日本語文書処理用文字盤配列). Japanese Standards Association. 1989.

————. *JIS X 9052-1983 24-dots Matrix Character Patterns for Dot Printers* (ドットプリンタ用24ドット字形). Japanese Standards Association. 1983.

————. *JIS X 9051-1984 16-dots Matrix Character Patterns for Display Devices* (表示装置用16ドット字形). Japanese Standards Association. 1984.

KS C 5601-1992 Code for Information Interchange (Hangul and Hanja). Korean Industrial Standards Association. 1992.

KS C 5861-1992 Hangul Unix Environment. Korean Industrial Standards Association. 1992.

X/Open Consortium. *X/Open CAE Specification: Commands and Utilities, Issue 4*. X/Open Company Limited. 1992. ISBN 1-872630-48-0. X/Open Document Number C203.

————. *X/Open CAE Specification: System Interfaces and Headers, Issue 4*. X/Open Company Limited. 1992. ISBN 1-872630-47-2. X/Open Document Number C202.

————. *X/Open CAE Specification: System Interface Definitions, Issue 4*. X/Open Company Limited. 1992. ISBN 1-872630-46-4. X/Open Document Number C204.

————. *X/Open Guide: Internationalisation Guide*. X/Open Company Limited. 1992. ISBN 1-872630-20-0.

Xerox Corporation. *Xerox Character Code Standard 2.0*. Xerox Systems Institute. 1990. Xerox part number XNSS 059003.

Periodicals

Association for the Internationalization of Computing Resources (AICR). *I18N*. Technical University of Brno Press. Published quarterly.

Chinese Language Computer Society (CLCS). *Computer Processing of Chinese & Oriental Languages (CPCOL)*. World Scientific Publishing. Published quarterly. ISSN 0715-9048.

Font & Function. Adobe Systems Incorporated.

KanjiLink Japanese Macintosh Report. Concord International, Inc. Published quarterly.

MANGAJIN (漫画人). MANGAJIN, Inc. Published 10 times per year. ISSN 1051-8177.

Multilingual Computing. Multilingual Computing North America. Published quarterly. ISSN 1065-7657.

SESAME Bulletin. Sesame Computer Projects. ISSN 0950-2025.

U&lc. International Typeface Corporation. Published quarterly. ISSN 0362-6245.

最新ワープロ大百科. 実業之日本社. Published quarterly.

Papers and Articles

Chon, Kilnam et al. *Korean Character Encoding for Internet Messages*. Internet Draft. May 1993.

Dillard, Troy & Ken Lunde. *Japanese Text Processing and Electronic Mail on the IBM PC and Macintosh*. Sesame Computer Projects. SESAME Bulletin, Summer 1992, Volume 5, Part 2, pp 40–48.

Huang, Jack Kai-tung. *Status of Digitized Chinese (Hanzi) Font Manufacturers in Taiwan*. April, 1993.

Lunde, Ken. *Using Electronic Mail as a Medium for Foreign Language Study and Instruction*. CALICO Journal, March 1990, Volume 7, Number 3, pp 68–78.

————. *Electronic Transfer of Japanese*. ATArashii, September/October 1990, Volume 4, Number 5, pp 19–27.

————. *JAPAN.INF: Electronic Handling of Japanese Text*. Distributed and maintained electronically since 1989.

———. *The History of the Japanese Character Set and its Encoding*. 1993. To appear in Computer Processing of Chinese & Oriental Languages (CPCOL).

Morita, Masasuke. *Japanese Text Input System*. IEEE Computer, May 1985, Volume 18, Number 5, pp 29–35.

———. *Development of New Keyboard Optimized from Standpoint of Ergonomics*. Work with Computers: Organizational, Management, Stress and Health Aspects, Proceedings of the Third International Conference on Human-Computer Interaction, September 18–22, 1989, Volume 1, pp 595–603.

Murai, Jun et al. *Japanese Character Encoding for Internet Messages*. RFC 1468. June 1993.

Miyazawa, Akira. *Character Code for Japanese Text Processing*. Journal of Information Processing. 1990, Volume 13, Number 1, pp 2–9.

西村恕彦. 漢字のJIS. 標準化ジャーナル. 1978.5, pp 3–8.

野村雅昭. JIS C 6226情報交換用漢字符号系の改正. 標準化ジャーナル. 1984.3, pp 4–9.

Open Software Foundation, UNIX International, and UNIX System Laboratories Pacific. *OSF, UI, and USL Standardize on Japanese Language Support*. UI-OSF-USLP Joint Announcement. Press release dated December 12, 1991.

Schilke, Steffen. *Japanization—An Introduction to Software Japanization*. Thesis. Summer, 1992.

田嶋一夫. JIS漢字表の利用上の問題—漢字処理システムにおける漢字のデザインと管理. 情報管理. 1979. Volume 21, Number 10, pp 753–761.

Index

About the Author

Ken Lunde was born in 1965 in Madison, Wisconsin, grew up in Mount Horeb, Wisconsin, and entered the University of Wisconsin-Madison in 1985 as a freshman. He graduated with a Bachelor of Arts degree in linguistics in 1987. He received his Master of Arts degree in linguistics in 1988. He then entered the PhD program with an area of specialization in Japanese linguistics, passed the PhD preliminary examination in 1990, and is currently a PhD candidate. He joined Adobe Systems in 1991, and is currently the Project Manager for Japanese Font Production. Ken aspires to complete his PhD thesis soon after this book is written.

The author's Japanese pen-name is 小林剣 (*Kobayashi Ken*). The Norwegian surname *Lunde* means "small woods" or "grove." The Japanese surname 小林 conveys these same meanings, and was thus chosen. The Japanese given name 剣 was chosen phonemically, and from the author's fondness for edged weapons.

Ken currently resides in Union City, California with his family, and works in Mountain View, California.

Colophon

Our look is the result of reader comments, our own experimentation, and feedback from distribution channels.

Distinctive covers complement our distinctive approach to technical topics, breathing personality and life into potentially dry subjects. Computer systems and their attendant programs can be unruly beasts. Nutshell Handbooks help you tame them.

The animal on the cover of *Understanding Japanese Information Processing* is a blowfish, also known as a globefish, swellfish, puffer, and porcupine fish. It exists in tropical waters throughout the world. In Japan it is known as *fugu* (河豚), and is a treasured delicacy, usually eaten raw in thin slices. While parts of the blowfish are deliciously narcotic, other parts contain a deadly toxin. Because of this, only specially certified and licensed chefs are allowed to prepare the fish for people to eat. The skin of the blowfish is often used for making lanterns and other decorations.

Edie Freedman designed this cover and the entire UNIX bestiary that appears on other Nutshell Handbooks. The beasts themselves are adapted from 19th-century engravings from the Dover Pictorial Archive. The cover layout was produced with Quark XPress 3.1 using the ITC Garamond and Heisei Kaku Gothic W5 (平成角ゴシックW5) fonts.

The original text was input using Nisus 3.45 running on Apple Macintosh SE and IIci computers. Japanese text entry was performed using MacVJE Version 2.5 and MacVJE-γ Version 1.0. Illustrations were created using Adobe Illustrator 3.2J, Adobe Photoshop 2.01J, and Aldus FreeHand 3.11. Custom typefaces were created with Altsys' Fontographer Version 4.0. Intermediate drafts of the manuscript were printed at 300-dpi resolution on an Apple LaserWriter IINTX-J printer. Typesetting was done by the author on an Apple Macintosh IIci computer running Aldus PageMaker 4.0J, and camera-ready mechanicals were produced on a Linotronic L300-J set at 1270-dpi resolution.

The English textface is 10-point ITC Garamond Light. Chapter and section titles are set in ITC Garamond Book Italic. The Japanese textface is 10-point Heisei Mincho W3 (平成明朝W3), which was developed by FDPC. All of these typefaces are available in digital format from Adobe Systems.

A special offer from Adobe Systems on select PostScript™ Japanese typeface packages!

Now that you have learned how Japanese is processed on computer systems, choose from two PostScript Japanese typeface packages. Better yet, choose both packages and get even more!

Order Information

YES, send me ValuePack日本語版! (*a $350 value*)

☐ $129 $ _____

☐ For Macintosh® ☐ For 日本語Windows™

Also send me the 平成明朝W3™ GaijiPack! *Available for Macintosh only.*

☐ $99 $ _____

Shipping (*outside USA and Canada only*) $ 20.00

Sales tax (*residents of FL add appropriate sales tax*) $ _____

Total amount $ _____

Payment Information

☐ Check/money order (*make payable to SystemSoft America in U.S. dollars*)

☐ VISA   ☐ MasterCard   ☐ American Express

Card Number _____

Expiration Date _____

Name on Credit Card (*please print*) _____

Signature (*required for credit card purchase*) _____

Shipping Information (*in English, please*)

Name _____

Company _____

Address (*no P.O. boxes please*) _____

City _____ State _____ Zip/Postal Code _____

Country _____ Telephone (___) _____

ValuePack日本語版 includes:

平成明朝W3™
あいうえおかきくけこアイウエオカキクケコ亜唖
娃阿哀愛挨姶逢葵茜穐悪握渥旭葦芦鰺梓圧斡扱宛

平成角ゴシックW5™
あいうえおかきくけこアイウエオカキクケコ亜唖
娃阿哀愛挨姶逢葵茜穐悪握渥旭葦芦鰺梓圧斡扱宛

Barmeno™ Extra Bold

CASTELLAR™

COPPERPLATE GOTHIC

Goudy Text™ Lombardic Capitals

LITHOS™ REGULAR

Rockwell® Extra Bold

Bellevue™

Nuptial Script™

Carta™
✳✲⚓☆⛪🛤◻☐✈️⚙▲★⛵⚓⚓▲★⛵⛵✈️►◻☐

Minion™ Ornaments
☙❦❧◉❧☙❧❦❦❧

Adobe Type Manager™日本語版 software

平成明朝W3™ GaijiPack includes:

JIS X 0212-1990 (*6,067 characters*)
丂丄丅丌丒丟丠两丨丫刋丰丯挙乁乁乄乇承乚乱
乢乣乤乥乧乨丷乲乴乺乻乼乽乿仈仚仛仜仠仢仦

JIS C 6226-1978 (*250 kanji*)
啞逢芦飴溢鰯淫迂欝厩噂餌焰襖鴎迦恢拐晦喝葛鞄
噛澗翰翫徽祇俠嶇僅喰櫛屑靴祁慧稽繋荊隙倦嫌

Adobe Type Composer™ software

For fastest delivery, call SystemSoft America at 800-882-8856 (outside the USA call 407-770-3371).

To order by fax: cut or photocopy this order form and fax completed with payment to 407-569-1937.

Or mail to: SystemSoft America, Incorporated, P.O. Box 4260, Vero Beach, FL 32964 USA.

From the best-selling The Whole Internet *to our Nutshell Handbooks, there's something here for everyone. Whether you're a novice or expert UNIX user, these books will give you just what you're looking for: user-friendly, definitive information on a range of UNIX topics.*

Using UNIX

Connecting to the Internet: An O'Reilly Buyer's Guide   **NEW**

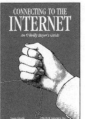

By Susan Estrada
1st Edition August 1993
188 pages
ISBN 1-56592-061-9

More and more people are interested in exploring the Internet, and this book is the fastest way for you to learn how to get started. This book provides practical advice on how to determine the level of Internet service right for you, and how to find a local access provider and evaluate the services they offer.

!%@:: A Directory of Electronic Mail Addressing & Networks   **NEW**

By Donnalyn Frey & Rick Adams
3rd Edition August 1993
458 pages, ISBN 1-56592-031-7

The only up-to-date directory that charts the networks that make up the Internet, provides contact names and addresses, and describes the services each network provides. It includes all of the major Internet-based networks, as well as various commercial networks such as

CompuServe, Delphi, and America Online that are "gatewayed" to the Internet for transfer of electronic mail and other services. If you are someone who wants to connect to the Internet, or someone who already is connected but wants concise, up-to-date information on many of the world's networks, check out this book.

Learning the UNIX Operating System   **NEW**

By Grace Todino, John Strang & Jerry Peek
3rd Edition August 1993
108 pages, ISBN 1-56592-060-0

If you are new to UNIX, this concise introduction will tell you just what you need to get started and no more. Why wade through a six-hundred-page book when you can begin working productively in a matter of minutes? This book is the most effective introduction to UNIX in print. This new edition has been updated and expanded to provide increased coverage of window systems and networking. It's a handy book for someone just starting with UNIX, as well as someone who encounters a UNIX system as a visitor via remote login over the Internet.

The Whole Internet User's Guide & Catalog

By Ed Krol
1st Edition September 1992
400 pages, ISBN 1-56592-025-2

A comprehensive—and best-selling—introduction to the Internet, the international network that includes virtually every major computer site in the world. The Internet is a resource of almost unimaginable wealth. In addition to electronic mail and news services, thousands of public archives, databases, and other special services are available: everything from space flight announcements to ski reports. This book is a comprehensive introduction to what's available and how to find it. In addition to electronic mail, file transfer, remote login, and network news, *The Whole Internet* pays special attention to some new tools for helping you find information. Whether you're a researcher, a student, or just someone who likes electronic mail, this book will help you to explore what's possible.

Smileys

By David W. Sanderson, 1st Edition March 1993
93 pages, ISBN 1-56592-041-4

Originally used to convey some kind of emotion in an e-mail message, smileys are some combination of typographic characters that depict sideways a happy or sad face. Now there are hundreds of variations, including smileys that depict presidents, animals, and cartoon characters. Not everyone likes to read mail messages littered with smileys, but almost everyone finds them humorous. The smileys in this book have been collected by David Sanderson, whom the *Wall Street Journal* called the "Noah Webster of Smileys."

UNIX Power Tools

By Jerry Peek, Mike Loukides, Tim O'Reilly, et al.
1st Edition March 1993
1162 pages
(Bantam ISBN)
0-553-35402-7

Ideal for UNIX users who hunger for technical—yet accessible—information, *UNIX Power Tools* consists of tips, tricks, concepts, and freely-available software. Covers add-on utilities and how to take advantage of clever features in the most popular UNIX utilities. CD-ROM included.

Learning the Korn Shell

By Bill Rosenblatt
1st Edition June 1993
363 pages, ISBN 1-56592-054-6

This new Nutshell Handbook is a thorough introduction to the Korn shell, both as a user interface and as a programming language. Provides a clear explanation of the Korn shell's features, including *ksh* string operations, co-processes, signals and signal handling, and command-line interpretation. Also includes real-life programming examples and a Korn shell debugger (*kshdb*).

Learning perl

By Randal L. Schwartz, 1st Edition November 1993 (est.)
220 pages (est.), ISBN 1-56592-042-2

Perl is rapidly becoming the "universal scripting language" Combining capabilities of the UNIX shell, the C programming language, *sed*, *awk*, and various other utilities, it has proved its use for tasks ranging from system administration to text processing and distributed computing. *Learning perl* is a step-by-step, hands-on tutorial designed to get you writing useful perl scripts as quickly as possible. In addition to countless code examples, there are numerous programming exercises, with full answers. For a comprehensive and detailed guide to programming with Perl, read O'Reilly's companion book *Programming perl*.

Programming perl

By Larry Wall & Randal L. Schwartz
1st Edition January 1991, 428 pages, ISBN 0-937175-64-1

Authoritative guide to the hottest new UNIX utility in years, co-authored by its creator. Perl is a language for easily manipulating text, files, and processes.

Learning GNU Emacs

By Deb Cameron & Bill Rosenblatt
1st Edition October 1991
442 pages, ISBN 0-937175-84-6

An introduction to the GNU Emacs editor, one of the most widely used and powerful editors available under UNIX. Provides a solid introduction to basic editing, a look at several important "editing modes" (special Emacs features for editing specific types of documents), and a brief introduction to customization and Emacs LISP programming. The book is aimed at new Emacs users, whether or not they are programmers.

sed & awk

By Dale Dougherty, 1st Edition November 1990
414 pages, ISBN 0-937175-59-5

For people who create and modify text files, *sed* and *awk* are power tools for editing. Most of the things that you can do with these programs can be done interactively with a text editor. However, using *sed* and *awk* can save many hours of repetitive work in achieving the same result.

MH & xmh: E-mail for Users & Programmers

By Jerry Peek, 2nd Edition September 1992
728 pages, ISBN 1-56592-027-9

Customize your e-mail environment to save time and make communicating more enjoyable. *MH & xmh: E-mail for Users & Programmers* explains how to use, customize, and program with the MH electronic mail commands available on virtually any UNIX system. The handbook also covers *xmh*, an X Window System client that runs MH programs. The new second edition has been updated for X Release 5 and MH 6.7.2. We've added a chapter on *mhook*, new sections explaining under-appreciated small commands and features, and more examples showing how to use MH to handle common situations.

Learning the vi Editor

By Linda Lamb, 5th Edition October 1990
192 pages, ISBN 0-937175-67-6

A complete guide to text editing with *vi*, the editor available on nearly every UNIX system. Early chapters cover the basics; later chapters explain more advanced editing tools, such as *ex* commands and global search and replacement.

UNIX in a Nutshell:
For System V & Solaris 2.0

By Daniel Gilly and the staff of O'Reilly & Associates
2nd Edition June 1992, 444 pages, ISBN 1-56592-001-5

You may have seen UNIX quick reference guides, but you've never seen anything like *UNIX in a Nutshell*. Not a scaled-down quick-reference of common commands, *UNIX in a Nutshell* is a complete reference containing all commands and options, along with generous descriptions and examples that put the commands in context. For all but the thorniest UNIX problems this one reference should be all the documentation you need. Covers System V Releases 3 and 4 and Solaris 2.0.

An alternate version of this quick-reference is available for Berkeley UNIX.
Berkeley Edition, December 1986
(latest update October 1990)
272 pages, ISBN 0-937175-20-X

Using UUCP and Usenet

By Grace Todino & Dale Dougherty
1st Edition December 1986 (latest update October 1991)
210 pages, ISBN 0-937175-10-2

Shows users how to communicate with both UNIX and non-UNIX systems using UUCP and *cu* or *tip*, and how to read news and post articles. This handbook assumes that UUCP is already running at your site.

System Administration

Managing UUCP and Usenet

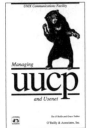

By Tim O'Reilly & Grace Todino
10th Edition January 1992
368 pages, ISBN 0-937175-93-5

For all its widespread use, UUCP is one of the most difficult UNIX utilities to master. This book is for system administrators who want to install and manage UUCP and Usenet software. "Don't even TRY to install UUCP without it!"—Usenet message 456@nitrex.UUCP

sendmail   NEW

By Bryan Costales, with Eric Allman & Neil Rickert
1st Edition October 1993 (est.)
600 pages (est.), ISBN 0-937175-056-2

This new Nutshell Handbook is far and away the most comprehensive book ever written on *sendmail*, a program that acts like a traffic cop in routing and delivering mail on UNIX-based networks. Although *sendmail* is the most widespread of all mail programs, it's also one of the last great uncharted territories—and most difficult utilities to learn—in UNIX system administration. The book covers both major versions of *sendmail*: the standard version available on most systems, and IDA *sendmail*, a version from Europe.

termcap & terminfo

By John Strang, Linda Mui & Tim O'Reilly
3rd Edition July 1992
270 pages, ISBN 0-937175-22-6

For UNIX system administrators and programmers. This handbook provides information on writing and debugging terminal descriptions, as well as terminal initialization, for the two UNIX terminal databases.

DNS and BIND

By Cricket Liu & Paul Albitz, 1st Edition October 1992
418 pages, ISBN 1-56592-010-4

DNS and BIND contains all you need to know about the Domain Name System (DNS) and BIND, its UNIX implementation. The Domain Name System (DNS) is the Internet's "phone book"; it's a database that tracks important information (in particular, names and addresses) for every computer on the Internet. If you're a system administrator, this book will show you how to set up and maintain the DNS software on your network.

Essential System Administration

By Æleen Frisch, 1st Edition October 1991
466 pages, ISBN 0-937175-80-3

Provides a compact, manageable introduction to the tasks faced by everyone responsible for a UNIX system. This guide is for those who use a stand-alone UNIX system, those who routinely provide administrative support for a larger shared system, or those who want an understanding of basic administrative functions. Covers all major versions of UNIX.

X Window System Administrator's Guide

By Linda Mui & Eric Pearce
1st Edition October 1992
372 pages, With CD-ROM: ISBN 1-56592-052-X
Without CD-ROM: ISBN 0-937175-83-8

This book is the first and only book devoted to the issues of system administration for X and X-based networks, written not just for UNIX system administrators but for anyone faced with the job of administering X (including those running X on stand-alone workstations).

The *X Window System Administrator's Guide* is available either alone or packaged with the XCD. The CD provides X source code and binaries to complement the book's instructions for installing the software. It contains over 600 megabytes of X11 source code and binaries stored in ISO9660 and RockRidge formats. This will allow several types of UNIX workstations to mount the CD-ROM as a filesystem, browse through the source code and install pre-built software.

Practical UNIX Security

By Simson Garfinkel & Gene Spafford
1st Edition June 1991
512 pages, ISBN 0-937175-72-2

Tells system administrators how to make their UNIX system— either System V or BSD—as secure as it possibly can be without going to trusted system technology. The book describes UNIX concepts and how they enforce security, tells how to defend against and handle security breaches, and explains network security (including UUCP, NFS, Kerberos, and firewall machines) in detail.

Managing NFS and NIS

By Hal Stern
1st Edition June 1991
436 pages, ISBN 0-937175-75-7

Managing NFS and NIS is for system administrators who need to set up or manage a network filesystem installation. NFS (Network Filesystem) is probably running at any site that has two or more UNIX systems. NIS (Network Information System) is a distributed database used to manage a network of computers. The only practical book devoted entirely to these subjects, this guide is a must-have for anyone interested in UNIX networking.

TCP/IP Network Administration

By Craig Hunt
1st Edition July 1992
502 pages, ISBN 0-937175-82-X

A complete guide to setting up and running a TCP/IP network for practicing system administrators. Covers how to set up your network, how to configure important network applications including *sendmail*, and discusses troubleshooting and security. Covers BSD and System V TCP/IP implementations.

System Performance Tuning

By Mike Loukides, 1st Edition November 1990
336 pages, ISBN 0-937175-60-9

System Performance Tuning answers the fundamental question, "How can I get my computer to do more work without buying more hardware?" Some performance problems do require you to buy a bigger or faster computer, but many can be solved simply by making better use of the resources you already have.

Computer Security Basics

By Deborah Russell & G.T. Gangemi Sr.
1st Edition July 1991
464 pages, ISBN 0-937175-71-4

Provides a broad introduction to the many areas of computer security and a detailed description of current security standards. This handbook describes complicated concepts like trusted systems, encryption, and mandatory access control in simple terms, and contains a thorough, readable introduction to the "Orange Book."

UNIX Programming

Understanding Japanese Information Processing   **NEW**

By Ken Lunde
1st Edition September 1993 (est.)
450 pages (est.), ISBN 1-56592-043-0

Understanding Japanese Information Processing provides detailed information on all aspects of handling Japanese text on computer systems. It tries to bring all of the relevant information together in a single book. It covers everything from the origins of modern-day Japanese to the latest information on specific emerging computer encoding standards. There are over 15 appendices which provide additional reference material, such as a code conversion table, character set tables, mapping tables, an extensive list of software sources, a glossary, and much more.

lex & yacc

By John Levine, Tony Mason & Doug Brown
2nd Edition October 1992
366 pages, ISBN 1-56592-000-7

Shows programmers how to use two UNIX utilities, *lex* and *yacc*, in program development. The second edition of *lex & yacc* contains completely revised tutorial sections for novice users and reference sections for advanced users. The new edition is twice the size of the original book, has an expanded index, and now covers Bison and Flex.

High Performance Computing   **NEW**

By Kevin Dowd
1st Edition June 1993
398 pages, ISBN 1-56592-032-5

High Performance Computing makes sense of the newest generation of workstations for application programmers and purchasing managers. It covers everything, from the basics of modern workstation architecture, to structuring benchmarks, to squeezing more performance out of critical applications. It also explains what a good compiler can do—and what you have to do yourself. The book closes with a look at the high-performance future: parallel computers and the more "garden variety" shared memory processors that are appearing on people's desktops.

ORACLE Performance Tuning   **NEW**

By Peter Corrigan & Mark Gurry
1st Edition September 1993 (est.)
650 pages (est.), ISBN 1-56592-048-1

The ORACLE relational database management system is the most popular database system in use today. With more organizations downsizing and adopting client/server and distributed database approaches, system performance tuning has become vital. This book shows you the many things you can do to dramatically increase the performance of your existing ORACLE system. You may find that this book can save you the cost of a new machine; at the very least, it will save you a lot of headaches.

POSIX Programmer's Guide

By Donald Lewine
1st Edition April 1991
640 pages, ISBN 0-937175-73-0

Most UNIX systems today are POSIX-compliant because the Federal government requires it for its purchases. However, given the manufacturer's documentation, it can be difficult to distinguish system-specific features from those features defined by POSIX. The *POSIX Programmer's Guide*, intended as an explanation of the POSIX standard and as a reference for the POSIX.1 programming library, helps you write more portable programs.

Understanding DCE

By Ward Rosenberry, David Kenney & Gerry Fisher
1st Edition October 1992
266 pages, ISBN 1-56592-005-8

A technical and conceptual overview of OSF's Distributed Computing Environment (DCE) for programmers and technical managers, marketing and sales people. Unlike many O'Reilly & Associates books, *Understanding DCE* has no hands-on programming elements. Instead, the book focuses on how DCE can be used to accomplish typical programming tasks and provides explanations to help the reader understand all the parts of DCE.

Guide to Writing DCE Applications

By John Shirley
1st Edition July 1992
282 pages, ISBN 1-56592-004-X

A hands-on programming guide to OSF's Distributed Computing Environment (DCE) for first-time DCE application programmers. This book is designed to help new DCE users make the transition from conventional, nondistributed applications programming to distributed DCE programming. Covers the IDL and ACF files, essential RPC calls, binding methods and the name service, server initialization, memory management, and selected advanced topics. Includes practical programming examples.

Power Programming with RPC

By John Bloomer
1st Edition February 1992
522 pages, ISBN 0-937175-77-3

RPC, or remote procedure calling, is the ability to distribute the execution of functions on remote computers. Written from a programmer's perspective, this book shows what you can do with RPC's, like Sun RPC, the de facto standard on UNIX systems. It covers related programming topics for Sun and other UNIX systems and teaches through examples.

Managing Projects with make

By Andrew Oram & Steve Talbott
2nd Edition October 1991
152 pages, ISBN 0-937175-90-0

make is one of UNIX's greatest contributions to software development, and this book is the clearest description of *make* ever written. This revised second edition includes guidelines on meeting the needs of large projects.

Software Portability with imake   **NEW**

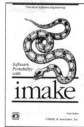

By Paul DuBois
1st Edition July 1993
390 pages, 1-56592-055-4

imake is a utility that works with *make* to enable code to be complied and installed on different UNIX machines. This new Nutshell Handbook—the only book available on *imake*—is ideal for X and UNIX programmers who want their software to be portable. It includes a general explanation of *imake*, how to write and debug an *Imakefile*, and how to write configuration files. Several sample sets of configuration files are described and are available free over the Net.

UNIX for FORTRAN Programmers

By Mike Loukides
1st Edition August 1990
264 pages, ISBN 0-937175-51-X

This book provides the serious scientific programmer with an introduction to the UNIX operating system and its tools. The intent of the book is to minimize the UNIX entry barrier and to familiarize readers with the most important tools so they can be productive as quickly as possible. *UNIX for FORTRAN Programmers* shows readers how to do things they're interested in: not just how to use a tool such as *make* or *rcs*, but how to use it in program development and how it fits into the toolset as a whole. "An excellent book describing the features of the UNIX FORTRAN compiler *f77* and related software. This book is extremely well written." — American Mathematical Monthly, February 1991

Practical C Programming

By Steve Oualline
2nd Edition January 1993
396 pages, ISBN 1-56592-035-X

C programming is more than just getting the syntax right. Style and debugging also play a tremendous part in creating programs that run well. *Practical C Programming* teaches you not only the mechanics of programming, but also how to create programs that are easy to read, maintain, and debug. There are lots of introductory C books, but this is the Nutshell Handbook! In the second edition, programs now conform to ANSI C.

Checking C Programs with lint

By Ian F. Darwin
1st Edition October 1988
84 pages, ISBN 0-937175-30-7

The *lint* program is one of the best tools for finding portability problems and certain types of coding errors in C programs. This handbook introduces you to *lint*, guides you through running it on your programs, and helps you interpret *lint's* output.

Using C on the UNIX System

By Dave Curry
1st Edition January 1989
250 pages, ISBN 0-937175-23-4

Using C on the UNIX System provides a thorough introduction to the UNIX system call libraries. It is aimed at programmers who already know C but who want to take full advantage of the UNIX programming environment. If you want to learn how to work with the operating system and to write programs that can interact with directories, terminals, and networks at the lowest level you will find this book essential. It is impossible to write UNIX utilities of any sophistication without understanding the material in this book. "A gem of a book. The author's aim is to provide a guide to system programming, and he succeeds admirably. His balance is steady between System V and BSD-based systems, so readers come away knowing both." — SUN Expert, November 1989

Guide to OSF/1

By the staff of O'Reilly & Associates
1st Edition June 1991
304 pages, ISBN 0-937175-78-1

This technically competent introduction to OSF/1 is based on OSF technical seminars. In addition to its description of OSF/1, it includes the differences between OSF/1 and System V Release 4 and a look ahead at DCE.

Understanding and Using COFF

By Gintaras R. Gircys
1st Edition November 1988
196 pages, ISBN 0-937175-31-5

COFF—Common Object File Format—is the formal definition for the structure of machine code files in the UNIX System V environment. All machine-code files are COFF files. This handbook explains COFF data structure and its manipulation.

Career

Love Your Job!   NEW

By Dr. Paul Powers, with Deborah Russell
1st Edition August 1993
210 pages, ISBN 1-56592-036-8

Do you love your job? Too few people do. In fact, surveys show that 80 to 95 percent of Americans are dissatisfied with their jobs. Considering that most of us will work nearly 100,000 hours during our lifetimes (half the waking hours of our entire adult lives!), it's sad that our work doesn't bring us the rewards—both financial and emotional—that we deserve. *Love Your Job!* is an inspirational guide to loving your work. It consists of a series of one-page reflections, anecdotes, and exercises aimed at helping readers think more deeply about what they want out of their jobs. Each can be read individually (anyplace, anytime, whenever you need to lift your spirits), or the book can be read and treated as a whole. *Love Your Job!* informs you, inspires you, and challenges you, not only to look outside at the world of work, but also to look inside yourself at what work means to you.

O'Reilly Online Services

How to Get Information about O'Reilly & Associates

The online O'Reilly Information Resource is a Gopher server that provides you with information on our books, how to download code examples, and how to order from us. There is also a UNIX bibliography you can use to get information on current books by subject area.

Connecting to the O'Reilly Information Resource

Gopher is an interactive tool that organizes the resources found on the Internet as a sequence of menus. If you don't know how Gopher works, see the chapter "Tunneling through the Internet: Gopher" in *The Whole Internet User's Guide and Catalog* by Ed Krol.

An easy way to use Gopher is to download a Gopher client, either the tty Gopher that uses curses or the Xgopher.

Once you have a local Gopher client, you can launch Gopher with:

```
gopher gopher.ora.com
```

To use the Xgopher client, enter:

```
xgopher -xrm "xgopher.rootServer:
gopher.ora.com"
```

If you have no client, log in on our machine via telnet and run Gopher from there, with:

```
telnet gopher.ora.com
login: gopher  (no password)
```

Another option is to use a World Wide Web browser, and enter the http address:

```
gopher://gopher.ora.com
```

Once the connection is made, you should see a root menu similar to this:

```
Internet Gopher Information Client v1.12
    Root gopher server: gopher.ora.com

->1. News Flash! -- New Products and
     Projects of ORA/.
  2.About O'Reilly & Associates.
  3.Book Descriptions and Information/
  4.Complete Listing of Book Titles.
  5.FTP Archive and E-Mail Information/
  6.Ordering Information/
  7.UNIX Bibliography/

Press ? for Help, q to Quit, u to go up a
menu                        Page: 1/1
```

From the root menu you can begin exploring the information that we have available. If you don't know much about O'Reilly & Associates, choose About O'Reilly & Associates from the menu. You'll see an article by Tim O'Reilly that gives an overview of who we are—and a little background on the books we publish.

Getting Information About Our Books

The Gopher server makes available online the same information that we provide in our print catalog, often in more detail.

Choose Complete Listing of Book Titles from the root menu to view a list of all our titles. This is a useful summary to have when you want to place an order.

To find out more about a particular book, choose Book Descriptions and Information; you will see the screen below:

```
Internet Gopher Information Client v1.12
    Book Descriptions and Information

->1.New Books and Editions/
  2.Computer Security/
  3.Distributed Computing Environment
    (DCE)/
  4.Non-Technical Books/
  5.System Administration/
  6.UNIX & C Programming/
  7.Using UNIX/
  8.X Resource/
  9.X Window System/
  10.CD-Rom Book Companions/
  11.Errata and Updates/
  12.Keyword Search on all Book
     Descriptions <?>
  13.Keyword Search on all Tables of
     Content <?>
```

All of our new books are listed in a single category. The rest of our books are grouped by subject. Select a subject to see a list of book titles in that category. When you select a specific book, you'll find a full description and table of contents.

For example, if you wanted to look at what books we had on administration, you would choose selection 5, System Administration, resulting in the following screen:

```
        System Administration

  1.DNS and BIND/
  2.Essential System Administration/
  3.Managing NFS and NIS/
  4.Managing UUCP and Usenet/
  5.sendmail/
  6.System Performance Tuning/
  7.TCP/IP Network Administration/
```

If you then choose Essential System Administration, you will be given the choice of looking at either the book description or the table of contents.

```
        Essential System Administration

->1.Book Description and Information.
  2.Book Table of Contents.
```

Selecting either of these options will display the contents of a file. Gopher then provides instructions for you to navigate elsewhere or quit the program.

Searching For the Book You Want

Gopher also allows you to locate book descriptions or tables of contents by using a word search. (We have compiled a full-text index WAIS.)

If you choose Book Descriptions and Information from the root menu, the last two selections on that menu allow you to do keyword searches.

Choose Keyword Search on all Book Descriptions and you will be prompted with:

```
Index word(s) to search for:
```

Once you enter a keyword, the server returns a list of the book descriptions that match the keyword. For example, if you enter the keyword DCE, you will see:

Choose one of these selections to view the book description.

```
Keyword Search on all Book Descriptions: DCE

-> 1.Understanding DCE.
   2.Guide to Writing DCE Applications.
   3.Distributed Applications Across DCE
     and Windows NT.
   4.DCE Administration Guide.
   5.Power Programming with RPC.
   6.Guide to OSF/1.
```

Using the keyword search option can be a faster and less tedious way to locate a book than moving through a lot of menus.

You can also use a WAIS client to access the full-text index or book descriptions. The name of the database is

```
O'Reilly_Book_Descriptions.src
```

and you can find it in the WAIS directory of servers.

Note: We are always adding functions and listings to the O'Reilly Information Resource. By the time you read this article, the actual screens may very well have changed.

E-mail Accounts

E-mail ordering promises to be quick and easy, even faster than using our 800 number. Because we don't want you to send credit card information over a non-secure network, we ask that you set up an account with us in advance. To do so, either call us at 1-800-998-9938 or use the application provided in Ordering Information on the Gopher root menu. You will then be provided with a confidential account number.

Your account number allows us to retrieve your billing information when you place an order by e-mail, so you only need to send us your account number and what you want to order.

For your security, we use the credit card information and shipping address that we have on file. We also verify that the name of the person sending us the e-mail order matches the name on the account. If any of this information needs to change, we ask that you contact order@ora.com or call our Customer Service department.

Ordering by E-mail

Once you have an account with us, you can send us your orders by e-mail. Remember that you can use our online catalog to find out more about the books you want. Here's what we need when you send us an order:

1. Address your e-mail to: order@ora.com
2. Include in your message:
   * The title of each book you want to order (including ISBN number, if you know it)
   * The quantity of each book
   * Method of delivery: UPS Standard, Fed Ex Priority...
   * Your name and account number
   * Anything special you'd like to tell us about the order

When we receive your e-mail message, our Customer Service representative will verify your order before we ship it, and give you a total cost. If you would like to change your order after confirmation, or if there are ever any problems, please use the phone and give us a call—e-mail has its limitations.

This program is an experiment for us. We appreciate getting your feedback so we can continue improving our service.